Charles James Rowe

Bonds of Disunion

English Misrule in the Colonies

Charles James Rowe

Bonds of Disunion
English Misrule in the Colonies

ISBN/EAN: 9783744752695

Printed in Europe, USA, Canada, Australia, Japan

Cover: Foto ©Suzi / pixelio.de

More available books at **www.hansebooks.com**

BONDS OF DISUNION

OR

ENGLISH MISRULE IN THE COLONIES

BY

C. J. ROWE, M.A.

BARRISTER-AT-LAW

AUTHOR OF 'QUESTIONS OF THE DAY IN VICTORIA'

LONDON

LONGMANS, GREEN, AND CO.

1883

CONTENTS.

———•◦•———

BONDS OF DISUNION;

OR

IMPERIAL MISRULE IN THE COLONIES.

———◆◆◆———

INTRODUCTION.

It seems but a poor compliment to the correct choice of a title for a book that the author should have to devote a few introductory lines to explain its meaning. It appears, at first sight, to be a confession that the book does not fit in with the title, and that the connection between the two must be justified by apparent apology for a want of correspondence between them.

My belief, however, is that no such apology is called for in the present instance, and I have therefore no further intention in penning these introductory lines than to briefly advance, for the sake of convenience and clearness, a statement of the objects sought to be attained in the ensuing chapters.

It is difficult to form a just estimate of the bearing of results where the end to be subserved is not clearly indicated: while, on the other hand, the mere statement of the object in view ought of itself to suffice to ensure a correct appreciation of the means used to effect it, of the facts employed in illustrating it, and of the comparative value of the general line of reasoning.

I wish, then, as shortly as may be, to explain to the reader, at the outset, the general scope of a work which, in its subject, need not fail to interest, however defective the treatment of that subject may be, and however small the attention which

B

the average Englishman may nerve himself to bestow upon a
work which concerns itself mainly with well-worn matters of
bygone colonial history.

With reference to the title of this book, it may be well at
once to proffer the explanation that, in my meaning, the
' Bonds of Disunion ' of which I treat are to be taken as expressive of those political measures for the government of our
Colonies which, while intended to weld the empire into one
harmonious whole, whereof each part should derive its laws
from a common centre, were, and under any circumstances
would be, so many centrifugal forces tending to disunion
between England and her Colonies.

Every now and again we are regaled with some elaborated
scheme of quasi-legislative union between Great Britain and
her Colonies wherever situate. We are told of the formidable
front which would be presented to the universe by the vast
Imperial Federation thus formed; of the immeasurable benefits that would be conferred by it on a world prone to dis-
ordered dreams of wild ambition; of the millennium of peace
and prosperity such union would inaugurate, and of the boundless authority the federated empire might exercise and claim.
Utopian theories these—wild, feverish, vague, high-sounding,
and raised on the flimsy foundation of unreasoning fancy.
To those who lend themselves to the advocacy of such schemes,
numbers the number of square miles, the number of people
to be confederated—are everything. The greater the number
brought under the influence of a central legislative body at
half the globe's distance from those colonies most specially
sought to be included in the happy union, the greater is to be
the might, the more real and overwhelming the power, of the
united whole. The individual dispositions, wants, jealousies,
and ambitions of particular colonies, of individual members
of colonial populations, are to the Federalists considerations
to be advanced only in order to be dismissed as unworthy of
the high dignity they claim for their loftiness of view. And
yet it is just those very individual whims, caprices, or call
them by what names you will, that must ever form the insuper-

able impediment to the realisation of the most likely-looking of federation schemes.

The necessity for complete local self-government, the wish to give local expression to individual wants, and to provide local remedies for local grievances, must always be too urgent in our autonomous Colonies to allow us to suppose that any one of them will ever again permit the interference of any foreign legislative body to regulate matters for the management of which the colony can itself provide a competent directing body. The term 'foreign' may seem misapplied, but it is not easy to see how a Federal Imperial Parliament could occupy any other relation to any single colony than that of a foreign Controlling Board. The extent of its interference would, we are assured, be limited to questions of imperial import, but who can doubt the sheer impossibility of drawing an accurate distinguishing line between imperial and purely local questions, or of adhering to it when sketchily defined. The disputes of a parish vestry may come to have a truly imperial signification, and the most general of measures providing for proportionate rates of expenditure on federal armaments may be justly regarded by colonial populations as grossly interfering with the minutest local rights. A Federal Union, Consulting Board, Parliament, or whatever it is proposed to call it, for even limited, strictly defined purposes, can therefore mean nothing less than a body endowed with competency to intermeddle with the internal details of colonial administration, and as such it could never by possibility be carried into actual practice.

But what is it that the strenuous advocates of Imperial Federation wish to protrude into notice? Is it some new system that has never previously been placed on its trial? or is it an old, old policy which it is sought to rejuvenate under some speciously modern guise? The answer, clear and decisive, I trust, may be found in the following pages, which show by admitted fact, by historical illustration, and by reasoning which, whether it be weak or strong, both fact and illustration spontaneously supply, that the centralisation involved in the principle of federal union has been pertinaciously tried. And not in vain, for if there is one broad result that stands out marked as the indisputable outcome of the happily superseded experiment, it is that the more tightly each legislative tie was drawn between England and her Colonies, the greater became the enfeebling strain upon it. The closer the connection attempted to be established, the more weakly grew the fine-spun link between exacting parent State and indignant dependency, and each fresh assertion of imperial authority or of the right of imperial interference was an additional instalment of ' Bonds of Disunion.'

The mere fact of the Colonies being governed from a distant unsympathetic centre was of itself enough to alienate from England the affections of colonists revelling in a sense of their own power and importance; and even though the rule inflicted on them had been as free from fault as it was fraught with injustice and mistake, its continuance would, in all probability, never have been tolerated beyond that preliminary stage which precedes the formation of local government institutions in the colony itself. But the proceedings of the Imperial Government in regard to the Colonies were certainly not free from blame, nor would it be easy to point to any one of them as not being in truth, at one time or another, an impolitic irritant to the easily aroused passions of jealous colonial populations. Injurious as most of them were to the colonies on whom the main burden of injudicious and perpetual home interference fell, they operated still more efficiently against the maintenance of union, or even harmony, between England and the Colonies. What were the main errors, and worse than errors, that formed the most noteworthy portion of the record of the imperial government of the most important colonies left to us, after our attempts to reduce the then North-American colonies to the position of London-governed provinces had produced their natural results, it has been my endeavour to narrate in this book. The examples I have given are those alone which appear to me most typical of their kind, for to have adduced a multitude of others would have done little but encumber with useless detail a chain of illustration in itself all powerful to prove, that both in Canada and in Australia, the necessary tendency of prolonged imperial rule was, to provoke in both a bitter discontent that only the concession of the right of self-government could assuage or remove.

Perhaps the general scope of my book has now been sufficiently indicated, but it seems advisable to discuss a little further the question of Imperial Federation, since the consideration will give a more pointed significance to the deductions I wish to be derived from the chapter immediately ensuing.

An important requisite of the federal project must evidently be, that the country claiming to exercise the chief share of authority in the Federal Council should have given proofs of its capacity for conducting the administration of its own affairs on principles likely to be conducive to the best results, and that from the history of its more recent past it should be able to furnish a guarantee that the preponderating share of power to be confided to it will only be used to the advantage of the imperial domain. For this purpose it should be ready to show a record of a consistently beneficial course of internal legislation, not calling for the sudden substitution of political and social changes of extraordinary magnitude; and further, it ought, in order to support its claim to the federal leadership, to be able to give ample evidence of as great a willingness to reform glaring defects in its previous conduct of colonial administration as it has given of its desire to destroy what is rotten, unjust, and hopelessly corrupt in its own institutions. Can such assurance be furnished from the comparatively modern domestic legislation of Great Britain? Can it be assumed that the future course that might be pursued towards the Colonies by England, if to her was entrusted the managing directorship of the Federal Council, would differ in spirit from the course she has persistently adhered to in the past? The change would be unlikely, and in the nature of things next to impossible. If so—if the sole answer to these questions must be a decided negative, and such it cannot fail to be—then England's claim to the controlling headship of the Federal Council is indeed a poor one, and as in the view of the Federalists the superior authority of the mother-country in the Councils of the vast Union is the end-all and be-all of the

imperial scheme, the denial of England's claim to effective
precedence would ensure the hopeless wreck of the crude
design.

The portion of England's history that I have chosen for
cursory review is one which typifies the period of transition
from oligarchical despotism gaudily decked out with a false
similitude of free institutions, to a time when the people of
England, roused at length to a knowledge of their own irresistible power, made a bold and partially successful bid for the
popularisation of the Constitution, and for comprehensive reform in all departments of administration. In the former
period, the country was being rapidly conducted by the glaring
misgovernment of a class to the alternative between ruin and
rebellion; in the latter period, the conviction of absolute
necessity had forced an unwilling ruling class to concede to
peaceful revolution those popular reforms which might otherwise have been extorted by unreasoning violence, and when,
like a faded leaf, the structure of privilege, corruption, and
hereditary right that had uniformly opposed an audacious
denial to the people's will, had crumbled to powder under the
vigorous touch of the reforming hand.

Unreformed England was certainly not a guide whom the
Colonies would have willingly chosen. Is it probable that
their experience of their government by Reformed England
would render her more acceptable to them as a counsellor
and leader? Here, again, the answer must be framed in no
doubtful negative. Clear and decisive it should be, if reasonable inference from hard facts be not altogether valueless. In
this book I have endeavoured to demonstrate that, whether
England was bound or free, whether oppressed and mismanaged by a clique or governing herself to her own advantage, each and all of her efforts to govern her Canadian and
Australian colonies, or to interfere in the management of their
local and general concerns, were productive of an ever-growing
want of confidence in the purity of her intentions, of an increasing disapproval of her measures—of so bitter and widespread a dislike as to make it in the highest degree unlikely
that the Colonies would ever consent to yield up to England

the smallest share of right to intermeddle once more in their domestic concerns. Not even as a co-partner would they willingly admit her into Federal Union with themselves; far less, then, as a Power entitled to precedence and headship.

Between Reformed and Unreformed England the difference was an enormous one. Slow, tentative, and incomplete though most of the early reforming measures were, the mere initiation of them was an immeasurable breach with the past life of the nation. Regeneration had been evolved from decay, and hopeful vigour had succeeded to paralysing decrepitude. But, vast as the difference was, it had little or no effect in improving the system of imperial government exercised over the Colonies. The nation had its hands full with the work of reconstructing its own public institutions in new forms, and public opinion in England, always careless and ill-instructed in regard to colonial matters, was too much occupied with the difficult task of substituting orderly liberty for old-established conditions fraught with iniquity to be able to lend to the study of colonial grievances even that limited degree of languid attention which the Englishman of to-day can, on occasion, be wrought up to bestow on colonial topics. On the other hand, the officious meddlesomeness of the Colonial Office was in no whit relaxed. With mistaken vigour it pushed the principle of centralisation into an active operation which became more nauseous to the colonial populations in proportion as they increased in numbers and self-esteem; and the right of self-government was only conceded to them when at length it became apparent to the slow reasoning powers of fussy officialdom that the concession of the right afforded the only means of keeping the Colonies in even nominal subjection.

It may now be apparent why the period of English history treated in the ensuing chapter should have been the one selected for brief review. Of all periods of our national history of modern date, none brings more closely into striking contrast the difference between the condition of the people before and after the Reform era, and the very extent of the difference effected at home furnishes an instructive commentary on the entire absence of alteration in our contemporary system of colonial government.

From the point of view of the national welfare it seems to be as desirable as it is natural that, within certain limits, people should regard their own individual interests as paramount to those of their neighbours. National prosperity flows primarily from the efforts of individuals to better their own condition, and not from a national striving after a philanthropic interference in the affairs of other people or other countries. England would probably not have worked out her own reforms as thoroughly as she has done had she not been too intent upon them to have had either time or inclination for taking into serious consideration the wants of the Colonies. It was well for England that she did not concern herself about them ; it was well also for the Colonies themselves, for it ingrained into them the conviction that they had nothing to hope from the sympathy of the public at home, and that upon themselves alone they must rely if they would gain the legislative independence they so eagerly desired. It taught them, in fact, to look closer to their own business than they had hitherto done. The bearing of these considerations upon the question of imperial federation is pertinent enough. The British public took no thought for the Colonies, and made no provision against their continued misgovernment, at a time when all other government institutions in Great Britain were condemned to radical reconstruction because of their corruptness and inefficiency—excepting alone the Colonial Office, the congenial home of red-tape, corruption, and incapacity. For the Colonies the public cared nothing then, and it cares nothing for them now. Test the last statement, reader, if you will. Inquire how many of your acquaintance know the political or geographical divisions of Canadian or Australasian colonies ; how many of them have the rare patience to wade through a single volume relating to colonial history, or to peruse a single newspaper article bearing on the most important colonial questions. Go to the civic or political banquet where the toast of ' The Colonies ' figures last on the speech list, and where only a few uninterested loungers linger while the utterances

of colonial representatives form an unheard accompaniment
to the delayed pleasures of the table. Find out what sort of
knowledge of the Colonies is imparted to the rising generation
at school or at home. Collect all the evidence possible, and
you can but conclude that of interest in colonial matters
there is amongst Englishmen *absolutely none*. A new
colonial loan may be discussed with fervour by acute stock-
brokers or by investors desirous of a new security. The ex-
ploits of a cricketing team may attract momentary attention
to the physical capabilities of antipodean colonists, but of
interest in the vast political and social problems every day being
thoughtfully and peacefully worked out in the Colonies for
future precedent and example to the parent State there is no
solitary vestige. And why should there be? Are we not
fully enough occupied at home in reconstructing our own
present and in framing our own future? Are we not, in
short, paying that salutary attention to our own business
which precludes the possibility of our giving a passing thought
to the concerns of distant countries? Fortunately, so it is,
so it must ever be, as long as the nation is free to exercise its
political intelligence for the furtherance of internal reform.
New questions of ever-increasing complexity are inevitable
attendants on the growing prosperity around us, for each new
opportunity gives rise to some freshly-born desire, and each
reform granted is but the harbinger of others to be demanded
in turn. The hands of a nation blessed with free power
to regulate its own affairs on a popular basis must always be
full to overflowing, and in applying itself to set its own house
in order England has enough, and more than enough, to do.
Why then should she concern herself about the internal
affairs of Colonies of whose condition and circumstances the
mass of her people know nothing and care nothing? Let the
Imperial Federalists explain this, and let them prove, if they
can, that any attempt on England's part to direct in the
smallest degree the external policy of a colony would not be,
in reality, an intermeddling with its domestic policy. Let
them demonstrate, if they can, that such a course would not
be prejudicial to the best interests of England itself, as in a

measure tending to withdraw her attention from plans for the amelioration of her own condition, and that it would not furnish a dangerous irritant to the easily excited animosity of the colonial community.

It is not my intention to discuss at any further length, in this introductory chapter, Imperial Federation schemes. Each page in this book should furnish arguments against them, and reference to the subject directly would best find place in its concluding pages. The facts set forth in the following chapters are proofs of an apathetic indifference to colonial interests on the part of England's people in times past, and of the unavoidable tendency of colonial government from a distant centre to produce the rapid severance of the tie by which it was sought to bind the Colonies in subjection to an English Government department. I have alluded here to the visions of federal schemers, because at the root of all their plans is the maintenance of the principle of centralised government. Can we hope that the consequences of the application of that principle in the future would differ in kind from the ascertained results of its previous trials? Do the teachings of experience allow us to suppose that a system that has broken down in every detail, wherever put into active operation, can ever furnish a more favourable record of success if refurbished under a deceptive title indicative of mutual co-partnership? It cannot be that it should; but if, on the other hand, an all-powerful ' Bond of Disunion ' is to be urgently desired, if the complete disruption of our colonial empire is an object to be attained with certainty and speed, then let us energetically promote the formation of a Federal Union and Council for matters of imperial concern.

But one word more by way of introduction. The miserable condition of England in the opening decades of the present century was, truly enough, alleged by the reformers, to be due to the domination of a landowning class. Every effort was made by the popular leaders to reduce the power of the landowners, for such a limitation was seen to be a condition necessarily precedent to the establishment of a rational system of popular government. Yet it was just when the nation had begun to acquire a certain amount of control over its former rulers that it was deemed just and wise to impose upon the Australian colonies measures for the encouragement of a greater and more injurious monopoly of landowning than England herself had been called upon to grapple with. The curse of England, landowning monopoly, was at a pen-stroke transplanted to the soil of the antipodes. There, alas! it has struck deep root, and may in time furnish, in the sad consequences of an embittered struggle between the acred few and the landless many, the most fitting tribute to the iniquitous folly of English colonial rulers.

Do English Ministries, to whatever extent of Liberalism they may pledge themselves in home politics, perceive the evil their predecessors have created in Australia? If so, they do their best to intensify it by conferring titles and distinctions upon the many-acred shepherd king; and, worse than that, by introducing into Australia the principle of *hereditary* title.[1] Heretofore the colonial landowner has looked upon his extensive property from a commercial point of view, as a means for the acquisition of wealth, and has shrunk from the prospect of letting his eldest son grow up in idleness in expectation of a paternal inheritance. To-morrow he may regard his acres as necessary to be kept together for the maintenance of the dignity of the title which his heir will succeed to. Eldest sons, aristocratic customs, and class hatreds—these are the injuries which England still has it in her power to bestow upon the Colonies, and the infliction of which affords conclusive proof that to-day, as in times past, the mother-country continues to give evidence of hopeless incapacity to comprehend the conditions of colonial life.

[1] I allude to the baronetcy recently conferred on Sir W. J. Clarke, reputed to be the largest landowner and richest squatter in Australia.

CHAPTER I.

A TRANSITION PERIOD OF ENGLISH HISTORY.

GLANCE for a moment, if you please, at the long list of measures
passed within the last fifty years for the relief of the English
labouring and middle classes. Look at the sweeping nature
of the reforms contained in those measures, and remember
that they were extorted from Parliaments bitterly hostile to
change. Read how concessions for the people's benefit were
wept for, clamoured for, struggled for, before being finally
wrested from rulers callous to the misery that they themselves
had caused. What must have been the condition of the people
whose necessities claimed such reforms, yet could not obtain
them except at the cost of such constant suffering and agitation? What must have been the character of the Government which persistently withheld the meanest instalment of
reform until extracted by the force of no longer resistible urgency? See, even to-day, around us a mass of humanity, fighting
for profit, for employment, or only for bare existence, and un-
ceasingly calling for legislative reforms. If with untrammelled
trade, with the universe pouring its wealth of produce in keen
competition on an English market, with an unshackled press
thundering out its mandate of 'popular rule,' in accordance with
a public opinion which encourages to the full the ventilation
of grievances and remedies, the Englishman of to-day is still
discontented and restless, how must the bulk of the community
have fared in the earlier years of the present century, before a
single remedial measure had been passed?—when, out of their
scanty earnings, a narrow oligarchy of borough-mongers maintained themselves in power and place as the 'elect of the

people; ' when they turned their power to account to oppress the poor, to enrich themselves, to rob the public purse, to stifle trade, to proscribe cheap food, to promote jobbery, monopoly, venality, and corruption, to burke discussion, to foster crime, to perpetuate and maintain, as the most sacred bulwark of the nation, the grinding religious, social, and political inequality from which for half a century or more the country has been trying to extricate itself?

Let us make the picture as bright as possible. See then, first, population increasing, borough-mongers in course of being overthrown, trade expanding, invention in powerful swing, and the people at last on the high road to freedom and self-government; and let the very magnitude of these changes point the misery which necessitated their accomplishment.

The population of the United Kingdom had increased from 19,000,000 in 1819 to 24,000,000 in 1831. This was made up by an increase of the population of Great Britain from 13,000,000 to 16,500,000, and of that of Ireland from 6,000,000 to 7,750,000. Between these periods, again, the gross taxable income had increased by over 50 per cent., or from 150,000,000*l.* to about 250,000,000*l.*, so that the national income had improved in a geometrical ratio to increase of population. Moreover, the cheapening of every manufactured article, brought about by the use of labour-saving inventions, by vastly improved modes of communication, and by the greater facilities for exchange afforded by them, had increased the purchasing power of the enlarged income by 70 to 80 per cent.

The power-loom and the spinning-jenny had taken the place of the hand-loom, the threshing-machine had been substituted for the tedious manual work of the labourer, and invention was busy in all departments of industry. Steam railways, after having been laughed out of court by all that was wise, great, powerful, and official in the land, were at length fairly started in 1830, and with what vast results on the peace, prosperity, and progress, not only of England, but of the universe, we now know. As men travelled quicker, so they thought quicker. A closer contact was established between different parts of the kingdom, and the nation for the

first time began to discover its real condition of suffering and
stagnation. Long-landed blessings began to be regarded as
unmitigated evils, and England at last positively set to work
to cleanse the Augean stable in which it was living—nay, even
to upset the glorious Constitution of 1688. Long and bitter
was the struggle, but the nation was getting rid of leading-
strings, and was beginning to find out its own power. As
soon as it did so it became irresistible, and bit by bit the
wonderful framework raised a century and a half before was
reformed, overturned, and finally reconstructed out of all
recognisable existence.

Religious dissent had been formerly regarded as a grave
offence, and was still punishable by the exclusion of Dissenters
from all offices of trust. This must be altered, and a reluctant
Legislature was forced to declare that the country should be
allowed to claim the services of Dissenters of all kinds, and
that formal subservience to an established religion was no
longer to be the test of magisterial capacity.

Blood relationship or family connection with those in
power, had been generally held to constitute a right to live on
the public purse. This, however, was not the view of the reformers, who saw no virtue in the arrangement, and insisted
that not only should public officials be rewarded in proportion
to the work to be done by them, but also that highly-salaried
State servants should no longer be permitted to procure cheaply-
paid substitutes to do the work entrusted to them. Nor were
the reversions to public offices of trust to be vended in future
for the benefit of the privileged few to whom the public service
was a profitable gamble.

The venerable Church, too, was to be reformed. Good
fellowship, unclerical habits, and good birth were no longer
to be the sole qualifications for Church dignities. The
Church must thenceforward exist for the people, and not the
people for the Church.

The courts of justice in their turn were attacked, though
with no great success. We all know that the laws of England
represent the perfection of human reason, that they are
known to all, and that there is and ever has been free access

to the courts of justice for the meanest subjects of the realm. The respectability of these maxims was to a great extent thrown away upon the reformers who turned their attention to the complicated and expensive nature of legal proceedings. They saw in them the evidence of the falsification of all true principles of administration of justice. Each court of common law had its own peculiar procedure, clashing with that of the courts around it, and chaos, confusion, and glorious iteration reigned at Westminster in honoured supremacy. Each step in a proceeding at law was so tedious, slow, uncertain, and costly, and it was also capable of such indefinite protraction that only the man endowed at once with the longest purse and the greatest share of obstinacy could hope to succeed in a lawsuit. The law should be the guarantee of liberty, and that it can only be if the poor man has the same chance of getting justice done for him as the rich man has. This, it was evident, he had not. He was told that the courts of law were open to him for redress, ' but so,' said Horne Tooke, ' was the London tavern—to any one who could pay.' As a consequence the risk run by a rich man in defrauding a poor one was rendered infinitesimally small.

But the justice of the law courts was speedy and cheap besides the dilatory proceedings of the Court of Chancery, where the length of suits was measured by decades and half-centuries, where people were born in Chancery, lived and died in Chancery, and left therein their descendants for as long as there was any corpus possessing a value over which Chancery could claim cognisance. The constitution of this court, originally devised to deal with less than a million of money, had been in no whit altered, though the property within its tenacious grasp amounted in value in 1831 to more than 40,000,000l. sterling. Honest and capable as most of the judges were, both at law and equity, they had no interest in conducting the business before them either quickly or well, so long as they were paid by fees and not by salary. The inferior officers of the courts, who were paid in like manner, for their part had a lively interest in throwing impediments in the way of expeditious termination of suits.

But the system, or rather want of system, was dear to the lawyers long taught to consider legal procedure, as well as the law itself, the highest perfection of human reason. Up to 1832 but slight improvement had been effected in law procedure beyond the substitution of payment by salary to the judges instead of payment by fees. Venerable fictions were too powerful for the reforming spirit to contend against with success, and it was not till the Common Law Procedure Act of 1852 came into force that legal proceedings began to be conducted on a fairly intelligible basis.

While such was the state of our civil courts, the evils of the 'justice' dispensed by the criminal courts were quite as apparent and far more terrible. The criminal laws were indiscriminate slaughter enactments. Our legislators at the beginning of the century had but one remedy for crime. 'Hang! hang!' was their guiding rule, as if hanging was the best use to which a human being could be devoted. Nowadays it is thought that punishment should be but a means to an end—a process to be applied to reform a community and to discourage from crime. Not so thought our forefathers. They were, in fact, too careless of either the moral or physical good of the people to reason out schemes for the prevention of crime. One of the most humiliating chapters of our national history is that in which the House of Lords and the bench of Bishops, headed by a Lord Chancellor and supported by the voice of a Lord Chief Justice of England, appear as banding their energies together in the cause of judicial murder, and successfully denouncing the noble efforts of Romilly and Mackintosh to remove the capital penalty from trivial offences as the hallucinations of crack-brained 'theorists.'

Till 1833 the very barbarity of our criminal laws continued to furnish powerful incentives to crime by the reaction their severity produced in public feeling. In the clearest cases juries over and over again refused to convict when a punishment grotesquely disproportioned to the offence charged would follow a verdict of 'guilty.' In a large number of cases they gave verdicts involving deliberate perjury—by reducing the amount sworn to as the value of stolen property, in order to avoid the capital conviction. Prosecutors and witnesses could hardly be induced to come forward at all when their evidence might hang some unfortunate, guilty of a trumpery offence committed in a moment of weakness or under the pressure of starvation.

As evidenced by the statistics of half a century ago, the chances of a prisoner being convicted at all were only about six or seven to four, and the odds of the quality of his offence being reduced by the verdict of a jury were largely in the prisoner's favour.   Taking, for instance, the criminal statistics for 1832, we find that the number of people committed for trial in that year was 20,829. of whom only 14,947 were convicted.   No fewer than 1,449 were condemned to death.   But so opposed was public opinion to the barbarity of the criminal system that the death sentence was but rarely permitted to be carried out, and it had become a mere formal method of terminating a trial for the graver kinds of offences.   In 1832, it appears that only 54 people were executed, and 15 of these executions were for murder.   It was evident that the criminal law had fallen into utter contempt, and nothing can furnish a clearer proof of this, and of the consequent increase of inducements to crime furnished by Draconian rigour, than the rise in the number of criminals from 4,605 in 1805, to 9,091 in 1816, and to 20,829 in 1832 —a quickly ascending rate of increase altogether disproportionate to the increase of population over the period.

The Game Laws were held up to the nation as sublime achievements of statesmanship, and as corner-stones of the glorious Constitution. Under these laws only landed proprietors and their heirs apparent, as also their gamekeepers, were allowed to kill game. Any one found transgressing the Game Laws was liable to be sentenced and tried by the magistrate, who was at the same time his accuser. The poacher, judged and sentenced by the landowner on whose preserves he had trespassed, was sent to herd with the worst of criminals. Smarting under a sense of injustice, he formed a ready tool for his new companions, and rarely did the man convicted of the dire offence of putting his toil-worn hand on a pheasant or a partridge emerge from prison without having irrevocably committed himself to association with the gallows-birds he left behind him.

But, however severe and unfairly administered the Game Laws were, they did little or nothing to check poaching, especially when, as too often happened, the mass of the population was sunk in the deepest distress.

It was made a penal offence to sell game. This enactment naturally drove up the price of game, and acted as a further stimulus to poaching. The brains of landlordism were, however, quite equal to the occasion, and erected the buying of game into a penal offence. The nation could not take this last feat of legislative wisdom *au serieux*. People laughed at it for awhile, and then bought more game than ever.

After 1831 some of the feudal privileges attaching to a landowner's monopoly of game were swept away, and the game-licence system was adopted which is now in vogue. But until very recently poaching was still considered as one of the most serious of offences in the eye of the law, and it doubtless is so rated still by many a Squire Western of modern times.

A step forward in the lessening of landowners' privileges was taken ere long. By 1830 the nation had become obtuse enough to be unable to see why landowners should continue to have the sole and exclusive privilege of defrauding their creditors, while ordinary debtors were thrown into prison for indefinite periods, not unfrequently embracing a lifetime. So in that year it procured the passing of an Act providing that the proceeds realised from the sale of landed estates should be liable to be attached in payment of debts contracted on it, and in 1833 real estate was for the first time subjected to liability for the payment of simple contract debts. These reforms may seem but small ones compared with the evils arising from landowning monopoly, and which future generations, if not the present, will still have to assail ; but considering that the Parliaments of those days were composed of landlords and their nominees, it was then infinitely more difficult to effect trifling reforms in the laws relating to land than it would be at the present day to procure complete and sweeping changes.

If by the measures above mentioned the defensive positions of the landlords were still left almost inviolate, the thin edge of the wedge of reconstruction had been introduced, and, further, the offensive powers of acred magnates were sadly curtailed by general legislation.

The time had at length arrived when landlordism in England was no longer to be treated as an absolutely inviolable principle. The standards of right were now declared to be standards of wrong, misrule, and iniquitous oppression. The people proclaimed their intention of setting up an entirely different set of principles for the conduct of legislation and for the government of the country. This could only be done through the medium of a Reformed Parliament, so Parliament was reformed.

It is not my intention to go into the details of the oft-told tale of Parliamentary Reform, but it will be necessary to advert to it in order to throw light upon the condition of the people and of the government of the country at the time it was effected, by pointing out some of the more glaring evils attaching to the representation of the people which required immediate attention.

The position of Members of Parliament was in many respects an enviable one. They revelled in the privilege of exemption from arrest for civil process, so long as they continued Members, and they also enjoyed an immunity from submission to decrees and from paying the cost of suits, in the Ecclesiastical Courts.

These privileges were equally agreeable to large capitalists as to the landlords, and rightly so, for they furnished to both a safe and simple relief from pecuniary difficulties. Thus a man desirous of defrauding his creditors would often purchase a seat in Parliament from some influential borough-monger, who welcomed the profitable transaction. Then, as the 'elect' of the people, he would lift up an indignant voice against the crime of indebtedness, and give a senatorial vote for drastic measures for filling the prisons with insolvent debtors. For these, however innocent or unfortunate, no punishment could be too severe. Or from the safe obscurity of Boulogne or

Calais he might resell his seat for a profit on the original transaction.

Public opinion had gradually come to consider these practices as objectionable ; at last they became scandalous, when in 1820 a debtor in the Fleet, for debts amounting to 7,600*l*., was by one of those judicious arrangements returned for Beverley. The prison doors were opened at once to the honourable Member ; but truth compels us to relate that, instead of adorning with his presence the Parliamentary arena, he betook himself to the retirement of a Continental retreat.   On the other hand, a seat in Parliament might be made the means of liquidating a just debt, for an influential owner of a borough might hand it over as an asset to some importunate creditor. If unembarrassed, he might satisfy the claims of conscience and relationship by handing the seat over for a time to a younger son or a needy relative for whom it was incumbent on him to make suitable provision.

The jurisdiction of the Ecclesiastical Courts at that time extended to grants of probate and suits for divorce.   The probate proceedings might involve expensive issues directly chargeable to the inefficient administration of a trustee, who yet, if a Member of Parliament, could not be called upon to pay one iota of the costs, to carry a decree into execution, or to make good damage caused by a breach of trust.   Or an heir-at-law might, if a Member, refuse to produce a will setting aside his claims or creating a charge in favour of some one else.

Where elections were contested, the electors became marketable commodities, to be bought up at fancy prices. The polling sometimes went on for weeks at a time, and the grossest bribery, corruption, and intimidation were freely indulged in and as openly boasted of.   The expenses of these elections were enormous, and, except through the avenue of a pocket borough, only a very wealthy man could dream of getting into Parliament.

Political discussion was the last thing to be thought of at election time.   It was a season of drunken orgies for the intelligent freeman and the enlightened burgess.   In some.

boroughs, the privilege of returning a Member to Parliament was confined to the Mayor and Corporation. In others, a limited body of freeholders were the only ones entitled to exercise the franchise. In at any rate one borough, an individual was known to have proposed, elected, and returned himself as duly elected, and, as he at the same time held the office of sheriff, his proceedings were strictly within his right. The anomalies were abundant, and to us are probably more startling than they appeared to a generation which regarded them as grateful indications of the eternal fitness of things.

If there was any principle at all regulating the distribution of electoral privileges, it would seem to have been that the larger the population of any particular place the fewer should be the number of voters allowed to it ; and that representation should, as far as possible, be made to bear an inverse ratio everywhere to the numbers of the people and to the magnitude of their interests. Nominally, there was a House of Commons representative of the people, but actually, a House representative of the Lords. It furnished the latter with places and pensions, imposed taxes on the people to provide for these, and presented the nation in return with Corn Laws, Navigation Laws, criminal laws of undiluted savagery, and penal laws of varying hues of absurdity and cruelty. But ' the eternal fitness of things ' was now to undergo alteration even in the sacred abode of legislative incapacity, and in 1832 a House of Lords, the palladium of our Constitution, though deaf to the wants of the people, consented to the reform of the House of Commons in order to prevent the extension of its own privileges to others more worthy of them.

Now let us look at the dark side of the picture. Hitherto we have seen progress and reform effected or about to be effected ; now we have to deal with poverty and suffering, with folly rampant and unrelieved by remedial change.

The prosperity of the nation from the beginning of the century up to 1832 was far more apparent than real. Above a certain line, was improvement and increasing comfort ; below, grinding distress but a short remove from starvation.

The substitution of machinery for hand labour had facilitated
and cheapened production. Improved agricultural and farming implements were raising a larger produce from the land,
but a rapidly increasing population had produced a demand
far more than the increased produce. In consequence, poorer
lands had been brought into cultivation, and the rent of land
had greatly risen. But the enlarged farming area had not
sufficed to bring into employment more than a comparatively
small number of the thousands of agricultural labourers
thrown out of work by the introduction of threshing-
machines.

In manufactures too, many thousands of people had been
thrown out of employment by the introduction of the power-
loom and the spinning-jenny, and the demand created by the
cheapness consequent on facilitated production had not yet
become sufficiently great to allow of the re-engagement of
these destitute toilers. Amongst manufacturers and merchants,
the competition engendered by the increased cheapness of
production had lowered profits all round for the time being,
and the fifty per cent. rise in the taxable income of the
country represented little more than a rise in the incomes of
the landowners and of the greater capitalists. For a while
the industrious Lancashire men refused to recognise the signs
of the times, and stuck patiently to their superseded hand-
looms. At one time it was estimated that at least 41,000 of
them were endeavouring to subsist on as little as twopence
per diem. But this could not last long, and in the rage of
infatuated despair many of them joined the bands of unemployed labourers then devoting their energies to indiscriminate rick-burning and general machine-breaking. Over
this untoward state of things the powers that were resolved
to triumph. They set about the laudable endeavour by
enjoining upon the parishes to extend the operation of the
Poor Law, by supplementing the labourers' pay out of the Poor
Rates. Whether a labourer was able-bodied or not, the rates
were to be expended in supplementing his earnings, if insufficient for his own support. He was to be entitled to
relief, not according to the value of his services, but in pro-

portion to the number of his progeny—therefore the larger his family was in point of numbers the greater would be the amount of relief afforded him.

The effect of these provisions soon became painfully apparent. Families had become lucrative investments, giving rates of profit or livelihood increasing progressively with the numbers and helplessness of their members. For the first time in his life, the labourer found himself authoritatively encouraged in extravagance and improvidence. Young people could look forward to State endowments on their marriages ; the older people found the necessity for work superseded by an amiable State mechanism.

The parishes were startled when they perceived the extent of the growing burden thus thrust upon them. The labouring population, by degrees, came to look upon the parish allowance as their inalienable freehold, and in consequence the emulation of parish officials was directed to shifting on to each other their expensive pauper bills. Proud indeed of its diplomacy was the parish that could contrive to marry off some aged female pauper to a pauper of the opposite sex in some adjoining parish. But the last parish, where the happy pair now acquired a new domicile, was not so satisfied with this connubial arrangement. Every scheme of petty ingenuity was brought into play to return the compliment, and pauper marriages in order to transfer liabilities to other parishes, became practical jokes of exquisite humour. A pauper was estimated to cost 25l. per annum, and as every case of doubtful settlement was hotly contested before the courts of law with all the careless profusion incidental to spending other people's money, the burden caused by the local Poor Rates soon became intolerable, so much so that the lower classes of ratepayers were themselves becoming rapidly pauperised.

Under the old state of things the landlords had often come forward to render temporary assistance to their tenantry, and between the loftiest and the lowliest in the rural districts there had always existed a certain bond of sympathy. Absolute power on the one hand, absolute submission and obedience on the other, almost always coexist with a feeling of obligation on the part of the superior, of entire dependence on that of the inferior, which prompts occasional acts of benevolent charity from the one to the other. But the new administration of the Poor Law made the tenant to a large degree independent, and whatever sympathy might have existed between the landlord and his tenants, or between the farmer and his labourers, was rudely severed. The landlord, seeing his tenant in receipt of parish relief to which he too had to contribute, promptly turned his tenant out into the cold. But, still desirous of doing something to allay the widespread misery thus occasioned, the landlords, honestly enough perhaps, embraced the theory that the enclosure of commons, by bringing more land into cultivation, would afford additional employment. So they procured Enclosure Acts, which had the effect of enclosing no fewer than 1,751,310 acres of common land in the squires' ring-fences between 1811 and 1830. But this was in reality diminishing and not increasing the cultivated area.

On the common land, labourers had been used to live in cottages on small plots of ground which they considered as their own. One of these small occupiers would have in his little domain a cow or two besides a few pigs and poultry, and could raise from it as much vegetable produce as he and his family could consume. Nay, he might often supplement his wages by an appreciable income from the sale of his surplus produce. All his spare hours were spent in the cultivation of his little terrain, and he was sober, industrious, and wealthy as compared with his after lot when these small productive holdings had gone to swell his squire's domain. The produce was now to find its way entirely to his landlord's behoof, and so at one blow the labourer was levelled from the position of a small but industrious and hopeful farmer, to that of a lodger on sufferance, at the mercy of a landlord who had robbed him of his all. Now, instead of being an energetic producer, his chief desire was to be an unthrifty consumer of parish sustenance, supplemented by what he could procure for the miserable pay doled out to him for unwilling negligent work on his stolen property. Despite, or probably because of, the enclosure policy, pauperism went on increasing, until in 1832 the Poor Rates of the kingdom for the year amounted to 7,000,000*l.*, and it was calculated that the proportion of paupers to population in England and Wales was as one to seven.

But it is an ill wind that blows nobody good, and it is certain that a considerable portion of the enormous sums devoted to pauper relief found its way into the receptive pockets of parish officials. Porter, in his 'Progress of the Nation,'[1] observes:—'Plunder and jobbing of all kinds were the usual accompaniments of the system, and it is by no means surprising that persons who were allowed to benefit themselves in this manner should have become violent opponents of a change which has introduced order and economy into the various branches of parish expenditure whence they had previously drawn their irregular gains.' The change, however, was to be deferred till 1834.

The enclosure system not having proved efficacious, the ingenuity of the squires was equal to a new remedy. 'The land is over-populated,' they said, and, with a view to reduce the fancied excess of numbers, they proceeded to pull down houses and cottages on their estates. But population was by no means reduced by these remedial methods, for the Poor Law was far stronger in promoting increase than misery and high-handed oppression were potent to check it.

The farmers were hardly better off than the labourers. Threshing machinery had come to their aid; the researches of Davy had given to farming a more scientific character; a better system of cropping by rotation had come into use, and improved means of communication had cheapened the carriage of produce to market, besides facilitating the means of exchanging it. Their produce was eagerly demanded, and the demand kept pace with the increase of population. But, despite all these considerations, farming had become a thoroughly bad business, a mere scheme for throwing good money after bad. Why this was so will be obvious enough if we briefly examine the operation of the Corn Laws.

Previous Corn Laws having failed of their nominal object

[1] P. 94.

of keeping the price of agricultural produce high and even while at the same time adding to the prosperity of the nation, the cry of distress among the owners and occupiers of land became exceedingly urgent. Accordingly, an Act was passed in 1815, under which the importation of corn was absolutely prohibited until the price of home-grown corn should have reached the famine height of eighty shillings per quarter. Also the monopoly of the home market was secured by the Act to the British grower, for all other grain until the price had reached a proportionate height. Further, the introduction of all foreign meat, flesh or fish, living or dead, was absolutely forbidden, and to give completeness to the system, it was decreed that imported butter was only to be used for washing sheep or for greasing carriage-wheels, and the revenue officers received stringent instructions to stir the butter round with tarred sticks so as to ensure its not being used as food. A notable exception, however, was made, by which turtle, turbot, and sturgeon were to be admitted, so as to afford cheap and nutritious food for the million!

It was expected that these enactments would keep the price of home produce permanently high, and would prevent fluctuations in price. Eighty shillings was thenceforward to be the invariable price of corn. So likely did this appear, that the bounties on the exportation of grain were done away with.

The effect of a rise in the price of produce in a settled country, is to raise the rent of the land on which it is grown if, in consequence of the rise, inferior land is brought into cultivation. In prospect, then, of the high prices promised by these Corn Laws, the farmer, if he wished to remain a farmer, was called upon to pay an increased rent for the expected value of his monopoly—an additional tax to his landlord to nullify the extra profit he might possibly derive from his business.

The farmers were in 1815 promised eighty shillings a quarter for their corn, and their farms were valued on that supposition. The hope of high profits held out by the Corn Laws created competition for high-rented farms, and caused abandoned and inferior soils to be brought into cultivation. So much the better for the landlords. But the dreams of continuous high prices were quickly dissipated. The average price of wheat in 1816 was 76s. 2d., in the following year 94s., and in 1818 it was 83s. 8d. With these prices came a further extension of tillage. The price of wheat dropped very materially in consequence, and continued rapidly to descend, until in October 1822 it was no more than 38s. 1d., while the average for that year was only 44s. 7d.[1]

Not much of constancy about these prices.

Protection had executed its natural function of first stimulating artificial prices and profits, and natural competition, unnaturally extended, had reduced them again to a non-paying level. 'Distress' became again the farmers' cry, and a Commission was appointed to inquire into its causes. 'Depreciate the currency again,' shrieked the landlords, 'and all will go well.' But even a landowner's Parliament at its wits' end for any impracticable panacea, could not go this length. In 1822 Lord Liverpool's Administration passed an Act allowing importation at high duties when the price of corn should reach 70s. But this enactment was inoperative, because till 1828, when it was superseded by the famous, or infamous, sliding scale, the price never rose higher than 66s. 6d.

A new set of Resolutions, moved by Mr. Charles Grant,[2] was passed and embodied in an Act in 1828. The Act provided that the duty was to be 23s. 8d. when the home price of corn was 64s., gradually declining to 16s. 8d. when the price was at 69s., and to 1s. when it was at or above 73s. On this shifting principle the duties were based till 1841, when the law was altered with a view of securing a price of from 54s. to 58s. per bushel, and in 1846 the Corn Laws were at last totally repealed.

Let us look at the condition of the farmers when the system of Corn Laws was in full swing. Their rents were based on the supposition of constant high prices being maintained. As a matter of fact, under the system prices fluctuated incessantly, and under its influence they were declining enormously, taking a comparison over a period of a quarter of a century. The farmer was crippled and often ruined, by the

---

[1] McCulloch's *Commercial Dictionary*, tit. ' Corn Laws.'
[2] Afterwards Lord Glenelg.

conjoint operation of high rents, Poor Rates, and low prices.
Rents fell again in 1818, but not in the same proportion as
prices of farm produce fell, and the farmers were therefore
worse off than before.   Farming had become a pure speculation
instead of a steady trade.   The land was of necessity cropped
to its utmost ability, and an incoming yearly tenant would
too often find that the basis of his rent, previous prices and
previous crops, was one which must absorb whatever profits
he might hope to make from exhausted soils.   He could not
get a lease, so improvements were out of the question.   Close
cropping was everything.   The distress of the farmers at the
beginning of the third decade of the century was more serious
than it had been in 1815, because of the increased number of
farmers verging on ruin, who had been induced to rush into
agricultural pursuits by the grant of a State monopoly, as it
was thought to be.   The sliding scale of 1828 was still to
secure this monopoly, but its main effect was to induce
enormous speculations in foreign corn, which was always ready
to come out of bond and so to depress the price of the home
supplies.   Foreign corn had never been entirely kept out, even
under the most absolute form of prohibition, but now it was
always lying in wait to wreck the farmers' hopes, as we shall
see later on.

It may be remarked here, that it was this attempted exclusion of foreign produce that was ever, in reality, the farmers'
bane.   At the period now under consideration, the length,
uncertainty, and risk of sea voyages, inefficient stowage, &c.,
made importation of grain by sea a very expensive and speculative business.   The importer, therefore, could only have
afforded to sell at prices far above the home level, if that level
had been a low and regular price.   The home farmer would
have had nothing to fear from a foreign competitor except
when crops were unusually deficient at home, and when in
consequence his own produce rose in value.   As a matter of
fact that rise would not have been a great one, because foreign
supplies would have rushed in to meet a deficiency.   The
nation, cheaply fed, would have been able to devote to extension
of productive industries vast sums which, though nominally

paid in giving encouragement to agriculture, in reality went to swell the rent-rolls of the landlords. A prosperous nation would have keenly competed for increased supplies of agricultural produce, and would, by a healthy demand, have prevented corn prices from falling below a paying level. Steady prices would have operated largely in favour of a disposition to grant leases, rather than yearly tenancies, which placed the tenant at his landlord's mercy. With the guarantee afforded by a lease, as well as with the stimulus to improvement given by average low prices returning no more than a regular fair margin of profit, would have come economical and careful cultivation, while invention would have received the spur it needed. Lands would have risen steadily in value. Rents would have been punctually paid. Prosperity would have gained the day over Poor Rates; and even with all the startling contrasts between progress and poverty that dog the footsteps of prosperity, England might have been energetic, industrious, and contented, instead of being merely restless, miserable, and starving.

Low prices and free competition were not, as was the supposition, the causes, but they *were the true remedies*, for agricultural distress. The legislative medicines for the disease were high prices and monopolies.

The competition founded on expectations of the value of an exclusive market, was of itself sufficient to reduce farming profits below the average limit that competition, not artificially stimulated, would have driven them down to. When to this circumstance we add the burden of crushing rents, pauperising rates, and a sliding scale so constructed as to promote the flow of foreign grain into England at the maximum of expense and risk to the farmer, to the nation, and to the importer himself, we can see that the lot of the British farmer, under the operation of the laws nominally devised for his express benefit, was not an enviable one.

Rents had dropped in 1818 after their previous rise, but, notwithstanding bad farming seasons, fast-dropping grain prices, and the restoration of a metallic currency, they were maintained at double the height to which they had reached in

the earlier years of the century. In 1803 the assessments to
the Income Tax upon real property in Great Britain were
made upon an annual value or rental of 38,691,394*l.* In
1812 the annual value was estimated at over 46,000,000*l.*,
while in 1842 Sir Robert Peel, in bringing forward his proposals for an Income Tax, estimated the rents of the previous
year at 72,800,000*l.* So that, even on *his* showing, rents must
have almost doubled in thirty-eight years. But Sir Robert must
have underestimated, or the growth of rental must have been
extraordinarily rapid during 1842-3, for we find that the
annual value of real property assessed to the tax for the
year ending April 5, 1843, was for England and Scotland
alone 95,284,497*l.*, although properties of less yearly value
than 150*l.* were excluded from the assessment. Deducting
from this total 2,598,943*l.* as the assessed value of railway
property for the year, we have still a formidable total left,
which shows an actual increase in rent of about 150 per cent.
since 1803.

It may readily be believed that relatively to the other
classes of the community—that is, to the people, and to the
farmers in especial—the landlords were doing very well for
themselves, and, on the principle of letting well alone, were
exceedingly unwilling to allow of any legislation which might
produce a change for the better in the circumstances of the
nation. Selfishly blind to their true interests as the landlords
were, while striving exclusively for the promotion of their own
wealth and influence, they failed to see that the prosperity of
the country would give a far higher value to landed property
than it had ever known before. The abolition of the Corn
Laws inaugurated a Free Trade era which the landlords bitterly
opposed, and which was in nothing more remarkable than in
the immensely increased value it gave to landed property.
Moreover, since the adoption of free-trading principles, the
rise in the value of land has been on a far sounder and more
permanent basis than previously, for it has not, as then, been
caused by the increase of population faster than its means of
subsistence, but by the large increase of the population in
numbers and wealth, resulting from the cheapness of food and

extension of employment that followed on the substitution of a world-wide market for the local supplying ground.

It is quite unnecessary to show how an already starving people failed to derive advantage from Corn Laws which curtailed an already existing insufficiency of food. The condition of the nation was so deplorable that, but for the effects of the Poor Law in destroying the growth of independence and manliness, the down-trodden population would probably have forced the repeal of the Corn Laws within a very few years after their imposition. It is only by considering the people as utterly deficient in spirit, and utterly wanting in the self-reliance which leads to organisation for the redress of evil government, that we can cease to marvel at their endurance of food taxation till 1846, or to wonder that they should for so long have consented to a twenty per cent. tax on their bread, whilst, according to Richard Cobden, ' the family of a nobleman paid to the Bread Tax about one halfpenny for every hundred pounds of income.' True it was that ' political discontent, revealing itself in occasional riotings, rudely repressed by violence and bloodshed, was rife throughout the country. But in the Legislature its voice was little heeded, for it was not the people but a class which was then represented in Parliament.' [1]

The people had gone off on a wrong scent, clamouring for Parliamentary Reform. That was desirable and necessary, but the repeal of the Corn Laws was far more so. That the great mass of the nation did not altogether starve was in great part owing to importations of foreign wheat. In 1825, 1826, and 1827, partial admissions of foreign corn were made under Orders in Council and special Acts, but under the sliding scale of 1828 a vast speculative import trade in grain grew up, which benefited the consumer if it did little good to the farmer or to the trader himself. The sliding scale appears to have been expressly drawn up with a view to promote risky speculation. It certainly had that effect, and thereby diverted a great deal of commercial enterprise into a hazardous foreign corn trade, from channels where more regular profits might

---

[1] Montgredien's *History of Free Trade in England*, p. 9.

have been made at far less than the average of risk involved
in the importation of foreign corn. With regard to this, Mr.
Jacob, in his evidence before the House of Commons Committee in 1833, says :—'The supplies of foreign corn came
in by jerks in large quantities at once, not according
to the immediate wants of consumption, but according
to the perpetually varying duty, and according to the
opinion among the importers of a probable rise or fall of the
averages.'

Mr. Henry Ashworth, in his valuable little book ' Cobden
and the League,' summarises as follows :—' Let it be supposed
that, following an unfavourable season, the average price of
wheat in the English market had become 73s. per quarter,
and the import duty consequently 1s. per quarter. This low
duty would attract the notice of the merchant and induce him
to refer to the prices of wheat abroad. If he concluded to
send out orders, the operations had to be hastened, in order to
escape payment of a higher rate of duty on arrival, in consequence of earlier arrivals inducing lower prices and higher
duties, at the instance of other importers. He would not
consider it safe, under the circumstances, to make his out-
going remittance in manufactures or home produce, lest his
delay in the sale of such produce abroad should cause his
import of wheat to arrive (in an extreme case) when, in consequence of other large imports, it was worth only 36s. a quarter,
and when the duty to be paid would be 50s. 8d., making
the total cost to the importer 86s. 8d. a quarter. With
such an array of hazards before him a large venture might
be his ruin. He might, however, take his chance of a profit
by sending out gold—the effect of which would be to facili-
tate his purchases of grain abroad, and at the same time to
derange our currency, instead of increasing our exports of
manufactures.'

Again, Mr. David Salomons, in his ' Reflections on the
Operation of the Present Scale of Duty on Foreign Corn,'
observes, after alluding to the risks run by corn importers :—
' Their [the speculating importers] gain is calculated not only
in the advance in the price of corn, but also in the fall in the

scale of the duty, and as the duty falls in a greater ratio than the price of the corn rises, the duty operates as a bounty to withhold sales until it reaches its highest protecting limit, when the duty is also at the lowest. . . . When the averages are at 73s., the extreme limit is attained, the duty being only 1s. per quarter; so that if an importation were made that might be sold at or about 60s., paying a duty of 20s. 8d., by withholding the supply until the extreme limit of 73s. be reached, a gain of 7s. not only would be made by the rise in the averages, but also a profit of 19s. 8d. by the reduction of the duty, making a total increased profit of 26s. 8d. . . . The tendency of the fluctuating scale is, not to promote, but to withhold the supply, not to keep corn from fluctuation, but to offer a bounty for raising it to that extreme point when the mere nominal duty is imposed.'

So not only had commerce been induced by the sliding scale into a risky and too often ruinous business, at the expense of more regular trade, but also at the cost of our out-turn of manufactures, which ordinarily form the medium of payment for our foreign imports ; at the cost of the farmer, whose hopes for compensation for bad seasons in the shape of occasional high prices were dissipated by the certainty of a sudden glut of corn being let loose from bond on to a bare market, which immediately became fully supplied ; at the cost of the nation, whose food supplies were withheld when there was the greatest need for them ; and at the cost of the revenue, which only received the lowest rate of duty payable when the corn was taken out of bond.

In consequence, too, of the drain of gold, used instead of manufactures to pay for foreign corn, the Bank of England had at one time to borrow largely from the Bank of France, 'and the rate of interest rose to the then unprecedented amount of six per cent., while many articles of produce fell to extremely low prices.' [1]

On the shipping interest too the effects of this corn specu-lation were disastrous, as concisely shown in the following

[1] Ashworth's *Cobden and the League*, p. 9.

remarks culled from Tooke's ' History of Prices : ' [1]—' On the occasion of a prospect of the opening of our ports at the low duty, such is the suddenness and the extent of the demand for shipping that not only are vessels very unsuitable for corn carriage engaged, but a deficiency of tonnage is experienced, to the inconvenience of other branches of trade. . . . But the mischievous working of the system is again felt in this very interest, for no sooner are the ports again shut than there is a sudden cessation of all such extra demand for shipping; vessels are built under the influence of the casual demand and high freights ; hence, by the subsequent competition the rate of freights is reduced temporarily below its ordinary level, and the shipowners, who, like the landed interests, consider themselves entitled to apply to the Legislature on occasions of any considerable decline from a previous adventitious rise in the value of their property, become loud in their complaints of a decay in British shipping, and pray for additional protection, as was the case between 1819 and 1822, and again between 1832 and 1833.' And yet with all its evils this foreign importation was necessary if the people were to be kept from starving—a compensation which in some degree atoned for the untoward result of trading adventures, made hazardous to a degree by the action of a beneficent Legislature.

Whilst an unhealthy stimulus was given to speculation in one direction, where the intention of the stimulating laws had been to minimise speculation and to equalise prices, an equally unhealthy prohibition was put on the development of general foreign trade by laws designed to enrich the mother-country and her Colonies. These last were the celebrated Navigation Laws. The effect of these when conjoined to that of the Corn Laws, and even without taking into account the enormous and multifarious duties imposed on every article of commerce, was to interpose a barrier to trade beyond which no lawful enterprise could penetrate.

The foundation of the Navigation Act was laid during the Protectorate, and the system was perfected in the time of

[1] Vol. iii. p. 31.

Charles II. The Act provided that no merchandise of either Asia, Africa, or America should be imported into England in any but British or colonial-built ships, navigated by an English commander, and having, at least, three-fourths of their crews English. Besides this exclusive right conferred on British shipping, discriminating duties were imposed, so that goods which might still be imported in foreign ships from Europe were in that case to be more highly taxed than if brought in under the English flag.

The reasoning of the upholders of the Act was somewhat as follows:—' The Act will encourage British shipping, and with increased shipping will come an increase of trade. Thus it will serve as a fostering ground for a naval marine, and a naval marine means commercial supremacy.' By this reasoning cause and effect were reversed with a vengeance. The present accepted way of looking at the matter would lead us to suppose that commerce would create a demand for ships, ships for sailors, and, judging by experience, that the number of British sailors employed under a free system of shipping would always bear a proportion of at least three-fourths to the number of foreign sailors. Thus a large, well-trained body of men would always have been ready to respond to the exigencies of the naval service. Nowadays we should further suppose that if European countries had been permitted to bring their own goods in their own ships at the same rates of duty as in English ships, an active trade would have sprung up between England and the Continent which would have led to a largely increased employment of English bottoms. The comparatively quick and recurring profits of that trade, as compared with the slow and doubtful returns of distant commerce, would have stimulated production at home for a market of which the wants could have been sufficiently accurately gauged to ensure the minimum of waste. London would have become an infinitely larger emporium of commerce than she actually had become previous to the repeal of the Navigation Laws, and would have been enabled to do a far larger trade in consequence with her Colonies and with the world at large.

More British ships and more British sailors would have been called into active requisition, and the nursery for our navy might probably have been great enough to obviate the necessity for the excessive amount of 'crimping' put into force during war time. A naval supremacy would have been acquired, all the stronger because based upon commercial supremacy.

But these were not the views of our rulers at the commencement of the century. The Navigation Laws were to be observed to the letter. With regard to the United States the consequence was that, very soon after acquiring their independence, they copied our own Act word for word, and put it in force against us. They refused to allow British ships to take produce over to their shores. For several years the contest was carried on with vigour ; British ships bringing home produce from the States and taking back nothing in return, while American ships took our manufactures to their own ports and returned again in ballast. So the game of making two ships do the work of one went on—a game which, if unproductive of benefit to shippers, was still more expensive to the populations on either side of the Atlantic, who found the cost of goods brought across the ocean either way more than doubled to them.

The gain was a doubtful one even to the shipowners. In 1815 both the Home and United States Governments gave way, and a mutual reciprocity treaty was drawn up, putting the shipping of either country on an equal footing with regard to the carriage of goods between English and United States ports.

The Continental nations were not slow to avail themselves of the tactics of the United States, and extracted from England certain modifications of the Navigation Laws in 1821 and 1825, but the hardship of the previous rules, though materially reduced, remained in great measure unremedied. The importation of European goods continued to be practicable only in British ships, or in ships of the country of which the goods were the produce, or of the country from which they were shipped. So that if a Dutch ship, for instance, could only get partially loaded in a Dutch port, she could not fill up at a neighbouring Belgian port, but must come to England partly empty. Freights of foreign ships went up in consequence of the perpetual recurrence of such cases as these ; the cost of imported articles was increased thereby, and for this the British consumer paid handsomely.

But this was not all. The measures of 1825 still prohibited the produce of Asia, Africa, and America from being imported from any European port, and these goods could not be brought in in foreign bottoms except when imported direct in ships of the country of which the goods were the produce. ' In consequence, though the ports along the English Channel might have been glutted with the corn and cotton of America, the sugar of Brazil and Cuba, the coffee of Java, and the tea of China, and though all or some of these articles might at the time have been deficient here, not one of them could be imported in a foreign ship unless, as was sometimes the case, it was carried back to the country where it had been originally shipped ; nor even in a British ship, unless it was first carried from Europe to some other continent.' [1] Notwithstanding the harm entailed by these arrangements, the shippers fancied themselves benefited by them—certainly no other class was. They therefore strenuously opposed the repeal of the Navigation Laws, and not till January 1, 1850, was their baneful operation put an end to.

In addition to Corn Laws and Navigation Laws there were the customs duties by which heavy tolls were levied upon every import, and which contributed effectually to prevent the expansion of our foreign trade. Girt in by this network of protectionism, any extension of external commerce was a sheer impossibility, and we find that while from 1801 to 1832 inclusive our imports of foreign and colonial merchandise had only risen from the value of 31,786,262l. to that of 44,586,741l., the declared values of British and Irish produce and manufactured goods exported had positively declined from 39,730,659l. in 1801 to 36,450,594l. in 1832. It is true enough that these figures show that we were buying in 1832 at a cheaper rate than in 1801, but under unfettered conditions we should doubtless

---

[1] McCulloch's *Commercial Dictionary*, tit. 'Navigation Laws.'

have been able to export a great deal more of both produce
and manufactures, and to buy with them a far larger proportion of foreign merchandise. That this effect actually followed
the removal of restrictions may be shown from the fact that
in 1847, the year after the repeal of the Corn Laws, we
bought close on 100,000,000*l.* worth of imports with less
than 59,000,000*l.* worth of exports. Such was the declared
value of exports in that year, but it may be mentioned, as a
curious fact illustrative of the obstinate opposition to change
pervading our fiscal administration, that the official values of
our exports had ever since 1818 been largely in excess of the
declared values; the official values, until a recent period,
having been based on a scale drawn up in 1694, and blindly
persevered in ever since, notwithstanding the great fall in
prices since the peace. The official value of exports in 1847
was therefore put down at 126,130,986*l.*, instead of at their
real value of 58,842,377*l.*

Within the period from 1801 to 1832 the volume of our
foreign trade had been almost, if not quite, stationary. Indeed, considering that the population of Great Britain had
during the period increased by nearly one-half, and that of
Ireland by about a seventh, it is evident that by comparison
the volume of outside commerce had positively diminished.
Estimated per capita of traders, independently of increase in
population, it certainly had done so, for between 1811 and
1832 the number of families engaged in trade increased by
27½ per cent.—figures which mean that a greatly increased
number of traders had not succeeded in enlarging the volume
of foreign trade. That many of these families were engaged
in internal trade only, in no way affects the truth of this assertion, since in a country like our own internal and external
trade are merely the complements of each other.

That trade should decline was inevitable at a time when,
as Mr. Montgredien says :—' There was hardly an article
obtainable from abroad that was admissible here without the
payment of import duties, always heavy, sometimes excessive,
and in certain cases all but prohibitory. It mattered not
whether it was a raw material or a manufactured product,

whether it was an article of luxury or of universal consumption, whether it came in masses like cotton, or in driblets like orchilla—everything foreign which an Englishman might use was withheld from him till its cost had been enhanced by a customs duty. The tariff list of the United Kingdom presented a tolerably complete dictionary of all the products of human industry.' [1]

The excise laws were a fitting counterpart to these restrictions. Not only everything foreign, but everything native. was heavily taxed. ' Wherever you see an article tax it,' might have been appropriately posted up as the principle of our fiscal legislation. Wherever there was anything taxable it was taxed, and the exciseman practically took charge of our chief industrial occupations. He was an effective ally of his co-spoiler the custom-house officer. It was to the interest of both to hamper business as much as possible, since the more they did so the more they might hope to exact as blackmail from people desirous of getting their goods to market.

Manufactures of woollen and cotton goods, silk and flax ; paper mills, calico-printing, brick-making or soap-making works, every branch of industry that most effectually administered to the bare wants of the people, were ruthlessly supervised by revenue harpies. Until 1825 silk goods had to be looked after and taxed in order to keep them from coming into the country to compete with the home manufacture. Wool, too, had to be similarly supervised and taxed in order to prevent it from going out of the country. Drawbacks were here and there allowed, and, being complicated in their nature, afforded excellent opportunities for tampering with officials. The greater the demand for anything—that is, the greater the necessity for it—the more inquisitorial were the regulations for the supervision of its production, manufacture, or importation, and the higher the tax charged for its use.

It is in the distribution of the incidence of taxation that its pressure is to be found, and whatever the nominal amount of a particular tax, it must inevitably press with infinitely greater weight upon the poor than upon the rich when im-

---

[1] *History of the Free Trade Movement*, p. 4.

posed upon the necessaries of life. Judged by a standard so taken, the duties on soap, candles, sugar, paper, and coal were far heavier than those upon pure luxuries, because they fell with disproportionate severity upon the poorest substratum of the population.

Coal is an article necessary alike to existence and to manufactures, and yet till 1831 a glaringly unjust and oppressive duty was imposed upon sea-borne coal ; unjust, inasmuch as it fell only upon those parts of the kingdom to which coal had to be carried by sea ; oppressive, inasmuch as the duty amounted to full fifty per cent upon the price paid to the coal-owner by the purchaser. Moreover, the duty varied in different parts of the kingdom, and in Scotland there was no duty upon coal at all. Further, until 1830 various troublesome distinctions were in vogue, under the customs regulations, as between large and small coal, between coal and culm, and between coal and cinders, all engendering delay, expense, and judicious bribing, the cost of which had to be recouped to the merchant by the consumer. Coal, too, was sold by measure and not by weight, a method fraught with golden opportunity to the coal dealer to defraud the public, and of which he eagerly availed himself with a dexterity begot from practice.

The expense of coal must have operated very powerfully to diminish the out-turn of manufactured goods, and to prevent the cheapening of their prices to a level easily payable by the mass of the community, as well as contributing to minimise in other ways the meagre comforts of the poor. Still, manufactures showed signs of prosperity ; not such signs as we should expect now with a world-wide market for our manufactured goods, but sufficiently marked to be indicative of a gradual progress in the prospects of manufacturing industries due to improvements in machinery and in means of communication. The great increase of population, too, created an extra demand, and through the conjoint operation of these various causes upon his business the manufacturer had been able to extend his works, and in some sort to triumph over the difficulties interposed in his way by the Legislature.

It may be said that in the ten or fifteen years immediately

following the peace, manufactures of all sorts increased *pari passu* with the population of the kingdom. It is a contention that cannot be readily admitted when we reflect on the numbers of manufactured articles then looked upon as almost unattainable luxuries that are now regarded as necessary adjuncts to existence. But, even admitting the truth of the assertion to the full, I maintain that the *proper* rate of increase of English manufactures is not in proportion to the increase of the population of the United Kingdom, but in proportion to the development of the entire universe. Making our calculations on the latter basis, then, there need be no hesitation in asserting that, though our manufacturers made progress in their business before the Free Trade era despite impeding restrictions, the statistics on the subject for the antecedent period fail to furnish any very healthy signs of positive prosperity.

The excessive rates of taxation afforded irresistible temptations to smuggling. If, on the one hand, there was an army of revenue officers, on the other was an imposing navy of smugglers. Each was in turn heavily subsidised by the trader, who by the exigencies of his position was almost forced to bribe the one and subsidise the other. Rare indeed must have been the merchant who, while honestly paying the duties on his imports, had not at the same time an interest in some smuggling venture. Sympathy with smuggling in an overtaxed country is as natural and general as sympathy with poachers in a country hedged in with Game Laws, because it is there, justly enough, considered that the vocation of the smuggler is the natural corrective of excessive duties. Hence smuggling itself was looked upon by the majority of the people as a risky but far from dishonourable species of adventure ; while each successful shift or evasion of the customs regulations was held to confer a badge of merit on the transgressor of the revenue laws. ' To pretend,' says Adam Smith, ' to have any scruple about buying smuggled goods, though a manifest encouragement to the breach of the revenue laws, and to the perjury which almost always attends it, would in most countries be regarded as one of those pedantic pieces of hyprocrisy

which, instead of gaining credit with anybody, seems only to
expose the person who affects to practise them to the suspicion of being a greater knave than most of his neighbours.
By this indulgence of the public the smuggler is often encouraged to continue a trade which he is taught to consider
as in some measure innocent, and when the severity of the
revenue laws is ready to fall upon him, he is frequently disposed to defend with violence what he has been accustomed
to regard as his just property ; and from being at first rather
imprudent than criminal, he too at last has become one of the
most determined violators of the laws of society.'

The high tariffs were an enormous premium on smuggling
and on the criminal state to which repeated violations of the
law too constantly lead. The bad associations into which a
man must necessarily enter when forced into opposition to
oppressive fiscal laws by the hope of gain would in all probability, in time, induce in him an opposition to all laws, good
or bad. Even where the most virtuous men have associated
themselves together for the purpose of remedying some glaring
defect in the political condition of their country, ostracism
and persecution have rarely failed to impart a reckless and
lawless character to their after lives ; but when the smuggler
enters upon the hazards of his profession, he bands himself
together with men inspired from the outset with no more
noble motive than that of filling their pockets at the expense
of the revenue. Theirs is not a lofty spirit of patriotism, but
an ignoble and lawless passion which leads to crime for crime's
sake, and to violence as an assertion of lawful right.

The wise men who imposed the duties were not only
encouraging smuggling, and through smuggling crime, but
they were also stimulating immorality in the mercantile
classes, through them amongst the small local traders, and
through these again in the people. Te defraud the revenue
by making false declarations, which a revenue officer was
bribed to endorse, had become an ordinary part of the routine
of trade, and who can doubt that the spirit thus engendered
would ultimately make its way into all business dealings of
whatever kind. Integrity in business matters is the test of

honour and truth in all social relations. Let the first be tampered with ever so little, and the others are worth—well, nothing at all. We believe that to-day commercial, social, and political morality all stand on a higher footing than they did some fifty years ago, and I cannot but think that we owe this improvement largely to the discouragement given to smuggling and open fraud that has supervened upon the reform of our fiscal system. True, our newspapers are full enough of commercial and other frauds, but it must be borne in mind that much of what is now called 'fraud' in the world around us has been authoritatively so denominated by very recent statutes, and that it was considered as mere sharp practice half a century back. If many frauds go unpunished for every one detected, the reflection arises that the proportion of them that were never discovered or punished must have been substantially greater when the police and detective forces were worthless in point of organisation and competency, when railroads were in their infancy, and when the telegraph did not exist to annihilate distance between the furthest limits of the globe, and to check the craftiest combinations of calculating villany.

At that time, too, only a very partial and occasional publicity was given to actions which to-day are exposed to the full blaze of public and private criticism in every detail, It was *then* easy to hush up a fraud or pass over an indiscretion on which nowadays the criminal courts, or at any rate popular opinion, would not be slow to pass an adverse verdict. That fraudulent practices are now more widespread in their disastrous effects cannot be doubted, but the same causes which render them so widely injurious are also those which tend to prevent their frequent recurrence. In this way increased facilities of communication act and react on each other. They augment the ill effects resulting from commercial immorality, while they diminish the temptations to unfair dealing by the increased risk of exposure and punishment. Reasoning thus deductively, it would appear that commercial and general immorality was more prevalent formerly than now.

If we owe much of that spirit to the prevalence of a protectionist *régime*, to preventive laws whose severity was a premium on their infraction, we may also debit it in part to the difficulties attending the dissemination of information. The rate of postage was then estimated by the distance over which a letter had to be carried. From 1827 to 1831 the lowest rate was:—4d. for any distance not exceeding 15 miles; 8d. for 50 and not exceeding 80 miles; 9d. for 80 and not exceeding 120 miles; and so on until it rose to 16d. for 600 and not exceeding 700 miles. For distances over 700 miles the postage was 17d.

'It appeared that the actual cost to the Government for carrying each letter between the most distant parts of the empire was only a fractional part of a farthing; and that to charge, as in many cases was done, more than 480 times the actual cost was equivalent to the imposition of a heavy tax upon communications of all kinds, whether carried on for purposes of business or for gratifying the sympathies of family affection and friendship.' It was well said by one of the advocates of postal reform, 'that if a law were passed forbidding parents to speak to their children till they had paid sixpence to Government for permission, the wickedness would be so palpable that there would be an end to the tax in that form of exaction in twenty-four hours! Yet what difference is there in principle when parents are prohibited from writing to their children, or children to their parents, unless they pay the tax under the name of postage?'[1] Until 1839, however, the high postage rates indicated above were charged on letters, and for the twenty years immediately preceding that date the Post Office revenue was stationary.

It must not be supposed, nevertheless, that Parliaments particularly skilled in shifting burdens from their own shoulders on to those of a suffering people would consent to impose taxation on themselves for the conveyance of letters. We fully expect to find, and *do* find, that the principal officers of Government and the members of both Houses of Parliament

[1] Porter's *Progress of the Nation.*

enjoyed the privilege of ' franking '—that is, of sending letters by the post free of postage, and this privilege was very extensively exercised, to the manifest injury of the revenue.   It will be found that in 1839 the estimated number of letters sent through the post in the ordinary way was 75,907,572, while the number of those ' franked ' was no less than 6,563,024, and thus some eight per cent. of the total number of letters, and a far larger proportion of the postal revenue, was remitted to those who ought at the time to have contributed most largely to the latter—namely, to Members of the Legislature, their friends and sycophants.   Let us not disparage the charity of our legislators, where the exercise of that virtue cost them nothing. It must be admitted that ' franks ' were freely issued by them to personal friends, influential voters, importunate creditors, or needy relatives.[1]

Nor could newspapers supply the deficiency of news caused by a dearth of letter-writing.   Besides that the paper on which they were printed was heavily taxed, a stamp duty of fourpence was placed on each printed sheet.   When to these taxes, postage at exorbitant rates was added, it becomes apparent that but few could afford to buy newspapers, and that those few would be mostly wealthy residents near the metropolis, or near the place of local publication.

A press so heavily hampered is hardly likely to attract or develop much literary talent or thoughtful reasoning.   The heavy expenses to be paid in taxes, and the risk of prosecution run by the proprietors and editors of papers for venturing to give utterance to Liberal sentiments, were considerations sufficiently powerful to prevent capital from being attracted to the newspaper business.   The newspapers were nothing more than ' prints ' meagrely supplied with news, wretchedly printed, and badly got up.   They afforded but little scope or

---

[1] The Post Office revenue continued stationary during the twenty years ending with 1839 ; though from the great increase of population and commerce during that period it is obvious, had the rates of postage not been so high as to force recourse to other channels, such as sending letters in parcels, the revenue must have rapidly increased from the termination of the war downwards.

attraction to writers of ability, for neither was much to be gained from contributing to the spiritless columns of an almost powerless press, nor did the handicapped finances of newspaper proprietors permit of their giving pecuniary encouragement to rising talent. Consequently, violence of language too often took the place of argument; scurrility of useful comment; personality of criticism; and the buyer of a newspaper did not usually take much by his high-priced purchase. It certainly could not be said of newspapers of half a century ago that:—' The advertisements or notices which they circulate, the variety of facts and information they contain as to the supply of commodities to all parts of the world, their prices and the regulations by which they are affected, render newspapers indispensable to commercial men, supersede a great mass of epistolary communication, raise merchants in a remote place to an equality with those in the great marts, and wonderfully quicken all the great movements of commerce.'[1] All these good points were notably conspicuous by their absence from the newspapers of the period.

The power of combination to redress bad laws is one which can best be given by a free and speedy circulation of news. Such a power was necessarily of slow and halting growth when impeded by the absence of general, regular, and trustworthy information on the affairs of the day. The long acquiescence of the people in the ascendency of a small ruling class who kept their means of information in so backward a condition may perhaps be ascribed as much to their want of knowledge of their own condition, and of their own power to remedy it, as to anything else. Narratives of passing events were mostly rumours culled from some letter or newspaper of possibly not too recent date, and circulated by word of mouth. Each local centre had its own opinions, no doubt, on matters pertaining to itself, but there was little or nothing of that irresistible power nowadays termed public opinion, acting in close alliance with an intelligent, carefully edited, and well-informed public press.

Where we find a heavily taxed press we need not expect

[1] McCulloch's *Commercial Dictionary*, tit. ' Newspapers.'

much excellence of national education.   As a matter of fact there was no system of public education at all.   It was far too resolutely opposed by those in power, especially by the Bishops, who never scrupled to quote Scripture against the policy of allowing the labourer to be educated into the belief that he was in any way better than a slave, and that he had a right to be dissatisfied with his situation in life.   Independent efforts did a little ; Lancaster and Raikes, Bell and others fought sturdily for the education of the people, and nobly devoted themselves and their purses to the cause, but my Lords were too careful of the happiness of the labourer to permit him to have the chance of being educated into dissatisfaction with his own condition.   And yet, ' if one tithe of the expense that has been incurred to so little purpose during the present century in punishing criminals had been employed in preventing crime by means of education, what a different country would England have been to what our criminal records show it to have been.' [1]

An uneducated, uninformed population may for long be persecuted with impunity.   That they revolted against the yoke even as soon as they did, miserable though their condition was, was perhaps owing to a considerable extent to the influence of American and colonial notions of freedom wafted across the Atlantic, and gradually permeating into the remotest nooks and corners of the kingdom.

I may hereafter have occasion to refer to the effect produced upon the internal legislation of the British Isles by the close association with the United States and the British Colonies developed under Free Trade.   At the period under notice such effect was, by comparison, almost unrecognisable, although doubtless to a certain degree operative in stimulating the growth and the strength of a national demand for popular government.

With reference to education, again, it would appear to be as advantageous from an economical as from a moral or intellectual point of view.   ' Of all obstacles to improvement,' says the late Dr. Sumner in his ' Records of the Creation,' ' ignorance is the most formidable, because the only true secret of bettering

[1] Porter's *Progress of the Nation*, article ' Education.'

the poor is to make them agents in bettering their own condition, and to supply them, not with a temporary stimulus, but with a permanent energy. As fast as the standard of intelligence is raised, the poor become more and more able to co-operate in any plan proposed for their advantage, and more likely to listen to any reasonable suggestion, and more able to understand and therefore more willing to pursue it. Hence it follows that when gross ignorance is once removed and right principles are introduced, a great advantage has already been gained against squalid poverty. Many avenues to an improved condition are opened to one whose faculties are enlarged and exercised; he sees his own interest more closely, he pursues it more steadily, and he does not study immediate gratification at the expense of bitter and late repentance, or mortgage the labour of his future life without any adequate return. Indigence therefore will rarely be found in company with good education.'

Education not only increases the scope of employments open to men and women by giving them greater power of utilising their opportunities, but it also augments the productive energy of each worker. Hence comes greater material prosperity, a just pride, reliance on oneself, and the corollary, a demand for a voice in the legislation of the country, follows as a matter of course. Of the tendency of education to prevent or check crime there can be no serious doubt. I agree with Herbert Spencer that it is not an unfailing panacea for crime, for education cannot annihilate the misery from which crime mainly springs; but as an adjunct to other means of improving the condition of mankind its efficacy is hardly deniable.

In treating of the general effect of environing trade with a close-drawn network of restrictions, one refers, as a matter of course, to a few powerful sentences in which John Stuart Mill concisely summarises the necessary results of the maintenance of a system of duties and disabilities in commercial dealings. He tells us : [1]—' That a tax on any commodity, whether laid on its production, its carriage from place to place,

---

[1] *Principles of Political Economy*, Book V., chapter v., § 32.

or its sale '—the ' tax on its sale ' being taken to include postal and newspaper taxes, the imposition of which has the effect of interfering with facilities of exchange—' or whether the tax be a fixed sum of money for a given quantity of the commodity or an *ad valorem* duty, will, as a general rule, raise the value and prices of the commodity by at least the value of the tax. There are few cases in which it does not raise them by more than that amount.' In order to prevent and check evasions of the tax the supervision of revenue officials is necessary, and the producer has to carry on his operations in the way most convenient to the revenue, ' though not the cheapest or most efficient for the purposes of production.' Of course these restrictions increase the price of the article. ' Further, the necessity of advancing the tax obliges producers and dealers to carry on their business with larger capitals than would be necessary, on the whole of which they must receive the ordinary rate of profit, although a part only is employed in defraying the real expenses of production or importation. . . . A part of the capital of the country is not employed in production, but in advances to the State to be repaid in the price of the goods. . . . Whatever renders a larger capital necessary in any trade or business, limits the competition in that business, and gives something like a monopoly to a few dealers.'

It must be apparent that trade has, under the freest conditions, an invariable tendency to become gradually monopolised in comparatively few hands. Until fresh areas of production are made available, competition in dealing in products from existing fields lowers by degrees the rate of average profits, until the margin of gain on small transactions is swallowed up by the losses incidental to average risks. Only on large ventures can the return be a paying one when profits generally are so reduced. The small principals then become middle-men, and, until fresh fields of production are brought within reach, a comparatively small number will maintain a monopoly of the trade, and will thus be enabled ' to keep up the price beyond what would afford the ordinary rate of profit, or to obtain the ordinary rate of profit with a less degree of exertion for improving and cheapening the commodity.'

E

These are tendencies distinctly observable even where trade is perfectly free, and they must be greatly strengthened and quickened in their operation where trade is fettered on all sides by high duties and multitudinous restrictions. These duties, and the other expenses connected with State supervision of industries, had to be advanced by the seller before he could be recouped by the buyer. The price requisite for giving a profit to the former undoubtedly restricted the demand. With a small demand and a large cost to be incurred prior to the article being put on the market, only large capitals could yield fair average profits by way of return. Smaller capitals would not give a profit at all without some fresh opening for their employment, and until access was found to this, the comparatively small number of large capitalists would be surely acquiring a complete control and monopoly of the market. Besides, the larger a man's capital, the more he could hope to advance in encouraging smuggling and in bribing revenue officers ; so the unscrupulous large capitalist had here an additional and powerful lever for use in pushing a small competitor out of business as a principal on his own account. Natural and artificial causes were thus combined against the small trader, and the normal tendency to monopoly was artificially hastened, and that too with the maximum of injurious result. When, then, we read of the great increase in the general income of the country for several years after the peace in 1815, we may unhesitatingly apportion that part of the increase which did not go to the landowners to a comparatively small band of large monopolists.

That as large a number of small traders as possible should make fair average profits, is evidently far more desirable than that a small number of men should make high profits. To allow of the free extension of the area of production, is to permit of the possibility of the first result ; to limit that area, is to necessitate the last. And yet, every attempt to increase the field of industry—or area of production and employment —by reducing or abolishing the infamous regulations which circumscribed the range of employment, was strenuously and even bitterly opposed by a landowners' Parliament. One may search in vain for any widespread evil amongst those above enumerated which were not directly brought into being and maintained, in utter indifference to a nation's misery, by land-lord and capitalist legislators. Equally vain is the search for any reform devised for the people's benefit which has not had to bear the brunt of fierce, uncompromising, relentless opposi-tion from the combined ranks of wealthy monopolists ever ready to live on the people, to sponge on the people, and to persecute the people, fraudulently filching from them their hard-won wages under the false guise of the 'elect' of the people, their 'natural,' 'heaven-born' legislators, &c.

Had the 'unworking aristocracy,' as Carlyle termed the mass of our unprincipled law-makers, been content with the privileges assured to them at the commencement of the century by then existing arrangements, framed in accordance with the theory of the 'glorious Constitution' of 1688, the verdict of posterity might be more lenient to the clique than it is or will be. But the continuous exercise of unfair privi-leges must infallibly produce, if not obliquity of the mental vision, at any rate an exaggerated notion of their own rights in those enjoying them. The 'unworking aristocracy' became more grasping, more tyrannical, more jealous than ever of any appearance of national prosperity which threatened to interfere with their monopoly of power and wealth, and launched boldly forward into Corn Laws, Game Laws, pro-tecting laws, and what not. 'What looks maddest, miser-ablest, in these mad and miserable Corn Laws,' said Thomas Carlyle, ' is independent altogether of their " effect on wages," their effect on " increase of trade," or any other such effect ; it is the continued maddening proof they protrude into the faces of all men that our Governing Class, called by God and Nature and the inflexible law of Fact, either to do something towards Government or to die and be abolished, have not yet learned even to sit still and do no mischief.' [1]

In the foregoing pages little has been done beyond exposing the framework of the picture which displays the misery caused by the ascendency of unworking aristocrats. As for their

---

[1] *Chartism Past and Present*, p. 208.

acts and all that they did, are they not written in indelible letters even in the signs around us ? Is not our enormous national debt a monument to their carelessness of national suffering, of national blood and treasure, and of their callous indifference to the national thrift ? Are not our Primogeniture Laws, Laws of Distress, and the encouragements given by law to entails and perpetual settlements, still potent remnants of their dearly-prized rights of defrauding their humble creditors ? Is not a Land Tax levied on a scale of valuation of no later date than 1692, a proof of their power to resist the burden of taxation, and to oppose the spirit of the principles of 1688 to the progress of improving innovation ?

What does a system of unfairly large proportionate representation to counties and small boroughs show ? What the acred wealth of the House of Commons ? What the maintenance of a House of Lords by right of birth, and of a bench of Bishops by right of State subsidy ?

They show that the ' glorious principles ' of 1688 still flourish with the vigour of a green old age, still powerful with the spirit of mischief, still a dangerous menace to the peaceful progress of the nation ; and they will continue to manifest their baleful presence amongst us so long as an hereditary and irresponsible House of Lords has the conceded right of maintaining even its outward semblance of irresponsible power, and so long as wealth rather than worth continues to furnish the House of Commons with a majority of legislators of strongly anti-popular sympathies.

Let our Colonies at the furthest ends of the world take these lessons to heart. Land, the possession of land, is and ever was the only true basis of an aristocracy. As population increases, land acquires a value not to be defined by figures of arithmetic. Social privileges, customary privileges, and statutory privileges therefrom arise. The smaller the number of those who acquire them, the worse relatively will be the condition of the remainder of the people, the greater the influence of the landowner. From influence comes power ; from power exclusive rights and ' Les droits du plus fort sont toujours les meilleurs.' Let the rising nationalities who now control their own destinies at the Antipodes and elsewhere, take warning from the bitter experience of the English people. Let them grasp clearly the lesson, that a landowning monopoly is the cause of all other monopolies ; that it raises up a class whose interests are made to run in a different groove from that of the landless multitude ; and that its office is to check progress by taxing its onward movement. The growth of the landowners' power is unchecked because gradual, and for the while unperceived. The small squatter, who may justly base his claim to his 640-acre block on his right of reward as a pioneer of early settlement, becomes in a short space the proprietor of vast estates of almost unlimited extent. As he encloses more land, so he becomes increasingly jealous of his self-asserted privileges. The neighbour who was formerly a welcome guest now finds his cattle impounded for breaking through some encircling fence or for trending on straggling ill-kept boundaries. The shepherd king becomes a territorial magnate, and, clothed with magisterial power, judges the cause of the luckless trespasser who has violated the sanctity of his territorial limits. As population presses further forward on the virgin soil, he exacts rent and yet more rent.

His scant and hard-earned sustenance becomes a princely income, and from the fount of honour, a landowning Council at home, he receives as the reward of wealth distinctions, not for himself alone, but for his children and his children's children. The colonist whose great possessions have procured his translation into a baronet, transmits his honours to his eldest son. He stands in a privileged position in the eyes of the vulgar wealthy, who are stimulated into sycophancy to the institutions of a mother-country ever ready to reward by the offer of ribbons and titles the wealth of a landowning monopolist wherever found. A landed aristocracy springs into being, and with it the curse of hereditary privileges, hereditary legislators, and hereditary monopoly.

Fervently is it to be desired that the attempts to establish a titular aristocracy in the Colonies may fail. Already the struggle between land monopolists and the great bulk of the

colonial populations is becoming dangerously embittered.   Let
the Crown enlist itself on the side of the landowners by giving
them titular distinctions as evidence of its sympathies, and in
far larger proportion than it gains the attachment of the
privileged few will it alienate the affections of the unrecognised
many.   Then the landowners' cause will become that of the
Crown.   At any rate the people will identify one with the
other, and will have none of either.

CHAPTER II.

IMPERIAL MISRULE IN CANADA.—'DIVIDE ET IMPERA.'

'WHEN legislating for a new and unsettled country, the provident ruler would lay his plans with a view to attract and nourish future populations, rather than with regard exclusively to the interests of the few individuals who happen at the moment to inhabit a portion of the soil.'[1] Nothing, however, could have been further from the intention of the legislators who towards the latter end of the eighteenth century took upon themselves the management of England's colonial empire, than to found their rule on so reasonable a plan. To establish peculiar privileges for a handful of individuals in the Colonies as well as in England, to initiate and maintain the rule of a small dominant class, and to invest it with the odious power of grinding monopoly in matters commercial, social, and political, were the principles of colonial government ignorantly advanced by them, and adhered to with an infatuated tenacity that argued more for their obstinacy than for their intelligence or capacity.

Until a comparatively recent date, the *raison d'être* of colonies was believed to consist exclusively in the peculiar facilities which their existence afforded to commercial monopoly. 'The only use of American colonies or West Indian Islands' to England, was heralded forth by short-sighted statesmen as consisting 'in the monopoly of their commerce and the carriage of their produce.'[2] To quote from Adam Smith :—'The maintenance of this monopoly has hitherto been the principal, or more properly perhaps the sole,

[1] Lord Durham's *Report on Canada*, 1839.
[2] This was the much applauded view put forward by Lord Sheffield.

end and purpose of the dominion which Great Britain assumes over her Colonies. In the exclusive trade, it is supposed, consists the great advantage of provinces which have never yet afforded either revenue or military force for the support of government or the defence of the mother-country. The monopoly is the principal badge of their dependency, and it is the sole fruit which has hitherto been gathered from that dependency. Whatever expenses Great Britain has laid out in maintaining this dependency have hitherto been laid out in order to support this monopoly.'

It was only to be expected that rulers so peculiarly apt at mismanaging the affairs of their own country should display at least equal ability of misrule when dealing with far distant colonial dependencies. Fortunately it was not within their power to inflict upon Canada and the West Indies, the most important of our colonies after the revolt of the United States, the extent of suffering which they inflicted upon the home population, but in so far as in them lay they contrived to cripple the rising colonial trade, to prevent the natural development of the colonies, to create amongst them bitter discontent, at times swelling into violent outbreaks, to prevent the flow of emigration to them, and to render them heavy and dangerous burdens to the nation at large.

In pursuance of this ' monopoly ' theory—the most mischievous groundwork of the Comedy of Errors known as the mercantile system, entailing, as it did, a double loss on the Colonies and on the mother-country—it was decreed, that the trade between the two was to be carried on exclusively in British or colonial-built ships. By means of protective or exclusive duties, which operated to shut out any cheaper produce of other countries, the monopoly of the home market was secured to the colonial producer, and an artificial basis of ' solid prosperity ' was thus given to home and colonial trading. So thought the inept legislators of the day.

To make of the system a consistent whole, by far the greater quantities of the produce of the Colonies, under the denomination of ' enumerated articles,' were to be prohibited from being sent direct to any foreign country. They were first to be sent to Great Britain, and there unladen, before they could be forwarded to their final destinations. In addition, the Colonies were to be compelled to buy such foreign articles as they might require, entirely from the merchants and manufacturers of England, and all attempts to establish manufactures in the Colonies were to be persistently discouraged. So essential was the enforcement of this last principle deemed to be to the just management of a colony, that Lord Chatham did not hesitate to declare in his place in Parliament, with all the fervour and indiscreetness of a harebrained schoolboy, that ' the British colonists of North America had no right to manufacture even a nail for a horseshoe '—a braggart assertion and fitting preface to the successful efforts of the colonists to manufacture for themselves an independent Republic.

One of the chief grounds on which this policy of contempt for and constant interference with the Colonies was attempted to be justified, was, that it would keep the Colonies in firmer dependence 'on the mother-country. It is needless to say that historical facts have conclusively belied this anticipation.

So long as our North-American colonies were allowed a large share of local self-government, the loyalty of their inhabitants to England was one of their most characteristic features. The very belief in that loyalty was perhaps the main cause of those attempts to interfere in the purely domestic legislation of the Colonies which led to the disintegration of our colonial empire. When Franklin offered to supply Gibbon with materials for a chapter on the ' Decline and Fall of the British Empire,' he doubtless had in view the pernicious consequences to the imperial dominion inseparable from the logical carrying out of our colonial system. The logical sequence of endeavours to regulate the *external* trade of the Colonies was to be found in maladroit meddlings with their *internal* exchanges, with their fiscal laws, and with their inmost political and social regulations.

The Americans had always been loyal, so they would always continue loyal. They had been so accustomed to have their external trade and politics regulated for them, that they would cheerfully submit to imperial dictation in all local

matters. This was the view taken and acted on in deciding
that the Colonies were to be locally taxed from St. Stephen's,
in order to keep them in 'firmer dependence.' The result
was the embittered and exhausting struggle which terminated
in the establishment of the complete independence of the
United States, and in a bill of 100,000,000*l.* which John Bull
had to pay for losing them.

This was a heavy cost to have to pay for the maintenance
of a vicious principle, but it had not the effect of modifying
the views of our rulers with regard to our remaining dependencies. On the contrary, the colonial system was more
rigorously administered than ever. The United States were
promptly added to the list of foreign countries tabooed to the
trade of the loyal Colonies, and the nearest and best market
and exchange centre was thereby sternly interdicted to
colonial producers. The trade of the empire was contracted
within a narrower zone, and the injurious effect of monopolies
within it were now rendered all the more apparent by
the contrast between expanding wants and an increasing
artificial contraction of the trading area. Of the restricted
trade done, the monopolists conducted a greater proportionate
share, and as peculiar trading privileges were assured to them
they became careless as to the quality of the commodities
from which, at unnaturally heightened prices, they reaped
extravagant profits.

If we would form a passing estimate of the injuries
inflicted both on England and her Colonies by this system of
fostered monopoly, let us briefly glance at two prominent
and typical cases—the West Indian monopoly of the sugar trade,
and the Canadian monopoly of the timber trade. No illustrations could be found reflecting more fairly the iniquitous folly
of the colonial system.

A trade in sugar was stimulated between the West Indian
colonies of Great Britain and the mother-country; and a
large amount of capital and labour diverted into sugar-grow-
ing by the favourable differential duties accorded to importations
of West Indian sugar as compared with those imposed upon
sugar from foreign countries proper.

For a lengthened period prior to 1845 the duty on foreign-grown sugar was maintained at 63s. per cwt., on West Indian colonial sugar at 25s. 2d. per cwt. The former rate of duty was of course prohibitory on foreign sugars ; although, exclusive of duty, the price of Brazilian and Cuban sugar was only half that of colonial sugar. The *direct* cost of this arrangement over a series of years has been variously estimated at from three to five millions per annum—an amount equivalent to cent. per cent. upon the totals paid for colonial sugar imported during those years. At one time, the colonial supplies of sugar were sufficient not only to supply the home market, but to afford a surplus for exportation. Not, however, that this meant a supply at all in accordance with the home demand for sugar, as we should estimate that demand nowadays, for Mr. Huskisson's statement in the House of Commons on Mr. Grant's motion in 1829 for a reduction of the Sugar Duties was undeniable. Mr. Huskisson alleged that, ' in consequence of the present enormous duty on sugar, the poor working man with a large family, to whom pence were a serious consideration, was denied the use of that commodity, and he believed he did not go too far when he stated that two-thirds of the poorer consumers of coffee drank that beverage without sugar.' But after the emancipation of the slaves, the supply fell to one-half of its previous dimensions. On the one hand, therefore, we had a rapidly increasing population, and on the other, we had that population confined, by an oppressive duty, to a market for sugar in which the supply had been materially diminished. ' The consequences were such as every man of sense might have anticipated from the outset. The business of refining for the foreign market and our export trade in sugar were all but annihilated, while the average price of Muscavado sugar admissible to the English markets amounted during the three years ending with 1844 to about double the price of foreign sugar, in bond, of equal or superior quality.' [1]

The slave trade had been abolished by Act of Parliament in 1807, but an active trade in slaves was notwithstanding

[1] McCulloch's *Commercial Dictionary*, article ' Sugar.'

kept up by the colonial sugar-growers, and, however much it
might be discouraged, slavery itself was recognised as essential to the development of the sugar plantations.   Sugar
cultivation and slavery went hand in hand, and in encouraging
the one we were maintaining the other.   The 20,000,000*l.*
paid to colonial sugar-planters as compensation for slave
emancipation may therefore fairly be added to the three to
five millions annually expended directly by the home consumer, in fostering the sugar monopoly.   As to the effects of
the abolition of slavery upon the colonists themselves, we
know how widespread was the ruin caused by it.   Had it
not been for the injudicious bolstering up of a large sugar
monopoly by legislative enactments, emancipation would have
been effected many years prior to 1834, and at a comparatively
trifling cost.   As it was, when it came it struck a deadly
blow at an artificially enlarged interest, and by the ruin it
caused it deprived us of much-needed customers, who, if
prosperous, might have afforded a valuable purchasing market
for articles of home manufacture.

The benefits (?) of monopoly were not all to be on one
side.   A monopoly accorded must coexist with reciprocity
enforced.   Besides the obligation imposed on the West
Indian colonies of sending *home* all produce destined for
foreign countries, it was made incumbent on them to aid in
encouraging British and Canadian shipping.   To this end,
American and foreign merchandise was prohibited from entering West Indian ports directly, by crushing duties.   But it
might be imported there duty free (in some cases), if shipped
from a British home or colonial port, and thence exported in
British or colony-built ships.   The hardship of these provisions was most keenly felt where American produce was
dealt in, since with New Orleans, Baltimore, and other United
States ports close at hand, no advantage could be taken of
their vicinity.   Everything bought in the States for the West
Indian colonies had first to bear the cost of transport to
Quebec or Montreal before it could be sent to our other
possessions, and trade was handicapped by being forced from
the shortest and cheapest into the longest and dearest routes.

In papers laid by the West Indian merchants and planters before the House of Commons,[1] they estimated the increased expenses they thus incurred in procuring lumber, staves, flour, shingles, fish, &c., at fifteen per cent. on the entire value of these articles, or at the enormous sum (to them) of 187,575l. a year. No part of this sum went into the pockets of any British merchants. It went wholly to indemnify the Americans and others for being obliged to bring their produce by the most circuitous route.

One object of our rulers—the steady discouragement of a direct trade between America and the West Indies—had been apparently attained, but this involved other consequences on which it was difficult to look with absolute complacency. For the contraction of trade had the natural effect of diminishing instead of increasing the tonnage of British and colonial shipping engaged in it, while, on the other hand, the restrictive laws had given a fine impetus to smuggling where the articles of trade were not bulky and inconvenient of carriage. The British West Indian ports swarmed with semi-piratical smugglers, and abundance of profitless employment was given to the large and expensive naval establishment maintained for the purpose of preventing and checking them.

The sugar monopoly collapsed as soon as the artificial protection was withdrawn from it. Widespread ruin followed, the moment the prop was taken away. The smuggling which had been fostered by preventive folly, resolved itself into piracy for want of other occupation, and for many years after the equalisation of the Sugar Duties the condition, on land, in the West Indies, was one of helpless despondency; on the sea, one of perilous insecurity.

Canadian timber, was an article to which especial preference was shown by our pseudo-economist governors. For some years previous to 1843, the differential duty in favour of Canadian timber was 45s. per load. The effect of this preference was to encourage the growth of a lumber trade in Canada

---

[1] No. 121. Session 1831.

and to turn the agriculturist into a lumberer—that is, to turn
him from an occupation where thrift and industry were
indispensable to success, to one where these qualities became
so conspicuous by their absence, that lumberers were justly
stigmatised as the ' pests of the colony.' Apart from this
demoralising tendency, the lumber trade actually put impediments in the way of the agricultural development of the colony,
since the cutting down of the trees engendered so great a
growth of brushwood, that it actually cost more to clear the
land where the lumberers *had* been than where they had *not*
been.

The immediate consequence of the differential duties to
the home country was, that at a stroke it almost annihilated
all trade between England and Norway and Sweden. Those
countries had little besides the finest timber to exchange for
our commodities. When prevented by the high duties against
them from exporting it to England, they were driven to resort
to the markets of France and Holland for the articles they
had formerly imported from us. Thus our manufacturers
lost a profitable market, and numbers of English workmen
employed by these manufacturers were thrown out of employment, while other countries thereby gained good customers,
and developed their own industries to meet the Scandinavian
demand. The loss to ourselves in pounds, shillings, and
pence was for the times very considerable. The exports to
Sweden, which in 1814 had amounted to 511,818*l*., declined
in 1819 to 46,656*l*., and even in 1842, after great efforts had
been made to re-acquire the Swedish trade, they totalled no
greater value than 199,313*l*. The like with the export trade
to Norway, which fell from a total of 199,902*l*. value in 1815,
to the value of 64,741*l*. in 1819, and in 1842 was still not
estimated to be worth more than 134,704*l*.[1]

During all this period of differential Timber Duties, the
price of timber from the North of Europe was cheaper than
that of Canadian timber by nearly the difference in the
amount of the differential duties. Not only that, but the
quality of the European timber was far superior, if we are to

[1] McCulloch, ' Timber Trade.'

believe the first Report of the House of Lords on the foreign trade of the kingdom, where it is asserted that ' the North-American timber is more soft, less durable, and every description of it more liable, though in different degrees, to the dry rot than is timber of the North of Europe.' And, further, ' that the timber of Canada, both oak and fir, does not possess, for the purpose of shipbuilding, more than half the durability of wood of the same description, the produce of the North of Europe.' And yet it was of this Canadian timber that we had been for years building bad ships instead of good ones, in order to give an artificial stimulus to supposed colonial requirements. We had been heavily taxing ourselves and putting an incubus on the real development of the Canadas, in order to build of the worst materials procurable, at extravagant rates, two ships where one would have done better at largely reduced cost, if built with untaxed ' durable ' European timber.

Independently of the direct pecuniary losses inflicted upon both mother-country and the colonies of Canada by the maintenance of this ridiculous monopoly, the indirect losses on either were certainly far greater. Each had to purchase in the dearest market, and each, therefore, lost the sound unbolstered trade which might have been utilised in developing fresh industries to which capital on either side would naturally have flowed. The purchasing power of each, not only for the products of the other, but for the products of all other countries, was diminished by at least the extra cost which each had to incur for buying in markets kept artificially dear by monopoly. That this was a benefit to individual monopolists is probable enough, but that only in a comparative degree, and it is evident that it could involve nothing but heavy loss to the bulk of the smaller traders on each side, and that both colonial and home consumers were distinctly impoverished by it.

The colonial system was exactly calculated to generate feelings of jealousy and dislike of imperial rule amongst both Canadian and West Indian colonists. In Canada, in especial, where there was a gradually increasing European-born labouring population, the injury and injustice of the system was

keenly felt, but it was, as we shall see, but the groundwork of
far more strenuous efforts to make the intermeddling despotism
of the imperial authorities more hateful to the colonists and
more dangerous to the maintenance of the tie between Great
Britain and her down-trodden dependencies.

Until we began to colonise with convicts towards the close
of the last century, the imperial power of England never attempted to rule *locally* in every detail from the vast distance
of the breadth of the globe, a body of its subjects who had
gone forth from England and founded a colony. The charters
of Maryland, Massachusetts, Connecticut, and Rhode Island
gave to those colonies unlimited powers of local self-government. Within their own boundaries the colonists had the
right to administer their own affairs on the freest and most
popular basis.

So long as the Colonies were poor and struggling communities, they were enabled to thrive under the ' beneficent
neglect of the home Government.' [1] When, however, it
became evident that they were rapidly advancing in wealth
and resources, England, or, rather, the body of Englishmen
that had arrogated to itself the power of imperial rule, was
prompt in asserting claims to the appropriation of the local
colonial revenues to its own purposes. This clique of auto-
cratic managers would perhaps, had it been possible, have put
into practice Sancho Panza's maxim of selling the colonists
for slaves, and appropriating to themselves the proceeds.
This being out of the question, the attempt was made to deprive the colonists of what Wakefield terms their ' dearest
municipal right,' and to submit the regulations of colonial
life and the control of the colonial purse to an unsympathetic,
careless, and irresponsible set of officials at home. This line
of policy was, as I have before attempted to show, the necessary outcome of the principles on which the colonial system
was based. The smaller and more irresponsible the body of
rulers, the easier was it to conduct unchecked a policy of

[1] Professor Thorold Rogers's *Essay on the Colonial Question.* Cobden
Club Essays, 1872.

meddling and spoliation. The system was not long in costing us the allegiance of the North-American colonies as an early instalment of its natural consequences, and the shock so rudely given imposed upon the clique the necessity of caution in the immediate future. A penal colony was, therefore, reserved for the theatre of our first experiments in thoroughly centralised government, and *there* the local or municipal form of self-government was wholly inapplicable so long as the population was entirely composed of convicts and their gaolers. It was deemed as inapplicable to the helpless communities in Canada which came under our dominion by conquest.

To French Canada was accorded a delusive shadow of free institutions without any of the reality of freedom ; the power of representation in a popular assembly without any of the natural consequences of representation. The central system was triumphant for awhile, and every portion of our vast colonial empire was liable to the most serious injury from an oversight, a misapprehension, a want of right information, or an error of judgment, on the part of a gentleman sitting in Downing Street, instructed by irresponsible, unknown officials wedded to red-tape by the law of their being. Communities of which the main characteristics, indeed the elements of whose existence, were perpetual changes and ever-onward progress, were ruled by an authority as ' laborious, heavy, busy, blind, and bold ' as the veriest Goddess of Arch-Stupidity.

So long as we made no attempts to interfere with the local self-government of our North-American colonies, their attachment to the British connection was genuine and deep. They presented in this respect a remarkable contrast to the centrally governed Spanish colonies of America. Both English and Spanish colonies have now forcibly separated themselves from their parent countries, and both have established Republican forms of government. The immediate causes of separation were in either case similar. The English colonies revolted against the attempt to impose upon them a central bureaucratic system which proposed to take from them the power of controlling their inmost fiscal arrangements. The

F

Spanish colonies rebelled against the intolerable continuance of the system. There was, however, one notable difference in the course of the hostilities in either case. In the former, education in the self-governing principle had developed a spirit and a power which speedily made the North-American colonies more than a match for the immense resources of the British empire. In the latter, a long continuance of unintelligent and unsympathetic bureaucratic despotism had enfeebled the powers of the South-American colonists to such an extent that only after a long series of feeble throes, at times quite unavailing, was the grip of impotent Spain released from the throat of her exhausted dependencies.

Again, compare the results. The United States came out of the contest ready and able to profit to the uttermost by the training which experience in local self-government had given them. The colonies of South America became the homes of perpetual revolution and incessant anarchy.

If a world-wide empire such as ours derives strength from its Colonies, it is not through the strengthening of the legislative tie between them, but through the deep-rooted loyalty which the unfettered exercise of local self-governing power implants in the affections of the most far distant colonists. Just as the North-American colonies derived from their local institutions a basis of unconquerable strength, so did the free exercise of local authority make them loyal staunch allies and subjects of the parent country. On the other hand, the one universal cause of weakness in an extensive dominion has always consisted in the disaffection of its outlying portions, arising from the maintenance of the central principle. Of the salutary principle of decentralisation, Burke himself was at one time a strenuous advocate, and yet it could hardly have been without a feeling of the deepest humiliation that, in order to illustrate the necessity of relaxing our powers over the borders of the empire, so as to strengthen it at the centre, he should have found himself forced to appeal, in an English Parliament, to the politic example of the Turk.

The Spanish colonies were a constant and fatal drain on the resources of Spain. Long before the latter had been reft of her South-American colonies she had lost all internal vigour and all her weight in European councils, chiefly because of the weakness and demoralisation her colonial system entailed upon her. On the other hand, so long as the municipal rights of the English colonies were left unmolested the colonists were at all times prompt to take up arms on behalf of the mother-country.

It is unnecessary to multiply instances of the political benefits resulting to the imperial State from the establishment of local self-government in colonies, as opposed to the evils to be expected from the maintenance of the central system. From the days of the Roman empire, whose chief dependence was in her municipalities, to the time when the self-governing Fueros of the Basque Provinces of Spain herself fought to the ast rather than submit to a revolution which deprived their egitimate sovereign of his throne, history abounds with nstances to point the moral and adorn the tale of the guarantee afforded by widespread, free-born local governing institutions for the loyalty and cohesion of the separate parts of the State: of the inevitable tendency of centralisation to violent disruption of peaceful relations between rulers and ruled.

The unwisdom of our ancestors in forcing on the separation of the States was still more glaringly conspicuous in their attempts to perpetuate in their Canadian colonies the policy which had given rise to the Declaration of Independence. The central system in a form which was bureaucratic as well as central was applied to Canada with redoubled vigour, and but for the utter want of training in self-government fostered by it throughout the Canadas, and the irreconcilable jealousies promoted by the system between the French and English-speaking divisions of the Canadas, the occasional revolts against our dominion by the colonists would most certainly have eventuated in violent separation.

Of all the evil results of centralised government there is none more pronounced than its effect in destroying, by the process of preventing, the growth of a spirit of self-reliance. If there is one quality above all others desirable for a young community to cultivate, it is implicit self-reliance from its earliest infancy. Our centralised form of government was not only calculated to, but was framed expressly to, repress the first indications of this quality. The colonist was to have no will of his own, and was to have no indiscreet aspirations in the direction of bettering himself. He was a toddling infant to be kept in leading-strings to an official high priesthood. At times he might be ' pleased with a rattle, tickled with a straw,' but the serious business of trying to get along in his own way was not for him.

The Canadians were to have representative assemblies to play with, but they were not to be permitted to have either hand or real voice in their own government. The Colonial Office would see to that, and everything would be administered in the best possible way. Canada was not to be governed for its own benefit, otherwise it might take the leading-strings into its own hands and run clean away, as the United States had just done. No! dominion over Canada was a recompense given by Providence to the Colonial Office, its relatives and friends, to make up for the field of patronage of which they had been pitilessly despoiled by the unreasoning conduct of the ' wicked rebels ' of the erst North-American colonies.

Canada was divided into two provinces, Upper Canada and Lower Canada. In the latter division the bulk of the inhabitants were French, and between them and the English population prevailed a fierce and consuming hatred. ' That liberal institutions and a prudent policy might have changed the character of the struggle I have no doubt,' says Lord Durham.[1] ' Unhappily, however, the system of government pursued in Lower Canada has been based upon the policy of perpetuating that very separation of the races, and encouraging those very notions of conflicting nationalities, which it ought to have been the first and chief care of government to check and extinguish.'

Up to so late a period as 1816, the nationality of the

---

[1] Lord Durham's Report on the Affairs of British North America, p. 13.

French Canadians was confessedly cultivated as a means of isolating entirely the inhabitants of British (Upper) Canada from those of the revolted colonies. To keep the former loyal, they were to be kept from contact with the populations of the United States—a device sufficiently puerile to be well worthy of the statesmen who supported it as a sound principle of government.

The policy of the Colonial Office was to govern its colonies by means of internal dissensions, and ' to break them down into petty isolated communities, incapable of combination, and possessing no sufficient strength for individual resistance.' [1] It was with this object in view that Canada was divided into two provinces, the settled portions being allotted to the French, and the unsettled portions being set apart for British colonisation. ' Had the sounder policy of making the Lower Province English in all its institutions been adopted from the first and steadily persevered in, the French would have been speedily outnumbered, and the beneficial operations of the free institutions of England would never have been impeded by animosities of origin.' [2] But it was found impossible to exclude the English race from a province where the great rivers afforded the most convenient highways for commercial enterprise. The attempt, therefore, to preserve a distinctive French-Canadian nationality in the midst of Anglo-American colonies and States proved a signal failure in respect of its object, but it succeeded in producing a jealous contest of races which was largely responsible for the long unprogressiveness of the Canadian Dominion. Every measure of the Imperial Government seemed shaped with special intent to aggravate the evil to the extremest degree. Alternate concessions to either of the contending races only irritated both, and, while intensifying the animosities of race, brought the vacillating and unwieldy Government system into utter contempt.

The defects of government in the Canadian colonies were briefly and pithily summarised by Lord Durham as follows : [3] -

---

[1] Lord Durham's *Report on the Affairs of British North America*, p. 46. [2] *Ibid.* p. 47. [3] *Ibid.* p. 51.

' It may fairly be said that the natural state of government in all the Colonies is that of collision between the executive and the representative body. In all of them the administration of public affairs is habitually conceded to those who do not co-operate harmoniously with the popular branch of the Legislature ; and the Government is constantly proposing measures which the majority of the Assembly reject, and refusing its assent to Bills which that body has passed.'

In Lower Canada the practical working of the Representative Assembly commenced with the imprisonment of its leaders for freedom of speech—no very auspicious initiation of free institutions ! By degrees the Assembly acquired a partial control over a portion of the public revenue ; and an unceasing struggle ensued with the Executive, until by 1832 the Assembly had gained an entire control over the whole revenue of the colony.[1] But it still found itself deprived of all voice in the choice, or even designation, of the persons to whom was to be confided the administration of affairs.

The constitution of the Assembly was unworkable. It might refuse or pass laws, vote or withhold supplies, but it could exercise no influence over the nomination of a single servant of the Crown. In the selection of officials no regard whatever was paid to the wishes of the people or of their representatives ; indeed, hostility to the Assembly was usually the ground of the elevation of the most incompetent persons to posts of honour and trust. The actual government of the colony was placed in the charge of officials bitterly opposed to the popular will, and who were deputed to carry into operation the legislation which they most strenuously opposed.

It is difficult to imagine a greater mockery than representative institutions coupled with irresponsible government. The opposition of the Assembly to the Crown was an unavoidable result of such an arrangement. The popular leaders, relieved of all the responsibilities of opposition, made the business of legislation and the practical government of the province subordinate to the struggle for power, and the necessities of the community were used for the purpose of

----

[1] *Report*, p. 52.

extorting the concession of whatever demands they might choose to make.

As to the Legislative Council, it is described in the ' Report '[1] as ' hardly anything but a veto in the hands of public functionaries on all the acts of that popular branch of the Legislature in which they were always in a minority.' This veto was used without much scruple, and the time which should have been devoted to wise legislation was spent in a contest for power between the Executive and the people ' which a wise Government would have stopped at the outset by submitting to a legitimate responsibility, and which a wise people would have ceased to press when it had virtually attained its end.'[2]

This Council was vowed to secresy. None of its members were answerable for the working of any department. Therefore there was no individual superintendence over, as there was no responsibility for, any department. Still it was from the advice given by these officials that the edicts of the Colonial Office were drawn up.

Considering these circumstances, it would be indeed surprising if it should be found that any department was carried on advantageously for the colony.

While the money voted for public works was unblushingly scrambled for, the works themselves were rarely commenced, and more rarely completed. Next to the power of disposing of the land in a new country, there is no more important function than that of forwarding and controlling the public works. But unless there exist municipal authorities to interest themselves in, and see to the proper administration of, the sums voted for those works, the department charged with their execution can hardly fail to utilise its opportunities for its own private ends. It is not too much to say that jobbery, robbery, and criminal inefficiency were the most conspicuous features in the administration of the public works of Canada.

There was no such thing as local or municipal government throughout the length and breadth of the Canadas. All

[1] *Report*, p. 58.　　　　　　[2] *Ibid.* p. 49.

regular administration appeared to cease immediately beyond
the walls of Quebec and Montreal.   In the rest of the country
there was 'no sheriff, no mayor, no constable, no superior
administrative officer of any kind.'[1]   Nor were there any
county, municipal, or parochial officers, either named by the
Crown or nominated by the people.   The people, accustomed
to rely entirely on Government dictation, had no power of
doing anything for themselves, and were but little disposed to
yield assistance to the central authority which presumptuously
thought itself above the necessity of local aid to enable it to
carry its measures into practice.   It was not deemed fitting to
the scheme of government that the colonists should be allowed
to regulate their own local affairs.   And yet, though declared
to be unworthy of managing the business of a parish, they
were, with an inconsistency characteristic of the system,
entrusted with the power of influencing, by the votes of their
representatives in the Assembly, the highest destinies of the
State.   It would have been indeed surprising had the self-
contradictory parcelling out of duties terminated in anything
but discontent, disaffection, and failure.

Canada was hedged around with a network of customs
duties.   But the collection of these was not entrusted to the
colonists themselves.   None were permitted to dip into the
'pickings and stealings' of the customs revenue except the
officers of the Imperial Government.   This revenue again was
a source of endless dispute between the two great provinces
of the Dominion.   Almost the whole of the imports of Upper
Canada came through the ports of Lower Canada, and the
former therefore insisted on receiving a portion of the revenue
from duties.   The revenue of Upper Canada being totally
inadequate to the expenditure, the province found itself
obliged to raise the scale of customs duties in order to pay the
interest on its debt.   These duties being levied in Lower
Canada, the taxation of that province had also to be raised,
although it enjoyed a large surplus revenue.   It may be
readily believed that this arrangement did not tend to produce
harmony between the two provinces—a result entirely in

_____
[1] *Report*, p. 78.

accordance with the motto ' Divide et Impera ' specially
adopted by the Imperial Government for application to the
circumstances of the two Canadas.

The principle of centralisation did not stop at the Custom
House. It was carried into the Post Office. The Colonial
Post Office was subordinated to the General Post Office in
London, and its every detail was regulated and administered
by the rulers and servants of an establishment several weeks'
sail from Canada. The increased cost of the postal service
was thus very great. The direct part of the cost was, in the
first place, borne by the English office, and, in order to recoup
the expense to that institution, the revenue from the colonial
etters was paid over to it. The indirect cost was probably,
n those days of slow-going sailing-ships, a still heavier
burden, and it fell chiefly upon the Canadians themselves.
But this was what was intended. Much letter-writing or ex-
ended business relations might have given the colonists a sense
of their own importance which it would have been presumptuous in them to entertain. Besides, what mattered the injury
done, if the object of good colonial government was attained—
namely, if money was somehow screwed out of the colony to
pay for the cost of officialism at home ?

Officials in England enjoyed the privilege of franking their
letters, on presumed grounds of public policy, but then *there*
they made their own laws. The Canadian officials would
doubtless have gladly conferred the privilege on themselves,
their relatives and friends, but this they were not allowed to
do, for reasons of public policy were not considered as applying to Canada ; and besides there was the all-sufficient reason
that the postal revenue was an English perquisite.

The colonial officials, however, availed themselves of a
remedy ready to hand. The funds derived from the sale of
Jesuits' estates had been dedicated to public educational
purposes. By way of reimbursing themselves for paying
postage and other vexatious charges, the Council diverted the
money derived from these sales—from education, for which
nothing was done—to a secret service fund by which the
official members of the body were enriched, at the same time

that their influence was sensibly enlarged. The obstinate
struggle which was for long maintained with the Assembly in
order to continue this gross misappropriation furnishes a
vivid illustration of the difficulty of curtailing the powers for
evil of an irresponsible and therefore corrupt clique of
officials.

The 'Family Party' which ruled Upper Canada had in
some respects an easier task before them—politically—than
had the small band of officials who administered to their own
wants in the Lower Province. There were no questions in
Upper Canada arising upon the jealousies of rival nationalities, so the only problem in politics to be solved was how to
set the different classes and interests in the community most
completely by the ears.

The 'Family Party' or 'Family Compact' was composed
of native-born as well as of English officials. So the party
had always a strong local connection, out of which it could,
in case of necessity, manufacture a good deal of support.

The small knot of officials who composed the 'Party'
adhered with great fidelity to the example set them by the
parent State. Conscious that unless the whole patronage of
the colony was at their disposal, they could not hold together
in defiance of the representative body, they divided between
themselves all places of office and trust, and endowed these
with salaries equivalent to their belief in their own merit.

A dominant Church is always one device of a ruling
oligarchy for giving to its position the weight of a religious
sanction. So the party set to work to bolster up an Established Church, representative perhaps of one-fourth of the
population. This move, from the point of view of their own
interest, was probably a wise one, for it enabled them to
count·on the support of a proportion of the people which,
though a small one, comprised the wealthiest and most
influential settlers. It was the countenance given by these
last that permitted of the continuance of the rule of the
Family Party. Religious government is government through
religious differences, and just as the Colonial Office based its

rule on local hatreds, so the Party founded its strength on religious animosity.

The Assembly repeatedly passed Bills appropriating the moneys from the sale of reserve lands which had been lavished on the Church, to education ; but all such Bills were summarily rejected by the Family Party, bent as it was in making up to the Church in endowments what it lacked in popular sympathy.

The members of the Party were supreme in the chartered banks. They therefore most persistently opposed any extension of the banking system which might compete with their own monopoly. Most of them, too, were lawyers. The legal fraternity has invariably distinguished itself by a close trades-unionism which has made the entrance into its own profession as narrow and exclusive as possible, and the Canadian lawyers, true to tradition, secured themselves from competition by refusing to allow even English barristers or solicitors to practice in the colonial courts without a long local apprenticeship, whatever might have been their standing at home.

As for the conduct of public works, it was of course far too abounding in lucrative chances to be permitted to be carried on except by the few individuals forming the Party, who, by getting the management entirely into their own hands, ' deliberately encouraged a system of carelessness and profusion by which they were enriched at the public expense.' [1]

With government in the hands of wreckers, trade must always lack confidence and enterprise. However anxious the rulers may be to promote it, its expansion will be impossible where political integrity is altogether non-existent. But the Family Party officials had no intention of encouraging the development of trade. It was, they thought, contrary to their private interest to do so, so they scrupled not to hamper the operations of commerce by imposing heavy duties, by retarding the settlement of the country, and by systematically neglecting those public works which are as the breath of life to a young community struggling into being.

Had there been any system of local government at all, we

<hr>

[1] *Report*, p. 109.

may feel certain that, despite every effort of the Family Party, roads, bridges, and communications would have been established over the face of the country, and would have neutralised to some extent the effects of detestable misgovernment ; but of local government there was not the faintest shadow, and, not having the fear of local control before its eyes, the Family Party pursued unchecked the even tenor of its way.

For the establishment and maintenance of this state of things the Colonial Office must be held directly responsible. The office had created the Family Party in Upper Canada and the Bureaux in the Lower Province, and between Office, Family Party, and Bureaux was the freemasonry of anti-popular interest.

The Colonial Governor was usually the mere creature of one or other of these powers, and his position was never a very enviable or secure one. The representations of the officials in either province were, as a rule, accepted by the Colonial Office as the basis of its instructions to the Colonial Governor. The information which thus formed the ground-work of the instructions given to him emanated from small knots of men systematically hostile to the wishes of the great majority of the colonists. The policy he was required to carry out was therefore that which the colony was the least prepared to accept. The details of the directions given to him were models of precision, and laboriously dictated to him the course he was to pursue in every particular of his administration. If he did as he was told, he became unpopular with the colonists, who clamoured for his recall. If he acted as he thought best in the interests of the colony, he earned the dislike of the local official class, who lost no time in procuring his deposition by malignant representations to the Colonial Office. In self-defence, then, he as a rule refrained from doing anything until he had taken the opinion of the Office, even in matters of a strictly local nature, of which none but those immediately interested could possibly know anything. Of the instructions that he received from time to time, the best that could be said of very many of them was, that they were quite inoperative. Either they had been outrun by time and events in the colony, or from some reason, which a moment's intelligent consideration might have rendered apparent, they were inapplicable to things real in the colony. Thus a glance at a map might have taught the Colonial Office that it was by no means necessary to send out a cargo of casks filled with *fresh* water for the use of ships floating on the fresh-water lake of Ontario. 'I have seen the House of Assembly,' says Wakefield, 'incapable of restraining their mirth while the Speaker was gravely reading instructions to the Governor which his Excellency had been desired to communicate to them. They laughed at the ludicrous inapplicability to Canada of the views expounded in these despatches.'[1] Such escapades as these had naturally the effect of bringing the home Government into contempt in the colony.

The greater part of these instructions, however, never saw the light without being marked 'secret' or 'confidential.' The Colonies were in fact ruled by a power which had an absolute choice between making known and concealing all the grounds of its laws and orders. 'The most important business of government was carried on in a secret correspondence between the Governor and the Secretary of State for the Colonies, and the Colonies were frequently the last to learn the thing, that most concerned them by the tardy publication of papers on the order of the British Parliament.'[2]

The Canadas were to be kept in firm dependence by being prevented from framing laws and institutions for their own local government. The entire management of the country was therefore to be centralised in a London office. It may be interesting to glance at the inner working of the system, together with some of its more obvious consequences.

Supposing a distant and centralised form of government to be conceivably necessary for the welfare of the Colonies, it would before all things be requisite that it should be administered by those 'who sympathise with their subjects, whose glory is in their prosperity, to whom their misfortunes are at least a discomfort, and whom . . . they can check in cases of

---

[1] Wakefield's *Art of Colonisation*, p. 243.
[2] *Report*, p. 75.

great need by threatening them with the *ultima ratio* of popular despair.' [1] But the very opposite was the case. The Colonial Office staff, who in reality ruled the roast, had not a sympathy in common with the bulk of the people in any one of the colonies, and the course of policy adopted towards the latter had reference merely to the state of parties in England and to the maintenance of antiquated office traditions, rather than to colonial wants and circumstances. The staff was a permanent body without responsibility to its unfortunate subjects, and could not be made amenable to pressure exercised by them.

Neither party in the colony could calculate upon the probable result of their mutual struggles; because, though they might be able to estimate accurately enough their strength locally, they could never tell how or when some hidden spring might be set in motion by the Colonial Office, which would defeat their best laid plans, and render utterly unavailing whole years of patient effort. [2]

The fact was that the business of the Colonial Office was conducted entirely by permanent clerks responsible to no one. It was quite beyond the power of any Secretary of State for the Colonies to make himself acquainted, even in the most perfunctory way, with the real requirements of the Colonies, or to decide satisfactorily upon the conflicting statements and claims brought before him. In his dilemma he sought the aid of his permanent staff, men of great ' tact ' in dealing with their superiors, and owing their elevation to that desirable social accomplishment, coupled with length of routine service. Frequent changes of government might bring as many changes of Colonial Ministers with widely varying views on the subject of the policy of their department, but the best of them could do little against the ' tact ' and *vis inertiæ* of the permanent clerk, under whose dominion they rapidly but surely fell. These clerks had from long practice grown up to regard the Colonies as so many empty pigeon-holes which it was necessary from time to time to fill up with perfectly rounded phrases and

---

[1] Wakefield's *Art of Colonisation*, p. 231.
[2] *Report*, p. 137.

metaphors on the subject of filial duty, with didactic discourses on morality and ethics, or with carefully penned essays on political economy. For them the Colonies existed only on paper. They represented nothing more than the opportunity for some gracefully turned composition, in which the reciprocal duties of Colonial Governors and peoples were pointed out in unexceptionable language, and quite in accordance with the most ancient office forms. The characteristics of this system of ' paper government,' as it was called by Burke, were vacillatory measures varied by tyrannical edicts. Caprice in everything, consistency in nothing, was the rule of conduct in Downing Street.

The chief object of the permanent clerk, the ruler of a domain besides whose vastness the empire of Imperial Rome dwindles down to a provincial centre, was to save himself trouble. If some obscure intriguer at home appeared likely to make himself troublesome in his efforts to procure for himself some exclusive privilege or piece of patronage in the permanent gentleman's territories, it was given to him as a tribute to his skill in bringing backstairs influence to work. But a deaf ear was turned to the colonist who could train no heavier metal to bear than the history of private wrongs or public misadventure, due to the ignorant rule of the Colonial Office. But, with all his desire of saving himself trouble, the permanent gentleman had contracted an inveterately bad habit of writing despatches and instructions, the effect of which was, often enough, to deprive Colonial Assemblies of their just functions, and so to irritate them and force them into violent proceedings, such as political impeachments, the stoppage of supplies, and personal attacks on the local representatives of the Crown. But where the permanent gentleman did save himself a world of bother was in his treatment of important Colonial Bills sent home for the royal assent. On these he bestowed but scant notice, except when impelled by some burst of virtuous indignation to recommend their disallowance. ' The number of colonial laws which have been disallowed . . . would.' says Wakefield, who wrote with an intimate knowledge of the subject, ' form the subject of an incredibly curious return to the House of Commons.'[1]   But often enough the permanent official omitted altogether to present the Bill for assent, as in one very characteristic case, where, through his delay, the royal assent was so long postponed that when the Bill was sent out to the colony as an Act,[2] the question was raised, whether the assent had been delayed beyond the two years allowed for it by law : whether, having been so delayed, it was valid ; and whether all the proceedings already taken under it were not thereby invalidated.   The Bill had been passed in March 1829, and the royal assent was not given till May 1831.[3]

The reasons for enforcing the reservation of Colonial Bills for the royal assent are alleged to be founded on considerations of State policy.   Unless the Bills so reserved are limited to those of a nature likely to involve the welfare of the parent State, as is in effect done under the Constitutions accorded to the Australian colonies, the requirement of the royal assent acts prejudicially on the social and political condition of the Colonies.   As it renders the validity of laws doubtful, since the royal assent may be capriciously exercised, obedience to them is not implicitly given.   The Colonial Ministry whose principal enactments are vetoed is either brought into contempt with the people, to the detriment of its legislative position, or else, if the measure disallowed be of great importance locally, the home Government comes to be looked upon with a dislike and jealousy which prompt the colony into a persistent defiance until its end has been achieved and the veto withdrawn, to the loss of Imperial political credit in the colonial mind.   The home Government is, in the end, always forced to submit to the colonial will, and the veto is practically worthless except as an irritant to the passions of the dependent community.   Even supposing the right to be exercised in a direction clearly for the good of the colony— for example, were it to be used to restrain enactments subversive of Free Trade principles—still, colonial jealousy would be excited by the fact that the veto was the act of a distant authority, who would be considered as much less qualified to

[1] *Art of Colonisation*, p. 254.   [2] 9 & 10 Geo. IV., c. 77.
[3] Lord Durham's *Report*, p. 75.

judge of the law than were those by whom it was made. Hence a certificate of popularity would probably be earned by the party whose work the vetoed measures were, and their hands would be strengthened for further efforts of similar tendency, however pernicious.

There can, moreover, be no temporary finality or certainty about legislation liable at any moment to be thwarted by the decision of a faction at home, and the party in the colony which has objected to the passing of any law is always on the alert to gain its own point by means of secret intrigues with the Colonial Office.

Colonial government, under the practice of an indiscriminate reservation of Bills, became a tissue of intrigues ; and yet the practice was absolutely necessary to the maintenance of a government at once bureaucratic and central.

This would be the case even where the colonial government was carried on by means of free and representative institutions. The evil was intensified in the Canadas in consequence of the initiative of rule being centred in the hands of officials who, as a rule, were the lowest types of their class. We all know the celebrated letter of O'Connell to one of his 'tail,' who had been ostracised from decent society at home, offering him a ' place ' in the Colonies, if for the sake of the party he would retire from Parliamentary life. It was on this principle that most of the colonial officials were selected. Doubtless there were exceptions, great and striking *as exceptions*, but the badge of qualification for a colonial appointment was too often that of incapacity for one at home.

Any one was good enough to be a colonial official magnate who was decidedly not good enough for public employment at home. Let a man but have displayed sufficient skill in preying upon the weaknesses of the British public ; let him have indulged in some indiscretion, which forfeited for him his place in English society ; let him have thoroughly proved himself unfit for some position of public or private trust at home ; then, if possessed of influence with the permanent gentleman, either through himself, or through relatives desirous of getting him out of the way, he was straightway

G

invested with powers over the destinies of some distant and
struggling fragment of the empire—powers absolute save in
so far as they were checked by his own integrity. His acts
and all that he did were invariably upheld by the Office at home,
so long as he exercised his authority in his own quiet way at
the expense of his subjects, and sent home no remonstrances
or suggestions. Sometimes a knowledge of the most flagrant
of his proceedings filtered home, and in the light of even an
indifferent public opinion were voted scandalous. He was
then requested to resign in favour of some other Colonial
Office *protégé*, whose retirement abroad had been rendered
necessary by circumstances. Wakefield asserts [1] that if the
truth were known regarding the conduct, character, and
manners of colonial officials in the palmy days of the tribe,
' John Bull's hair would stand on end. We should hear of
judges deeply in debt, and alone saved by the privilege of
their station from being taken to gaol by the officers of their
own courts. We should hear even of Governors landing in
secret on their arrival, and getting hastily sworn into office
in a corner, for the purpose of hindering officers of the sheriff
from executing a writ of arrest against his Excellency. We
should learn that in the single colony of New South Wales,
of which the population was at that time under 200,000,
many high officials passed through the Insolvent Court in a
single year.' Their insolvency was caused by their speculating
in the public land, of which they were trustees for the people,
but they continued to hold office as though nothing had
happened. ' The Colonial Treasurer at that time was a
defaulter. At the same time the Colonial Secretary was
obliged to resign his appointment in consequence of a discovery that a lady who passed as his wife was not married to
him. An office, the duties of which required very high and
peculiar qualities—that of a sole judge of law and conscience—
was held by a country attorney whose chief business in
England had been the dirty work of elections, and who by that
means got the appointment. Another office, of still more difficulty and delicacy, was given to an awkward, half-educated lad
of eighteen. Two principal officers of the Government fled the

[1] *Art of Colonisation*, p. 207.

country—the one for robbing the pool at cards; the other for a yet more disgraceful offence.'

And yet the class composed of people such as these—the official class—was the only one possessing any privileges in the Colonies. The Canadian officials had not the same opportunities for misconduct as were open to the bureaucrats of the convict colony, but it was the absence of opportunity and not any moral superiority which enabled the one set to maintain a more respectable appearance than the other. Mentally and morally the two sets of officials were probably on a par.

Thrift and intelligence, even the acquisition of wealth, never operated to raise the worthiest settlers to the height of the lowermost steps of the official thrones. In Upper Canada one of them might struggle into a family relationship with the Family Party, but as a rule he was inclined to indulge in a spirit of independence that rendered him peculiarly obnoxious to the Party. Not only did the members of the ruling faction set their faces against the introduction of such men to offices of trust, but they used also to affront and injure them by every means in their power. They assiduously strove by similar means to discourage the immigration of people of the better classes. In short, it may be said that respectability, wisdom, or any prominent virtue acted as a proscription in respect to the enjoyment of distinction and power. The man possessed of these attributes found himself placed in the colony in a mortifying position of inferiority to the lowest officials. Debarred from the chance of bettering himself, even perhaps from a money point of view, the more intelligent he was, the less likely was he to look upon the colony as a permanent home where he might assist in establishing a happier and freer England than the one he had left behind him. Such ambition was of no use at all, so he contented himself with making money as fast as possible, in order to return at the earliest possible moment from colonies which official stupidity, tyranny, and meddlesomeness had rendered ' unfit abodes for any but convicts, paupers, and desperate or needy persons.' [1]

By the operation of the central system, enterprise had been benumbed and creative legislation forbidden in societies whose natural business was adventure and creation. Ground down under the heel of an officialism ignorantly and secretly impelled, colonial parties had degenerated into factions, colonial politicians into demagogues. Amongst them the injustice and oppression of the system had begotten slavish means of self-defence, prominent throughout which was ' hypocrisy, crafty intrigue, and moral assassination of opponents.' [1] Can we wonder that even the practice of integrity had been banished from public life in the Colonies, and that the standard of private honour had been brought far below that of the mother-country ?

Natural advantages of climate and soil were of slight benefit where enterprise was deliberately discouraged. Prince Edward's Isle might, in Lord Durham's opinion, in *his* time have become the granary of the British colonies in Canada. Instead of that, it barely sufficed to support some 40,000 people. Although the whole island was pre-eminently rich in agricultural resources, and required but little labour in clearing, while at the same time it was blessed with a more genial climate than that of the other provinces, only one-fourteenth of the surface of the island had been brought into cultivation. The cause of this lamentable waste of national wealth was owing partly to the possession of almost the entire island by absentee proprietors ; but mainly to the influence of the absentees at home in preventing the royal assent from being given to remedial Acts of the local Legislature.[2] Prince Edward's Isle, New Brunswick, Nova Scotia, and Newfoundland, although among the oldest settled colonies in the North-American continent, could only show a population of one person to every hundred acres. Yet all the land was easily cultivable, and the coast fisheries were enormously valuable, but in consequence of the lack of enterprise due to the vicious working of a centralised bureaucratic system of government, these fisheries were practically monopolised by the fishermen of

[1] Wakefield's *Art of Colonisation*, p. 156.
[2] *Report*, p. 141.

the United States. Such was the depth of apathy into which colonists, whom every surrounding circumstance of climate and opportunity combined to spur into healthy vigour, had been forced by the unwisdom of their Colonial Office wet-nurse.

'In all these provinces,' says the 'Report,' [1] 'we find representative government coupled with an irresponsible Executive; we find the same constant collision between the branches of the Government, the same abuse of the powers of the representative bodies, owing to the anomaly of their position, aided by the want of good municipal institutions, and the same constant interference of the imperial administration in matters which should be left wholly to the provincial government.'

The tendency amongst all young colonies when left to themselves has been towards centralisation to a far greater extent than is desirable, but it has, on the other hand, been largely neutralised by the control exercised over Government proceedings by an unrestricted franchise and by unlimited freedom of speech. The centralisation has never taken the form of a concentrating of power in the hands of a small knot of officials, but rather that of grouping in the hands of a popular Assembly a great deal of the business which might more advantageously be conducted by private enterprise.

Where the work of the politician is mainly constructive, and where, side by side with central business management, a vigorous principle of local self-government is to be found, the danger that looms ahead is not perceived because not immediately apparent, but it is nevertheless, even there, a very real one. There is always the imminent risk of the central Government, entrusted with a large share of the national business, extending the area of its influence by increasing the amount of patronage at its disposal. A class of officials is created which, as it is dependent on Government employment, so it influences the proceedings of Government. As the circle of State employés becomes larger, so they will fetter the free action of a Ministry by claims for an increase of the area of employment for their services—claims which, with each fresh

[1] *Report*, p. 139.

concession, become increasingly more difficult to be resisted. An official class nominally dependent on the State may thus at some future period become its controller, even in those countries rejoicing in the freest institutions.

Local institutions for self-government are worth little unless invested with a full share of responsibility. The principle of responsibility is weakened if the central Government is allowed to take upon itself any part of the local business for which the smaller authority is able satisfactorily to provide. Thus in the matter of local roads, local improvements, and local expenditure, the central Government should not be permitted to interfere, at least not to such an extent as to lessen the responsibility of the local officers. That principle is recognised and acted upon now in England, if not in Ireland. Unfortunately, in our free colonies the tendency is towards encouraging the assistance and interference of the central body , in district business.

It may be that the causes of this difference are not far to seek. At home a bitter experience has given an irresistible impulse to decentralisation. In some of our colonies, inexperience of the evils of centralised government has perhaps been the cause that has prompted a resort to it. But in truth the habit was implanted in many of the colonies by the circumstances of their first foundation, as immediately dependent on the Crown, and the traditions of the Colonial Office may have thriven in antipodean soil unconscious of the parentage from which they sprung. There is, however, quite enough in the history of the natural development of a colony, however free, to account for an indisposition on the part of individuals to burden themselves with the cares of government on even the smallest scale. They generally live far apart from each other, and concern themselves little about the business of neighbours the nearest of whom are remotely situated. The new settler usually considers himself a mere bird of passage—encamped, not settled—and he takes no more than a passing interest in the affairs of the country as a whole, or in the local concerns of his own part of it, so long as he is left in peace and quiet. In Australia, where there has never been a dangerous assemblage of savage hordes fringing the borders of the squatters' run, the reasons which stimulated local association in the American colonies to prevent molestation, and which ultimately led to a degree of local organisation, do not exist. The Australian squatter was left in peace, and had little inducement to associate closely with fellow-settlers in his vicinity. He had neither motive nor wish to do so, and he was still more unwilling to take long and tedious journeys to the seat of government in order to discuss matters colonial, or to arrange for local institutions in which he did not consider that he, as an individual, was personally and directly interested.

Again, in a new colony the majority of the early settlers, especially if the country is a pastoral one, are fairly prosperous, and therefore are not easily worked up to political agitation. They are content to leave the rule of the country in the hands of those in the vicinity of the seat of government; and thus it is that the leading centre of population first absorbs the representation of the colony, then undertakes through its Assembly the conduct of public works, and gradually usurps the authority of the local ruling bodies.

These are evils which will, in the Colonies, doubtless find their remedies, but they must first have produced sufficiently injurious effects to make a remedy a pressing necessity. That is to say, the evils consequent on centralisation will not be thought worthy of being cured until they have worked a good deal of harm to the colonial community.

Let us not underrate the politics of a vestry. The interests of a nation are those of the individuals composing it. The desire to better one's own self is at the root of national success; individual efforts in the direction of the promotion of private interests form the only groundwork of natural prosperity, and these efforts are better capable of being seconded by small local bodies in the business of which each member is personally concerned than by an Imperial Parliament or a Representative Public Legislature.

A system of local and municipal self-government, if

properly guarded from encroachment, promotes the growth and spread of the very virtues which the official central system represses. If the area of local rule be sufficiently limited, the settlers enter with ardour into questions of every-day life, where it is in their own power to promote their own well-being. Every new district institution or improvement settled or discussed is a fresh step onward in the political and general education of men who perhaps for the first time find their voices influential in the resolution of measures affecting others besides themselves. They learn that if they take they must also give, that if they live they must also let live. So a spirit, if not of sympathy, at least of toleration, is generated, while collectively a sense of responsibility and self-reliance takes the place of sulky obedience to the central power. As local privileges become more extended, so the jealousy of any interference with them becomes more pro-nounced. The interest as well as the duty of a people en-trusted with the making of its own local regulations is to maintain the laws and preserve order. From liberty, the liberty of complete local self-government, and from that alone, spring order, contentment, and prosperity.

CHAPTER III.

MALADMINISTRATION OF CANADIAN LAND. PAUPER EMIGRATION
TO CANADA.

IN new countries the business of deepest moment to all, upon
which indeed everything else depends, is the disposal of the
public land. If it be doled out sparingly with niggard
hand, the community, however small, may be pinched for
room even in the wilderness. New-comers may be prevented
from choosing the most fertile soils and favourable situations
within reach, and the society may, even at its foundation,
endure the evils of an old and overpeopled State.

Or large tracts of land may be lavished upon speculators
and favourites, who leave their lands unsettled and untouched
while they may forbid the use of them to others. By acts
such as these the *bonâ fide* settler may be cut off or far
removed from markets in which to dispose of his surplus
produce and procure other commodities ; and the greatest obstacles may be opposed ' to co-operation in labour, to exchange,
to the division of employments, to combination for municipal
or other public purposes, to the growth of towns, to public
worship, to regular education, to the spread of news, to the
acquisition of common knowledge, and even to the civilising
influences of mere intercourse for amusement. Monotonous
and stagnant indeed must ever be the state of a people who
are permanently condemned to such separation from each
other.' [1]

Of the two methods, the evils of the latter are unquestionably the greater. It may at first attract population and
generate a delusive appearance of prosperity over the youthful
colony, but it will certainly ultimately retard settlement to a

---

[1] *Report* of Lord Durham, p. 145.

much greater degree than it originally stimulated it. Further, it will inevitably leave behind it a train of unfortunate consequences, of which the history of land settlement in Canada furnishes numerous examples. It is not the intention here to point out the pernicious policy of the lavish system further than it is illustrated by the state of the Canadas under it. In treating of land settlement in Australia, I propose to discuss briefly the merits and demerits of different modes of alienation of public lands. Suffice it to show, in the present chapter, how pregnant with mischief was the course actually pursued in our Canadian dominions. No better example could be chosen, and none has been more exhaustively treated by the Report of a high official whose interest no less than his inclination furnish a sufficient guarantee against his sweeping condemnation being dictated by prejudice or couched in terms unnecessarily strong.

A lavish mode of free granting of land involves a careless dealing with it. The physical features of a new and vast country, heavily timbered and abounding in every variety of natural formation, require careful and intelligent surveying in order to figure in accurate scale on the plan which points the new-comer's destination. If the boundaries of property are incorrectly described, the settlement of land may be the signal for a plentiful store of litigation, which, though it may furnish an irresistible attraction to lawyers, must be prejudicial to the order and harmony of the settled districts. Men engaged in lawsuits with each other will be unlikely to form associations for purposes of local management of the affairs of a district, or even for recreation. Moreover, the intending immigrant will be deterred from a colony where the decision of a law court may at any time divest him of the fruitful farm which he hopes to wrest from the wilderness. From these considerations it would seem that the importance of accurate surveying can hardly be overrated. Its absolute necessity, indeed, becomes apparent enough from the mere reflection that, without certainty of limits and boundaries, there can be no security of title to property in land. How the officials in whose hands was the disposal of public lands in Canada recognised that obligation we shall presently see.

Even supposing land to be unexceptionably surveyed, and alienated under the best possible system, the entire virtue of the plan may be wrecked by there being unnecessary delay in the granting of titles to land. Whatever delay takes place in perfecting the titles of individuals occasions uncertainty and consequently insecurity of property. Circuitous and expensive modes of application for titles are of themselves productive of delay, and produce other evil consequences of their own, not the least of which are those 'backstairs' dealings so savoury to official senses and so unlikely to be practised with effect except by wealthy colonists of the speculator class.

It is eminently desirable that land alienation should be conducted on a coherent plan, and that that plan should as far as possible be uniformly applied. 'If very different methods of proceeding have effect in the same colony, or in different parts of the same group of colonies, the operation of some can hardly fail to interfere with or counteract the operation of others.'[1]

However dear conflicting differences of system may be to the legal mind, they undoubtedly operate injuriously on the dispositions of men not brought up to regard the technicalities of varying forms of land tenures as affording ready means of subsistence. The thrifty emigrant, the man who calculates his future carefully beforehand, is the one whose entrance into a colony it should be the object of any colonial Government to encourage, and it is just this class of immigrant whom an absence of system, a total want of uniformity, or a frequent change of system will most tend to discourage. On the other hand, variations of system are no bar to the advent of people of the 'shovelled-out' pauper class, equally careless of the future as improvident in the present. 'Frequent changes of system,' observes Lord Durham, 'are apt to be very injurious, not only by probably displeasing those who either obtain land just before, or desire to obtain some just after, each change, but also by giving a character of irregularity,

[1] *Report*, p. 145.

uncertainty, or even mystery to the most important proceedings of Government. In this way, too, settlement and emigration are discouraged, inasmuch as the people are deprived of all confidence in the permanency of the system and are unacquainted with any of the temporary methods.' [1]

A lavish mode of disposing of the public lands is sure to be accompanied with an extreme absence of impartiality in effecting the distribution. The authority which gives away the land in vast areas at a time will most certainly select as the recipients of its gifts only those who are likely to be useful to it. Relatives and friends are provided for in this way, and those influential and wealthy settlers whose opposition is likely to prove troublesome are appeased by large grants of the public estate. Thus a comparative few, and those in all probability with the least power and the least intention of turning their properties to good account, are favoured at the expense of the mass of the community. A dangerous system of political and purely speculative landlordism is early brought into prominence. The sturdy cultivators, whose labour is the greatest benefit that can be derived by the State, and who, however harshly repressed, will in time constitute the most powerful party in it, get at best but a scant unremunerative share in the pickings. The inevitable result is a feeling of distrust of all Government proceedings, eventuating in the general unpopularity of the ruling powers, if not in positive acts of secret or open rebellion against them.

Nothing is more requisite to the well-being of a young colony than that the disposal of its lands should be administered by authorities trusted by and in sympathy with the people. It is only under such a condition that the population can either demand or expect a constant and regular supply of new land in proportion to its wants, an equitable distribution of it, a ready adjustment of claims, uniformity or constancy of system, or, in fact, any encouragement worthy of the name being given to immigration and settlement. Lord Durham's testimony is only that of one of a cloud of witnesses to the statement that ' in the North-American colonies, as in

[1] *Report*, p. 146.

the United States, the function of authority most full of good or evil consequences has been the disposal of public land.' ' Therefore,' he might have added, ' it should be delegated to those on whom the consequences fall.' The authorities selected to superintend that business should therefore have been composed of those individuals whose knowledge of and sympathy with the people's earth-hunger was shown by the popular choice having fallen on them as being peculiarly fitted to deal with the question. Even Merivale, who certainly cannot be accused of any antecedent prejudice against the Colonial Office, where he drew an official salary, advocates the necessity of giving up to the Colonies the charge of their own land administration. Fortunately that has been done long since, and the question once so fiercely debated has ceased to possess more than a curious interest for the present generation, but up to thirty years ago it was fiercely debated, both in the Colonies and at home. However, at the period we are treating of, the entire power of the disposal of the public lands was confided to the grasping hands of a set of officials distrusted and detested by the people. Their acts furnish ample proof of the vigour with which they set to work first to deserve and then to repay that hatred by such ruinous misconduct in the great charge committed to them that Merivale indignantly asks, ' What public body after all could mismanage the lands of its own demesne more than those of our American colonies have been mismanaged by the Imperial Government ever since their foundation ? '

Let us thoroughly grasp the meaning of the term Imperial Government. It was imperious rather than imperial. It was the remorseless sway of the permanent unknown official that was here typified. Between him and colonial Officialdom there was a secret all-powerful bond—kept alive by patronage on the one hand, by the fruits of patronage on the other. For the official mind the vast colonial estates of the empire represented only opportunities for private corruption, jobbery, and plunder, and these it utilised to the very uttermost.

We shall see how systematically every principle that we consider it necessary to observe in alienating the public land was violated in Canada, to the infinite detriment of that colony, and side by side we may use for comparison the progress of the adjoining United States under a consistent plan based on rational, because natural, maxims.

In the United States ever since 1796, the disposal of land not already appropriated to particular States had been strictly regulated by a law of Congress. In British North America, with one partial exception, there never was any law on the subject till 1827. The Imperial Parliament only interfered once to enact the ' unhappy system '[1] of Church Reserves. The Provincial Assemblies never exercised any control in the matter, so that the Lords of the Treasury and the Colonial Secretary for the time being—that is, the permanent unknown official—were the only legislators, and the provincial agents of the permanent gentleman, responsible to him alone, were the only executors.

' The system of the United States,' says Lord Durham,[2] ' appears to combine all the chief requisites of the greatest efficiency. It is uniform throughout the vast federation ; it is unchangeable save by Congress, and has never been materially altered ; it renders the acquisition of new land easy, and yet by means of a price restricts appropriation to the wants of the settler ; it is so simple as to be readily understood ; it provides for accurate surveys and against needless delays ; it gives an instant and secure title ; and it admits of no favouritism, but distributes the public property amongst all classes upon precisely equal terms.'

The British North-American colonies, on the other hand, suffered from the entire want of *any* system. Many different methods had been practised, not only in the different colonies, but in every colony at different times, and within the same colony at the same time. The greatest diversity and the most frequent alterations would almost seem to have been the objects in view. In one respect there was uniformity, and in one alone. Everywhere the greatest profusion had taken place, so that in every colony and almost in every part of each colony more, and very much more, land had been alienated

<hr />

[1] *Report*, p. 148.   [2] *Ibid.* p. 148.

by the Government than the grantees ever could have the means of reclaiming from a state of wilderness, or the opportunities for attempting to cultivate. Yet in all of the colonies it was difficult and sometimes next to impossible for a person of no influence, however willing to become a *bonâ fide* cultivator, to gain a title to any land against the superior claims of unscrupulous speculators.

The man who was fortunate enough to obtain a promise of a land grant after much intriguing had, in addition, to undergo a harassing delay before the title was made out to him. In the United States the title to land purchased of the Government was obtained immediately and without delay. But in the British Colonies there was always a great deal of useless formality to be gone through before a complete title could be procured, even to land that had been paid for. These formalities were accompanied with expenses in the nature of fees to lawyers and costs to officials which, of course, had to be taken into account in estimating the price paid for the land. The longer the delay and the more complicated the formal proceedings, the greater the legal and official perquisites. It is not surprising, then, to learn that, although eight years was considered an utterly abnormal length of time to perfect the process of the completion of the title, the average period requisite for that purpose, after the whole of the purchase-money had been paid, was fully fifteen months. During all these months the purchaser would have no right to enter on the land, and the labour which might have been employed in raising a surplus produce capable of extending industries at home was exercised in dangling listlessly about in official ante-rooms.

When the settler had at length secured his right to take up his land, he found that in consequence of the almost 'incredible' [2] inaccuracy with which it had been surveyed, it was next to impossible for him to claim his supposed boundaries without trespassing on the limits of his neighbour's properties. Or else he discovered that he was liable to be divested at any time of his holding by some later comer

[1] *Report*, p. 149.   [2] *Ibid*. p. 167.

whose boundaries, as delineated on the Government plan, conflicted with his own. Litigation therefore became the first and most important business of each settler. It was the interest of the official class to further the litigious spirit, for the members of it were themselves lawyers as a rule, and devious were the traps they laid for stimulating that spirit into existence. This was effected by selling lands as nominally surveyed where in fact there never had been any survey taken ; or, again, by making grants to different purchasers for the same lot of land. Purchasers were circumvented in every way. In some places ' the lots, instead of running perpendicularly according to the diagram, actually ran diagonally. In others, again, the lots dividing the ranges were so irregular as to give to some lots several times the contents of others, although all were nominally equal in extent ; and in places the area of some lots was taken up entirely with lakes which had been altogether omitted from the plan.' So inextricable was the confusion into which the surveying department had been allowed to fall, so inefficient was its constitution, that Lord Durham abstained from interfering with it, believing it to be ' incapable of any valuable improvement.' [2]

It was not till 1827 that any attempt was made to supersede the old system of free grant by that of sale. Up to that date the scandalous proceedings connected with lavish grants to official favourites had been allowed to go on unchecked. About half of the surveyed lands in Upper and Lower Canada had thus been alienated, not to thrifty husbandmen, but to loyalists—i.e. refugees from the United States who settled in the provinces before 1787—and to their children, to militiamen, discharged soldiers and sailors, legislative councillors and their families, to naval and military officers, to barristers and solicitors, to contractors, to favourites or their heirs. To Mr. Cushing and another were given upwards of 100,000 acres as a reward for giving information in a case of high treason. In short, half of the .surveyed land, comprising the most fertile and best situated portions, was given to just those very people who were utterly unfitted by their station, sex, or

---

[1] *Report*, p. 171.   [2] *Ibid.* p. 159.

infirmities from dwelling on their grants or cultivating them
with success. Many of the grants to loyalists were to unmarried females. It was estimated that not one-tenth of the
lands granted to loyalists had been ever occupied by the
grantees. Of the remaining grants it was asserted that nine-
teen-twentieths had hardly ever been approached by their
owners. Had the proprietors simply been incapable of work,
and so had they indulged in the practice usual with them of
selling their holdings for a trifling sum or a few bottles of
rum to others who could, and would work them, the injurious consequences might not have been so great. But the
purchasers for rum were the officials themselves, who thus
monopolised in their own hands most of the grants, in addition
to those they had conferred upon themselves by free gift.
These they held as land-jobbers in view of the value which
future settlement would give them.

It has been urged by Merivale that purely speculative
purchases of land are economically disadvantageous only where
the capital employed in the speculation has been withdrawn
from some productive use.[1] But the disadvantage is, in
reality, far more serious, and consists in the prevention
offered by land speculation to putting labour, which in
new countries is the highest form of capital, to the productive use of land cultivation. The land-jobbers in Canada
not only did not work their own estates, but they prevented
others from doing so until the pressure of increasing population made it worth their while to sell small portions.
Further, they put every obstacle in the way of permitting
roads or bridges to be made across their extensive wastes,
in order to force up land values by restricting the colonists
within a small centre, and also with the object of preventing the acquisition of ' rights of way ' by the general public,
which might be considered as taking away from the price
that an intending purchaser might be willing to give. In
this way alone, amongst others, land-jobbers can effectually
retard settlement, and prevent the development of the resources of the country. In doing so they enforce the loss of

[1] Merivale on Colonisation, Lecture XV.

H

infinitely more wealth than the capital expended on the purchase of land would have represented if otherwise productively
employed. It must be remembered, too, that the enhanced
price on the resale of portions goes entirely into the land-
jobber's pocket, who thus enriches himself at the expense of
the *bonà fide* cultivator, and thereby subtracts from the power
of the latter to accomplish his ends. Economically considered,
land speculation is a tax upon progress in a new country
which, if not utterly destructive of its prospects in the immediate future, is deeply injurious to its ultimate well-being.

Of the moral evils of speculation, Mr. Merivale takes a
view with which there can be no disagreement. To use his
own words, 'it consists in the feverish excitement which it
communicates to all transactions of ordinary business; the
impatience of slow results; the restless disposition; the languid inattention to regular labours which it infuses into the
spirit of all classes; the enormous and discreditable puffery
to which speculators resort to increase the value of their
lands, which is sure to raise extravagant expectations in the
first instance, and then to end in discouragement and disappointment.'

The land-jobbing class ruled supreme in all the British
North-American colonies, and in no case was their influence
more marked than when practically the whole of Prince
Edward's Island, comprising an area of over 1,500,000 acres,
was granted away to a few individuals, chiefly absentees, in
the course of a single day.[1]

The local Executive could always calculate on the indifference of the home Government to its proceedings so long as
it confined oppression and injustice to the most defenceless
members of the community. It made bold, therefore, to
modify provisions made by the home Government for land
grants to disbanded militia-men who had served throughout
the great European wars at the commencement of the century. By interposing expensive and harassing delays in the
way of the grants, which made them worth nothing at all,
the local Executive, in fact, violated the instructions received

[1] *Report*, p. 175.

from the mother-country as effectively as if obedience to them
had been deliberately refused.

Of course, with a Governmental clique straining every
point so as to adjust the systems of land alienation to the
wants of its individual members, the people were willing
enough to imitate their example for their own private benefit.
Accordingly, we find that provisions made after the passing
of the Constitution Act that grants should not in general be
of more than 200 acres, and that under special circumstances
1,200 acres were to be the maximum of each, were most successfully evaded. This evasion was effected by the system of
'Leaders and Associates,' and was managed as follows :—A
petition signed by from ten to forty or fifty persons was presented to the Executive Council praying for a grant of 1,200
acres to each person, and promising to settle the lands applied for. Such petitions were always granted, the Council
being perfectly aware that under a previous agreement between
the applicants—of which agreement the form was prepared by
the Attorney-General of the colony, and sold publicly by the
law stationers of Quebec—five-sixths of the land was to be
conveyed to one of them, termed the ' leader,' by whose means
the grant was obtained.

It is to be regretted that history should abound with instances of the desire of the clergy of a dominant Church to
extend the influence of their order by founding it on their
power as landowners. A spiritual power basing its authority
upon temporal wealth is but too likely to lose in reverence
what it gains in worldly resources. Be that as it may, the
clergy of established religions in Canada, if not possessed of
the former, were certainly favoured with a fair share of the
latter.

The system of clergy reserves was established by the Act
of 1791, commonly called the Constitutional Act, which
directed that in respect of all grants made by the Crown a
quantity equal to one-seventh of the land so granted should
be reserved for the clergy. These clergy reserves alternated
with Government reserves like the squares on a chessboard,
and the effect of both was to withhold so much land from

settlement and to keep it in a state of wilderness. A perpetual contest was kept up between the clergy of different denominations for the exclusive monopoly of the reserves, and the Protestant Established Church got the best of the struggle, inasmuch as the forms of its religion were most out of harmony with the views of the colonists. In violation of the Constitutional Act a quantity equal to one-sixth of the land granted in Upper Canada was set apart for clergy reserves, and in the Lower Province the clergy had reserved for them half as much again as they ought to have had. The method of making these reservations was as bad a one as could have been devised. Every second or third lot was reserved alternately—one for the Crown, one for the Church—so the settler found himself hedged in on either side by unoccupied wastes, across which it was neither within his ability or legal right to make roads. Even if roads were constructed by Government there was no machinery for keeping them in repair. There was not in Canada any local taxation for local works, and the modes adopted for raising funds for those purposes were, in Upper Canada, frequent turnpikes, to which in the Lower Province was added the venerable plan of *corvée*, or statutory compulsory labour for so many days in the year. It is stated in the ' Report ' that, solely in consequence of the badness of roads but a little way from the great towns, it cost more to send wheat a distance of eighty or ninety miles, in many places, than it would have cost to send the same quantity of wheat from Montreal to England, and to have it ground there and returned. A barrier wider than the Atlantic itself was thus interposed between places which in these days of swift communication would be next door to each other, and might even then have been near neighbours. After 1821 a certain amount of consolidation of the blocks was effected, but with little beneficial result ; and although a part of the reserves were sold from time to time, the last vestige of the system was not swept away by the absorption of the funds resulting from the sale of the reserves into the general revenues of the colony till 1856.

In July 1827 instructions were sent out by Lord Goderich to discontinue grants of land in future, and to substitute a uniform system of sale. This was a well-directed purpose to which the home authorities had been compelled to give their attention through fears of rebellion in Canada. These instructions were further confirmed in 1831, and further evaded, to such a degree, indeed, that between 1827 and 1839 the quantity of land disposed of by free grant in Upper Canada in respect of real or pretended antecedent claims was twenty times that of the land sold. Two million acres were granted against one hundred thousand sold. In Lower Canada also, the object of the new rule of selling was completely defeated by the large number of free grants.[1]

As a result of long misgovernment, the administration of the public lands, instead of always yielding a revenue, cost for a long while more than the land sales produced. 'But this is,' says the 'Report,'[2] 'a trifling consideration when compared with others. I allude to the striking contrast which is presented between the British and American frontier lines in respect to every sign of productive industry, increasing wealth, and progressive civilisation.'

On the American side all was activity and bustle. The forest had been widely cleared; every year numerous settlements were formed and thousands of farms were created out of the waste; the country was intersected by roads; canals and railroads were finished, or in the course of formation; the ways of communication and transport were crowded with people and enlivened by numerous carriages and large steamboats. Bridges, artificial landing-places, and commodious wharfs were formed on the lake frontages as soon as required. Townships were growing apace, and the stability and magnificence of their buildings might have done credit to populated centres of the Old World. On the British side, with the exception of a few favoured spots where some approach to American prosperity was apparent, all was waste and desolate.[3] There was but one railroad in all British America, and that one was only fifteen miles in length. The ancient city of Montreal could not bear comparison with some of the most recent American cities. The difference was, however, most

[1] *Report*, p. 165.   [2] *Ibid*. p. 150.   [3] *Ibid*. p. 151.

manifest in the country districts. On the Canadian side was a widely scattered population, poor, and apparently unenterprising, though hardy and industrious, separated from each other by tracts of intervening forest, without towns or markets, almost without roads, living in mean houses, drawing little more than a rude subsistence from ill-cultivated land, and seemingly incapable of improving their condition. In the eastern townships of Lower Canada, upon the border line, it was a common practice for settlers when they wished to meet, to enter the State of Vermont, and make use of the roads there for the purpose of reaching their destination in the British province.[1]

Throughout the frontier the market value of land was much greater on the American than on the British side. The average difference was 'notoriously several hundred per cent.,' and in some cases amounted to over a thousand per cent. The price of wild land in Vermont and New Hampshire, close to the frontier, was five dollars per acre, and in the adjoining British *townships* only one dollar. In Canada a great deal of land was totally unsaleable even at such low prices, while in the States property was continually changing hands. Not only was land almost unsaleable, but it was impossible to obtain money on mortgage of land, because when a sale was forced there was no certainty as to the value, since at the time there might be a perfect glut of land in the market, and no purchasers. And this though, on the whole, superior natural fertility belonged to the British territory. In Upper Canada the whole of the great peninsula between Lakes Erie and Huron, comprising nearly half the available land of the province, consists of gently undulating alluvial soil, and, with a smaller proportion of inferior land than probably any other tract of similar extent in that part of North America, it was generally considered the best grain country on the whole continent. The soil of the border townships of Lower Canada was allowed to be superior to that of the neighbouring American States; while the lands of New Brunswick, equal in natural fertility to those of Maine, enjoyed superior natural

[1] *Report*, p. 152.

means of communication.[1]   If there had been any difference
between the two countries due to natural causes, it ought to
have been in favour of Canada.   The difference, such as it
actually was, was the result of radically bad misgovernment,
and the same cause drove a large proportion of the people out
of the colony and into the United States, where the inducements offered to emigrants by a beneficial system of local self-
government were so far superior.

The theory of the day was that Colonies existed only for
the benefit of the home country—an estimable theory and one
worthy of being thoroughly worked out.   The only way in
which the mother-country could benefit by her Colonies was
through *their* prosperity ; yet they were regarded as useful in
promoting the prosperity of England by being themselves made
unprosperous.   Infirm paupers, of the class least capable of
helping themselves, were to be shovelled out to colonies
where self-help was a *sine quâ non* of existence, in order that
England might be supplied with a new and profitable market
for her surplus manufactures.   The rulers of the day ignored
entirely the fact that without exchange there can be no commerce, that non-producing colonists can never be customers
at all, and consistently strove to foster a colonial market by
remittances of paupers physically incapacitated from earning
their own livelihood, much less of raising produce wherewith
to purchase even articles of necessity from home.

The labour of a young and active man is worth far more
in every way in a new and fertile country than it would be at
home.   Under favourable conditions he can soon hope to
raise far more produce than suffices for his own consumption.
He quickly finds himself in want of home commodities, which
the results of his own labour enable him to purchase, at a
handsome profit to the provider of his necessities.   The more
capable he is of work, the greater becomes his purchasing power,
the more ambitious is his scale of requirements and the larger
are his demands upon the home market.   Business at home
is quickened and extended by the new and remunerative call
upon it.   The area of employment is enlarged, and goes on

[1] *Report*, p. 153.

enlarging in proportion to the increased activity of labour on
the soil of some far distant settlement. Whole families who
previously were starving from want of employment, or impelled to criminality by insufficiency of food, now find constant
occupation at paying wages, and widespread pauperism is
resolved into general prosperity. Such is the true development of the theory that our Colonies ought to exist for the
benefit of the home country. Let our object be to induce our
most vigorous and intelligent labourers to emigrate and so to
improve the lot of those left behind, if we would not make of
colonisation what it has too often been—a disgrace and a
burden to the kingdom, as well as a scarecrow to the working-
man.

But there is another benefit, which, though less easily
apparent, accrues with unfailing certainty to the country from
the freedom and prosperity of such colonies. It is to be
found in the moral effect exercised upon the home population
by the constant intercourse with societies freer and happier
than their own. As their standard of living is raised by more
constant and better-paid work, so also is the desire strengthened of securing for themselves more advantageous situations
in life. The more prosperous the condition of the working
classes, the more they are likely to claim for themselves a
share in the legislation which affects them as the bulk of the
community—that is, in *all* legislation. Not by those violent
measures which are the sole resort of a proletariat, to
whom misery and oppression have left no other resource, but
by the gradual assertion of rights which flow naturally from
the improved intelligence to which prosperity gives birth.

It would be a small gain, were the working classes merely
made contented with a better state of things. What is to be
desired is that they should be made more active in interesting
themselves in the regulation of their own affairs, as being the
affairs of the nation. That this is certain to follow on 'prosperity' is evident if we consider the actual meaning of the
term. Greater commercial activity is productive of improvements in means of communication, and with them of improved
facilities for information. As the opportunities for exchange

of commodities are rendered easier and more plentiful, so also will ideas and aspirations be more freely exchanged. Social meetings will embrace a wider circle, anomalous or unjust conditions of life will be rendered more apparent and more intolerable by comparison with those of others more fortunately situated, while combination for purposes of redress will be more influential because more numerously supported, and because capable of being illustrated by a greater number of individual instances. The social meeting is the germ of the political association, and this last can now speak with an authority which lends weight to its assertions, while the knowledge of its power procures for it leaders of worth and ability fitted to achieve its ends by moderation and firmness. For example and guidance they cast their eyes to distant lands where a free and vigorous British nationality has established popular institutions and popular laws. Out of the colonial statute-books they cull precedents for English use, and laugh at the venerable fictions or convenient metaphors which once did yeoman duty for political maxims. In all these results the meaning of national 'prosperity' is involved. Thus it is then that our Colonies may benefit us by improving our social conditions, as also by giving us back precedents of legislative virtue and wisdom in return for the boon of encouraging a healthy vigorous emigration and of leaving them unhindered to manage their own affairs. Had not our rulers of a few decades back been alike indifferent to the wants and sufferings of the people, this must have been the basis on which they would have promoted colonisation, for their failings were more due to an entire absence of sympathy with national requirements than to deficiency in reasoning powers.

Not so very many years ago, however, the view generally taken of emigration is clearly enough expressed in some of the conclusions arrived at by the Select Committee of 1827, on Emigration. Referring to the proposal of the Manufacturers' Relief Committee to subscribe 25,000*l.* for the purpose of assisting emigration, provided a further sum of 50,000*l.* could be obtained from other sources, the Commissioners lay down as a rule ' that private or local contributions in some shape ought to form the basis of any system of emigration to which it may be expedient for this Committee to recommend any assistance from the national funds.'[1] But they immediately proceed to break through the salutary principle so pretentiously laid down by recommending a national grant of 50,000l. from the rates for an ' immediate ' emigration, on grounds of the peculiar urgency of the prevailing distress. In truth, the Committee does not seem to have clearly understood the meaning of its own rule, for, while deprecating State assistance, it advocated the application of parish rates to ' shovelling-out ' redundant population. That there is a distinction between the two methods may be admitted, but it is one of degree and not of kind. The one is a form of State aid as well as the other, and that of the parish was the more objectionable of the two because of the greater power and desire of the local body to make emigration compulsory.

On economical grounds the exportation of paupers or other emigrants by the State is not easily defensible. If compulsory, no condemnation can be too strong for the practice ; if voluntary, it will be accompanied either by the retention of a lien on the emigrant's labour as a security for the repayment of the passage-money, or by the offer of a free grant of land as an inducement to him to pay for his own passage.

In the former case he must be subjected to occasional supervision by some subordinate official whose duty it is to collect his instalments ; and usually he ends by refusing to pay them at all, justly regarding their payment as an unfair tax on his labour, while learning the lesson of dishonesty by evading the fulfilment of his contract. In the latter case the offer of a free grant is nothing short of a bonus on emigrants exactly on a par with a bonus on the exportation of any commodity.

The recommendations of the Commissioners were, however, of too careless a nature to allow us to suppose that they founded them on economical reasons. Throughout the Report

[1] Second Report.

it is evident that their object in deprecating State aid was to shift the responsibility of the conduct of emigration from Parliament on to local bodies.

A Board of Emigration was to be appointed whose first duty would be to examine into the claims of would-be emigrants. The man who could claim to be in a state of ' permanent pauperism ' [1] would be considered as most worthy of a passage out to the Colonies. It seemed hardly necessary to add that ' the emigrant chosen should be a person in consequence of whose removal no diminution of production would take place, although by such removal the expense of his maintenance would be saved to the community,' because people in a state of ' permanent pauperism ' would, if judiciously chosen with regard to that principle, consist very largely of the aged and infirm, incapacitated from work of any kind.

It was anticipated that the number of English incapable ' permanent paupers ' would not be sufficiently great to materially lessen the burdens of the home population ; so Ireland, as being the principal pauper field, was first to be resorted to for emigrants, and preference was to be given to Irish claims. The Irish, it was alleged, were responsible for a great deal of English misery by their constant influx into the United Kingdom. This stream must be diverted elsewhere, and what way could be better than by sending out shiploads of Irish as burdens for colonial backs. Now this Irish influx was of immense benefit to England and Scotland, for it furnished a cheap and abundant supply of labour at harvest-time. But for Corn Laws, this autumnal immigration would have helped to considerably reduce the price of bread. The allegation that these Irish harvesters added to the distress and misery of the population was absurdly untrue. They were not paupers who came over, and whilst in England they made and saved money. They were, in fact, prosperous and well-to-do, as compared with the mass of the English labourers in the northern counties. It is fair to suppose that the Commissioners were misinformed, for they emphatically declare that ' it is vain to hope for any permanent advantage from any system of emigration which

[1] Third Report.

does not primarily apply to Ireland, whose population, unless
some other outlet be opened to them, must shortly fill up every
vacuum created in England or in Scotland, and reduce the
working classes to a uniform state of degradation and misery.'[1]

The Committee recommended that ' no assisted emigration
should be anything but voluntary.'[2] The capital advanced
for the purpose was to be repaid by the emigrant, but no able-
bodied paupers were to be assisted to emigrate. So, with the
obligation thrown on them of physical labour in order to repay money advanced, only those were to be chosen who were
altogether incapable of work. This was the first regularly
appointed Parliamentary Committee, and its recommendations
ought to be engraved on a monumental tombstone raised by
some intelligent colonial community as a tribute to the legislative incapacity and heartlessness of their former masters.

Paupers abounded in Ireland, and were to be picked up for
the choosing by emigration agents, not from amongst those
who had the enterprise to voyage across St. George's Channel
in order to find temporary work for themselves in England
and Scotland, but amongst the most helplessly debased and
unthrifty earthworms of the cottier class. Ignorant and helpless at the same time, they furnished a ready prey for the unscrupulous contractors whose business it was to make a profit
for themselves out of the pauper cargoes exported. These
contractors got so much a head on each emigrant, and, despite nominal regulations to the contrary, compressed as many
emigrants as possible into the smallest available ship-room.

The tendency of these pauper shovellings-out was to make
the common people think of emigration with dislike, nay, even
terror. It was looked upon as a degradation, and its very
name was associated with a feeling of shame. And how could
it be otherwise when ' hundreds and thousands of pauper
families walked in their rags from the quays of Liverpool and
Cork into ill-found, unsound ships, in which human beings
were crammed together in the empty space which timber was
to be stowed in on the homeward voyage. Ignorant themselves,
and misinformed by the Government of the requisites of such a

---

[1] Second Report.   [2] Third Report.

voyage, they suffered throughout it from privation of necessary food and clothing ; such privation, filth, and bad air were sure to engender disease ; and the ships that reached their destination in safety deposited some contagious fever together with a mass of beggary on the quays of Quebec and Montreal.' [1]

So abominable had the condition of the emigrant ships become before the termination of the voyage, that the Inspecting Physician of the Port of Quebec alleged in evidence before a colonial committee, that the 'harbour-master's boatmen had no difficulty, either when the wind was favourable or in a dead calm, in distinguishing by the odour alone a crowded emigrant ship.'

The death-rate on board, from typhus fever alone, at times amounted to nearly ten per cent. of the total number of passengers, and from the same cause a far larger proportion were afterwards received into hospital on shore, after having been ruthlessly disgorged from their floating pent-house without a shilling in their pockets, and with clean bills of health. For six weeks at a time, the witness had known the shores of the river along Quebec to be crowded with these unfortunate people, the places of those who might have moved off being constantly supplied by fresh arrivals, and ' there being daily drafts of ten to thirty taken to the hospital with infectious disease.' The consequence was its spread among the inhabitants of the city, especially in the districts in which these unfortunates had established themselves. Those who were not absolutely without money got into low taverns and boarding-houses and cellars, where they congregated in immense numbers. and where their condition was not any better than it had been on board ship. This state of things existed for many years prior to 1832.

According to Dr. Skey,[2] a regular importation of contagious disease was continuously occurring. It originated on board ship and was, in his opinion, occasioned by bad management,

---

[1] Speech of Mr. Charles Buller in the House of Commons on Colonisation in 1843.

[2] Deputy Inspector-General of Hospitals, and President of the Quebec Emigrants Society.

in consequence of the ships being ill found, ill provisioned, overcrowded, and ill ventilated. 'I should say,' he adds, ' that the mortality during the voyage has been dreadful ; to such an extent that in 1834 the inhabitants of Quebec, taking alarm at the number of shipwrecks, at the mortality of the passengers, and the fatal diseases which accumulated at the quarantine establishment and the Emigrant Hospital of this city, involving the inhabitants of Quebec in the calamity, called upon the Emigrant Society to take the subject into consideration and make representations to the Government thereon.'

These occurrences took place under the Passengers Act, which had been passed in 1825 and re-enacted in 1828. In 1835, in consequence of the strong remonstrances of the colonists, an amended Act was passed containing some excellent provisions, but so rarely were they enforced that under it things went on pretty much as usual. It attempted to establish and maintain a proportion between the tonnage of ships and the number of passengers to be carried. This direction was simply ignored altogether in practice. No emigrant was to be allowed on board without a sufficiency of some sorts of provisions. Beyond those of the Act of Parliament, however, they seldom took enough on board, despite the duty imposed upon emigration agents of seeing to their sufficiency. Vessels were chartered for emigration purposes by contractors whose sole object was to make their cargoes pay, and in this laudable endeavour a great part of their business operations consisted in evading the Act.

The Act required that the name, sex, age, and occupation of each passenger should be entered in a list, certified to by the customs officer at the outport, and delivered by the captain with the ship's papers to the customs officer at the port of arrival. These lists were systematically falsified, especially as to the ages of emigrants, so as to defraud the revenue by avoiding the full payment of the Emigration Tax, which was levied in proportion to age ; and also for the purpose of carrying more persons than the law allowed, by counting grown persons as children, of which last the regulations permitted a greater proportion than of grown persons, to tonnage. 'This fraud,' says Lord Durham, 'is very common, of frequent occurrence, and it arises manifestly from want of inspection at home.'[1]

In 1837, after many thousands of innocent emigrants had fallen victims to official inattention and private avarice, some improvement was effected in the shape of a Passenger Tax, imposed in order to provide medical attendance, shelter, and some means of transport on arrival to destitute emigrants. Also a quarantine station was establish at Grosse Isle, where arriving ships were to be regularly detained 'as if the emigrants had departed from one of those Eastern countries which are the home of the plague.'[2]

Will it be believed that in the Report of the Emigration Agent from the United Kingdom,[3] it is stated, with reference to that emigration to the Canadas before 1832 which has been above described by eye-witnesses of the miseries and calamities that then took place, that ' these great multitudes had gone out by their own means, and disposed of themselves through their own efforts, without any serious or lasting inconvenience '? 'A practice,' it is added, ' which appeared to thrive so well spontaneously.'

The same Report states, with reference to the operation of the Passengers Act of 1835, that the duty of the officers employed by the Colonial Office to superintend its execution was ' to give ease and security to the resort to the Colonies and to promote the observance of the salutary provisions of the Act. . . . In all that relates to emigration they constitute, as it were, in every port, the appointed poor man's friend. They take notice whether the ship offered for his conveyance is safe and fit for the purpose; they see to the sufficiency of the provisions on board; they prohibit overcrowding, and they make every effort to avert or to frustrate those numerous and heartless frauds which are but .too constantly attempted at the moment of departure upon the humbler classes of emigrants. Every effort is made for the ease and safety of their transit.'

---

[1] Report, p. 180. [2] Ibid. p. 181.
[3] Ordered by the House of Commons to be printed, May 11, 1838.

The Colonial Office confessed that 'heartless frauds' had been perpetrated, that they could not have been effected except through the incompetence and venality of officers appointed by itself; and yet it prompted this gross tissue of falsehoods as a monument to its own integrity, forethought, and humanity.

These were not the views taken by people at Quebec, where the majority of the passengers were landed. After the date of this Report, Dr. Poole, who had been in charge of the quarantine station at Grosse Isle for the preceding six years, stated in his evidence before the Commissioners of Inquiry on Crown Lands and Emigration, that ' the poorer class of Irish and the English paupers sent by parishes were, on the arrival of vessels, in many instances *entirely* without provisions—so much so that it was necessary to supply them with food from the shore ; and some of these ships had already received food and water from ships with which they had fallen in. The state of destitution to which they were thus brought, combined' with dirt and bad ventilation, invariably produced fevers of a contagious character, and besides the deaths on the voyage, numbers were admitted to hospital on arrival as suffering from contagious diseases. The emigrant ship was almost invariably a mere sponging-house, in which the captain utilised his position to extort their little all from the emigrants, by inducing them to lay in only a small store of provisions for the voyage, and when these supplies were exhausted he seized the opportunity to supply them out of his own private stock at 400 per cent. profit, until he had robbed them of their last shilling. Yet, no doubt, there were plenty of respectable captains employed in the lumber trade, and a proper selection by the emigrant agent at home might have prevented this abuse.

Another evil which Dr. Poole pointed out—namely, that of employing as emigrant ships unseaworthy vessels, which consequently, being unable to carry sail, made very long passages, might easily have been minimised by very little expenditure of trouble at home, since the tonnage of vessels coming to Canada was in excess of emigration requirements. He alludes in conclusion to the incapacity of the medical officers appointed to superintend the physical ailments of emigrant cargoes. The majority of them were unlicensed students and apprentices or apothecaries' shopmen, without sufficient knowledge to be of any service to the emigrants, either for the prevention or cure of diseases. To conceal their ignorance they often combined with the captains to give false reports at the quarantine station with respect to their ships. In one instance amongst others, a vessel containing 150 emigrants was returned as having a clean bill of health. On inspection being made, upwards of forty cases of typhus fever were sent to the hospital, of whom nine were then below in bed unable to get up. 'Many of the others were placed against the bulwarks to make a show of being in health, with pieces of bread and hot potatoes in their hands.'

Sometimes the proofs of their utter want of the first rudiments of medical knowledge were ludicrously illustrated by their mode of treatment. Thus one of them returned the captain of a ship and three passengers as suffering from fractured arms. These fractures, however, turned out on examination to be simple bruises. The surgeon, however, insisted on his own mode of treatment, alleging as proof of its correctness that ' in the case of the captain ' both the tibia and fibula of the arm were broken. As is well known, the tibia and the fibula are both bones of the leg.

This, however, was not a laughing matter for thousands of emigrant families suffering from many forms of disease, complicated by lowness of diet, and whose condition required skilful and unremitting medical attention. Under the circumstances of utterly incompetent medical officers being those generally selected for these ships, probably the death-rate on board would have been even higher than it was had the proportion of surgeons to emigrants been sufficiently large to permit of anything like attendance on individual invalids.

A Government which induces thousands of people to emigrate ought to look after the means of transport, and it ought to take at least as great care of the comforts, or at any rate necessities, of those whom it sends abroad as a reward for faithful service to the State. But nothing of the kind was

I

done. In the years 1832 and 1833 some 3,000 old soldiers, termed Commuted Pensioners, to whom grants of land had been apportioned in Canada in lieu of their claims upon Government, were compressed into hulks and shipped away. No instructions with regard to them had been remitted to the colonial authorities, and the pensioners consequently landed at Quebec in an almost penniless condition and without any provision having been made for them. 'Many of them spent the amount of their commutation money in debauchery, or were robbed of it when intoxicated.' Many never attempted to settle upon the land awarded to them, and of those who made the attempt, several were unable to discover whereabouts in the wilderness their grants were situated. Many of them sold their right to the land for a mere trifle, and were left within a few weeks of their arrival in a state of absolute want. Of the whole number who landed in the colony, probably not one in three attempted to establish themselves on their grants, and not one in six remain settled there at the present time; the remainder generally lingered in the vicinity of the principal towns, where they contrived to pick up a subsistence by begging and occasional labour. Great numbers perished miserably in the two years of cholera, or from diseases engendered by exposure or privation and aggravated by their dissolute habits. The majority of them have at length disappeared.'[1] Thus the ignorant tools employed in manufacturing military glory for a triumphant nation were first robbed of their earnings by an appreciative Government, and contemptuously tossed away to die in degraded misery in a distant grave.

In most transactions of human life a balance between good and evil may be allowed for. In the Government conduct of emigration the balance is weighed down heavily on one side, for the inhumanity of their actions was uncompensated by one good deed or one good result. Merciless injustice was unrelieved by one single achievement of sound policy or one solitary gleam of right principle. Enfeebled paupers were shovelled out to territories where youth and activity might

[1] *Report*, p. 189.

have raised a golden harvest as well for the Old World as for themselves. If our rulers could have known anything, they must have known how large a proportion of the British population depended at the time on the trade with the United States. Without that trade what would have been the size, wealth, and population of Manchester, Liverpool, or Glasgow—in fact of all our great towns? These were hard facts which they must have seen, and had brought under their notice day by day. Even at that time it could not have been doubted that a prosperous Canada might have maintained a large proportion of the home population.

Could the Governments of the time have in fact believed that the ' over-peopling ' of the kingdom, while 300,000 helpless mouths were every year being added to the population, could ever be seriously diminished by even systematic and gigantic emigration schemes? It is only too probable that they were sufficiently acquainted with the true principles on which colonies could be made beneficial to the mother-country. If so, they showed an indifference to the prosperity of England, as well as of the Colonies, a general hatred of the human race so great as to be almost incredible. They were well aware that the effect of emigration must be to increase the home population, unless the emigrants should be physically incapable of becoming producers at all. They could not hope to prevent the increase at home which the rapid spread of trade with the United States portended, but within their own limits of authority they did their best—a best which was verily the worst—by making the Canadas as barren and unproductive as possible. Let us by preference lay the discredit as much to their want of intelligence as to any other cause. Far be it from us to decry the consummate ability or the vast powers of the orators and statesmen whose names are still with us household words; but there is abundant evidence that on the great economical questions of the day Governments had for long no wish to learn the salutary truth. It was a medicine for which they had no taste. Men learn with difficulty what they have no wish to believe. Economical remedies for suffering, prescribing equality of rights and raising of conditions, found unwilling advocates even in those members of the ruling classes who professed a cold sympathy for the labouring population. To raise the condition of those below them was, in their view, to lower their own to an intolerable level. Education, custom, and the long assertion of a superior position had built up a barrier of pride which opposed an almost impregnable bulwark to the teachings of economical science.

Let us admit all this. Let us further allow that the business of government is in the main transacted by hirelings who, whatever may be their zeal, ability, or good-will, lack the minute supervision which alone can assure attention even to the dull routine of their daily duties; that their work is systematically scamped, or regulated by precedents framed for a bygone age; that the Minister of the day is delivered over, bound hand and foot, into an inextricable web of formalism woven by the traditions of generations of incompetent officialism. Let us allow that superior intelligence has been cramped, enterprising schemes baulked, and noble aspirations checked by the withering breath of official red-tapeism. Allow all this, and when every excuse has been made and every palliation suggested for the crimes and the follies which made up the sum of our colonisation policy, let the responsibility be laid to the charge of those who undertook its direction. *Respondeat superior*; let each titular chief in whose name these things were done answer for them. By just so much as man is the most difficult piece of luggage to transport, does he require to be handled with greater care in the transporting. Yet he was badly packed, insecurely stowed away, and with abominable cruelty shot away as rubbish on Canadian shores, to the great injury of himself, his fellow-subjects and fellow-creatures, and to the lasting infamy of his unnatural parent.

CHAPTER IV.

CRIME RAMPANT—TRANSPORTATION TO NEW SOUTH WALES.

IT may or may not be that there is a time and place for everything, but it is certain that neither the one nor the other is discoverable until experience has demonstrated how mistimed and misplaced everything actually is. It is possible that there may have been a period when the transportation of criminals might have been productive of the best results, and there may have been a locality exactly suited to develop the system to the greatest advantage. We may assert with confidence, however, that the history of criminal transportation to the Australian colonies does not furnish a single shred of evidence in proof that there ever was a time when the wholesale exportation of cargoes of felons directed to them was productive of anything but an infinity of evil.

Transportation first began to be practised as a system by England in the reign of Queen Elizabeth,[1] when it was decreed that rogues and vagabonds were to be banished. It apparently mattered little where to, for the place of exile was not particularly specified. In the reign of James I. this omission was rectified by the direction that criminals were thenceforward to be sent to the southern colonies of North America and to the West Indian colonies—to just the very places where the labour of white men was least likely to be of use to themselves or to any one else. The great abuses that then arose under the practice of transportation were tentatively dealt with in the reign of George I.[2] by a Parliamentary enactment, the necessitating causes of which were stated to be · the failure of

---

[1] 39 Elizabeth, c. iv.   [2] 4 Geo. I.

those who undertook to transport themselves '—as they well might do—and ' the great want of servants in His Majesty's plantations.' They were to be taken out by contractors, who were empowered to hire the convicts out—in other words to sell them—to the planters at the highest possible profit. The price given by the purchasers varied according to the length of sentence which had yet to run, and the most heavily sentenced convicts, who were presumably the worst offenders, brought the best prices. Both the home Government and the con-tractors thus made handsome profits out of the worst forms of vice, and this Parliamentary slave trade flourished as a national institution till the War of Independence. As the average number of criminals so disposed of was about 2,000 per annum, and as the average market quotation was 20l. per criminal, the Government for many years made an annual gross revenue of 40,000l. out of the national vices.

The suggestions as to the future disposal of criminals after the revolt of the States were characteristic of the light views of their public duties prevailing among our political leaders at the time. Mr. Eden, for example, proposed ' that the more enormous offenders be sent to Tunis, Algiers, and other ports for the redemption of Christian slaves; while others might be compelled to dangerous expeditions or be sent to establish new colonies and settlements on the coast of Africa and on small islands for the benefit of navigation.' Another statesman, still more sweeping in his intentions, would have it that criminals should be thrown ashore on the Guinea Coast —a proposition that had, at any rate, the merit of simplicity. The latter suggestion was to a certain extent acted upon, and it was deemed wise and expedient to make the West Coast of Africa the future destination of convicts. But the deadliness of the climate there soon awakened the spirit of humanity throughout the kingdom in favour of the lives of the convicts, and procured the speedy abandonment of. a system of trans-portation which, under the pretence of ' correction and im-provement,' was found almost equivalent to an indiscriminate sentence of death.

The discovery of Botany Bay by Captain Cook came just

in the nick of time to relieve the Government of that date
from undertaking the responsibility of dealing with its own
criminals at home. Thenceforth, the vast resources and the
infinite capabilities of Australia were to be subordinated
to the supposed requirements of the felonry of England, and
only the most degraded forms of crime were to be allowed
to confer the right to emigrate to the newly-discovered
continent.

The objects of transportation as put forward at the time
were :—

1. To rid the mother-country of the intolerable nuisance
arising from the daily increasing accumulation of criminals
in her gaols and houses of correction.

2. To afford a suitable place for the safe-conduct and
punishment of these criminals, as well as for their ultimate
and progressive reformation ; and

3. To form a British colony out of those materials which
the reformation of these criminals might gradually supply to
the Government, in addition to the families of free emigrants
who might from time to time be induced to settle in the
convict territory.

Brave words, bravely spoken, and making a fine show of
philanthropic intention never meant to be acted up to. Gloss
it over as the Government might with humanitarian sentiment, its real object in promoting transportation to Australia
was its desire to avoid doing its plain duty to the country. It
was far simpler to evade all obligations connected with the
proper punishment, right discipline, and the reformation of
criminals by turning them out of the country, neck and crop,
to the remotest corner of the universe, from whence neither
complaint nor remonstrance could penetrate home, than to keep
alive before an indignant people the spectacle of defects of
prison management so gross that the reform of the system
would soon be imperatively required. If the convicts were
indiscriminately transported, the home population would not
realise the amount of vice and crime prevailing in their midst,
and would consequently be less likely to turn their attention
to the unequal and iniquitous laws which forced so large a

proportion of men and women into criminal habits. Out of sight is out of mind, and a colony of convicts might soon be expected to fade out of popular memory; while complaints of oppressive treatment, or of incompetent and tyrannical administration on the part of the Government gaolers sent abroad to safeguard (and reform!) the prisoners, could be altogether suppressed, or represented as the lying tales of discontented felons. Such, in plain English, divested of its sickly philanthropic guise, were the objects which Government had steadily in mind when advocating the establishment of a penal colony in New South Wales.

The reformation of the transported criminals may, indeed, have been hoped for by many of the advocates of transportation, but the *Government*, at any rate, never made the slightest effort to achieve it. On the contrary, their aim seems to have been, as we shall presently see, to render the condition of the prisoner as degraded, demoralised, and hopeless as possible. As for the forming of the basis of a free colony out of convicts, the merit, if any, of the intention completely disappears when we reflect that the ordained system of convict management in New South Wales effectually precluded all possibility of reform, and that the free colonists who from time to time proceeded thither were neither encouraged to emigrate by the home Government, nor in any way assisted to do so until the absolute necessity for free emigration was repeatedly called for by the local authorities. Then a few pauper families were sent out, whose advent was a doubtful gain to the settlement, and all the future efforts of Government in that direction were fitful, forced, and of futile utility.

Free emigrants to Australia were, in fact, considered objectionable on various grounds. They gave trouble from the commencement by not being contented with the means of transport when lamentably deficient in the requisites of decency or comfort. They grumbled at this, that, and the other arrangement that was unfit for human beings; they found fault with the conduct of things in the colony, and were perpetually trying to effect alterations in every department of local administration. Besides, they occasionally wrote home to friends in England, and every now and again questions were asked in consequence which it was disagreeable for Ministers to have to answer. Free emigrants were therefore on no account to be encouraged.

'Imagine the case of a household most carefully made up of picked specimens from all the idle, mischievous, and notoriously bad characters in the country! Surely the man who should be mad or wicked enough to bring together this monstrous family, and to keep up its characters and numbers by continual fresh supplies, would be scouted from the country he so outraged, would be denounced as the author of a diabolical crime against his people, and would be proclaimed infamous for setting at naught all morality and decency. What is it better that, instead of a household, it is a whole people we have brought together, and are so keeping up? that it is the wide society of the world and not of a single country against which the nuisance is committed?'[1]

Such was the condition to which the English Government diligently strove to reduce New South Wales; such was the crime against humanity of which England may claim the sole and exclusive credit of precedent amongst modern nations.

People may differ widely as to their conceptions of those forms of penal discipline which are ideally the most efficacious for the double purpose of punishing and reforming. Still, all would agree that the essential requisites of any effective reform would comprise certainty of punishment or reward—that is, the assurance that definite consequences would follow upon particular acts or omissions—and also the maintenance of as equable a proportion as possible between offence and penalty, between merit and guerdon. Without these requisites every penal system must break down.

It is desirable also that the persons put in authority over the prisoners should be those who, from the weight of their moral characters, are in some way fitted to give examples of decorum, self-restraint, and good conduct to the contaminated mass around them. Especially is this advisable when gaolers

[1] *Essay on Colonisation*, by Dr. Hind.

and their charges are not brought into contact with each other merely in the ordinary routine of prison discipline, but are associated together more closely, as master and servant for instance ; so that the latter has continuous opportunities for profiting or otherwise by the private as well as by the official character of the former.

The system ultimately adopted with regard to the convicts transported to Sydney was to ' assign ' them to masters who were practically free to make of them what use they pleased. They employed them in every department of their business ; slave-drove them to their hearts' content ; spoiled some by over-indulgence ; hardened the evil dispositions of others by unfair treatment ; and being entirely unrestrained by any pretence of responsibility, were quite careless of the physical pain or the moral injury their practice or example might inflict on those whose lives had been made over to their keeping.

A bad system can never be made to give good results, and if the assignment system was a radically vicious one, it must be remembered that it was almost a necessary consequence of convict colonisation as actually practised. In promoting transportation the home Government had, in effect, laid down the broad principle that the most convenient way to treat criminals was to save themselves the trouble of looking after them by getting rid of them *anyhow*. When they had sold a cargo of convicts to contractors, they considered that they had fulfilled their duty as guardians of the national rights, and it mattered not at all to them that the mortality on board the transport ships was frightful, and that a large number of the survivors of the voyage landed but to find a grave. We are told that days and even weeks elapsed without their deliverance from the reeking hold. ' Ventilation was ignored ; discipline was lax or brutal. It was to the interest of merchants that rations should be reduced. Every death on the voyage was a gain of so many pounds to the contractors. The officers on board were often partners in the traffic, personally interested in landing as few as possible.' [1] We learn from the official report of the surgeon superintendent of

---

[1] Bonwick's *First Twenty Years of Australia*, p. 18.

one of the convict fleets how the poor wretches might well have complained of hard fare and hard usage :—' Stowed below in fetid quarters, half-clad, lying in wet places with insufficient covering or absolutely destitute of it ; stripped of the few comforts which had been provided by friends, bullied by brutal officers, beaten without cause, conscious of exposure to disease and death, helpless and hopeless in their half-starved condition. Did they complain, the remonstrance was made the ground for inflicting fresh torture. Chains and flogging added to their horrors. . . . A great number of them lying, some half and others nearly quite naked, without either bed or bedding, unable to turn or help themselves. Some of these unhappy people died when the ships came into the harbour, but before they could be taken on shore. Part of these had been thrown into the harbour, and their naked bodies cast upon the shore were seen lying naked on the rocks. The misery I saw amongst them was inexpressible.' [1]

In the case of one ship the convicts were put in irons during the *whole voyage* in consequence of some *conjecture* that they meant to seize the ship and murder the officers; and Dr. White relates many instances of finding, on his visits to convict ships on their arrival, dead bodies below ' *still in irons.*'

On board the ten transports that formed the second convict fleet there had been embarked in England 1,763 convicts, male and female, of whom no fewer than 198 died on the passage out ; and such was the state of debility in which the survivors landed in the colony, in consequence of the insufficient quantity and bad quality of the food supplied to them during the voyage, that 116 of their number died in the Colonial Hospital shortly after their arrival.[2] It is a fitting commentary, however, upon the inhuman recklessness with which the convict colony had been settled that this calamitous mortality actually prevented the annihilation of the inhabitants from absolute starvation. ' Had not such numbers died,' observes Colonel Collins, ' both on the passage and since the

[1] Bonwick's *First Twenty Years of Australia*, p. 195.
[2] Lang's *History of New South Wales*, vol. i. p. 42.

landing of those who survived the voyage, we should not at this moment have anything to receive from the public stores ; thus strangely did we derive a benefit from the miseries of our fellow-creatures.'

The colony at this period had been reduced to the greatest straits for want of food—a condition of things directly attributable to the action of the British Government in sending out convicts of whom not a single soul possessed the smallest knowledge of agriculture. Thus it was with the whole of the system and every detail in it—gross negligence everywhere ; and the example so given from home was speedily followed by the Colonial Governors, who found in the adoption of the assignment system the readiest means of minimising the trouble of looking after the convicts.

The first Governor of the colony, Captain Phillip, was fully alive to the duties of his position, and was unremitting in his efforts to ameliorate the condition of the convicts by supplying them with motives for exertion and with inducements to become thrifty settlers. To those who had satisfactorily worked out their sentences he gave grants of land, and by his firm, considerate treatment of those under sentence, tending as it did to give them an interest in their daily labour, he almost succeeded in imparting to the colony for the time being what, under the circumstances, may fairly be called—a moral tone. But the benefits attributable to his rule vanished with his departure, when the colony was left to the tender mercies of the New South Wales Corps.

This was a corps recruited for special service in the colony about three years after its foundation. Its officers were easily procurable out of the ranks of men who had failed to satisfy the by no means very stringent social requirements of those days, and whose habits and characters bore a general resemblance to those of the felons delivered over to their rule. Like officers, like men. According to Governor Hunter, ' Soldiers from the Savoy, and other characters who have been considered as disgraceful to every other regiment in His Majesty's service, have been thought fit and proper recruits

for the New South Wales Corps, which in my humble
opinion, my Lord, should be composed of the very best and
most orderly dispositions. They are sent here to guard and
to keep in obedience to the laws, when force may be necessary,
a set of the worst, the most atrocious, characters that ever
disgraced human nature ; and yet we find, amongst those safe-
guards, men capable of corrupting the hearts of the best
disposed, and often superior in every species of infamy to the
most expert in wickedness among the convicts. Our stores,
our provisions and granaries, must be entrusted to the care of
such men, and what security can we have in the hands of these
people ? '

It matters, in reality, but little for the purpose of this
chapter what or who were the members of the corps, except
as further proof of the indifference of the home Government
to the conduct of affairs in New South Wales, because it was
inevitable that even a regiment composed of the possessors of
all the virtues should, from the almost boundless power with
which they were invested over the offscourings of the English
gaols, become, in time, as brutalised as the hardened criminals
with whom they were hourly brought in contact.

If the vices of the individual members of the corps had been
more conspicuous than their virtues during their home career,
the exhibition of pettifogging rapacity and open profligacy
afforded by their behaviour as a corporate body, from the time
of the formation of the corps till its recall in 1809, was even
more noteworthy. True to its doctrine that the convict
colony was not worth looking after, the home Government
had neglected altogether to send out a successor to Governor
Phillip until nearly three years after his return to England ;
and in the meantime the corps ruled the settlement in undisputed supremacy.

In justice to the corps, it must be said, that its members
were placed in a position of great temptation to turn their
opportunities to purposes of private gain. The extraordinarily
high profits frequently realised by speculative importers on
the sale of articles of consumption were a strong inducement
to them to eke out an inadequate pay by speculating in com-

mercial transactions themselves. However widely their dealings might be known, it was in the highest degree unlikely that any notice would be taken of them at home. They were, moreover, in sole possession of the King's stores, and as these contained whatever was necessary for the subsistence of the settlement, useful articles might be procured from that source for nothing, or at worst at prime cost, which could afterwards be retailed at enormous profits. That their duty as the guardians of the stores was to deal with them as trustees for the population of the colony was not an argument likely to recommend itself to men oblivious to the sense of honour, and, in their case, the salutary principle of securing common honesty by a high scale of payment had never even been attempted. If any of them reasoned with themselves about the matter at all, they found their excuse in irresistible temptation, and what was at first a fraudulent misappropriation soon acquired the strength of a recognised laudable custom.

The article then and for many years after in most frequent requisition was Rum ; and in process of time it came to be established as a general rule that there should be certain periodical issues of rum to the officers of the corps, in quantities proportioned to the rank of each.[1] Rum-selling became the whole art of government, and the officers, from being buyers and sellers in general, gradually constituted themselves the *only* traders in rum in the colony, and then refused to content themselves with anything short of the entire monopoly of trade in every description of commodity, whether produced in the colony or imported from abroad. When a merchant ship arrived in the harbour, the officers got the first sight of her manifest and cargo, and in the sale of the latter they diligently and successfully copied the example of that other military trading association, the Honourable East India Company. The officers, having the sole command of every commodity that came into the colony, forced the farmers who had been established by the wise policy of Governor Phillip to bring their crops to them as soon as gathered. These crops they

[1] Lang's *History of New South Wales*, p. 50.

paid for in diluted rum, which they passed in exchange at the rate of 3*l.* to 4*l.* per gallon, and afterwards sold the crops at extravagant prices to the colonists.   The effect of these proceedings was so greatly to discourage attempts at agriculture that on more than one occasion the colony was brought to the brink of starvation.

In addition to the injurious effects resulting from the monopoly acquired by the misappropriation of the public stores, the whole corps furnished an example of licentiousness which must be held largely responsible for the gross immorality pervading the community.   Lieutenant Bond is but one of several who assure us that on the arrival of a convict ship in Sydney Harbour ' the commissioned officers come on board, and as they stand upon deck select such females as are most agreeable in their persons, who generally on such occasions endeavour to set themselves off to the best advantage. The non-commissioned officers then are permitted to select for themselves, the privates next, and lastly those convicts who, having been in the country a considerable time, and having realised some property, are enabled to procure the Governor's permission to take to themselves a female convict.'

When Governor Hunter arrived, at the end of 1795, he tried to counteract this monopoly of commerce and women by urging the recall of the corps.   Naturally his recommendations were unheeded.   After having nominally carried on the government in hostile subordination to the corps for five years, he embarked for England to represent the grievous state of the colony in person ; but backstairs influence was too strong for him, and he neither returned nor was able to procure any attention to his remonstrances.

Governer King arrived in the colony towards the close of 1800, and found himself at once imbroiled with the corps. He very soon gave up the attempt ' to make farmers out of pickpockets,' but the chief cause of the comparative failure of farming during his reign was the effect of the grinding monopoly of the corps in depriving the pickpockets of all inducements to become farmers.   No one will work if he is certain to be despoiled of the hoped-for reward of his labour, and the farmers who, while forced to take payment in diluted spirits for produce which, under the existing circumstances of the colony, might have been sold at a high profit, saw that those profits, raised by extortion to an enormous height, were quietly absorbed by the officers, gave up agriculture and became rum sellers on their own accounts. In thus changing their occupation they were assisted by the Governor, who hoped that by giving them licences to sell rum he might set up a counterpoise to the overbearing power of tyranny which the corps derived from its monopoly. Up to this time the superior officers had carried on the wholesale, and the non-commissioned officers the retail, trade in rum—a division of labour supported on the ground that by no other means could the surplus stores of rum be effectually disposed of. Under the system introduced by Governor King, expired-sentence men—'emancipists,' as they were called—were to compete with the non-commissioned retailers, and licences for the purpose were given out with such liberality and profusion that the population at the time was said to consist 'of those who sold rum and of those who drank it.' Even the chief constable of Sydney, whose business it was to repress irregularity, had a licence to promote it, under the Governor's hand, by the sale of rum and other ardent liquors ; and the chief gaoler had a licensed house in which he sold rum publicly on his own behalf right opposite the door of the gaol.

The natural result of this state of things was a general dissolution of the scanty moral feeling of the colony, and a general relaxation of penal discipline. There was now no pretence of either. 'Neither marrying nor giving in marriage was thought of in the colony ; and as the arm of the civil power was withered under the blasting influence of the miserable system that prevailed, the police of the country was wretchedly administered, and virtuous industry was neither encouraged nor protected. Bands of bushrangers, or runaway convicts, traversed the country in all directions, and, entering the houses of the defenceless settlers in open day, committed fearful atrocities.' [1] Several hundred convicts banded them-

[1] Lang's *New South Wales*, vol. i., p. 71.

selves together with the view of imitating the example set
them by their masters, of making the most for themselves
out of the existing chaos. They armed themselves, and after
devastating a part of the country gave battle to the military
at Vinegar Hill. Here they were defeated and broken up—
fortunately, it would seem, for the respectable portion of the
inhabitants, for the success of the convicts would have insured
a much more formidable insurrection, with the probable accompaniment of a general massacre.

Whatever may have been Governor King's capacity for
bringing the affairs of the colony to a more prosperous issue,
the antagonism of the corps was too strong to allow of any
reforms being even partially carried through. How uncompromising was the spirit in which his measures were counter-
acted by his nominal subordinates, may be gathered from the
following instance. His Excellency, having found it necessary
to prefer charges against a member of the corps to the Secretary of State, did so at considerable length, entrusting his
despatches to an officer proceeding to England for the express
purpose of carrying the complaint; but he was imprudent
enough to allow the circumstance to get abroad rather too
soon, and the *genius loci* was set to work to defeat his intentions. The despatch-box was deftly picked of its contents
before leaving the colony, and when opened in the Duke of
Portland's office in Downing Street, it was found to contain
merely a number of old newspapers.[1]

In August 1806, Captain Bligh, of the famous 'Bounty,'
succeeded King. At the time of his entering upon his duties,
the rum-selling practices of the corps had become so systema-
tised that rum had actually become the colonial currency,
or universal medium of exchange. Officers, civil and military,
the clergy, all sorts and conditions of people, were under the
necessity of paying for everything, even for labour, in ardent
spirits ;[2] and consequently every one in the colony was obliged

[1] Lang's *New South Wales*, vol. i. p. 71.
[2] Evidence of Mr. John MacArthur on the trial of Colonel Johnston
in 1811.

K

to be a trader in and for rum. Governor Bligh was specially
instructed to put an end to this monstrous system.

It was easy enough to make a show of morality by giving
these instructions, but if the Home Government had been in
earnest in its attempt to reform the colony, it might even then
have recalled the corps, as it had been repeatedly urged to do
by previous Governors and by indignant private remonstrances.
To send out Governor Bligh to curtail the privileges of a body
of men who, besides possessing absolute power in the colony
itself, were backed up by secret influences at the Colonial Office
far more potent than could be brought to bear on the side of
the Governor, was to hand over that official tied and bound
into the hands of the Philistines.

We need not concern ourselves with the widely varying
estimates of Governor Bligh's character with which colonial
historians have favoured posterity. Whether he was a monster
of iniquity as described by Wentworth or the much-injured
individual portrayed by Lang, by Bennett, or by himself, matters
little. It is certain, however, that he was called upon to con-
front a situation of infinite difficulty, and the fact that, during
his administration, he set himself resolutely to break down the
injurious monopoly of the corps, must plead in favour of his
action as Governor, whatever may have been his private
failings.

Only four months before his arrival had occurred the great
March flood of 1806. The agricultural operations of the
colonists had been carried on principally on the rich alluvial
soils bordering the river Hawkesbury. An extraordinary and
unexpected rising of the waters of the river swept away at a
blow the agricultural resources of the colony, and, save for the
Government stores, the inhabitants were deprived of the
ordinary means of subsistence. Maize, meal, and flour of the
coarsest description rose to two shillings and sixpence a pound ;
the price of wheat sprang up from seven and sixpence to eighty
shillings a bushel, and many families had no bread in their
houses for months together. The Governor under these circumstances endeavoured to alleviate the distress by encouraging the cultivation of as large an extent of ground as possible,

and with this view he engaged to purchase from the colonists, for the King's stores, all the wheat that might be disposable after the next harvest—at ten shillings a bushel. Besides this, he took upon himself to throw open the King's stores at very moderate prices, and he allowed these stores to be exchanged against produce at fair rates. These were certainly judicious measures, for, in the first place, a large extent of ground which had been enriched by recent floods was laid under fruitful cultivation, and, in the second place, a heavy blow was struck at the system of making rum the circulating medium of the country. But they drew down upon the Governor's head the dire vengeance of the corps, and of the numerous licensees to whom had been accorded by Governor King the privilege of retailing rum. The craft of those who fattened on the drunkenness of their fellows was endangered by these new-fangled arrangements. If they were allowed to get fairly into operation, the emancipated convicts might begin to take to agriculture in earnest, and might possibly acquire the habits of virtuous industry, as they would no longer have an almost irresistible temptation to do nothing but drink rum. The free settlers, too, if allowed to pocket the profits of their own produce, would probably become prosperous, and their prosperity might attract other free immigrants into the colony. A respectable community might thus grow into existence, with a gradually increasing power of its own, which would be too weighty for the rum sellers.

The wrath of these last culminated in 1808, the pretext being the alleged illegal treatment of Mr. John MacArthur, one of the officers of the corps, and the next step was the seizure of the Governor by the corps, his imprisonment for several months in Sydney, and his ignominious expulsion from the colony. But in procuring the downfall of the Governor the corps was but paving the way for a like calamity for itself. Not all at once, for the home Government was too completely indifferent to the welfare of the colony to take immediate notice of these acts of rebellion against its own representative.

The commanding officer, Major Johnston, took upon himself the government of the colony immediately on the deposition of Governor Bligh, and was not recalled to answer for his conduct, before a court-martial, till two years later.

For nearly a twelvemonth he governed the colony as he pleased. The acts of his administration and all that he did consisted of lavish distribution of rum, and prodigal grants of land to those of the free population who either approved of the late measures, or were likely to do so with proper management; of profuse granting of pardons and other lesser indulgences to the convicts. Major Johnston took credit to himself for having relieved the King's stores of the maintenance and clothing of three hundred persons, but this benefit was effected by no more sagacious a course of policy than was implied in the throwing open the doors of the gaols for the exit of hundreds of felons. In this way a number of persons of the worst character were let loose on the colony, ' and as an idea had also got abroad that the colony had now become free, and that it was no longer obligatory to labour, the result was a state of anarchy that produced a general neglect of the cultivation of the soil, and was otherwise distressing in the extreme to the well-disposed part of the population.' [1]

During Major Johnston's administration, and that of the two brother officers who succeeded him until the arrival of Colonel Macquarie, there was further opportunity for the display of governing talent, which was utilised for the purpose of levying and expending numerous duties on imports, and of completely emptying the King's stores, plentifully as those had been replenished during Bligh's superintendence.

At last, after a reign of fifteen years, the gentlemen of the New South Wales Corps were recalled. ' The evils that men do live after them,' and the effects of the profligacy and rapacity of the corps lingered long in the scene of their unsavoury triumphs. Progress had been effectually checked by a military despotism sanctioned and encouraged by careless masters at home. The support uniformly afforded to the corps in high quarters had enabled them to turn robbery of the public property into a recognised branch of their professional labours, and to establish habitual intoxication and promiscuous concu-

[1] Lang's *New South Wales*, vol. i. p. 126.

binage as the ordinary standard of morality. For fifteen years, at the most critical period of the history of the settlement, they had been aided and abetted by the home Government in making a hell out of what should have been a reformatory, and by the same influence they were stimulated to display in their own behaviour vices transcending those which they *should* have been selected to reform.

It was during Governor Macquarie's administration that New South Wales may be said to have entered on the initial stage of her future career of greatness and prosperity. Freed from the harassing opposition of the corps, the Governor now had to support him a regiment [1] which had not been corrupted by any previous connection with the colony. He had before him the task of completely reforming everything and everybody in the colony, and to a certain extent he succeeded. But, however great may be our admiration of the unswerving honesty of his purposes, it cannot fairly be said that the progress of the settlement during his reign was very largely due to the measures adopted by him.

Macquarie seems to have been actuated throughout by the sincerest desire to promote the prosperity of the colony. Unfortunately he thought that the surest way to achieve this was by keeping it up as a convict settlement and altogether excluding the free element. The latter object was plainly incompatible with the welfare of the colony, as became evident from the improvement manifested so soon as the free population began to preponderate over the bond. But in the Governor's eye convicts were the best colonisers. The surest claim to his favour consisted in having at some time borne the badge of conviction for felony. He held the opinion that the population was composed entirely of those ' who had been convicted and of those who ought to have been so,' and that the former, being more amenable to discipline—of a kind, furnished the more promising material of the two. At any rate, he could exact implicit obedience from the convicts, and that was a virtue of superlative merit to the soldier mind of the Governor.

[1] 73rd Regiment.

In order to better the condition of the convict class he adopted Governor Phillip's plan of giving grants of land to emancipists, but with this difference, that Phillip only gave to men of superior character, whereas Macquaire gave without making inquiry into character at all. But very few emancipists cared to become farmers, and almost invariably the donees sold their blocks for as much rum as they could get for them, and migrated to Sydney, where they could revel in the society of congenial spirits, and in one way or another find plenty of money, employment, and rum. There was every inducement for them to go to Sydney provided by the Government itself, in the shape of easy employment on public buildings of more than doubtful utility, and carried on on a scale so extensive that labour of any kind was gladly welcomed. This concentration of criminals in the capital was of itself a dangerous evil, and it was intensified by the practice of paying for labour as for everything else—in rum. Amongst other buildings erected at this 'period, utterly disproportionate in size and magnificence to the wants of the colony, was the General Hospital, commonly called the Rum Hospital. The terms made for its construction were that the contractors should have the right to purchase and retail 15,000 gallons of ardent spirits annually for four years. The contractors were men of ingenuity and resource. The financial part of their business they understood thoroughly, for first they bought rum abroad for 2s. 6d. a gallon, passed it through the customs at 7s. a gallon, and then they paid the wages due, partly in rum at the rate of two guineas a bottle, and in clothes, tea, sugar, &c., each of which articles was charged to the labourer at an enormous profit. Then they set to work to get the money part of the wages back again. This they succeeded in doing by the simple expedient of erecting public-houses close by the works, where the men might expend their money wages in more rum at two guineas a bottle.

The immense quantity of building that was carried on on similar terms for several years naturally made Sydney a very Paradise for emancipated felons, and while they flocked thither in drunken gangs, the country districts suffered from want of labour.   The blocks so freely granted to the emancipists found ready purchasers for rum in already extensively acred proprietors, and thus the foundation was laid of a land monopoly in the hands of a comparative few which was destined to furnish a crop of burning questions in the immediate future.

Even to the inhabitants of Sydney itself, the building mania of the Governor afforded a serious grievance, since, in consequence, they could only procure the labour of men judged incompetent to be employed on the Government works. Handy or industrious artisans were with difficulty found, to provide for the wants of the general public.   Their work was badly done, and so exorbitantly dear that it was cheaper to import the most ordinary articles of use from home than to buy them on the spot.   Private building operations were almost at a standstill, and newly-erected palaces, uninhabited and useless, stood side by side with the crumbling walls and wooden shanties where the residents lived and moved and had their being.

This was not the country for free labourers, nor did the Governor intend it to be so.   The actual cost of convict and emancipist labour might be four times as great as the cost of free labour, but Macquarie was prepared to charge that loss upon the British taxpayer in order to preserve the colony as the inheritance of felons, and the home Government was ready and willing to support his policy.

It is often asserted that the future prosperity of New South Wales was most materially assisted by the extensive roading and bridging operations inaugurated by Macquarie.   Without doubt it was.   Internal commerce was immensely benefited by them, and so, in time, was external trade, but it is equally clear that, had free immigrants been attracted instead of being repelled, the necessities of what would have been a brisk active population would have enforced the making of means of communication quite as extensive as those actually effected and at a large saving of expense.   The public works effected in New South Wales since free immigration became an accomplished fact on a large scale, have infinitely exceeded in magnitude, though at a largely reduced proportionate cost, even the great achievement of road-building across the Blue Mountains to Bathurst. Still, there is no denying that these roads and bridges were of great use to the country ; the chief, perhaps the sole, benefit attributable to the initiative of Macquarie.

Referring to him and to his general line of policy, Mr. Commissioner Bigge observes :—' It has been his misfortune to mistake the improvement and embellishment of the towns for proofs of the solid prosperity of the colonists, and to forget that the labour by which these objects have been produced was a source of heavy expense to the British Treasury, and that other means of employment might have been tried and resorted to, the effect of which would have been to regulate in a cheaper and less ostentatious form the progress of colonisation and punishment.' [1]

It is impossible to avoid the conclusion forced on us by the preceding sketch that a large proportion of the vast expenditure of British money in the Governor's building craze was, in reality, devoted to carrying on a growing process of demoralisation in the colony, and in thus preventing the attainment of the chief end for which the colony was nominally established—the reformation of the convict population. It acted adversely, too, on the free population by discouraging labour from finding its way to the country districts, whither free immigrants might otherwise have resorted ; and by raising up a powerful emancipist class who, basking in the sunshine of Government House, and rewarded for villany by official favours, were for many years able to combat the desires of the free settlers for necessary measures of reform.

Few people will be found to quarrel with Macquarie's honestly-meant wish ' to restore emancipated and reformed convicts to a level with their fellow-subjects.' But the mind revolts at the bare possibility of effecting the equality of footing by bringing down the reputable portion of the community to the level of the convicts. Yet this was what *was* done. The effort to raise the bond resulted in the degradation

[1] Commissioner Bigge's *Report on New South Wales.*

of the free. In 1814 the Governor lent his influence to an attempt to admit three convicts, who had been transported for perjury and forgery, to the privilege of practising as barristers and solicitors in the Supreme Court. The petition presented for the purpose to the judge, Mr. Hart Bent, was refused by him on grounds which accorded with the law he was bound to administer, if not with the views to which the Governor gave countenance. The immediate consequence was the deposition from office of the judge conscientious enough to oppose the mandate of authority, and the substitution of a more pliable instrument to preside over the administration of law thus lowered to the standard calculated to suit the proclivities of a criminal society. Had the convicts at that time possessed the opportunity or shown the desire to make their condition better or more virtuous, the counter-action might, in a measure, have mitigated the evil. But it was just at this time that the practice of ' assignment ' contributed most powerfully to degrade their aspirations, to minimise their opportunities, and to debase their characters by offering every inducement to criminality and worthlessness.

The practice of assignment grew up into great prominence during the reign of Macquarie. Convicts of all sorts were allotted as servants to whoever might care to take them off the hands of the Government. In the assigned service no wages were allowed to be given, and the servants were subjected to the most severe regulations, such as any master could invariably get enforced, on appeal to a fellow-magistrate and master, by equally severe punishments. At the end of the allotted periods, the convict might ask for, and according to the report made of him might obtain or be refused, a ticket of leave. Whether he would obtain this ticket or not was always a matter of uncertainty. The record kept of prisoners' conduct only embraced offences; no official notice being taken of good ordinary behaviour, such as diligence, sobriety, obedience, honesty, fidelity, zeal, or the like ; and thus, as only that appeared which had drawn down magisterial censure, a careless man, however good his disposition and intentions!

might, especially under an indifferent master, have a long list
against him and nothing in his favour ; while a thorough
villain, more happily circumstanced or perhaps because of the
very power of deception which his villany gave him, might
have few or no offences recorded against him.   When the
ticket was obtained, a particular district was assigned in
which the recipient was to reside, and within which he might
change his master and residence and receive wages.   It was
obligatory on him to attend certain musters and not to change
his abode without informing the police, to sleep constantly at
home, and to return thither before eight o'clock in the evening.
For very trifling irregularities he was liable to have his ticket
suspended or entirely taken away ; in either of which cases he
was usually sent to hard labour on a road party, thus being
suddenly reduced to the worst and most demoralising of all
penal stages.

As the periods of sentence respectively expired, whether
with or without the intervention of tickets of leave, the
prisoners became entirely free, and mixed as such in the
community.

This is a sufficiently accurate sketch of the course of the
assignment system.   Its operation was most distinctly injurious all round, if for no other reason than that the degree
of punishment inflicted by it was in the highest degree uncertain.   A bad master might make it fearful ; a good or weak
master might make it an indulgence rather than a punishment.   In the system was involved a position of utter degradation for those convicts possessed of a semblance of self-
respect ; whilst to irresponsible masters was given the most
absolute power for the abuse of tyrannical authority.

The assigned servants were, in fact, slaves.   The system
was slavery in its very worst form, for the New South Wales
slaveholders had no property in their slaves, nor consequently
had they any motive for improving their condition.   Besides,
the servants had not always held the same degraded positions.
Many had education, more ability, and the passions of all
were easily excited.   They were fitting enough subjects for
the exercise of moral influence, had it been forthcoming either

in precept or example ; but the discipline to which they were
subjected was purely physical. If the master so willed it, the
most minute offences against this discipline were visited with
further pains and penalties, and the frequent and gross injustice of the punishments thus inflicted had as demoralising a
tendency as the spectacle of the unrestrained vices of the free
portion of the community.

For some time after the establishment of the system, the
Government undertook to clothe and provision the assigned
servants for a specified number of months in each year.
Their labour was useful so long as it could be had on these
terms, but it frequently happened that the master would,
as soon as Government support was withheld, be undesirous of employing all those assigned to him. If he was a
farmer he would, as a rule, at that time, not care to raise a
larger amount of produce than was necessary for him and for
his family's subsistence. There was no market for any surplus
outside the colony, and inside it the number of inhabitants
was too small and the bulk of them too poor to absorb the
large grain crops, which grew almost without superintendence on the fertile soils in favourable years. The farmer
would take the convicts assigned to him, partly in order to
curry favour with the Government, partly because their
maintenance involved him in no cost, and possibly they
might be useful to him as domestic servants, or in other
capacities. When the time came for him to give them the
minimum of support required by law, he had a choice of ways
in which to rid himself of his burdens. Either he might
return them on the hands of the Government, by bringing
accusations against them which, whether true or not, he
could always contrive to get substantiated, and so manage to
procure them a period of labour with some road gang ; or
he might give them free indulgence to roam about the
country—that is to say, to form themselves into predatory
gangs pledged to the worst forms of lawlessness. When he
got them imprisoned, it was perhaps to satisfy a grudge, or
out of the promptings of a general malevolence of disposition.
Either dislike or revenge could be safely wreaked in this

form. If he turned them loose to prey upon society, the act may have argued kindliness of character, but, like many of the freaks of good-nature, this course was probably the more objectionable of the two, since those so sent abroad would be the most worthless of the lot assigned to him. The best he would probably reserve, as being worth their keep.

When free emigrants began to come into the colony in considerable numbers in Governor Brisbane's time, the status of the convict, considered as a labour machine, was greatly altered. He was no longer an incubus on Government hands to be forced off at any price, but he had become an article of value of which the Government had sole possession. A quickly increasing population with a gradually extending range of wants required an amount of food which could only be supplied by the active co-operation of all the labour force of the colony. Commerce generally was stimulated by the incursion of the free element, and the service of able assistants became a matter of necessity. The dispensers of convicts could now become coquettish, and were in a position to dispose of their human machines on favourable terms, as well as to make assignment a branch of special patronage. Thenceforth, servants were only to be granted to people who could give proof of capacity to maintain them. So far so good; the clearing of the gaols had become a matter of apparent saving of expense. The difference between the new and the old methods of assignment was that now the slave was not given, but sold. This saving of expense was only apparent as concerned the community at large, for the burden of maintaining the convicts had been merely transferred from the Government to individuals, and assigned labour was estimated at not more than one quarter of the worth of free labour under ordinary conditions. But such was the disinclination to direct payments in the shape of wages that the free labouring immigrants could only with extreme difficulty obtain permanent engagements, the masters generally hoping that they might get a prisoner assigned to them suited to their own particular purpose, and that they might thus save the direct expense of a free servant.'[1]   In consequence, the free servants, who might otherwise have formed a valuable labour force, in some cases either themselves became employers of a few convicts, or became small tradesmen in the towns, or more usually, through sheer inability to procure work, they sank deep into vicious modes of existence or into lazy dissipated habits.   Their very independence was a fatal bar to their employment by masters whose rule, whether conducted with tyranny or indulgence, was based throughout on the principle of physical coercion.   The free man was a contractor for a definite use of his services, and, before the law, had equal rights with his master, which he might enforce if occasion required. He was obnoxious therefore to men accustomed to the delights of slave-driving, and had consequently no chance afforded him of bringing his labouring power into competition with that of a convict.

It must, too, be remembered that the scale of a man's work will depend upon the general standard of labour around him.   The free labourer might have been competent to produce four times as much as the convict, but, unless a man of very exceptional force of character, he would usually content himself with doing no more than was necessary to raise the value of his day's work slightly above the convict level.   Be that as it may, one prominent effect of the assignment system was that it procured the discouragement of free labour and of the working power of the free labourer, besides powerfully militating against the influx of free immigrants.

Both as a punishment and as a means of reforming criminals, the failure of assignment was complete.   Its efficacy for either purpose was dependent upon the characters of individual masters.   By just so much as these differed from each other, the operation of the system was rendered uncertain.   Masters might be stern disciplinarians, ready to visit an offence against conventional regulations with all the heaviest penalties of a penal code so harsh that its extreme provisions were rarely carried into practice ; or they might regard breaches of discipline with a lenient eye, using them

[1] Captain Maconochie's *Thoughts on Convict Management*, p. 13.

only as convenient excuses for procuring the punishment of servants whom they disliked or feared. Others, again, might err on the side of over-indulgence either owing to good-nature or to weakness of character, or perhaps from a belief in the greater efficacy of easy treatment in inducing labour. The whole system was a lottery, in which the prizes, the good situations, were as often as not drawn by those least deserving of them, felons too hardened in vice to profit either by good treatment or good example. On the other hand, men more unfortunate in their fall than criminal in their habits might be assigned to masters—possibly themselves emancipists, of the lowest type, and deriving their rise from fortunate speculations in rum—whose treatment might be effectual in brutalising their miserable dependents.

The great majority of masters cared nothing about the punishment or reformation of their slaves—they viewed them merely as insensate instruments for business purposes, their object being to get as much work out of them as possible, and, whether they used the indulgent or coercive system, it was but as a means to the attainment of this end. Of the two the indulgent system was the one more generally employed, and those subjected to it might safely calculate on being better fed and clothed, and also on doing far less work than would have been demanded at home from healthy English labourers.[1] Captain Maconochie, in illustration of the indulgent system, mentions a case where the whole of an assigned staff sat down in a cornfield during harvest and refused to work because the supply of tobacco was exhausted. Some was hourly expected from a neighbouring town ; nevertheless it was found necessary to procure an immediate supply before the men could be induced to work. Tobacco was an indulgence which the master was not bound to allow them, and the men were at the time receiving as much flour and mutton as they chose to eat, and a bottle of wine a day. Instances of this kind were not very frequent, it is true—and why ? *Because masters took good care not to be without tobacco.*

When such was the pampered condition of convicts, it is

[1] Maconochie's *Thoughts on Prison Management*, p. 36.

not surprising to find that free men were occasionally found willing to exchange their freedom for bondage by committing some act which would subject them to the luxuries and indulgences of the latter state. An instance of this, much dwelt upon by the colonial historians, was furnished in the case of two soldiers of the 57th Regiment in Governor Darling's time, who, with the object in view of becoming assigned servants, committed a theft in such a way as to ensure immediate detection. The temptation was great; and the punishment, intended to be exemplary, was so disproportioned in fact to the circumstances of the case that one of the men convicted died within a few hours of its first infliction, and in consequence a popular revulsion of feeling was produced, alarming in its results.

It occasionally happened that assignment furnished a ready means of evading the ends of justice, as where the proceeds of robberies in England were remitted out to some unsuspected colonist, under a preconcerted arrangement or trust, that the thieves when transported should be assigned to the service of the consignee confederate, who might be relied upon, through fear of exposure, to make a fair distribution of the plunder.

If the nature and extent of the punishment of the assigned servant was uncertain and capricious, his reward—namely, the ticket of leave—was every whit as doubtful. It often happened that good behaviour *lessened* the chances of a man's obtaining his ticket when due, for the ticket was only given if there was no record of offences against the servant during his period of assignment. Consequently, good, useful servants were prosecuted by their masters for the most trivial, real, or fancied offences, in order that a record of crime might be procured against them, so that, their tickets being refused them, they would of necessity be continued in the assigned service. This practice became so common in Sydney that a regulation had to be passed making it impossible, by requiring all men to whom tickets were due for service to be returned to Government, whether they were entitled to them by conduct

---

[1] Maconochie's *Thoughts on Prison Management*, p. 43.

or not.[1]   On the other hand, by reason of the difficulties thrown in the way of masters parting with useless servants, men, otherwise unfit, would generally obtain tickets of leave. By procuring them that indulgence, the master immediately became entitled to another servant, who might turn out a greater acquisition. So the most worthless and hardened were rewarded with freedom and entitled to spread their demoralising influences through the colony as advertisements of the value of vice, while the thrifty, temperate, and industrious were made to furnish a warning against the cultivation of qualities deemed meritorious in all other communities but those of New South Wales and Van Diemen's Land.[1]

Of all the disgraceful features attending transportation, perhaps none was more glaring in its cruelty than the failure of the home Government to supply the local authorities with proper lists of the periods of transportation to which the convicts had been severally sentenced. It was thus often impossible, without a lengthened inquiry, that in those days of slow communication occupied many months, or even years, to ascertain the correctness of the assertions of the numerous convicts who claimed to have served the full lengths of their sentences; and, though the importance of sending out such lists with each convict ship was even imploringly urged by the Colonial Governors, it was not until ten years after the first foundation of the settlement that the Secretary of State for the Colonies condescended to state that ' *in future* lists shall be sent from England and Ireland of the terms of sentence.'

So far as the principle of the injustice thus done was concerned, it made no difference whether the worst or the best of the convicts were most affected by it. It was, however, naturally felt as a greater hardship by those prisoners who had been transported for political offences, and to whom any prolongation of their sentences meant a bitterly intense degree of mental suffering, than it was by those convicts to whom transportation or imprisonment was neither a disgrace nor a punishment. The studied neglect was, in the case of the former, a refinement of cruelty directed against political

[1] Now Tasmania.

opponents who had been transported for having dared to defend the liberties of their country ; and in the case of all it was a bitter heartless wrong.

With respect to the reformation professed as the main object of the system, the wonder was how it could ever have been expected. Assignment was, on the face of it, as has been shown, not only slavery, but slavery in its very worst form. The stimulus to labour or the punishment for indolence and insolence was usually the lash. Other modes of punishment were liberally provided, but masters generally preferred flagellation, as causing less interruption to their servant's work. Even under the indulgent system, the lash was frequently brought into use.

The effect of slavery has always been in the highest degree debasing to both master and slave, and thorough deterioration of general morality has been its invariable result. The following is the picture of the convict settlements under the assignment system of slavery, drawn by a careful observer :— ' In my opinion the effect is what ought to have been expected. I firmly believe that almost every prisoner who is submitted to its operation ' (that of assignment) ' is deteriorated by it. Every one of them may not be a bad man, but every one was a better one in England. I have directed considerable attention to this subject, and sought information from every available source. I have conversed with ministers of religion of various denominations, with magistrates and settlers, and my opinion has been everywhere confirmed. I hear one say that the prisoners invariably have money which they cannot honestly obtain. Petty thefts are so common that all appear to make up their minds to them. Drunkenness seems in most cases to be only limited by opportunity ; and lying and perjury are so fearfully prevalent that I believe we have the authority of a Judge and Attorney-General attached to the assertion that evidence may be readily obtained to convict any man of any crime laid to his charge for half-a-crown.' [1] Those who had obtained their tickets or had been completely emancipated had greater inducements to work and

[1] Maconochie's *Thoughts on Prison Discipline*, pp. 58, 39.

to revert to the ways of honesty, but the demoralising effects of the penal discipline which they had undergone were equally pronounced in their case. One of them, who since his emancipation had devoted himself entirely to sheep-stealing, had brought from the school of reforming discipline the maxim, ' An old thief must keep his hand in,' and this he alleged as his only motive. ' And,' continues Maconochie, ' of those who had been convicted of murder within the year preceding, all were of those who had been let loose upon society as penitent and reformed men.' [1]

The large influx of convicts during the reign of Macquarie and the supply poured in in Brisbane's time might not have been effective in reducing the demand for convict labour had the colony been making sufficient progress to be able to give employment to the extra arrivals. But, although the statistics taken at the end of Macquarie's administration compared favourably with those taken twelve years previously, the advance in material progress had been very small. The population had been swollen to three times its previous amount mainly by importations of convicts, and the increase in flocks and herds was the result of reproductive action in a country peculiarly well fitted for its operation. The acreage nominally under cultivation had been enlarged, but was still far from sufficient to feed a trebled population without large supplements of food brought at heavy expense from India and Batavia. Moreover, only about two-thirds of this acreage was actually under cultivation, a large proportion having been abandoned after having been cleared. To open a market for the employment of the convicts now rapidly accumulating on his hands, Brisbane stimulated the immigration of free settlers. With this view he offered, through the Home Government, grants of land to those intending colonists who could procure satisfactory certificates of their possessing a capital of at least 500l., the grants to be proportioned to the amount of their available property. Besides which, any one who would undertake to maintain twenty convicts was declared to be entitled at once, and without any further quali-

[1] Maconochie's *Thoughts on Prison Discipline.*

fication, to a grant of 2,000 acres, and so on at the rate of one hundred acres for every convict he might be willing to take on his hands. The result of these inducements was a large and continued influx of free settlers, and the colonial Government soon found that the demand for convicts was greater than the supply at its disposal could satisfy. The Government farms that had been laid out to give employment to the convicts had therefore to be abandoned. On these farms land had been cleared and buildings erected at great expense, and it is a striking commentary on the worth of convict labour--or of Government planning-- that the value of the land had been but little increased by the expensive work performed upon it, while the buildings were found to be of no value at all, and were suffered for the most part to go to ruin. These farms were now given up, and the convicts located in them were distributed forthwith among the free settlers.

It seems impossible to patch up an evil without creating fresh ones. The whole system of colonising with convicts was thoroughly bad, and although the necessity for the emigration of free people was at length admitted, even at home, it was promoted by means of encouragement productive of vicious results. The habit grew up among the free of getting large grants of land made to themselves by offering to maintain a larger number of convicts than the Government could supply, and they were nevertheless granted the full quantity of land proportioned to the whole number of convicts applied for. As an instance of the stimulus given by the ' encouragement ' plan to land-jobbing may be taken the case of an individual who, having come to the colony for a short while for the benefit of his health, bethought himself of benefiting his pocket as well as his health by applying for a grant of 2,000 acres. The grant was accorded, and he immediately sold his easily-earned property, without ever having seen it himself, for the sum of 500l. This was no extreme example, for Governor Darling afterwards found it necessary to devise regulations expressly to meet the frequent recurrence of such cases. Agreeably to these regulations land was thenceforth to be granted in proportion to the property or means of the applicant, but it was not to be granted to him at all unless there was reason to believe that he was able and willing and likely to improve it.

It may be suggested that Brisbane would have acted more wisely if he had done more to encourage the immigration of free labourers instead of confining his efforts to the introduction of capitalists. As it was, the class of men whom he induced to come to the colony were afterwards the strenuous supporters of the continuance of the transportation system, and by their insistance in that respect their influence in retarding the advance of the colony was very considerable. Not only were they advocates for transportation, but they uniformly did their utmost to keep free immigrants of the labouring class entirely out of the country, and thus they prevented the formation of a society intermediate between masters and convicts. Such a society would probably have prevented the pretensions of the former from acquiring a solidity dangerous to the welfare of the country, and would by the force of example and association have been effectual in raising the latter from their brutalised level.

The convicts had no chance of becoming reformed characters under actual conditions. It was not in Australia as it had been in America, where the felon transported to the plantations found himself an insulated rogue amongst honest men. There 'he imperceptibly glided into honest habits and lost not only the tact for pockets, but the wish to investigate their contents. But in Botany Bay, the felon, as soon as he got out of his ship, met with his ancient trull, with the footpad of his heart and the convict of his affections—the man whose hand he had often met in the same gentleman's pocket, the being whom he would choose from the whole world to take to the road, or to disentangle the locks of Bramah.' It was impossible that vice should not become more intense in such society. The most powerful instrument of reform —the public opinion of respectable men and women of a rank of life on a par with that of the generality of the convicts— was non-existent in New South Wales, and was sedulously kept at a distance f om a community where its steady operation was essential to the reformation which the ruling powers professed to have in view.

The fear that Brisbane's steps in the direction of free emigration might be but the thin end of the wedge which was to open out a path for the introduction of free labourers took possession of the Home Government. The emancipists, too, whom Macquarie's ill-judged schemes had raised up into a powerful class, might be always sure of a community of sentiment between themselves and the Colonial Office. They therefore pressed for Brisbane's immediate recall, and the Office gladly acceded to a proposition which gave opportunity for showing signal disapprobation of a course which, if unchecked, might eventually lead to the prosperity and independence of the colony. Fortunately, they were too late to prevent the influx of a goodly number of free labourers in the teeth of all discouragement, and during the governorship of Darling, Brisbane's successor, the preponderance of this class became so pronounced that from thenceforward convicts and their concerns dwindled into comparative insignificance, until brought prominently into notice again by the opposition of the Home Government to the demands of the colonists for the cessation of transportation. During Darling's time the emancipated convict mechanics gradually disappeared from the face of society in the towns, being replaced by skilled labour of a more reputable character from the mother-country, and being thus in the natural course of events pressed down to a lower level in the scale. The emancipist was obliged either to conform his habits to those of his respectable neighbours, or to be off as an outlaw to the inhospitable interior.

Governor Bourke, who succeeded Darling, found it necessary to mitigate the severity and the inequality of magisterial sentences on convicts by limiting the scale of punishment for any one offence to a maximum of fifty lashes. He also regulated the practice of assignment by refusing to bestow more than seventy convicts on any single individual ; and, by giving a second or casting vote in the Legislative Council, he procured the passing into law of his proposal to make convicts eligible to serve on juries on criminal cases. These measures, especially the one restricting the liberty to lash, brought the Government into very bad odour—a not altogether unhealthy sign in the latter case, inasmuch as it was significant of the growth of a free population. Some three years after the departure of Bourke, transportation to New South Wales virtually ceased; although, as we shall see hereafter, the Home Government was always anxious to renew the system. If not entirely killed, it was thoroughly scotched by 1840, and it only remains to sketch some of its salient features to which attention has not yet been called.

During the fifty-three years devoted to turning the colony into a reservoir of crime, no fewer than 59,788 felons had been transported from England to this distant shore. Of these only 8,706 were females—only about seventeen per cent. of the whole number—a fact which speaks volumes for the professed desire of the home Government to reform the morals of the prisoners. This arrangement prevented the natural increase of the criminal population by births—possibly a fortunate circumstance—but the fact must be debited to the culpable carelessness rather than credited to the good intentions of our rulers. This inequality between the numbers of the sexes was for fifty-three years the ready cause of the grossest forms of vice that civilisation has ever been called upon to reprobate.[1] And who shall say that felons, untended and untaught, inured to vicious lives, and brutalised by habit though they were, were to blame for these atrocious immoralities, rather than those Pharisees in high places in England whose measures were devices for depraving the depravity even of the noisome herd selected with care from the bestial offscourings of British gaols.

The expenses of the transportation system were enormous. The evidence given before the Transportation Committee in 1816 showed that the price paid for the *mere transport* of convicts had been on an average 37*l.* per head, exclusive of food

---

[1] The women who were sent out from time to time are described as being the most polluted of their sex ; as ' far worse than the men, and at the bottom of every infamous transaction in the colony.' *—Letter from Governor Hunter.*

and clothing *en route*; and it appeared that in 1814, 108*l.* per man were paid for the transport, food, and clothing of 1,016 convicts. Up to 1815 the total direct cost of the settlement to the mother-country had been 3,465,983*l.*, and whereas the annual expense of maintenance of each convict was calculated at 33*l.* 9*s.* 5*d.*, the value of his labour was stated to be not more than 20*l.* per annum.

What a reversal of the true functions of colonisation was shown in these figures. Instead of being the means of en-riching the home populations, New South Wales has been made a sink for the national wealth as well as for the national iniquities.

The local Governors were being continually urged to reduce the expense of maintenance, until they were harassed into the pernicious system of granting tickets of leave to convicts pro-miscuously, without any inquiry worth the name into their title to the indulgence. There was thus let loose a set of men who had been solemnly pronounced to be improper and dangerous members of society, and unrestrained opportunities were thus afforded them of committing fresh enormities before they had made the atonement affixed to their original offences. Such was the extension of the ticket of leave system, that although 4,659 convicts were transported between January 1812 and January 1817, the expenses of the colony for the latter year were 6,445*l.* less than for the year 1813. This violent and unjusti-fiable mode of retrenchment, however, was not put into such extensive practice with impunity; it was attended with its natural and inevitable results—proportionate increase of de-moralisation and crime. Robberies and other crimes of violence became so frequent that the Governor deemed it expedient 'earnestly to recommend to persons in general to travel only during the daytime.'

The 'ticket of leave' system may be made beneficial enough in its operation; for, if carefully administered, it may consti-tute a means of exceptional value for stimulating criminals to an industrious course of conduct which may ultimately be-come the habit of their lives. In a community composed ex-clusively of convicts, the adoption of the system is practically a necessity ; but just in proportion to the need for it is the danger lest carelessness in its application should furnish a premium to villany.

The home Government must have known that when they were insisting on the granting of tickets of leave as a device for economy, they were in fact directing the local authorities not to make good conduct the condition of granting. They were simply to use tickets of leave to diminish the number of convicts, so as to cut down the cost of their maintenance.

The local objections were contemptuously set aside, and the home creed forced upon the colony. Tickets were dealt out with lavish profusion and the grantees very soon required an increased police force to watch them or to take them into custody, unwilling though the authorities were to take any grantee on their hands again. For how were they to save expense if they had to re-arrest men as fast as they let them go ? Under the circumstances they pursued one or other of the two inconsistent courses of either waiting until the outrages perpetrated by the releasees became unbearable, or they kept up the stream of circulating criminality by fresh indiscriminate issues of tickets.

The felons released on tickets had not even the chance of obtaining an honest livelihood so long as the policy of the Home Government prevented the opening of fresh avenues of employment; and this prevention was, as will presently appear, a cardinal feature of Downing Street rule. So matters went on from bad to worse. Crime increased in a proportion higher by thirty or forty per cent. than the growth of population, for criminal cases trebled while population scarcely doubled itself ; and notwithstanding that, at times, the practice of assignment provided very largely for the expenses of convict maintenance, it was ascertained by a Transportation Committee of the House of Commons that up to the end of 1836, when transportation virtually ceased, the total average cost of maintenance had been for each convict 82*l.* The average cost of conveying each one to the colony during the whole of the transportation period had been 28*l.* Against this last item there was nothing to place on the other side of

the account, while, on the calculation given above, for every
33*l.* 9*s.* 5*d.* expended on his maintenance, the convict could
only show work to the value of 20*l.* It follows that the probable net loss incurred by England, taking simply cost of
transport and loss due to inefficient work, in establishing and
fostering this one convict colony for fifty-three years, amounted
to no less than 2,500,000*l.* exclusive of interest.

This is indeed in striking contrast to the prosperity that
might have resulted both to the colony and the mother-
country had free emigration earlier taken the place of convict transportation. The estimated annual value of a free
labourer's work in the Australian colonies is usually taken at
200*l.* Over and above the necessary cost of subsistence, a
good part of this represents the value in exchange to the
colony of the surplus produce which he annually assists in
raising. As this surplus is, as a rule, exchanged for home
goods, the value of the free labourer is almost as great to
the mother-country which supplies him as to the colony in
which he resides.

Suppose the conditions of the community, where labour is
so economically profitable, to be suddenly reversed. The
labouring man ceases to produce a surplus, or even has to
depend upon subsidies from home for the means of existence.
How many families at home would, in such case, inevitably
be thrown out of employment and driven to a criminality of
life on which in happier times they looked with abhorrence!
By seeing what a loss pecuniarily and morally such altered
conditions would involve, we can in a measure appreciate
the injury inflicted on the home community by the devoting
of one of the fairest portions of the universe to the exclusive
occupation of a society of unprofitable consumers, fed, clothed,
and lodged at the expense of the British taxpayer.

Every convict sent out increased the burdens of the English
poor; and so in turn transportation increased the propensity
to crime at home.

Transportation, as actually conducted, was as a punishment most unequal in its operation. ' Generally speaking, it
was most dreaded by those offenders against the laws of their

country who might be called accidental criminals; by persons who had not made a trade of crime, but who had been induced to commit crime by the impulse of the moment, or by some accidental combination of circumstances, or by some all-powerful temptation, and who might in many cases be possessed of good moral feeling.'[1] It fell with terrible effect on those who were least deserving of it, while hardened criminals viewed it as a golden opportunity for running riot in vice and lawlessness. The distance of the Antipodes from England made transportation, for most, a sentence of perpetual banishment, and that to a colony where, thanks to atrocious political and economical mismanagement, the successful exercise of honest industry was next to impossible. Some by force, fraud, or successful speculation in rum, managed to do well, and to find their way home again, to renew once more the criminal associations of their youth, or to furnish an example of the prosperity to which villany might attain in a place specially designed for its signal punishment and complete reformation. A few of those who remained behind, by strength of character or resolution, acquired for themselves wealth and regained the respect of their neighbours; but the vast majority lived on, hated, despised, degraded, and ever sinking lower into the darkest depths of helpless drunken imbecility; or, by indulging boldly in criminal adventures, remained a constant source of annoyance and danger to the community until their gradual extirpation by rum or the gallows.

Probably many of these last had, when transported originally, been of the class most easily accessible to reforming influences. They were the ' accidental offenders ' most keenly alive to the degradation of their situation, and most easily goaded to desperation by a sense of the unmerited degree of their sufferings.

In one way or another the convicts dwindled away with remarkable rapidity under the influence of a free emigration. Some were assimilated by the advancing wave, but generally they dropped out of sight and out of mind, much as the aboriginal withered away when brought into contact with

---

[1] Report of Committee on Transportation.

civilisation. But the taint remained for long in dissolute habits, in the disposition to look upon vices with a lenient eye, in the fashion of dependence upon the fiat of the ' some-body's cousin ' who ruled the colony as the nominee of the Colonial Office, and last, but not least, in the disinclination of labourers to emigrate from home to a place associated in their minds with every circumstance of infamy.

During all this time, the facilities afforded by the trans-portation system for getting rid of criminals had prevented any attention being given to criminal discipline at home. Alike at home and in our dependencies, the rule of a landowning oligarchy had promoted the growth of crime, and the draft of a few thousands of convicts annually to Australia seemed to have increased, rather than diminished, the call upon the foul accommodation of the English prisons. This was natural enough, for the prospect of transportation was attractive to the English criminal, and even without that inducement, misgovernment was there, too, an all-compelling cause of crime.

The chapter of transportation records a period of English history as disgraceful as any that obscures her annals. But it is with the impolicy rather than with the wickedness of the system that I am now mainly concerned. To make a colony look back with shame upon its origin is certainly not a likely way to promote an *entente cordiale* between it and the parent-country, or to generate a feeling of pride in the mutual tie that nominally binds them together.

If ever there was a system certain to be reprobated by a free colonial population, it was that of the transportation of con-victs. Nothing was so calculated to give reality to the rising threats to ' cut the painter ' as the blindly persistent attempts of the home authorities to give the system fresh vitality ; and until wiser counsels induced the abandonment of that policy, New South Wales was a formidable hotbed of rising disaffection.

CHAPTER V.

WHETHER we go back in search to remote periods of antiquity, or trace the course of history to times as recent as our own, we shall find that the prosperity of individual nations has ever been dependent on the freedom of their institutions rather than upon fertility of soil or benignity of climate. On the other hand, centralised and anti-popular forms of government have invariably had the effect of neutralising the benefits to be expected from the possession of natural advantages.

It mattered not at all that New South Wales was so plentifully endowed by nature that, even under the withering blight of convictism, she might speedily have become pre-eminent among our colonial possessions, so long as the despotism of the Colonial Office extended over her an influence more deadly than even convictism itself.

Canada possessed the shadow without the substance of free institutions. New South Wales, although inhabited entirely by Englishmen, could not show even the semblance of freedom. This was a condition of things which, however much it might have been warranted at the original foundation of the convict settlement, was totally inexcusable in its continuance as soon as the numbers and energy of the free non-convict population became capable of administering to local requirements.

It is not easy to lay down a rule for the point of time best fitted for handing over to a young community, composed largely of a convict element requiring constant supervision, the management of its own destinies. Where the colonists are

free men and women, they will probably fare best if left to
themselves from the outset. Self-government *ab initio* is there
the best, indeed the sole, means of developing local resources
and of acquiring local strength. The absence of leading-
strings undoubtedly gave rise to the great energy and vitality
of our North-American colonies, and enabled them to contend
successfully, not only in their war with the wilderness and the
savage, but at a later period against the imperial power
which would have ruthlessly robbed them of their hard-earned
heritage.

With regard to New South Wales the reasoning is more
involved. The case was unique in the history of English
colonial possessions, and it is therefore only by looking back
to the time when the evil effects of the general regulations
applied to her first exposed the incompetency of the Home
Government to legislate for her that we can point to a date
when her free inhabitants should have been entrusted with
the moulding of popular institutions. If it can be shown that
after a certain period the free settlers formed a considerable
proportion of the population, that their industry was retarded
by their absolute subjection to the decrees of a distant governing body, and that remonstrance was useless to avert or mitigate the course of injurious legislation, it may with reason be
asserted that that was the period at which local self-government became a necessity if the welfare of the colony was an
object to be considered.

But, as we know, New South Wales never *was* governed
by the home authorities with a view to its welfare. It was
to be repressed, not developed, and therefore the emigration
of free settlers, the *sine quâ non* of the uprising of free local
institutions, was to be perseveringly discouraged.

Had means been taken to further the prosperity of the
colony, it was but too probable that free emigrants would
have been attracted to it; that they would ere long have
asserted their right to refuse the cargoes of felons so freely
exported; and that the accumulation of such a mass of depravity at home might have directed a disagreeable amount of
attention at home to the misgovernment of England herself.

From the official point of view, then, it was not desirable to make the colony prosperous, so any measures tending to its benefit must be decisively tabooed. The subject of the most advisable time for granting a certain degree of local self-rule cannot, therefore, be treated from the point of view of the Home Government, since they had no wish to see the colony make forward progress at all, but must be considered by the light thrown upon it by the page of history.

The fact that about the year 1804 the free and the industrious freed inhabitants of the colony began to feel the weight of oppressive imperial restrictions on the every-day business of their lives, and that these settlers then bore a fair proportion in number to the general mass of convicts, would seem to mark out that year as an epoch when a measure of self-rule might have been properly accorded. It was then that agricultural produce had become in excess of the quantity required for consumption, and that farmers began to look around them for fresh openings for the exercise of their energies. A local representative governing body would doubtless have made vigorous efforts to help them by refusing to give effect to the monstrous restrictions with which the imperial rulers had environed the colony ; and the immediate future of New South Wales might then have been as full of promise as has been its subsequent career. As it was, the prayers, remonstrances, and arguments of the colonists fell upon listless ears ; the old restrictions were tenaciously adhered to, and until they were removed, many years afterwards, the colony remained in the stationary stage.

Never was there a country more fitted for diversity of occupation than New South Wales, and never was a better opportunity afforded to the home Government of stamping out enterprise than was afforded by the circumstances of the colony in the opening years of the century. This opportunity was utilised to the uttermost.

The means adopted were duties and disabilities. The duties were levied on all articles imported and on all articles exported, the tariff of duties on exports being, in the case of coal and timber, double the amount of the duty on the same articles

when imported. It made no difference that the imports liable
to duty came from ports in the same colony, for the coal and
wood on which a double export duty was levied came to
Sydney from other portions of the colony itself. That duties
on these articles should be levied equally on exportation as on
importation, and in two of the most material instances doubled,
was, says Wentworth,[1] 'so manifestly absurd that it would be
quite superfluous to dilate on the system. It is a system of
policy which, it may be safely asserted, is unknown in any other
part of the world ; and nothing but the indubitable certainty
of its existence would convince any rational person that it
could ever have entered into the contemplation of any one entrusted with the government of a colony.' Surely he would
have been justified in asserting that *only those* entrusted with
the government of a colony could ever have conceived such
fiscal measures.

Two great industries were thus nipped in the bud. But
for the duties, both coal and iron would have been largely
exported to India and to the Cape of Good Hope. As it was,
the vessels trading between those countries and the colony had
always to return from the latter in ballast, though the owners
or consignees would have gladly shipped cargoes of bark,
timber, and coals. if they could have derived the most minute
profit from their carriage or sale.[2] The colonists had, in consequence, to pay, in the increased price of imported articles, for
the double freight entailed by the importing ships having to
return empty. Will it be credited that a succession of
Governors should, under instructions from home, have pertinaciously adhered to a system of finance so monstrous and
absurd ?

The rising trade in coal, cedar-wood, and wattle bark was
thus extinguished—as a trade ; and survived only in the profitless form of an occasional fitful speculation on a limited scale.

There were, however, still more potent forces applied to
crippling any incipient development of industry. The home
duties on colonial produce were made to exceed the local

---

[1] Wentworth's *Description of New South Wales*, p. 289.
[2] *Ibid.* p. 290.

duties in severity. The southern coasts of Australasia abounded with fish, and within a few hours' sail of Sydney were extensive whale fisheries capable of being worked at a great profit to the colony. Here was a new field of employment lying ready to hand, and at so great a distance from England that the object of the Navigation Laws—the fostering of an English naval marine—could not possibly have been interfered with by allowing the colonists the run of their own fisheries. But it did not suit certain London merchants concerned in the South Sea fisheries that spermaceti oil should be introduced in large quantities into the home market. At the same time, so totally uninterested was the Home Legislature in the welfare of the colony that, at the instance of the merchants, Parliament passed an Act virtually prohibiting the colonists from the right whale as well as from the sperm whale fishery.

The *local* duty on whale oil was heavy enough—being 2*l.* 10*s.* on a ton of sperm oil, and 2*l.* on a ton of black whale or other oil—to act as a partial discouragement to the prosecution of the fishing; but, by the Act, the duties on oil imported into England, taken from whales caught 'by His Majesty's subjects usually residing in ' Australia, were raised to 8*l.* 6*s.* 3*d.* on the ton of train, and to 24*l.* 18*s.* 9*d.* on the ton of sperm oil. The duties thus imposed were twenty times greater on train oil and sixty times greater on spermaceti oil than the duties levied on similar substances taken by British subjects residing within the limits of the United Kingdom.

There can be no doubt that these enormous rates were devised specially to prevent the Australian settlers from even attempting the whale-fishing, and the proof, if proof were needed, is strengthened by the fact that the English import duties on oils brought from any other colony were a small fraction of those charged on the like matters imported from the Australian colonies. All the efforts made by the latter to utilise the whale fisheries for their own benefit were rendered futile by the enormous weight of unjust duties imposed upon their produce on its introduction to the only country where it would otherwise have found a ready and remunerative market,

while ships, manned by English crews, might explore the
Southern Seas in pursuit of a valuable property which the
residents hard by were forbidden to touch. These English
crews only found their way thither at rare seasons and intervals, and thus vast resources were rendered unavailing, a
struggling community was reduced to idleness, and the British
consumer was victimised, in order to prevent the convict
colonies from becoming enterprising and respectable, and so
that the pockets of a few grasping London traders might be
comfortably filled.

Had the colonists been encouraged to prosecute the whale
fishery on their own shores, a direct trade might have sprung
up between the mother-country and the Antipodes, which
might have called into existence a fresh demand for British
shipping, and which would have furnished a natural fostering-
ground for a mercantile and naval marine.

For other reasons, too, it was distinctly to the interest of
England herself to encourage the local prosecution of the
whale-fishing. The ropes, canvas, and gear of every description necessary for the outfit of the colonial vessels for these
fisheries would certainly have been furnished from home for
some time to come. Moreover, the supply of sperm oil in the
market would no longer have been so deficient as to keep the
price at famine height, or to afford an excuse for the bounties
held out by the Legislature for the encouragement of whale-
fishing. To argue thus, however, is to suppose that the Home
Government were capable of preferring the interests of mankind to those of small cliques of monopolists whose political influence was worth buying; or to suppose that they
troubled themselves to reflect upon the inconsistency of giving
bounties to individuals to promote whale-fishing, and inflicting
duties upon a whole community in order to prevent any such
fishing being carried on at all.

The duties created disabilities, but there were disabilities
proper in addition. By a clause in the East India Company's
charter it was provided that no vessel of less than 350 tons
measurement, with the exception of the Company's packets,
should be allowed ‘ to clear out from any port within the

United Kingdom for any place within the limits of the said
Company's charter, or be admitted to entry at any port of the
United Kingdom from any place within those limits.'[1] Unfortunately for the Colonies, 'those limits' included Australia,
and thus a death-blow was given to the Australian colonists'
chances of bettering their position. For the smallness and
poverty of the colonial population did not allow of a demand
sufficiently great to absorb cargoes of such magnitude, and
experimental shipments out there resulted in loss to the
owners, who very soon discontinued the hazardous speculation. Before the passing of the Act, merchants had been in
the habit of shipping cargoes in smaller vessels for the
colonial markets, but now they were compelled to abandon
their connection with the colony, which therefore had to
depend for its supplies of British manufactures upon the
captains of the vessels engaged in the transport of criminals.
' These supplies therefore naturally became unequal and
precarious ; sometimes being unnecessarily superabundant
and cheap, and at other times being so excessively scarce and
dear as to be entirely beyond the reach of the great body of
consumers.'[2]

The tendency of this Act was not less injurious to the
colonists with regard to the few articles of export which
they were enabled to produce or collect for the English
market. These were three in number—namely, wool, hides,
and sealskins, and their quantity was inconsiderable. These
articles represented a value for export to England of about
15,000l. annually. ' It may therefore be perceived,' says
Wentworth, ' that the whole of the annual export of this
colony would not suffice for half the freight of a single vessel
of the size regulated by the Act in question. It happens in
consequence that the different articles of export which the
colonists collect frequently accumulate in their stores for a
year and a half before it becomes worth the while of the
captains of any of the vessels which frequent the colony to
give them ship-room, and even then they do it as a matter of

[1] 53 Geo. III. c. 155.
[2] Wentworth's *Description of New South Wales*, p. 313.

favour, not forgetting, however, to extort an exorbitant return for that kindness and condescension. The owners, indeed, of the vessels are so well aware of the inability of the colony to furnish them with cargoes on freight that they generally manage before their departure to contract for freights from some of the ports in India—a precaution which increases still more perceptibly the difficulty which the colonists experience in sending their produce to market.'[1]

It was not until some forty years after its foundation that the colony found itself able to build and use, on its own account, vessels of the dimensions of 350 tons. Consequently, during the whole of that period they were prohibited from navigating their own vessels on their own seas. Of what possible benefit could this have been to the East India Company? At the best it could not have advantaged the Company so much as the operation of similar restrictions on vessels built at the Cape of Good Hope would have done; and yet, by an Order in Council in 1814, the Cape was expressly relieved from the disability, while Australia was still kept grovelling under its burden.

There seems to have been a wantonness in our dealings with the Australian colonies, a doing of mischief for mischief's sake, which is not accountable for solely by reference to the contemptuous tone in which it was customary for the Downing Street officials to set at nought the necessities of our Colonial Empire. Either the English statesmen who successively made absurd and injurious regulations for Australian colonies were careless enough of their duties to allow themselves to be kept in utter ignorance of the effects of the measures endorsed by them, or else their actions must have been dictated by a spirit of general malevolence.

Mated at every turn, the condition of New South Wales was indeed deplorable. The agriculturist, for whose produce there was no demand, might not have the capital wherewith to become a grazier. If he went to Sydney he could not get employment, and it was useless to set up as a

---

[1] Wentworth's *New South Wales*, pp. 313, 314.

trader for himself, except as a rum seller, in a country where
there was hardly any other trade than rum selling.   To do
even this he required capital, for he not only had to pay a
heavy duty on the imported rum, but he had to bribe the
authorities heavily in order to obtain a licence ; and being subjected to severe competition in his adopted calling, he could
not hope to do well except by selling a very large quantity of
spirits.   Thus he was driven by pressure of foolish fiscal
measures and by the arts of favoured Government officials to
stimulate widespread intoxication as his only means of making
a livelihood.

A certain amount of external commerce was, it is true,
carried on, and, strange is the irony of events, with China—a
country whom we afterwards forced at the cannon's mouth to
open her ports to foreigners.   While England was playing the
very part which she afterwards declared to be so immoral when
practised by China as to deserve exemplary punishment, a
small trade was being maintained between the latter country
and a few colonial merchants by means of American and
Indian-built vessels.   But this channel of industry, as well as
that furnished by the discovery of the Seal Islands, soon became
profitless, and they were consequently far from providing a
remedy for the unprosperous condition of the agricultural body.
The distress, therefore, of the colony continued increasing in
proportion to its increase of population, and rum selling grew
more and more into favour as an indispensable and natural
vocation.

The necessity of permitting the erection of local distilleries
was repeatedly urged upon the home Government, and apparently with excellent reason.   The principal agricultural soils of
the colony along the banks of the Hawkesbury river usually
produced far more grain and vegetable produce than the colony
could consume.   In consequence the crops were left rotting
on the ground for want of purchasers, and farmers were ruined
by the very fertility of the land.   Every now and again, however, came an inundation of the river which swept away all
he agricultural resources of the colony.   No produce had
been stored up, for there was no use for it, and of a sudden the

community was reduced nearly to starvation point. Then recourse was necessary to foreign supplies, and these had to be procured at famine prices from India and elsewhere, and very large amounts had to be paid away in freight duties and shippers' profits. Moreover, the colonial consumers were computed to have paid over a period of fifteen years, from 1804 to 1819, some 25,000l. per annum for rum, more than half of which amount went in payment of incidental duties and charges ; and if the amount thus disbursed benefited English and foreign distillers, it certainly did no good to the colony. If the colonists had been allowed to erect distilleries, an immediate use would have been found for surplus grain supplies, an inducement would have been given to store them, and so the risk of famine, with its attendant heavy expenses, would have been minimised, while farming would have received a healthy stimulus. It might have become a profitable business, and many a resourceless convict might have taken to it as an occupation preferable to vice and drunkenness.

It seems more probable than not that the liberty to distil would have tended to diminish intoxication, for there can be no doubt that part of the heavy consumption of spirits at the time in the colony was owing to the exceedingly high price at which they were retailed. This may sound paradoxical, but it is none the less true. It was afterwards found, when the importation of spirits was practically freed from duties, that general drunkenness diminished in a marked degree, and that too at a time when increased sobriety could not well be ascribed to superiority of education or condition among the classes forming the subject of the comparison. The reason of the difference effected by the fall in price may perhaps be found to rest on much the same ground as does the almost unvarying sobriety of natives of wine-producing districts; but a more potent cause of the sudden improvement may be suggested as arising from the natural lessening of desire in men to get full value out of a cheap common article than out of a dear one of comparative rarity. The purchaser of rum at two guineas a bottle would possibly conceive himself under a sort of obligation to drink the whole of it and to get the full result out of it as an intoxicant, but he might not consider it necessary to brutalise himself over a bottle at four shillings.

Besides the probable moral effect that would have resulted from the cheapening of spirits, it was in the highest degree likely that the stimulus given to agriculture would have favourably reacted on all other occupations, except perhaps rum selling. A certain measure of prosperity would have been imparted to each when the principal one was prosperous, and people would have had other things to do besides drinking. The community would in all probability have attained to a height of respectability which would have given it no interest in maintaining drunkenness as the normal phase of existence.

Apparently the colony had only to ask for a thing from the home Government in order to have it scornfully refused. The proposed scheme would affect the customs revenue, and beside that consideration the welfare of the colony sank into insignificance. So the colony was not to be permitted to employ and improve itself by distilling spirits.

It has ever been a characteristic of Colonial Office rule that the officials of the Colonial Department, though themselves utterly ignorant of perhaps even the geographical positions of the countries over which they exercise irresponsible sway, should steadfastly endeavour to regulate the manners, customs, and occupations of the inhabitants of the remotest dependencies after their own fashion. The Office was possessed of the idea that agriculture and nothing else was the true vocation of the Australasian colonist. Starting with that belief, it naturally went just the wrong way to work to contrive that it should be so. Instead of encouraging agriculture by fostering such a growth of population and general occupation as would have put the colony in a position to consume its own available produce, every obstacle was interposed to the growth of either population or occupation, so that every one might be forced into the losing business of farming. Magnificent crops were rotting on the ground for want of purchasers, farmers in despair were seeking for other pursuits; but the instructions from the Office were to induce settlers and expirees to take to nothing but farming by offering them free maintenance for themselves, their wives. families, and servants for eighteen months, on condition of their cultivating the soil. Of this offer, newly-arrived settlers, despairing of finding other employment, and many expirees, availed themselves ; and as soon as the helping hand of Government was withdrawn, the distress amongst them became as pronounced as it was among the original farmers, and they were reduced to the necessity of seeking the same expedients for relief. Of course. if these measures had been directed to attracting population, the maintenance of a large number of free settlers for so long a time might have afforded some excuse for the offer thus made of inducements to new arrivals to subsist in idleness. But even this excuse, bad as it would have been, as altogether uncalculated to effect its object, was altogether wanting ; for, despite all professions to the contrary. the home authorities made it clear by their acts that they wished to render the colony as unattractive as possible to free emigrants. The measure was never more than an ' Outdoor Relief Act,' and was about as well devised to promote prosperity as was the celebrated Poor Law in operation in England during the earlier portion of the century. It was indeed productive of such wide-spread distress in the colony that the period of Government maintenance had after a time to be reduced to six months. But the mere alteration in the number of months effected no change in a radically bad principle, and, after having been productive of an infinity of misery, the regulation was allowed to lapse into disuse.

The promotion of agriculture in' a country possessing,. in many respects, such peculiar aptitudes for it as New South Wales possessed on many easily accessible soils in the neighbourhood of Sydney was undoubtedly a politic object; and had requisite opportunities been afforded for its natural development, agriculture would speedily have become *the* most favoured and general of pursuits. Those opportunities would have consisted in allowing free exercise to the trading instincts of the community, but these were denied. The colony was ' cabined, caged, cribbed, confined ' on every side ;

its population was kept down ; its purchasing power reduced, and agricultural production altogether surpassed the local powers of consumption. The soil was too fertile, too easily responsive to the ' tickling of the hoe,' to permit of farming being profitable so long as the colony remained stationary, and thus a series of unjust laws had made of fertility a curse instead of a blessing.

The unsatisfactory results of farming turned attention to grazing; but cattle and sheep were scarce at that early period, and only men possessed of a certain amount of capital could become graziers. Those who did so found their occupation a lucrative one. They increased their acreage as their flocks and herds multiplied, and as they became possessed of land and wealth, so they acquired influence and unreasonable views of their own importance. They set themselves up as a separate order from the rest of the people, as an aristocratic body with peculiar privileges. These ' squatters,' as they were called, afterwards constituted themselves the bitterest opponents of all popular demands, and in no respect was their opposition more uncompromising than to the claim of the people to a fair share in the public lands. Whatever may have been the squatters' rights, the long and bitter struggles for their asser-tion between them and the people materially impeded and still impede the progress of the Australasian colonies.

It is probable that there would not have been so many largely-acred squatters if the profits of farming had kept pace with those from grazing. Those who succeeded in the last would, under circumstances favourable for farming, have persisted in their tillage over comparatively small areas, and so the commencement of the landowning monopoly of the squatters might have been delayed until free institutions had come into being, when such a monopoly would certainly not have been possible of acquisition.

Let us briefly review the chain of consequences. Duties and disabilities, by their injurious effects upon population and commerce, procured the ruin of the farmers. The latter would not have become graziers, or squatters let us call them, if they could have continued farmers working at a profit. As it was, they became squatters because they were getting ruined as farmers. In the former capacity they attained to an exceptional prosperity which attracted all the spare capital of the colony into their calling, and they thus possessed themselves of a monopoly of land and influence which was opposed to the popular interests. An irreparable injury was thus inflicted on the people, as the indirect but obvious consequence of the duties and disabilities imposed by the superlative wisdom of Downing Street.

It may with confidence be asserted that a colony in its infancy is peculiarly unsuited for the establishment of manufactories. Neither the requisite plant or skilled labour can be procured without great difficulty, and the labour of the description required must for long be so limited in quantity that the manufacturers must inevitably be dependent upon the good-will or caprice of employés well aware of the impossibility of replacing their services, rather than upon a carefully carried out system of superintendence. Even when initial difficulties have been surmounted, the articles turned out are almost invariably inferior in quality and dear in price. In consequence of the disabilities which prevented the home manufacturers and merchants from sending out cargoes of the most necessary manufactures, except occasionally and in very small consignments, the colonists found themselves obliged to erect small manufactories in order to supply themselves with the most ordinary articles of clothing. A certain amount of capital was invested in these concerns, which, through the medium of exorbitant charges, kept up a moderately prosperous existence until it became worth the while of the home shippers to supply clothing enough for the colony, when the competition from outside procured the ruin of the local manufactories, together with the loss of the capital sunk in them.

Ordinarily, the policy of the home Government was directed to the most uncompromising opposition to the establishment of colonial manufactories. In the view of the imperial authorities Colonies were chiefly useful as consumers of home manufactures. The prohibitions to manufacture imposed upon Colonies were probably ineffectual in promoting the sale of a single article of English make in the Colonies, since the English markets were naturally the best and most obvious centres for the supply of manufactured goods to the Colonies. But through the monstrous restrictions imposed upon trade with Australia, the settlers in the Australasian colonies were absolutely disabled from purchasing home commodities, and were forced to make for themselves on the spot articles which the home manufacturers would, in the absence of restraints and disabilities, have gladly exported there.

A review of the evils resulting from Imperial rule can hardly furnish any other conclusion than that it was in all respects the form of government least desirable and most injurious to the colony from the moment when she gave the first signs of having outstripped the conditions of a purely penal settlement. No hostile invader could have wrecked the country more effectually than did the measures of the British Government during the first twenty years of the century, during which the nominees of the Colonial Office, uncounselled, unchecked, and uncontrolled by any local body, lorded it over the destinies of the colony under the sole and irresponsible direction of the Office itself.

Utterly unfitted for his post although more than one of the Governors was, it is evident, from the urgent remonstrances repeatedly sent home by all of them against Imperial measures, that if left to themselves they would not have inflicted upon the colony a tithe of the damage due to ignorant home Government interference.

The Governor was left unfettered so far as regarded his power to inflict injury, for the only court in which his actions were cognisable at law was at a distance by sea of sixteen thousand miles from the colony; and while the expense of proceeding against him would have been quite beyond the means of any member of the community, an adverse verdict for the plaintiff was almost or quite a foregone conclusion. But his power to do good was most jealously watched by the scribes of the Colonial Office, who exhausted the ingenuity of official red-tapeism in the elaboration of rules for the suppression of virtue and prosperity in the Colonies.

The Governor might impose what duties he pleased, in violation of the fundamental maxim of British liberty that no one shall be taxed without his own or his representatives' consent ; nor, until Macquarie voluntarily undertook to furnish quarterly accounts of the public revenue and expenditure for public information, had those who paid the duties the satisfaction of knowing how any part of the proceeds were applied. From the secresy thus observed it was natural to conclude that a goodly portion of the funds so raised found their way into the Governor's private purse—a supposition which, whether just or not, was certainly entertained by the majority of the colonists. The power he thus possessed was enormous, for, though he was sufficiently sensible of his own interest to confine his duties to articles which in the then pauperised state of the colony might be considered luxuries, it was open to him to tax every article of consumption, and, on the plea of public contributions, to undermine the whole prosperity, such as it was, and happiness of the community. Gradually, as the free element in the colony acquired stability, the growth of an influential public opinion imposed an unwritten though very practical check upon the unjustifiable levying of taxation at the will of an individual—a check on the caprice of the Governor for the time being of far greater weight and utility than was the advice of the nominee Councils appointed, after Macquarie's time, to regulate the course of local legislation.

Again, the Governor had nearly absolute power over the lives and liberties of the colonists under his charge. Criminal cases were tried, not before a jury, but by a court-martial composed of military officers selected for the purpose by the Governor. Civil officers were rigidly excluded from these court-martials, and the accused was left to the mercy of judges whose professional training left little doubt that they would not be likely to run counter to the known or supposed desire of the Governor for the conviction of any particular prisoner. Macquarie wisely abandoned the principle of selecting the members of the court-martial himself, and during his time officers were made to serve in regular rotation; but it was open to him at any time to revert to the old practice of choosing as judges either those most easily amenable to Government influence or those who were known to have private reasons for punishing prisoners whom it was thought desirable to convict. In the time of Governor Bligh, his chief legal adviser, the Judge-Advocate General, was found incapable of advising on any point of law whatever. He had obtained his office as the relative of an influential man, though he had not even received a legal education. Such was the legal guide provided by a thoughtful mother-country for a Governor of naturally arbitrary disposition, and possessed of almost unlimited local power. He was, however, soon discovered to be useless for any purpose, so the services of a local attorney who had been prosecuted in the colony itself on a charge of swindling had to be called into requisition. Anomalous as it would have been anywhere else, a quondam convict of notoriously bad character was considered the fittest person to advise laws for a community of which even the free members were declared to be incapacitated by reason of the taint of convictism from exercising the usual right of British subjects—that of sitting on a jury. But in New South Wales it was quite in the order of things that an infamous swindler should pull the strings of justice, and prompt the selection of military judges—against whom, be it remembered, no ground of challenge could be urged by the accused—to work his own private purposes.

With the unchecked control over the purses and property of the colonists, joined to the right of disposing at pleasure of their lives and liberties, the power for evil of the earlier Colonial Governors resembled more those of an Oriental despot than of the vicegerent of a free nation. In no English-speaking community of modern times would the continuance of such unnatural authority have been tolerated for an hour had not every energy been paralysed by the closing of all avenues of enterprise to a people forced into a hopeless state of crime, idleness, and drunkenness.

If, on the other hand, a Governor wanted to contribute to the progress of the colony he found himself powerless, for in his good intentions he was checked at every turn. Macquarie was sincere in his desire to inaugurate a period of prosperity, and his adoption of measures which tended to prevent it were certainly due more to necessity than choice. He urged the allowance of local distilleries ; he wished to develop a taste for agriculture among the emancipists; he endeavoured to raise the physical and moral status of the convicts by giving them higher aims. True, his main principle, the keeping up the colony as a penal settlement to the exclusion of a free population, was a false one ; but in the main his views would, if put into operation, have largely promoted the reformation and respectability of the convict class. But, as has been seen, the fetters which had been riveted on the commercial enterprise of the colony had crippled the agricultural interest ; the expirees had no inducement to settle down as farmers ; and in order to give them employment the Governor was obliged to institute public works in Sydney. His scheme for dispersing the expirees had failed, and the concentration instead of the dispersal of the criminal element was thus in great measure forced upon him and upon the colony as the direct consequence of the commercial policy of the Colonial Office—a policy which met every attempt at reform or improvement, at the outset, with an obstinate negative.

Until Brisbane's time the administration of affairs was confided to the care of Governors who, as utter strangers to the colony, could know nothing about it, and yet who from the moment of their landing were under the necessity of carrying on the government without any advisers, except those whom, in their ignorance, they might choose to encourage. Nor were the Governors bound to act upon the suggestions of these if not disposed to do so, but they might, if they so inclined, pursue a course of their own from the outset, in defiance of all local advice.

We may imagine, if we cannot altogether realise, the numerous intrigues for private influence brought to bear upon a Governor who, according as he inclined to one individual or another, might ensure the success of private schemes or promote the discomfiture of an adversary. Bligh, as we have seen, guided his policy by the direction of a transported attorney. Macquarie evinced a decided preference for the counsel of convicts, when he sought for advice at all. Both were enclosed in a circle of corruption, intrigue, sycophancy, and dissatisfaction; for none but those in power for the time being at Government House could partake of the loaves and fishes; and the knowledge that favour was dependent on caprice stimulated them to help themselves as plentifully as possible during the short period of their ascendency. This state of things, however suitable to the morals of a reformatory, became intolerable when the first considerable driblets of free settlers began to arrive in the colony. This was in Brisbane's time, and it was then that the first Legislative Council was formed. It was at best a bad apology for a check on the proceedings of any arbitrarily-disposed Governor, for it consisted only of the Governor, the Lieutenant-Governor, the Chief Justice, the Archdeacon, and the Attorney-General— a crew of officials whose guiding principle was to pull together in subservience to the meddlesome decrees of the home Government. During Sir Ralph Darling's administration the numbers of the Council were extended to fifteen members, including the Governor and other officials, together with seven other members selected exclusively by the Crown. Naturally this nominee Legislature failed to command the slightest respect in a community in which the free element now figured largely. It was of considerable assistance to the Governor in aiding him to pass 'Gagging Acts' for the colonial press, and in countenancing numerous acts of petty tyranny and a system of espionage which produced a universal state of distrust, suspicion, and consternation throughout the colony. Darling's administration has been styled the 'Reign of Terror' in New South Wales, and, thanks to the opportunity given him of shielding his responsibility behind this flimsy device of a Council, he was enabled to give full vent to the promptings of a singularly arbitrary nature.

During the whole period of Darling's government there was a constant agitation kept up, in the shape of public meetings in the colony and petitions to the authorities at home, on the part of the majority of the colonists, for the concession of free institutions. 'But these efforts were uniformly and successfully opposed, chiefly in the way of secret communication with Downing Street by those whose personal interest lay the other way, and who professed to believe that the colony was unfit for such a boon.' [1]

A very simple but useful test of the fitness of rulers for their posts is to be found in the degree of willingness with which they lend their attention to the well-established complaints of their subjects, with a view to rectify grievances or to punish flagrantly unjust dealings. Judged from this standpoint, the home Government during Darling's reign proved itself thoroughly unfit for the task of governing New South Wales. Although reiterated complaints were sent home against Darling's measures, it was not till 1835, four years after his return from the seat of his government, that a Parliamentary Committee was appointed to investigate the charges against him, although various attempts had from time to time been made to procure one. Even then the Committee was only granted on the condition of its not dealing with the case of Captain Robison, which was the principal item in the list of accusations. The conduct of a British Governor at the other end of the globe must be peculiarly flagrant if it cannot be sheltered from the condemnation of a Parliamentary Committee in London, and Darling was not only honourably acquitted, but he received the distinction of knighthood as a mark of royal favour on the occasion. Had the Committee been appointed four years earlier, when the circumstances were still fresh in men's memories, when the sense of injury was strong, and when the evidence had not been weakened by the lapse of years, the conclusions of the Committee might have been different. But, however that may have been, the delay in investigating complaints of so · serious a nature was of itself sufficient to show how necessary it was that the colonists should not be governed from home.

The greater the extent and the more absolute the degree of power possessed by the Colonial Governors, the smaller was

---

[1] Lang's *New South Wales*, vol. i. p. 241.

the importance attached to their personal characters by those
who selected them. ' Who having lost his credit, pawned his
rent, is therefore fit to have a government,' seems to have
been the principle on which the supply of Colonial Governors
was provided, so long as their authority was unbounded and
unchecked. If one of them occasionally happened to be the
right man in the right place, this could not be laid to the
credit of a careful choice ; indeed, such a man would have
been looked upon as likely to prove troublesome if his good
qualities had been known beforehand, and he would have stood
small chance of becoming the chosen vessel of the Colonial
Office. And yet no nation can be safely indifferent to the
characters of its representatives abroad any more than it can
afford to blind itself to the imperfections of its own political
chiefs. ' If,' says a leader in an old Sydney newspaper,[1] ' we
wished ill to the personal character of our Queen, and to the
stability of her claims on the affections of her subjects, we
should promote, not resist, the wicked injuries of the Colonial
Office perpetrated in her name, and the appointment of immoral Governors to corrupt the people. A better mode of
undermining the moral respectability of Her Majesty's name
and the security of the throne we can hardly imagine than the
modes adopted for the government of most of the Colonies of
the Empire, and the appointments so favoured in Downing
Street.'   .

After Darling's retirement in 1835 the influence of the
Governor of the colony was not so important a factor in
colonial politics as it had been. Wakefield had at length received a hearing at home, and his suggestions as to the disposal of land by sale instead of by gift were to be put into
practice in New South Wales as well as in the projected
colony in South Australia. Governor Bourke, who succeeded
Darling, therefore found himself differently situated to his
predecessors in that he had no land to give away as a means
of dispensing patronage, and as ' land is everything ' in a new
colony, he was by no means so supreme and important a
personage as the holder of his office was wont to be. But

---

[1] *The Sydney Empire*

although the range of his power was thus curtailed, it was still competent to the Governor to interfere very prominently in the methods of disposing of the land by representing to the Home Government the necessity, to his mind, of the modification of existing rules to suit his own peculiar views, and he might always be assured of the support of the nominee advisers who yielded sycophantic obedience to the expression of his opinion. This mattered little under such a ruler as Bourke, who, except in one instance—that of his pet scheme for allowing emancipists to serve on criminal juries, when, after his vote had equalised the numbers for and against the proposed measure, he gave a second or casting vote in favour of his own proposition—was content to act the negative part of strictly conforming to his instructions from time to time; but it signified a great deal when the Government was in the hands of his successor, Sir George Gipps. How actively he made his own peculiar tenets influential in regulating the supply of land in the market will be treated of in another chapter, and the reader must turn to that if he would see how potent was still the authority of the local Governor over a matter that gravely affected the interests of the entire community. It is sufficient to show here how, by the help of the Home Government, despite the nominal check of a Council, the Governor continued to pose effectually as king—and certainly not to the benefit of the colony.

Acts of a despotic nature on the part of an individual ruler are more provocative of indignation when done counter to the wishes of a controlling body to a certain degree representative of the people, than when carried into operation either in opposition to, or by the assistance of, the vote of a mere nominee Council, so framed that the public reposes no confidence in its ability or willingness to counteract high-handed measures. The tendency of the legislation may, in either case, be the same; but popular feeling and expectation is more thoroughly aroused where the dicta of the people's representatives are contemptuously set aside than where there is no pretence of popular representation at all. Further, where the legislative body is partly elected by the people, questions of policy are keenly discussed by men who know that their future return by constituencies depends chiefly upon the thoroughness and bitterness of their opposition to despotic legislation ; and the assertion of supreme authority must therefore be carried through with a harshness proportioned to the degree of resistance offered. Where, then, the popular party possesses a numerical majority in the legislative body, its resolutions can only be overridden by proceedings of a highly despotic character, such as outrage the feelings of the community, and drive its representatives to a resort to the most ready means of obtaining their objects. Obstruction, vilification, and demagogy in its most extreme form take the place of the useless system of debate and vote ; and while the country has to bear the burden of laws imposed upon it in defiance of its own protest, it has also to bear the blame of the scandalous excesses too often laid to the charge of the local politicians. Yet the real responsibility for the intemperate course occasionally conspicuous in colonial politics must lie with those who promoted it by rendering none other possible, or at least efficacious.

The very extension of the Legislative Council in 1842 was calculated to discredit political strife by embittering the relations between the Governor's party and the bulk of the people, and so driving the popular representatives to avail themselves of every means at their disposal to check the exercise of arbitrary power. The Legislature, as then constituted, was to consist of thirty-six members, of whom six were to be Government officials, six to be Crown nominees, and twenty-four to be elected in the proportions of eighteen for New South Wales and six for Port Phillip. The qualification for these elective members was to be the possession of a freehold property valued at 2,000l. or rented at 100l. per annum. They were to be selected by men paying a 20l. rental or owning a freehold of 200l. value. That is to say, that the counterpoise to the twelve official and nominee members who were welded together by firm bonds of a mutual self-interest necessarily coincident with the maintenance of the existing *régime*, who were in the possession of the confidence of the Governor and of

Downing Street, and who were constantly associated together and always on the spot, was to be formed of double their number of men, chosen from the most distant points of a vast territory, unacquainted with each other, without cohesion as a body, not easily brought together from remote distances, representative of a multiplicity of conflicting interests, bound to possess qualifications so onerous as to ensure only a very limited range of choice, and chosen by a minority incapable from its constitution of giving fair representation to the wants of the great bulk of the population. The elective members might be earnest and zealous in their advocacy of the popular cause, but they were too few in numbers and too deeply engaged in their private business, many hundreds of miles away from Sydney, to be able either to devote very much of their time to the care of the interests of their constituents or to be in a position to bring the weight of their numerical majority to bear in case of necessity. The majority of the elective members was just large enough if united and on the spot to carry the day on a division, but it was not nearly large enough or homogeneous enough to supply a constant working majority. On many important questions the sympathies of some of the elective members were strongly with the official body, and their presence at a division could generally be self-excused by the pressure of private business, so that the official party by a little judicious management could usually contrive to put their opponents in a minority.

If, on the other hand, a popular measure was actually passed, it had to run the gauntlet of the Governor and of the Colonial Office; and if the one was ever ready to transmit the Bill home with an adverse criticism appended, the other was equally prone to veto it out of hand.

A legislative body so constituted was no more efficient for the assertion of popular rights than the Council composed entirely of nominees. It first raised the hopes of the people, and then excited their passions by disappointing expectation. This was the best result that could have been attained, paradoxical as the assertion may seem, when considered in its bearing on future results. For the unsatisfactory working of the

Council as reformed in 1842 stimulated the political dissatisfaction of the colonists far more quickly and in a greater degree
than a more smoothly working Constitution would have done ;
and so hastened on the time for the establishment of free representative institutions not only in New South Wales, but
in all the Australian colonies. At the same time the reflex
action of conviction gradually permeated the minds of the
home authorities, and made it evident to them that the unnatural combination of elective and official members in one
deliberative body was better calculated to promote the violent
separation of the colony from the mother-country than to
strengthen the natural tie between them. These results
furnish some consolation, but they were far from compensat-
ing for the evils with which the official system had saddled
the colony.

A few examples will be sufficient to illustrate the impotent
position of the elective members in the Council formed in 1842.
Their first struggle was to cut down the enormous expenditure of the colonial Government. Beginning with the
Governor himself, one of the elective members brought in and
carried through a Bill having for object the reduction of the
salaries of all future Governors from 5,000l., the amount at
which it had been fixed by the Secretary of State, to 4,000l. a
year. Although the salary in question was charged upon the
colonial revenue, this Bill was disallowed at home ; the intention of the Colonial Office being that the Governor of the
colony should receive as large a salary as the President of the
United States.

This was a bold attempt on the part of the colonists to
secure the services of the Governor for themselves, and to subject his actions to their own control. The Colonial Office, on
the other hand, was well aware that by allowing the colonists
to take upon themselves the onus of paying the Governor's
salary, sanction would in effect be given to the principle that
the Governors should be responsible to the colony instead
of remaining the mere tools of the Office. The obligation to
pay the Governor conferred the right to direct and to remove
him. It also gave him a direct interest in conciliating the

colonists—a consideration intolerable to the English official mind, and enough of itself to secure the rejection of the Bill.

When Hutchinson, the last royal Governor of the colony of Massachusetts, informed the Legislature of that province that 'he no longer required a salary from them, as the King had made provision for his support,' the Assembly informed him in reply 'that the royal provision for his support, and his own acceptance of it, was an infraction of the rights of the inhabitants, recognised by the principal charter, an insult to the Assembly, and an invasion of the important trust which, from the foundation of the commonwealth, they had ever continued to exercise.' This was the language of men reared to independence and self-help, and contrasts strongly with the acquiescence of New South Wales in the Downing Street veto.

Another grievance calling for immediate remedy was the withdrawal of a large portion of the ordinary revenue to the extent of 81,500l. a year—nearly half which was yearly appropriated for the support of religion, and the remainder for official, including the Governor's and the judicial salaries— from the control of the Council. The local Government, ' whose powers of absorption were somewhat extraordinary,' [1] having found the reservations in certain cases too small, applied to the Council to make good the estimated deficiency. This the Council refused to do unless every item of the expenditure should be submitted for their revision, and this condition having been acceded to, they went to work to cut down the salaries of certain officers. Immediately upon their doing so, however, his Excellency promptly checked their action, on the ground that the Council had no right to interfere with salaries fixed by the Colonial Office. The result was that the expenditure went on as before.

The duties on wines and spirits were, in Sir George Gipps's time, so exorbitantly high that great encouragement was virtually given by them to smuggling and illicit distillation, ' both of which were carried on on so large a scale as to give rise to extensive demoralisation.' [2] A large minority of

---

[1] Lang's *New South Wales*, vol. i. p. 329.   [2] *Ibid*. p. 350.

the Council was strongly in favour of reducing these duties, but the Governor's specific consisted in passing more stringent measures to put down breaches of the revenue laws, and in instituting a most abominable system of espionage, under which the excise and revenue officers were instructed to receive bribes from the principal distillers and to betray the fact to the Government, so that the police might be on the watch at the proper times and places to effect seizures. Despite the protest of the Council, these regulations were put into active operation, ' but they failed egregiously of their desired effect, smuggling and illicit distillation being practised more extensively and openly than ever.' [1]

The fact that the officials were always in opinion, and sometimes in voting power, in a minority in the Council produced no difference in the contemptuous treatment of that body by the Governor. For example, the Council by its vote declared itself strongly in favour of the adoption of a general system of education on an unsectarian basis. A Bill was passed through for the purpose of effecting the new arrangements, but the Governor, having an individual preference for the denominational system, refused his consent, and education had to be continued on the old limited lines. A measure for the extension of the electoral franchise to squatters and tenants, strongly recommended by a Select Committee of the Council, met with a similar fate, and a proposal to establish a uniform twopenny postage rate throughout the colony had to be withdrawn in consequence of the Governor's opposition.

So, whether the elective members secured the passing of a vote or were left in a minority, no alteration in the course of legislation was effected. The officials, not being responsible to the colony, kept their places and offices whether triumphant or defeated on any question, and everything went on in the Council as before.

The farce of representative legislation went even further. A popular measure, even if assented to at home, had still to penetrate through the pigeon-holes of the Colonial Office—

[1] Lang's *New South Wales*, vol. i. p. 350.

receptacles where colonial aspirations and royal assent might find equal oblivion. This was becomingly exemplified by the fate of the petition for the separation of Victoria from New South Wales. The Port Phillip members were unanimous in favour of the object of the petition, and it also received the support of Mr. Robert Lowe (now Lord Sherbrooke), who was at the time one of the New South Wales elective members. It was, moreover, acquiesced in by the then Secretary of State for the Colonies (1845). The favourable reception of the petition was a source of inexpressible delight to the inhabitants of Port Phillip, but they would have done well to reserve their transports till 1851, for it was not until six years had elapsed that the pigeon-holes gave up their prey and suffered Port Phillip to be at length proclaimed as a separate and distinct colony under the name of ' Victoria.'

No matter what the object that those members of the Council who wished well to the colony might have in view, it had apparently only to be pressed and backed up by colonial public opinion in order to be opposed by the Colonial Office, and by its pliant tool the Governor. Geographical discovery in Australia was, in 1845, in a very backward state, as a glance at more recent discoveries may render evident. At that time the Council recognised the importance of discovering an over-land route to Port Essington, and addressed the Governor in favour of that object, pledging itself to vote whatever funds might be necessary for its accomplishment. ' But his Ex-cellency, who was doubtless somewhat incensed against the Council at that time from the opposition he had himself experienced from that body ' (in the matter of the official and judicial salaries), ' and who probably wished to mortify the Opposition members, with whom the idea had originated, refused to place any amount on the Estimates for the purpose without the previous sanction of the Secretary of State. Such was the miserable state of thraldom in which the colony was then held under Downing Street domination.' [1]

Despotic, ignorant officialism had still to resort to a measure which exceeded in its unreasoning arbitrariness

[1] Lang's *New South Wales*, vol. i. p. 340.

almost anything that had been done before, and that in the
way best calculated at the same time to lower the character
of the home Government for ordinarily fair dealing, and to
stimulate the hatred of the colonists for the connection with
the mother-country. This was the manner of it. By an
Order in Council, dated May 22, 1840, for which Mr. Gladstone as the then Secretary of State for the Colonies was
responsible, it had been announced that a penal colony had
been designed in the north-east corner of Australia, north of
the twenty-sixth parallel of south latitude, to which convicts were
in future to be sent instead of to New South Wales. All the
necessary arrangements had been made for this change when
Earl Grey succeeded to Mr. Gladstone's office. His lordship
at once repudiated the idea of the new penal colony, and set
himself to work with might and main to revive and re-
establish transportation to New South Wales. ' The colonial
Government, of course, lent itself to the accomplishment of
this favourite object of Earl Grey's in every possible way, and
every species of influence was exerted in the cause to satisfy
his lordship. Indeed, till the final settlement of the question,
the colony exhibited the edifying spectacle of the local
Government pulling one way and the great body of the people
pulling another, as if their interests had been contrary and
irreconcilable.' [1]

A small but influential body of squatters was in favour of
the resumption of transportation. These squatters were men
of the aristocratic class of colonists, who held vast tracts of
country in temporary occupation under their squatting
licences—in not a few cases at the yearly rent of one-eighth
of a penny per acre—and they had therefore no permanent
tie in the colony. Very few of them were married; they had
no intention of becoming permanent settlers, and consequently
had no great interest in the moral welfare and social advancement of the colony. They disliked the idea of the growth of
a middle class of free emigrant settlers, which would be the
inevitable result of the cessation of transportation, and much
preferred the old division of dominant and slave castes to one

[1] Lang's *New South Wales*, vol. i. p. 357.

where general equality might have the effect of permitting any one to raise himself by hard work and good fortune to as lofty a position as their own. The Governor, Sir Charles Fitzroy, and the squatters employed themselves in sedulously misrepresenting to Earl Grey the feelings of the colonists on the transportation question, and that nobleman was only too willing to give ear to suggestions which accorded with his own wishes. Accordingly he announced in a despatch of September 8, 1848, ' that he proposed at once recommending to Her Majesty to revoke the Orders in Council by which New South Wales was made no longer a place for receiving convicts under sentence of transportation.' At the same time it was announced that a ship laden with convicts was about to be sent out from England to Sydney. The indignation of the colonists on receiving intimation of this breach of faith was intense. Crowded meetings were held in quick succession, at which the suggestion of ' cutting the painter ' was enthusiastically received ; and it is highly probable that, had the colony been brought up on that self-reliant system which was so influential in moulding the independent character of the early American settlements, the landing of the convicts would have been opposed by armed force. As it was, on the arrival of the convict ship in 1849, the landing of its criminal cargo was only effected under cover of the guns of the man-of-war in the harbour brought to bear upon the masses of people assembled on shore to protest against the disembarkation. This, by far the largest and most influential public meeting ever held in the colony, was described by the Governor in a despatch as ' an insignificant assemblage.' Upon the accidental discovery of this document a year later, a crowded meeting of the colonists unanimously resolved ' that, considering the faithless manner in which the colony had been treated by the Right Honourable Earl Grey, the meeting humbly prayed Her Majesty to remove that nobleman from her councils.' A petition to this effect and in protestation against the continuance of transportation was signed by nearly 40,000 colonists—an enormous consensus of opinion when the population of the colony, its sparse distribution, and the consequent difficulties of getting signatures are taken into consideration. The petition, too, was only one of several similar expressions of opinion, and in one of the principal of them the petitioners, in praying for the removal of Earl Grey from office, stated that ' they would not disguise from Her Majesty the persuasion that what was lately but a grievance was ripening into a quarrel,' and professed their opinion that ' the continuance of transportation in opposition to the united resolution of Australasia leagued together against it would imperil the connection of these colonies with Great Britain.' The wrathful, even insurrectionary, spirit of the colony had become too serious to be any longer treated with utter contempt, and on an Address to Her Majesty being moved in the Council in 1850 demanding the cessation of transportation, the squatters and official members, making a virtue of necessity, retired from the council-chamber, in imitation of a notable home precedent, and the Address was voted unanimously by the Liberal members. The consent of Her Majesty was given thereto, and the transportation system was settled by the ignominious defeat of the home Government. Earl Grey had not the grace to put up with his discomfiture manfully ; but as the logical consequence of the victory of the colonists had not been followed up, in his case, by his being deprived of office, he was still able to inflict considerable annoyance, and accordingly he vented his spleen by every now and again threatening the resumption of transportation during the remainder of his period of authority. However, the effect of the discovery of gold in May 1851 was to put a stop to all such efforts. There appeared to be no further necessity for any anti-transportation agitation, but the fears of the colonists were again aroused in 1852 by the intemperate language of his persistent lordship.

The four colonies of New South Wales, Victoria, Van Diemen's Land, and South Australia [1] had formed a league for the discontinuance of transportation, and Mr. King had been sent home as the delegate of the Victorian Government to lay before Parliament the views of his colony. An official report,

[1] Queensland was not then in existence as a separate colony.

corrected by Earl Grey himself, of a conversation between himself and Mr. King, furnished a full display of his obstinate infatuation on the transportation question, while his offensively contemptuous remarks on the occasion proclaimed his extreme unfitness for exercising even the most limited control over colonies super-sensitively alive to their own importance. In that interview, after expressing his belief that Pentonville and Portland convicts ' would in many instances be found to bear a very favourable comparison with the free emigrants who went out under the bounty system,' his lordship added that ' he could hold out no hope that transportation to the originally convict colony of Van Diemen's Land would be abandoned, nor that the Government would not continue to send transported offenders to such other of the Australasian colonies as had consented, or might consent, to receive them.'

On the receipt of this information in the colony, crowded meetings were held to applaud the idea of ' cutting the painter,' and but for the belief that Earl Grey's declarations were merely blustering ebullitions of temper, serious consequences would have certainly resulted.

The insult directed at the characters of the colonists was not one to be easily overlooked. It prominently revealed a want of tact which of itself ought to have incapacitated Earl Grey from ruling the Colonies. Young communities are apt to be peculiarly sensitive, and are only too likely to interpret outside criticism or suggestions as gross insults. Nothing more powerfully contributed to the disaffection of the North-American colonists than their contemptuous treatment by the home authorities. To take only two individual instances. Franklin when in London was laughed at, snubbed and cut by officialism and society ; and it is probable enough that the first feelings of disloyalty were planted in the breast of Washington by the contempt accorded to his position as an officer in the Provincial army. Earl Grey's expressions were scarcely less forcible and hardly more polished than were those of an Attorney-General of William and Mary's reign, who, being urged to prepare a charter for a proposed clerical college in Virginia, replied to the contention that the people of Virginia as well as the people of England had souls to be saved, ' Damn your souls—make tobacco ! ' But Earl Grey's language was infinitely more impolitic, because made in an era when official language was usually studiously courteous and ambiguous, and because it was certain to be known through the length and breadth of the colony almost as soon as published. It stood out by contrast to ordinary official communications as a deeply meditated insult, and it was addressed to a people of rapidly-rising power and importance, cherishing a healthy and to a large extent well-founded belief in their own supe-riority to colonists anywhere else. And yet this man, who ruled the colony by alternate threats and insults, was kept on as England's chosen colonial chief, and no succession of proofs of his hopeless incapacity could induce his removal to a humbler sphere more suited to the exercise of his peculiar talents.

Earl Grey's administration of the Colonies was eminently successful in promoting the accomplishment of the object to which he was most bitterly opposed—the establishment of local representative institutions in the Australasian colonies, on the present basis, with only a nominal, perfectly harmless, because inoperative, subjection to the mother-country. But the credit was not wholly his. On the contrary, the fact that the home Government kept him in office despite the colonial remonstrances was perhaps the ultimate exciting cause of the fierce indignation that gave strength to the demand for com-plete self-government. Between the one and the other, how-ever, sufficient cause of discontent was generated to make the Constitution Act of 1855 a necessity, and it accordingly was passed and came into operation in 1856. By that Act it was provided, *inter alia*, that the actual members of the Govern-ment should retain their respective offices until outvoted and relieved by a Parliamentary majority, in which event they were to be entitled to pensions or retiring allowances equal to the full amounts of their respective salaries. But the new Governor, Sir William Denison, was an instrument specially selected for his despotic tendencies by Earl Grey, and because of the universal detestation which his pro-transportation

principles had procured for him during his rule in Van Diemen's land. He was just the man to labour most sedulously
to counteract the free working of the newly-acquired Constitution. His first act went far to justify the confidence reposed in
him by his political sponsor, for, without subjecting the
members of the Government to any Parliamentary trial at all,
he relieved them of their offices at once, on his own authority
giving them their pensions forthwith and appointing to the
Ministry men entirely of his own choice, who had no other
claim to the distinction than that they had uniformly voted for
the resumption of transportation.

During the whole period of his government Sir William
Denison showed an utter indifference to the requirements of
the colony. He made no attempts to acquaint himself with the
actual condition of things by actually traversing the country;
but he was never weary of writing didactic despatches thereon to
the Colonial Office, who in return posted out equally instructive
documents of like tenor to his own. His power of making mischief was, however, minimised by the strong popular determination to work the new Constitution on a thoroughly liberal
and uncontrolled basis. But, like the boy who chalked up 'No
Popery' and then ran away, he distinguished himself at the
close of his administration by yet another arbitrary act. This
was in connection with a question as to whether the Great
Seal should be appended to a certain document, by which a
wealthy emancipist of the name of Tawell, who had been
hanged in England for the atrocious murder of his concubine,
had conveyed his property to his widow. The Ministry unanimously refused to append the Seal to the document, and re-
signed their offices rather than comply with the Governor's
orders to that effect. His Excellency, being thus left alone in
the Cabinet, went down to the Colonial Secretary's office and
appended the Seal himself—after doing which he left the
colony.

He was succeeded in 1861 by a very different stamp of
man—Sir John Young,[1] who wisely left the machine of

---

[1] Afterward Governor-General of Canada, and subsequently Lord
Lisgar.

government to its own unchecked operation, and who consequently earned in a high degree the confidence and respect of the public. The important Land Bill passed during his period of rule will be treated of in an ensuing chapter. It is only necessary to mention it here to point out an instance of the unhealthy working of the system of two Legislative Houses from the very commencement of their institution in New South Wales.

The Bill passed the Assembly, but was rejected by the Council. The country was in a fever-state of ferment for ' the Bill, the whole Bill, and nothing but the Bill.' In this emergency the Ministry took the bull by the horns. There was no law limiting the number of members of the Legislative Council in New South Wales any more than there was for restricting the number of Peers in the House of Lords, so the Ministry nominated a number of gentlemen of Liberal views to take their seats in the Council, in order to swamp the Opposition. The history of the closing scenes over the Reform Bill in England was repeated with scrupulous fidelity, for the President and the Opposition members of the Council walked out from one end of the House while the swampers walked in at the other prepared to take their oaths and their seats. No actual swamping took place, thanks to the virtual suicide of the Council, but that body had been effectually frightened into consenting to the Bill.

That the working of free institutions in Australia has been attended with considerable friction was only what was to be desired as well as expected. The Constitution Act was studded with anomalies, better suited to the temper of an old country abounding in well-established social distinctions than for countries where the fabric of society was to undergo constant and radical modification. The main blot was that two Legislative Houses were established by the Act where one would have done far better. Artificially restricted qualifications, partly pecuniary, partly educational and professional, were alone to confer the right to membership or to the privilege of electing members of either House. The elective bases and qualifications were speedily lowered by the colonists, but, notwithstanding, the conflicts between the two Houses have been bitter and lasting, and will become more so the longer the dual system lasts. So far, it has served the purpose of raising up and fostering distinct class prejudices, and its function in the immediate future will probably be to excite still further the hatreds of contending factions. The Upper Houses in all the Colonies have perseveringly and persistently thrown out, blocked, or mutilated the most important measures passed by the Lower Houses, in furtherance of their mission as the champions of the satisfied few against the discontented many; and the Lower Houses have, with periodical regularity, insisted on the total alteration of the constitution of the Upper as requisite to the carrying on of legislation at all; and so, unseemly wrangling has become the prominent feature of colonial politics until at length is reached the necessary point where agreement is possible or compromise unavoidable.

Ever since 1856 the colonists have had the undisturbed control of their own affairs. The vetoing power of the home Government was restricted by the Constitution Act to certain well-defined cases, and even where exercised it has been made to give way to any evident re-expression of colonial feeling. It is in the highest degree improbable that the nominal right of interdicting Colonial Bills will ever in future be insisted upon. Should it ever be made use of as in times past, as an instrument for checking, to any considerable extent, the passing of measures seriously demanded by the mass of a colonial population, the consequences are not difficult to forecast. So soon as the legislative tie becomes oppressive to any Australasian colony, so soon will it, and the other members of the group, in sympathy and in apprehension of a similar result to themselves, assert the right to settle for themselves their own course of legislation in every detail, freed from every vestige of parental control.

The experience of our troubles with the early North-American colonies is at length beginning to make itself apparent in counsels wiser than of yore. Sounder and more generally diffused economical knowledge, subversive of long-established heresies as to the functions of Colonies; the growth

of popular institutions at home, and of British popular feeling
in sympathetic admiration for the sturdy colonists working out
for themselves problems not yet considered in England as
being within the range of practical politics; above all, the
fast increasing belief in the present immense power and wealth,
as well as in the probable future of almost illimitable prosperity
in store for Australasia—all conspire against the likelihood of
home interference with colonial legislation being actively exercised.   It is, on the contrary, far more likely that even the
nominal right of veto will ere long fall into desuetude, and
signs are not wanting that England will, ere long, readily
turn for precedents to colonial statute-books instead of furnishing them herself.   Already we see how valuable to us are the
lessons taught by the continual struggles in the Colonies
between wealthy land monopolists and nations ranged in
opposition to their extravagant claims ; how the operation of
manhood suffrage at the Antipodes has paved the way for a
similar extension of the suffrage at home ; how the working of
the erst forbidden Deceased Wife's Sister Bill is called forth
in evidence by the English advocates of a like measure ; and
chiefly we see how the bold experimentalising spirit of the
colonists, in treating grave social and political questions, is
insensibly permeating the thoughts and actions of every section
of society at home.

CHAPTER VI.

Some of the writers on systematic colonisation have not
scrupled to express their desire to put into operation a scheme
of colonisation which should present as great attractions to the
upper as to the lower classes of the home population. In
their opinion the most ideally perfect colony is that which,
from the outset, imitates most faithfully the manners, customs,
and social gradations of the mother-country. Just as the old
Greek colonies were sent out ready-made and complete in all
the requisites of the older society—philosophers, musicians,
ancestral images, and gods inclusive—so the modern colony,
we are told, ought to start on its career with upper, middle,
and lower classes carefully pre-arranged and distinguished from
each other by regularly defined differences in their respective
scales of rights or ranges of duties. To a colony thus furnished
with all the inequalities, evils, and anomalies that in the
parent State have been the slow growth of countless ages
there need be no delay in imparting the privilege of self-
government, of course on the home model of Sovereign, Lords
and Commons. The Colonial Governor is to represent the
first, an hereditary legislative body is to be established in
imitation of the second, and the Lower House alone is to be
elective. It is assumed that such arrangements would suit
the wishes of the vast majority of emigrants, and would most
powerfully conduce to the welfare of the colony, as well as to
the future growth of emigration.

These speculations might have earned an honourable position for their authors at the University of Pagoda, as carrying

out the plan of housebuilding from the roof downward. That English colonies may in time furnish almost exact counterparts of the mother-country in their social usages and political institutions is probable enough, but that they should be founded as such and continue as such is the extreme of impossibility. The colonial copy, too, will never in any case be typical of the country from which the original colonists set out, but of an England whose usages, laws, and institutions will have undergone continuous and radical changes derived from the teachings of the colonies themselves.

The history of the first emigration movement of any importance from England is that of small bodies of men and women who made their way across the Atlantic in order to secure for themselves that religious and political ascendency which was denied to them at home. Far from seeking to perpetuate in a new country the likeness of the old, each of these bodies or sects at once set to work to organise itself on the most essentially democratic basis. Many of these emigrants were men who, in the country of their birth, could have claimed high social rank, but, except at the very outset, this availed them nothing in communities professing a strict equality of rights. The aristocrat, *as such*, ceased to exist from the moment he enrolled himself as a colonist. A certain concession might at first be made to the superiority of position he might have claimed at home, by emigrants not yet emancipated from the fetters of habit, but his after-maintenance of superior right had to depend entirely on the exercise of his own thrift and ability.

The North-American colonies were the most vigorous and flourishing that the world has ever seen. And that because they were founded on no plan or system ; because they were left to their own devices ; because, in effect, they recognised no distinctions of class, and because they held out no inducements to attract aristocratic rather than plebeian immigrants—because, in short, they ran counter to every one of the maxims which certain theorists have laid down as essential to the proper conduct of colonisation.

According to these, the emigration of a superior class—

superior either in point of wealth, social standing, or educaion—ought to be encouraged, and special inducements should
be held forth with that object. It is certain, however, that
the most successful colonies of modern times owe their prosperity entirely to the adoption of the very opposite course—
namely, to the encouragement given by their institutions to the
emigration of a lower rather than to that of a higher class.

Between the *free* emigration to the early North-American
colonies and that to Australia, there are many wide points of
difference. The former owed its origin to principle ; the
latter to cupidity. The American settlers were associated
together before their departure by the strongest bonds of
religious or political sympathy. The members of each body
of emigrants were well acquainted with each other, and joined
themselves together in companies for the purpose of seeking
new homes where their own peculiar tenets might be predominant. They looked upon emigration as a species of
perpetual banishment to a country where life would be beset
with peril and difficulty ; where individual resource must be
called forth to supply the means of existence, as well as to
furnish an organisation for mutual protection and assistance.
Whatever form of government they might ultimately resort to
was one which must of necessity be fashioned by the pressing
requirements of their position.

The early *free* Australian emigrants, on the other hand,
were men who went out on their own individual accounts.
They set forth with high hopes to a fondly imagined El Dorado,
where slave-driving would be their hardest task ; where they
were not to be called upon to devise schemes of government ;
where their sojourn would be brief, and their occupation easy,
profitable, and devoid of danger. That the nature of these inducements was likely to prove attractive to men of the upper
class can easily be understood. Convict labour and free land to
any one who would employ the one by cultivating the other
were the baits held out by the governing powers. Until free
emigration began to be conducted on a large scale, a large
proportion of the emigrants were of a rank above that of the
labourer or mechanic, and many of them were men of good

birth and education. Indeed, the very considerations which attracted these last were powerful to repel ' labourers ' in the ordinary sense of the term. A despotic form of government was unsuited to their tastes ; the great distance from England, which forbade the prospect of return ; the uncertainty of employment ; the necessity of having to compete with convict labour ; the association in their minds between emigration and transportation, which to their thinking made the one as unpalatable as the other ; the very fact that their betters in social position were wending their way thither—all conspired to check any aspirations they might have for going to the penal colonies. With the gentleman or small capitalist the case was different. He saw that in Australia he could at once secure a position beyond that which he might hope to attain to at home. As a landowner and slave-master at the same time, he would find things made tolerably easy for him immediately on his arrival in the new country. In comparison with America, Australia appeared to him a very Utopia. He would not there, as in Canada or the States, have to rub shoulders with men from the lower walks of life, who perhaps, from greater physical power or from a more natural aptitude for rough-and-ready conditions of existence, might soon surpass him in the struggle for wealth, and take up a position superior to his own. Besides, across the Atlantic his small capital would have to be devoted to paying high rates of wages to men over whose service he had but an uncertain and limited control, while any advantage that his command of capital might give him at the outset would almost certainly be quickly neutralised by the power which every labouring man possessed of becoming himself a greater capitalist. In Australia there need not be any wage-paying. A beneficent Government was ready to supply servants and labourers at the expense of the nation, and he had but to work them, or to exchange them for others out of whom he could force more work, in order to realise a fortune and return to England. The despotic form of government was far from disagreeable to him, for by repressing men of the lower class from rising higher, it secured the monopoly of his own set. Then, too, he had no intention of becoming a permanent settler, and had therefore no interest in the system of rule except that it should not be subjected to disturbing influences such as might depreciate the value of his colonial possessions. A set of free labouring immigrants would be certain to be dissatisfied with things as they were, and would agitate for representative institutions. The despotic system deterred such people from coming to the country, and in so far as it had that operation it was highly convenient and useful.

These were the chief reasons which determined the emigration of men, of far higher social rank than that to which the ordinary colonist can pretend, to Australia. Many of their hopeful anticipations were rudely upset by painful realities of experience, but in the main their expectations were in a great measure fulfilled.

That this class of emigrants was not the one most capable of advancing the progress of the colony is apparent enough from the stationary condition of New South Wales during the whole of the time that the squatter class predominated in proportionate numbers and influence over the rest of the free population. The reason is not far to seek. The squatters wished to keep themselves as a separate caste in the land, while they were absolutely indifferent to the welfare of the colony. Acting on this guiding principle, they ranged themselves on the side of the home authorities in endeavouring to render the colony yet more unwelcome to the English working classes.

They had good reason to be satisfied with their own position and to be undesirous of change. They could run their stock over unlimited areas, and they were too few in number to compete with each other in bringing down the prices of beef and mutton. Their wool, too, was acquiring a rising value which promised soon to be productive of great wealth. Whatever the depression from which the colony was suffering, they could always make sure of a good market for their produce, and until wool and tallow became staple articles of commerce, some thirty years after the foundation of the colony, they troubled themselves little about the removal of the onerous restrictions upon trade which environed the colony.

Few of them had wives; and in their dealings with the female convicts they set an example of depravity to the community which gave rise to the most hideous forms of vice.

Let it be granted that immigrants of good social rank and position are not undesirable acquisitions to a new colony. Let it be even asserted, in the most unqualified form, that men possessing these attributes ought to be welcomed as emigrants by reason of the ameliorating effect which association with them may cause in the manners of colonists of the usual type. But such benefits can only result from the *admixture* of such men with the ordinary tide of emigration. A large proportion of the early American colonists consisted of men of superior position, and there their presence was as conducive to good as in Australia it was productive of harm ; because in America social distinctions were altogether sunk in the struggle for existence, and because the energy and ability of the gentlemen colonists was devoted to the cause of the common weal, and not to the acquisition of exclusive rights and monopolies. In America, it was to the interest of every member of the immigrant body to frame a system of government which should allow to each and all the freest exercise of their powers, for relative positions were continually shifting. The master of to-day might be the servant of to-morrow ; the penniless labourer might become the local capitalist, and this last, in turn, might have to yield his pride of place to some more facile worker. Labour, too, was difficult to get, except on conditions of mutual advice and assistance—' log-rolling ' in its primitive and best form. The colonists were thus forced by their circumstances to mingle freely with each other, and on equal terms, with the result that the gentleman instinctively acquired the sturdy qualities and industrious habits of his lowly-born fellow-labourer, while he, for his part, imparted to the latter much of his own more cultivated manner and higher tone of thought.

In Australia there was no such community of interest between all sorts and conditions of men. The few labourer immigrants who made their own way out from time to time were not wanted by men who could get labour for nothing, so there was no mutual commingling between the free inhabitants of the colony. The squatters kept themselves apart as a holy caste whose special function it was to maintain its own sacred rights, at whatever cost of injury to the community. How the immigration of the squatter class *alone* affected the prosperity of New South Wales may be ascertained by comparing the respective rates of progress before and after Brisbane's time.

No immigrants could have been so useful to the colony in its earlier days as people of the working class. Not the shovelled-out paupers who have ever been the pet colonists of the Colonial Office, but men capable of undergoing hardship and toil. They would have been of special value to Australia not merely as workers, but as the most efficient instruments for reforming the convict population. Had large numbers of free labourers been introduced, the convicts would have had before them the spectacle of persons of a rank of life not inferior to their own working, prospering, and rising by honest toil to wealth and influence. Between the convicts and these immigrants there would have been a certain degree of association for social and business purposes, such as must have powerfully contributed to stimulate the better disposed convicts to aim at bettering their own condition. It may be said that the reverse effect would have been produced—that the free would have been contaminated by association with the bond—but even with every impediment cunningly devised by Government to prevent men of the labouring class from becoming anything but convicts themselves, it was not found that any large proportion of the one descended to the level of the other. On the contrary, the most adverse conditions failed to altogether check the tendency to moral improvement actually shown among the convicts as the result of the introduction of a mere handful of free labourers. If the colony had been freely supplied with such immigrants, it cannot be doubted that the bulk of the criminal population would have been won back by honest habits to their lost position.

Of the importance of the labouring class of immigrants from an economical point of view there can be no question.

There are those who think that emigration should be so regulated that labour and capital should be planted together and simultaneously on the virgin soil of a new colony, in certain definite proportionate quantities, and who maintain that the permanent disarrangement of these proportions must of necessity involve a young colony in hopeless disaster. It is impossible, however, to treat this argument seriously, for relations or proportions between capital and labour in a virgin territory are the very things which no human ingenuity can settle beforehand. Capital may safely be trusted to follow in the wake of labour, and the relations between the two must vary according to local requirements or development. To endeavour to establish such relations beforehand is to realise by anticipation the circumstances of an unknowable future. Wakefield and his followers, while bitterly and justly inveighing against Colonial Office red-tapeism, were themselves red-tapeists of the deepest dye. It is to them that we are indebted for colonisation schemes in which the useful suggestions are so bound around with reels of red-tape that sound principles and unsound theories are at first sight almost inseparable from each other. It is in these speculations that we find visionary pleas for the establishment of antecedent ratios between capital and labour, and between land and labour; and how mischievous were the consequences of the reduction of these rules to practice will appear in treating of the questions connected with the foundation of South Australia.

If it be desirable to attract capital to a new colony, the best inducement is the most natural—namely, a ready supply of labourers on the spot. The Colonial Office utilised the convicts as a labouring staff, and emigrants with capital came as of course. So they would have done, in smaller proportion to the free labourers, but in all probability in greater numbers, if a plentiful influx of free labourers had been encouraged. The opposite policy was, however, adopted, and a convict labouring staff, consisting of slaves who did only the modicum of work extorted from them, together with the taskmasters who considered the welfare of the colony as opposed to their own, formed the whole industrial population.

I have spoken of the inducements given by the forming of the convicts into a labouring staff as being 'natural' inducements. They were so only in the sense that the home Government, by maintaining the settlement as a penal one only, had closed the way to the more powerful inducement that would have been offered by the early and continuous introduction of *free* immigrants of the labouring classes. It was the natural result of a forced non-natural system of colonisation, and of the home policy which was responsible for having created conditions which could not produce a mixed colonisation of men and women of all classes, but only of one class. It was a natural inducement as regarded the small or large capitalist, but it was an unnatural one as regarded its formation.

From the very outset the home authorities were urged by the first Governor of the colony to send out free labourers. More labour, he told them, would have been performed by a hundred free labourers from any part of England and Scotland 'than had at any time been performed by 300 convicts with all the attention that could be paid them.' In consequence, a few pauper families were let out to contractors and transmitted out in driblets from time to time.

The lot of these emigrants was not, as a rule, a happy one. The produce they raised had to be exchanged against 'property,' as it was called—that is, against rum, tea, sugar, or such other goods as the purchaser, the Government, might choose to offer at an enormous over-valuation. These labouring settlers were objectionable to the squatters, hateful to the emancipists, and obnoxious to the Governor who exercised absolute power over the colony for a longer period than any of his predecessors or successors.[1] His Excellency's maxim was, 'New South Wales is a country for the reformation of convicts ; free people have no right to come to it ; ' and, in accordance with this maxim, he diligently strove to disgust free settlers with the colony by elevating emancipists to magisterial offices and special privileges. The dislike of both Macquarie and the emancipists to free immigrants of the

[1] Governor Macquarie.

humbler sort was founded on the opposition of these last to having whilom gaol-birds promiscuously set in authority over them. There was probably a certain amount of reason on both sides, but the Governor had his own way, as being possessed of the greatest power of inflicting annoyance—a process to which he resorted so effectually as to discourage any attempts at free immigration *by any class* until just before the close of his period of administration. Even the system of giving free passages and free grants of land to upper-class immigrants had been discontinued since 1818, thanks to Macquarie's action. Nevertheless, or rather in consequence, so greatly was his policy appreciated at home that he was kept in power for twelve years.

Towards the close of Macquarie's administration the capabilities of the colony became better known, and the tide of immigration began to set in towards its shores on the arrival of Brisbane ; but as the possession of a capital of at least 500*l.* by each intending colonist was insisted upon by the Government, labourers and artisans were precluded from emigrating. Slave-drivers were taken out instead of working-men. Of course a good many of these who failed to prosper had to descend to humble walks of life, and it was well for the colony that they did so, for they formed the nucleus of a labouring body which was of immense benefit in forming a counterpoise to the political preponderance of the convicts, and they did more by their influence to pave the way for free institutions than could have been done by a more highly-placed body of men or by any other means, under the circumstances.

Their united voice was the first expression in the history of the colony of a public opinion which regarded the interests of the community as matters of paramount importance. Gradually that voice grew powerful for remonstrance and then for control. By degrees the influence of the emancipists sank as that of the free working-men rose. In 1831 some fifty or sixty families of Scotch mechanics—stone-masons, carpenters, brick-makers, and the like—were brought out from home ; and, although in consequence of the bitter feeling that had grown up against them among the emancipists generally, under the fostering care of Macquarie and the Colonial Office, they were for months after their arrival subjected to gross abuse and to every form of petty annoyance, their patient and inoffensive demeanour gradually disarmed hostility and conciliated general respect.

The example of these immigrants worked wonders for the moral improvement, as well as for the material advancement, of the colony. The more meritorious of the emancipists now began to compete for an honourable position in a society now for the first time launched on a career of commencing prosperity. These in turn attracted others to industrious courses, while the success of the Scotchmen, together with the improved aspect their exertions and influence imparted to colonial life, was instrumental in procuring the emigration of many more, respectable, skilled labourers from the mother-country.

From this emigration dates the progressive rise of the country, and it seems almost unnecessary to remark that it was not assisted in any way by the Colonial Office, but that the labourers were brought out at the expense of private individuals anxious for the welfare of New South Wales. True, Lord Goderich, who was then at the head of the Colonial Office, ordered the advancement of a small sum of money from the Colonial Treasury to part pay the expenses of shipping out the first batch of the Scotch mechanics ; but even this much was done under protest, and by enforcing the condition that a like amount was previously to be expended for the purpose by the private promoters of the undertaking. This was in striking contrast to the readiness displayed by the home Government in shipping out cargoes of convicts sunk in the lowest depths of depravity.

The year 1831 was, as has been seen, a great epoch, or, perhaps, it might be more appropriately termed, ' a landmark,' in the history of Australia. It was then that the Wakefield theory of selling instead of granting land, and of devoting the proceeds of land sales to the promotion of free emigration, began to be put into practice. The change was eminently disagreeable to the Colonial Office, for it deprived that institution of a large amount of the patronage which was made to conduce to the solidification of its power in the colony. But public opinion had at last commenced to take a languid interest in colonisation, and the Office for the time being was suppressed. Unfortunately, the conduct of emigration was left in the hands of the Imperial Government, who, according to time-honoured precedent, let out the business to contractors. At the time of effecting the change in the mode of the disposal of land, a pledge had been virtually given to the colonists that the land revenue should be appropriated mainly towards the encouragement and promotion of the emigration of virtuous, industrious, and able-bodied persons. This pledge was incontinently broken. Not more than one-fifth of the land revenue was applied to emigration at all, and that amount was devoted to picking up paupers on easy terms from the workhouses. To remedy the disproportion of the sexes in New South Wales the Government appropriated part of the land fund in 1832, 1833, and 1834 to the purpose of exporting unmarried females. This delicate mission, though nominally carried out under the superintendence of a Female Emigration Board in London, was in fact handed over to a notorious speculator, who, looking at the matter on the strictest business principles, procured and shipped out the women who were most easily and cheaply procurable. These were, as a rule, to be found amongst those leading immoral lives, and without supervision or question they were shipped off; and in consequence the streets of Sydney and the public-houses of the colony swarmed with free immigrant prostitutes from the cities of London, Dublin, and Cork, the expense of whose passage had been defrayed from the land revenue of the colony.

Over and above what was expended on emigration, there was a large surplus remaining from the land fund. This, under conscientious management, might have been utilised for the purpose of introducing an active, intelligent, thrifty population, with the certain result of effecting an entire moral revolution in the characters of the colonists within a comparatively short period of time ; but the home Government was still hankering after the fostering of a penal settlement in preference to consulting for the good of New South Wales. The Secretary of State for the Colonies therefore determined to appropriate this balance for the maintenance of the police and gaol establishments of the colony, thereby diverting the funds which ought to have been applied for the furtherance of the colonial prosperity towards the perpetuation of its low and degraded condition as a sink for the criminality of the empire. The resolute opposition of the colonial population to the proposed measure was ineffectual to prevent the nominee Council from passing a vote in favour of it; but as the ordinary revenue of the colony proved sufficient to meet the whole expenditure of the Government during the last three years of Sir Richard Bourke's administration, that vote was in reality a dead letter, and the balance of the land revenue remained untouched. Yet the wants of the colony for several thousand additional free labourers and mechanics were, at the time, extremely urgent, and the absolute indifference of the Home Government to the necessity of promoting their emigration was extremely prejudicial to the colony. ' It checked the march of its general improvement by preventing the importation of the large amount of skilled labour which might otherwise have been secured to it ; it retarded the progress of its moral advancement by virtually repelling from its shores the numerous industrious, virtuous, and free emigrant population which would otherwise have been attracted to its territory ; and at a time when the colonial treasury was overflowing with funds available for the promotion of emigration, but locked up from the public under the hand of the Governor, it virtually compelled the colonial proprietors, very shortly thereafter, to enter into associations for importing, at their own private expense, Hill Coolies from India, Chinese labourers from Canton and Amoy, South Sea Islanders from the New Hebrides, and expiree convicts from Tasmania to fill the places that might otherwise have been occupied so much more advantageously for the colony in every respect by thousands of the redundant and comparatively virtuous population of the British Isles.' [1]

[1] Lang's *New South Wales*, vol. i. p. 251.

The indignation of the colony at this shameful misappropriation of its funds had now grown into so much positive discontent, especially on account of the expressed determination of the Home Government to apply the local revenue to extend the comfort and accommodation of the convicts, that in 1837, Lord Glenelg, then Secretary of State for the Colonies, organised an agency in England for the promotion of emigration to New South Wales at the expense of the land fund. For a while emigration was carried on on a better system, but the old evils crept in again ; and though, on the whole, large shipments of a more reputable class of colonists were exported, the pauper and immoral element still permeated the mass in no small degree. Colonisation was still looked upon as a convenient means of freeing the mother-country from the destitution her own laws had caused, and, under the pretence of philanthropy, the Highlands of Scotland were ransacked for the lowest types of pauperism procurable for export.

The dissatisfaction of the colonists with these arrangements became at length so deep and widespread that the Home Government found itself obliged to virtually relinquish the conduct of emigration. In consequence, the ' bounty ' system, as it was called, was inaugurated. If this change had been made simply with a view to meet the wishes of the colonists, and if the working of the details had been left to the guidance of the colonial public, the business of emigration might have assumed an improved character. As it was, the adoption of the bounty system was due to the hue and cry got up by a few mercantile houses in London and Sydney, who perceived that, if they could get the exclusive management of emigration to New South Wales into their own hands, they could easily turn the large revenue available and expenditure necessary for the purpose to their own private advantage. The whole business was now confided to the unscrupulous care of the speculators, who were to receive a certain fixed payment as a bounty for every emigrant of the whole number whose transmission had been previously authorised by the local Government.

The Home Government, during the time that emigration was

carried on by it, had occasionally, as has been seen, gone to some expense in ferreting out paupers from the most distant parts of the kingdom. The funds for this purpose came from the colony, and it was as well to find some employment for the numerous staff of fussy Government emigration agents. Therefore, remote districts were sometimes drawn upon for emigrants. The syndicate, however, to whom the business had, at its own suggestion, been assigned, thought only of working on the most unexceptionable commercial basis. As with commodities, so with emigrants; they were to be bought in the cheapest and sold in the dearest market. The cheapest market was undoubtedly the south and west of Ireland, and thither the contractors despatched business-like agents, or 'whippers-in,' to collect the refuse of the rural and workhouse population. The characters or capacities for work [1] of these wretched creatures was a matter of complete unimportance They were to be got on cheaper terms than sturdy unemployed Lancashire operatives or able-bodied but destitute Highlanders, and were therefore best fitted for export, as yielding the largest margin of profit. During the eight and a half years of Sir George Gipps's administration,[2] the bounty system was in full swing, and, mainly by its operation, the population was more than doubled in the time. But by far the greater number of the immigrants thus introduced consisted of the lowest description of Irish, while the remainder comprised the most depraved classes of English. 'The workhouses and the streets were ransacked, and certificates, both of kindred and character, were systematically forged. In one case, for example, a man and woman, both single, in another, a mother and her son, had lived on board in one berth, having in both instances been passed off as man and wife. One of the

---

[1] Bonwick quotes the following from the official correspondence of Captain Hunter, the third Governor of the colony :—' I have discharged a wheelwright sent out by Government at a salary of 105*l.* per annum. He had not earned 5*l.*, although he had cost the public 600*l.* or more. Anxious as I was to get a mill erected, I could not effect it until I found an ingenious Irish convict, who has finished a very good one, and as an encouragement I gave him 25*l.* and abolished the above salary.'

[2] From 1837 to 1846.

clerks employed in this emigration system appears to have held a conspicuous position for the facility and variety of his devices. He had been in the habit of directing single men who applied for a passage to obtain from the streets or brothels, or whence mattered not, the requisite appendage of an unmarried female; and it seems that in these golden days all that individuals had to do was to say that they would go, and the clerk would make it right for them. Many of the single women, according to the evidence of Mr. Merewether, the emigration agent in the colony, alluding to the same system and period, " proved to be of notoriously bad character ; and many have also been of a class much above that prescribed by the regulations, and in every way unsuited to the demand of the colony." '¹ Again, Westgarth tells us that 'large quantities of spirits were sold to the emigrants on board, and a promiscuous intercourse of the sexes frequently occurred to a shameful extent during the voyage, sometimes directly encouraged by the captain and surgeon, at others defying the authorities who were disposed to attempt restraint. The parties who were engaged in despatching the emigrants at the shipping port were also in the habit of living with the females who were awaiting the sailing of the vessels.' ²

Loud and long-continued were the complaints of the colonists at the glaring misuse which was thus being made of their money. Fervent and eloquent were the lengthy compositions of the Land and Emigration Commissioners in England, devoted to prove, in a style worthy of Pangloss, that all was for the best, that their efforts were laboriously directed to selecting only the most useful emigrants, and that it was the fault of the excessive demand for labour if Irish men and women of lower intellectual calibre than the Australian aborigines ³ were shipped as fast as they could be collected. The fact was that the nominal supervision of the contractors by the Commissioners was no supervision at all. The trans-

---

¹ Westgarth's *Australia Felix*, pp. 298, 299.

² *Ibid.* p. 300.

³ Evidence of Mr. Alexander Thompson before a Select Committee of the Legislative Council in 1843.

port of the emigrants was carried out in shocking defiance of all the rules of humanity and decency. A considerable percentage died on the voyage from putrid fevers, brought on by overcrowding, want of nourishment, and improper attendance, and Canadian emigration history was reproduced in all its gross details. As to those who landed at Sydney and Port Phillip, notwithstanding the great demand for labour that prevailed, not a few amongst them were so incompetent for work of any kind that they could procure no employment, and were thrown on the charity of the community. At last the colonial Government began to wake up to the necessities of the situation, and proclaimed its resolve to withhold bounties for such emigrants as were incapable of work, if men, or who, if women, were falsely described as married, or were notorious prostitutes. To meet the risk of losing the bounties on individual emigrants, the contractors raised the scale of freight, but the colony reaped the advantage of gaining a more carefully chosen and more reputable set of emigrants, though at great expense.

Let us listen to what the Land and Emigration Commissioners themselves say of the system : [1]—

The first theory was that private persons in the Colonies should be allowed to send for their own immigrants, and should be repaid the cost when the people safely reached the colony. It is evident that gentlemen residing at the distance of New South Wales had no peculiar facilities for selecting, fitting out, and despatching labourers living in the United Kingdom. They had to cast about for others to do the business for them; but the only others who had a motive to transact it were shipowners who looked for a return in the profits of their trade in the conveyance of the passengers. Hence it soon came to pass that one party sold and the other bought permissions which were useless to the one and valuable to the other. The bounty orders, as they were called, became notoriously vendible commodities, and the fortunate procurer of one of them from the colonial Government could put the price into his pocket without any further trouble or risk whatever. . . .

The next plan was that the business should avowedly be committed by the public to the hands of shipowners. These, who . . . might be

[1] Appendix to their Fourth Annual Report.

eminently qualified for supplying good ships, were totally unversed in the mass of miscellaneous business which had to be transacted in procuring, selecting, advising, and controlling the equipment of emigrants.

The evils which might otherwise have been apprehended were for some time avoided by contriving on one ground or another to confine the business to the hands of one or two respectable persons. . . . But by degrees other merchants complained of this virtual monopoly, and it became necessary to throw the business more open.

The result was, that every one concerned was a loser. . . . Intending emigrants were exposed to suffer from the incautious communications of persons not possessed of the requisite experience and knowledge, while unduly stimulating pictures of the state of the Colonies might be presented to them by private agents, ready to fill their employers' pockets, and, in case of complaint, there was no well-known administration likely to be strictly called to account, on which to come for redress. Shipowners, on the other hand, were saddled with a very unsuitable responsibility, after they had honestly and well furnished excellent ships and good provisions, at the sheer will of one or more public officers in the Colonies, because, more perhaps from inexperience than inattention, they had not procured people equal to the standard considered right in the Colonies. Before the practice came to an end, serious discontent had been excited in some of the shipowners who had the largest dealings in emigration, on account of the heavy pecuniary losses which were inflicted on them upon this ground.

The bounty system was a thoroughly bad one, and probably could not have produced satisfactory results—except possibly to the contractors—under any given set of conditions, even if conscientiously supervised. The essence of the system consisted in holding out temptations to the greed of the contractors, and yet these were relied upon as affording incentives to honest and careful selection. It threw into the hands of unprincipled speculators enormous powers for good or evil— the supplying materials for a new world—and provided no check against their flagrant abuse.

The colonial Government was to blame for having urged the adoption of the system, and for having adhered to it, but let it not be forgotten that the colonial Government until 1856 was utterly out of sympathy with the wants of the great majority of colonists, and was merely the complement of the Colonial Office.

Contemporaneously with the bounty system, the practice grew up of prepaying in part the outward passage of some nominee selected by the colonial payer. This 'remittance system,' as it was called, was a vast improvement on the bounty system, for the home nominee was in many cases the individual whom the colonial nominator knew to be fitted for colonial life. On the other hand, it was liable to be grossly abused by fraudulent or worthless nominees, who first intrigued for nomination orders for themselves, and, having got them for nothing, sold them to the highest bidders. Or, again, speculators in ' orders ' would, by practising on the fears or credulity of *bonâ fide* nominees, induce them to part with their orders for a trifle—a transaction which left a chance of a good profit on the resale. As this sort of thing grew into a regular trading operation, systematically indulged in by the numerous firms of shipping contractors, it followed that a goodly proportion of those who came out with assisted passages were not those for whom the colonist had gone to the expense of prepaying a passage ; and as the essence of the system was that the individual shipped out should be the one actually chosen by the nominator, its actual working was provocative of much dissatisfaction. Under the circumstances, remittances were not sent home by many colonists who would willingly have done so had they possessed the assurance that the money deposited by them would be expended in bringing out their nominees : but still the system grew into general favour, as was evidenced by the numbers of the persons for whose passages remittances were made. These rose from 20 in 1848 to 4,159 in 1853, and a total sum of between 15,000*l.* and 16,000*l.* was the value of remittances sent home from New South Wales, Victoria, and South Australia in the latter year. This does not at first sight compare favourably with the 1,439,000*l.* remitted home from North America in 1853 for the purpose of prepaying emigrants' passages out, even when the difference between the respective populations of the States and Canada, as compared with that of Australia, is taken into account, for the Australian settlers were more recently from home, and might therefore be supposed to have many more home relatives and friends whom they would be desirous of assisting to emigrate, and the average individual means of the Australians were probably at the time greater than were those of American colonists at a corresponding period of settlement.

A large proportion of the Australians were, in 1853, mere rovers, who had gone out to dig for gold, and had no idea of residing permanently in the colony. These men did not trouble themselves about introducing emigrants, so the remittances came from a very limited number of *actual settlers*—a fact which must be taken into consideration in estimating the comparative results of the remittance system in America and Australia. Nor should it be forgotten that, side by side with the remittances system, a large free-passage Government emigration was being briskly carried on.

The system had a very noteworthy effect upon the character of the emigration. As the Commissioners tell us:—' The labouring classes were in former years driven to emigration only by the pressure or the immediate fear of destitution ; they are now induced to do so by the hope of advancement.' [1] This change of feeling and of the standpoint from which emigration was regarded was undoubtedly owing to the proofs given, by the remittances, of the previous emigrants' prosperity. Thus, by means of the system, an *inducing* instead of a compelling cause was made the medium of promoting emigration, and that which Government had striven to press forward as a necessity for paupers had through the action of private enterprise become an advantage to be sought after by the best of the artisans and labourers.

There is nothing more instructive in the records of the remittance system than the prominent part played in it by remittances from Irish settlers. One of the most constant subjects of complaint against the home Government and the home Commissioners was that they sent out an undue preponderance of Irish emigrants to Australia. That the

[1] Fourteenth Annual Report.

colonists were justified in so complaining need not be doubted. At the same time nothing can more fully illustrate the advantageous effects produced upon the most ignorant and helpless of men by introducing them to a thriving colony than the fact that the major portion of the remittances for passages came from Irish settlers. Both in America and in Australia the Irish have ever been a disturbing element. The Bowery Boys of New York and the Larrikins of Sydney and Melbourne are unquestionably of Irish origin, and, as the rowdy and criminal class in both divisions of the globe, their proceedings have naturally excited comment far more than have the orderliness and industry of the large numbers of Irish by whom so much has been done to advance colonial and American prosperity. Let it be remembered that the large sums remitted home every year represent an available surplus of earnings after all the necessities, and probably many of the small luxuries, of life have been provided for by the remitters, if we would see how tangible a proof is supplied by the remittances of the improved condition of the emigrant Irishman. The comparison in favour of the emigrant as compared with his previous impecuniosity and worthlessness while in his native country is strengthened by the consideration that the great mass of Irish emigrants from whom the remittances came were at the time of their expatriation sunk in ignorance, poverty, and slothful habits, untrained to skilled pursuits, and totally devoid of the sense or habit of self-dependence. Yet these same people, when transplanted to American or Australasian soils, are quick to furnish examples of industrious thrift fully equalling those displayed by English or Scotch emigrants of far more cultivated intelligence, and are found powerfully to contribute by their conduct and prosperity to the welfare of the home population.

Great indeed must be the magic of colonisation, if it can produce results such as these out of the worst materials. That a considerable number of Irishmen should become the life and soul of rowdyism when suddenly transplanted to new and freer conditions of existence; that, unaccustomed to self-restraint, they should at once become pliable, willing instru-

ments for evil in their adopted countries ; and that, of a sudden
emancipated from serfdom, they should give the rein to the
indulgence of unbridled passions, ignorance, and vice—the
only qualities that their English governors have for centuries
endeavoured thoroughly to develop in them—is surely not to
be wondered at. But it is a matter of surprise that colonisation
should so effectually curb the evil propensities almost ingrained
into the characters of the lower orders of Irish as to resolve
the vast majority of indolent good-for-nothings into orderly
industrious citizens.

The remittance system had the great recommendation of
giving play to the operation of private enterprise. Economically the bounty system is hardly defensible, for it is difficult
to draw a line between bounties on the export of goods and
on that of human beings. The principle is practically the
same in both cases. But no objection on economical grounds
can fairly be maintained against private individuals bringing
out immigrants, partly at their own private cost, unless it be
that not *part* merely but the *whole* of the expense of immigration should be borne by them.

The objection was frequently raised in the Colonies against
the remittance system, that it occasionally brought out a glut
of immigrants, and that at other times it failed to bring out
enough labourers to supply the local market—in short, that it
was fitful and irregular in its working. For this, rapidly alter-
nating rushes of extraordinary speculation, followed by the inevitable reaction, were to blame rather than the remittance system
itself; moreover, the same irregularity of supply was at these
periods a feature of both assisted and voluntary emigration.

The frequent statements made in the respective Colonial
Legislatures as to 'gluts' of labour are totally unsupported
by any evidence worth the name. It was rather a protectionist
cry got up by colonial workmen, to prevent others of their
class from outside from coming in to break down their monopoly of high wages. We find, for example, that in 1857, when
the 'glut' cry had attained great prominence, a motion in the
Victorian Assembly to send a supply of labour to Villiers
County, ' in order to save the crops,' was carried in the House.

The terms offered by the local farmers were *thirty shillings per diem, and seven glasses of grog per man*, besides the payment of the labourers' expenses from Melbourne and back. Yet we find Mr. Childers[1] objecting to the motion, on behalf of the Government, on the ground that labourers ought not to be forced to go to Villiers. Imagine a country ' glutted ' with labourers, where they had to be *forced* to accept thirty shillings and seven glasses of grog per man per diem, besides having all expenses paid !

At that time, too, a great deal of philanthropic discourse was expended over the ' unemployed ' in Melbourne, and the Government, after taking the tenderest care of them for a few days, had to announce to the Assembly that some of the unemployed were still out of work. Here was evidence of a ' glut,' had it not been for the Ministerial explanation that the ' unemployed ' still left on their hands were men who refused to work for less than sixteen shillings a day. It may be added that the whole of the original ' unemployed,' about whom the devotees of the ' glut ' theory were so solicitous, were freshly landed immigrants, and that many of them, having been improperly selected at home, were quite unfitted for work of any kind.

But perhaps the strongest disproof of the ' glut ' theory is to be found in the following letter :—

Belvedere Hotel Lodge : May 27, 1857.

Gentlemen,—In answer to the notice issued by you, intimating your intention to lower the wages of the men now in your employ, we beg to say it was duly submitted to this Society for its consideration and discussed in all its bearings. It was resolved that a proceeding so unconstitutional and so repugnant to the feelings of the Society be strenuously and determinedly resisted ; and it was also further agreed that no member resume your employ without an advance of one shilling per day, should you persist in your intention by keeping the men out of your employ for more than three days, thereby incur-

---

[1] Now the Right Hon. Hugh Childers, Chancellor of the Exchequer, 1883.

ring expenses on the Society, and which we consider entirely uncalled for. We are, gentlemen, your obedient servants,

(Signed)   THE PRESIDENT AND MEMBERS OF THE
OPERATIVE MASONS OF MELBOURNE.

To Messrs. Bell & Co., Builders, Contractors, &c.

When to this are added instances of jobbing labourers refusing ten shillings per day and lodgings for simply cutting wood and drawing water, it seems impossible to doubt that, though it might be authoritatively declared by a majority of the Legislature that the colony was glutted with labour, the reason of the thing was in favour of those immigrationists who appealed to the foregoing facts in proof of an actual dearth of labourers.

The fact was that the labour was unequally distributed. The policy of keeping large numbers of workmen engaged on expensive public works beyond the requirements of the colonists caused the retention of many labourers in and about the capital towns; and the rushes to the gold-fields, besides their effect of turning the labourer into a miner, centralised the supply of labour in the neighbourhood of the gold-fields, while the rest of the country could not get labour for love or money.

If the remittance system was to blame, it was for not bringing out enough labouring immigrants at the times when it was said there were too many; and if not enough *then*, certainly not enough when it was admitted on all hands that the country was suffering from a dearth of labourers.

It would, indeed, be an unhealthy sign if the supply of labour in vast and wealthy territories, such as are the Australasian colonies, was at any time in the immediate future to be found more than sufficient to meet the demand for it. Now and again may come a commercial crash, which in its effects may throw every industry in the country, for a brief space, out of gear, as in 1842, but the check would be an insignificant one, and would but clear the air for a renewal of the normal state of industrial activity in which there is a constant cry for more and more labour. Therefore, to urge against the remittance system that it did not bring out enough labouring immigrants was merely to say that the Colonies were progressing satisfactorily. Still, their prosperity would have been augmented had the labour supply been larger, but there were several causes why this should not be so. First there was the fact that emigration, instead of being supervised by colonial agents at home—that is, by men whose chief interest lay in working for the Colonies—was regulated by the Land and Emigration Commissioners, a body composed of men desirous of doing well, and capable, perhaps, of carrying into efficient execution the important duties imposed upon them had they possessed any knowledge of the wants of the Colonies, and been at the same time under direct responsibility to them. But they were answerable merely to the English Parliament—a responsibility that might mean much or nothing, according as Parliament might take great interest or none at all in the matter. The Duke of Newcastle thought that he had made out an unanswerable case when, in reference to the complaints conveyed in a Report of the Legislative Council of Victoria on the conduct of emigration, he replied, on the question of responsibility, that ' it is enough to answer that every shilling of the Commissioners' expenditure is rigidly scrutinised by the Commissioners of Audit, . . . and that not an item, however small, is passed without the production both of vouchers and of an express written authority for the expenditure incurred. . . . I have merely to observe that the Emigration Commissioners are answerable to the Government, and are subject to the same penalties as all other public servants for any neglect or maladministration in their office ; that their Reports are in constant course of production to Parliament, and through that channel to the public ; and that their whole credit depends on the ability and success with which they may serve the interests of the Colonies for which they act.' [1]

How absurd was the principle of responsibility implied in the auditing of the accounts by the Audit Commissioners is apparent from the confession of the Duke in the same despatch [2] that no accounts had been furnished by the Land and Emigra-

---

[1] Despatch of September 19, 1853, to Lieutenant-Governor La Trobe.
[2] Paragraph 12 of Despatch.

tion Commissioners to the colonial Government since 1847—six years back. The auditors themselves, notwithstanding the formidable parade of a paraphernalia of vouchers and express written authorities, seem to have affixed their signatures to the statements of accounts as of course, without any examination. Had the auditing been done with any care or system, it is unlikely that the complaint would have been brought forward by the colonists, in July 1852, that a sum of 129,000*l.* was totally unaccounted for, and that the Duke, writing towards the end of the following year—an interval which gave him abundant opportunities for investigation—would have had to admit that 'respecting the sum of 129,000*l.* which the Committee described as totally unaccounted for, no sufficient information is afforded to admit of giving any clear answer.' [1]

The responsibility to a Parliament which manifested not the slightest interest in emigration may be dismissed as a stock phrase inured to useful service in many a Downing Street despatch, but without any meaning at all as a practical fact.

The Commissioners themselves would appear to have had but a scanty stock of local knowledge of the Colonies. New South Wales and Victoria were to them terms having a distinctive meaning as political divisions, but their geographical acquaintance with the two colonies was not sufficient to prevent their falling into errors which, being unaccompanied by a detailed statement of accounts, were productive of much intercolonial wrangling. For example, the Commissioners charged upon Victoria the expenses of sending emigrants to Twofold Bay, *in New South Wales*, an occurrence which would have been impossible had they troubled themselves even so far as to consult the maps at their offices.

The principles laid down by the Commissioners for their own guidance were extraordinarily incompatible with their own actions. Thus they declare that 'the character of a Government emigration should be mainly decided with a view to the permanent interest of the colony, and therefore to the infusion of the greatest possible number of active, healthy, and industrious colonists; yet,' they add, 'the peculiar exigencies of the

---

[1] Paragraph 6 of Despatch.

moment could not be properly neglected, and we were bound to remember that these exigencies rendered it of paramount importance to send out large numbers of persons possessing the now all-important qualification of unfitness for the gold-fields.' Instead, therefore, of sending out ' active, industrious, and healthy' emigrants, they despatched cargoes of weavers, spinners, and the like—men whose inferior physique would prevent their resorting to the gold-fields or dispersing themselves over the colonies. This was the application of the grand principle of conducting emigration for the best interest of the Colonies—to send out cripples incapable of enterprise. Could anything more conclusively show than this one fact does how utterly incompetent the Commissioners were to manage the momentous business of emigration ? It was of itself complete proof of their extreme ignorance of the real condition of the Colonies, and throws considerable doubt upon their vaunted solicitude for the prosperity of Australia. But it was also indicative of a deep-seated belief in their official minds—a belief worse than mere ignorance—that emigration should be conducted in the interests of only the small squatter class of colonists, consisting though it did, at that time, of men who had not bought their lands, and who therefore had contributed nothing directly towards the expenses of emigration. Further, it was significant of the attention given to squatter suggestions by the Colonial Office. For these invalid emigrants were selected with a view to their being physically incapable of wandering beyond the limits of their squatter-masters' sheep-runs, and thus it was hoped that a supply of shepherds might be always secured to the squatters. It seems almost incredible that this emigration of invalids should have been actively carried into practice, but it was so, until the colonists raised up their voices against the continued inpouring of men physically unfitted for the rough usages of colonial life. Then the Commissioners naïvely gave their reasons as above quoted, and actually concluded by expressing their surprise at the widespread dissatisfaction of the colonists with measures conceived ' in their best interests,' et cetera. Where the Commissioners had grievously erred was in mistaking the wishes and representations of a small body of wealthy landowners for those of the community, between whom and the landowners there was a complete disaccord of feeling on most subjects; an error of no trifling description when considered in connection with the vast importance to young countries of a proper understanding of their internal wants on the part of those to whom is confided the charge of emigration.

Another scheme of the Commissioners is especially noteworthy as significant of their non-appreciation of the practical working of things in the Colonies. In pursuance of an Act passed at their suggestion for the purpose, they endeavoured to inaugurate a system of ' deferred payments ' of passage-money. The Act provided that all emigrants sent out at the public expense should before embarkation enter into an agreement with the Land and Emigration Commissioners either to repay the amount still remaining due from them for passage-money, where a part had been originally paid, within fourteen days after their arrival in the colony, or to take service for two years with an employer who should guarantee to repay that amount out of their accruing wages. But a power was reserved to the emigrants to terminate such agreements after the first twelvemonths by giving three months' notice and paying up the unpaid instalments of the passage-money. It was also provided that the indentures of single women should be terminable at any time on their marriage upon the like conditions of paying up their unpaid instalments, and that where the parents of a young woman were in the colony, their approval of the person to whom she was to be indentured should be obtained.

Wherever and whenever this principle of deferred payments —or, as it practically was, a principle of loans to be repaid by instalments—had been tried, whether in America or Canada, or, earlier in date, in New South Wales itself, and whether applied to land purchases or payment of emigrant passages, it had thoroughly broken down, but Government official bodies possess a power of perseverance in revivifying exploded theories not easily separable from blinded infatuation, and the Colonial Office was for setting the ' deferred payment ' farce going again.

Mr. G. W. Rusden [1] thus characterises the working of the system in New South Wales:—' On the subject of promoting immigration on the principle of loans to intending immigrants, the experience of New South Wales seems by no means encouraging. . . . Immigration was to be provided of a partially self-supporting character—immigrants assisted under its terms engaging to pay the whole or a fixed proportion of the cost of passage out of their earnings in the colony. . . . In 1854 the experiment was tried, . . . but the Act must ere long become a dead letter. So averse were employers to engage servants under the bond, . . . and so little were immigrants inclined to respect those bonds, that as regards female immigration the Act was in a short time superseded with the hope of clearing the Government depôts and of inducing a more useful class of immigrants.

' It appears to me that it cannot be expected that a large number of promises to pay can be enforced against either themselves or their employers. . . . Then, too, the palpable absurdity of putting the community into court to sue for the balance of the passage-money against every recalcitrant immigrant shows that the defects of the system are not profitably to be evaded in the colony.'

Lieutenant-Governor La Trobe also states as his belief ' that in this colony [Victoria] such engagements are so much waste-paper; that in many cases the emigrants are not aware of what they have signed, and that experience has proved the futility of any attempt to enforce such undertakings.' [2]

The system was found unworkable. as it always had been and as it always will be, under similar conditions, to the end of the chapter. Had the Commissioners been allowed to have their own way they would have applied it to all the Colonies. Then every immigrant would have been the indentured slave of his master, every master would have been a Government debtor under bond, and in addition would have had to do the policeing of his entire working staff to see that none of them ran away to prospect for themselves. In the end, after a vast deal of

[1] Report on Immigration to Victoria, paragraph 32.
[2] Letter to Sir George Gipps, January 21, 1853.

vexation and despatch-writing, either the home authorities would by pressing for payment have forced the severance of the imperial tie, or, as is much more probable, the home Government would have had to consent to erase all pecuniary obligations on account of deferred payments, at a single pen-stroke.

It must be confessed that the path of the Commissioners was in some respects a thorny one. Jealous and easily irritable colonial populations were perpetually calling for more immigrants, and then volubly condemning the increased expenditure per head necessary to procure the extra supply. It is not to be supposed that the Commissioners were particularly economical in their distribution of funds for whose application they were not responsible to the providers. No one is, under such circumstances. But there can be no doubt that the cost of conveying immigrants was enhanced by the necessity for extra ship-room with every increase in their numbers. However, the attraction of the gold-fields furnished a far more efficient cause of expense, for not only was a voluntary emigration set on foot by the discovery of gold, but in 1852 it had attained to such dimensions that immigrants landed, in Melbourne alone, at the rate of 300 a day. This gigantic rush of itself raised the cost of the outward passage; but what added to it more than anything else was the fact that no sooner did ships arrive in the colony than their crews deserted *en masse* for the gold-diggings. In August 1852 there were no fewer than seventy-four vessels lying in Hobson's Bay emptied of all hands. The sailors scarce consented to remain on board till the cargoes were discharged before rushing wildly off to the diggings. 'The dropping of the anchor on every arriving vessel was the usual signal for a war between the captain and his impatient crew, who must be forthwith ashore in order to proceed to the diggings, and who were neither very nice in intimating their wishes, nor very long, of some fashion, of carrying them out. Entire crews, obstinate and refusing to work, were transferred to prison to be again put on board when their ship was about to leave the port.'[1] Or else—when tired of digging, or having spent in drink their newly-acquired wealth—

[1] Westgarth's *Australia Felix*, p. 155.

they could with difficulty be induced to re-engage for the home-ward voyage at 50*l*. or 60*l*. for the straight run home, and this was demanded to be put down in gold upon the capstan before a hand would be put to the cable. Under these circumstances freights, of course, rose. Tenders from contractors for the emigration business went up from 10*l*. per head in 1851 to 23*l*. in 1852—a sudden increase which excites little surprise when placed side by side with the increase in the numbers of emi-grants to Australia from 5,744 in 1851 to 57,268 in the follow-ing year; the numbers of Government emigrants out of the whole having risen to 20,313 in 1852, as compared with 3,724 in the preceding year.

There can be no doubt that the task of procuring the best descriptions of labourers and artisans for the Colonies was one of some difficulty, for home employers were unwilling to part with their good workmen, lest their example should be conta-gious, and so should produce a rise in wages all round. Em-ployers, therefore, were sedulous in circulating false statements prejudicial to the Colonies amongst their labourers; and the Commissioners were, by their official constitution, but little fitted to dissipate the prejudices against emigration carefully fostered by artful masters. Indeed, it is certain that the Commissioners did not possess that intimate knowledge of the Colonies which was necessary to enable them to rebut damaging statements privately circulated, and their efforts to do so were neither vigorous or well-directed. Still, even if the difficulty is admitted to the fullest extent claimed, it can-not excuse the conduct of the Commissioners in selecting the *worst* emigrants because they could not *easily* procure the *best*.

There appear to be, then, a formidable list of reasons for excusing the Commissioners from charges of paying unduly high prices for costs of passage ; and indeed it is likely enough that this matter of cost was one with which a body of men at home could deal more satisfactorily than could the colonists themselves. The functions of the Commissioners should have been confined entirely to the chartering of ships—a business which they had peculiar facilities for transacting on more

favourable terms for the colony than could have been made by
any agent sent home, at that time, by any of the colonies,
because of the superior credit granted to the Government
Department by virtue of its position. But, as has been seen,
they were eminently unfitted for the more delicate and infinitely more important business of gauging the real wishes of
the colonists, and of selecting, out of the multitudinous applications before them, the emigrants most likely to be of service
to the colony. The incapacity of the Department was perceived with growing distinctness every year, and when in 1857
Victoria notified her intention of sending home her own emigration agent to supersede the Commissioners—so far as she
herself was concerned—her action in the matter was in perfect
agreement with that of New South Wales and South
Australia. At that time the voluntary emigrants were coming
forward in considerable numbers, and the comparatively small
sums placed on the Estimates of New South Wales and Victoria
for immigration were almost entirely for the purpose of stimulating female emigration so as to equalise as far as possible the
great disproportion between the sexes.

There can be no question as to the disadvantages which an
exceedingly great proportion of men to women entails upon a
community. After the gold-field rushes the disproportion
became more marked than ever, and vigorous efforts were
made to send out single women. Here, again, the old iniquity
of faulty choice became painfully conspicuous, and it was
found that the carelessness of the authorities at home entrusted with the selection of the single women was so culpably
great that, until the colonists became seriously angry with
those who sent out immoral viragoes, and carried out the
resolution to take the matter under their own control, it is
probable that the female immigration left but small balance
of good as the result of its vigorous prosecution.

For several years after the colonists had begun to conduct
the immigration business themselves, the introduction of single
women into the Colonies was the chief business of the Immigration Department, and the appointment of colonial agents
at home, specially selected for their supposed aptitude

or the purpose, and immediately responsible to their employers, was instrumental in procuring a good-class female
immigration. Now, instead of prostitutes being brought out
at the expense of the Colonies, the women assisted with passages were respectable and useful either as wives or servants,
in both of which capacities they were eagerly snapped up.
The rapid social improvement consequent upon this extensive
well-chosen immigration naturally stimulated the voluntary
immigration of women of higher social position, and so by
degrees the relative disproportion between the numbers of the
sexes was reduced to a wholesome equality.

It is not within the scope of the present work to dwell upon
the improved suavity of tone between man and man that resulted from the gradual filtration of female influence through
the rough young colonial communities. Manners were
softened and improved as a matter of course, but probably
the greatest and best effect was that it induced rovers to
become settlers. Men married, found themselves surrounded
with increasing social and domestic comforts, and took thoughtful interest in the new colonial home, now furnishing attractions previously only dreamed of in connection with that
ultimate return to the old country for which every colonist
devoutly prayed. As their families increased, so the novel
allurements towards colonial life resolved themselves into
ties to the soil. The man who had to work for his children
now set to work in earnest if he had never done so before.
Australia had at length grown to be his home, by force of
circumstances, and it had become his business to do the best
for it and for himself. This, then, was the chief good effected
by the reduced disproportion between the sexes, that it made
the colonists settle down and work hard for the prosperity
of Australia, instead of roaming over the face of the land
Micawber-like, trusting to something 'to turn up,' or dashing
headlong into any fresh scheme that might suggest itself to a
fevered imagination as likely to lead to immediate fortune
with the minimum of toil.

In order to confer beneficial results on the Colonies, it was
above all things necessary that the female immigrants should

be respectable and virtuous, capable of becoming intelligent helpmates to men and to themselves in countries where self-denial and physical and mental activity were required for the enjoyment of life or even for procuring an existence. The combination of qualities required for the formation of a society is of a far higher order than that which should be possessed by those who administer the regulations of an existing community. The pioneer female immigrants to the Colonies had before them the task—which Governments cannot hope to achieve with success—of welding into a homogeneous whole innumerable discordant elements; of investing social relations at once with decorum and attractiveness; and of making respect for social observances a bond of cohesion between colonists of whatever grade. To pitchfork into the Australian colonies the most ignorant and abandoned females of the British Isles was not only to delay, but seriously to injure, the structure of society. Where the best women obtainable should have been chosen, the worst only were accepted as emigrants by Commissioners better fitted for the utterance of moral sentiments than for the work of carrying them into execution.

It would be superfluous to attempt to prove that to fill a colony from home with immoral and unintelligent characters of either sex is the most unlikely means of generating mutual feelings of esteem and confidence between the colony and the parent State. The conduct of emigration by the British Government never failed to excite the wrath of the colonists, and had not the former wisely relinquished its claim to control the management of emigration, wrath might have grown into hatred, and hatred into violent antagonism.

CHAPTER VII.

DENATIONALISATION OF THE LAND IN VICTORIA.

It has been seen how the home Government, where it encouraged emigration to New South Wales at all, evinced a marked preference for emigrants of comparatively high social position over those of the labouring and artisan classes. I have endeavoured to show how, under the peculiar circumstances of the convict colony, the aristocratic settlers were but ill fitted to secure the prosperity of the colony in comparison with the capacity and willingness of free labourers to attain that end; and that because the aristocratic class strove to maintain itself *as such*, and succeeded in establishing itself as a caste apart from the mass of the community. In its own exclusive view, therefore, its interests were identified solely with the pecuniary aggrandisement of members of its own body, and it was consequently generally to be found in alliance with those who devoted themselves to crushing popular aspirations by a consistently despotic policy. These aristocratic settlers had procured considerable grants of land to themselves, and by devoting themselves to grazing pursuits had gradually built up a foundation of wealth and possessory rights which, when added to their superiority of social rank, necessarily gained for them a far more overpowering influence with both the home and colonial authorities than was due to their small proportionate numbers. Their influence was unfortunately but naturally thrown into the scale which weighed down the counteracting balance of popular demands, except on the occasional questions in which they conceived their own interests to be identical with those of the population. All-powerful for good or evil, they were assured of governmental support in contesting any popular demand, while they were equally certain of gaining the respectful ear of Downing Street and Government House whatever might be the object to be attained. When free immigrants began to pour in at last, their power as a separate distinctive caste became gradually less and less in the ascendant, and although their existence as a body, separated from the people by class feelings and by their position as landowners, was at all times a menace to the welfare of the colony, the growth of wealth and freedom amongst the mass of increasing population would in all probability have effected the assimilation of the squatter class with the body politic as part and parcel of it, had the natural course of events been allowed an unimpeded issue. But it was not to be so, and the why and wherefore it is the object of the present chapter to narrate.

Previously to 1836 men had squatted where and as they listed. At that time the demand for agricultural produce was very limited as compared with the demand for wool, of which there was a large and growing export, and all the waste lands in the neighbourhood of Sydney were greedily taken up for the purpose of grazing. Attracted by the facilities for plunder afforded by large unfenced tracts sparsely overspread by sheep and cattle, runaway convicts and expirees soon began to ' squat ' on their own individual accounts, having in view the ready possibilities of sheep-stealing and sly grog selling. To admit the legitimate graziers on the lands and to drive away these bad characters was Governor Bourke's object in framing the ' Squatting Act,' as it was termed. By this Act, no one was to be allowed to depasture live stock on the Crown lands unless he had procured a licence for that purpose from the Crown Lands Commissioners. A 10l. fee was payable for this licence, which was renewable annually at the pleasure of the Crown, so that an official check might be imposed upon the character and doings of the licensees. Besides, small semi-annual assessment was, at the instance of the squatters themselves, imposed upon the live stock, in order to defray the costs of a body of police for the squatting districts.

It cannot be denied that sheep and cattle-farming first

brought the Australian colonies into favourable notice with
the outer world, and contributed enormously to secure the
prosperity of the colony ; so that regulations framed with the
view of giving fair play to the squatters were fully deserving
of the best consideration. In so far as grazing was instrumental in developing the resources of the colonies, and in
attracting population thither by giving proofs of the great
wealth-producing capacity of Australia, the pastoral interest
was synonymous with the general interest. That it was so
was in the sequel strangely unfortunate, for the first move
made in the matter of Crown lands occupation was of such a
nature as to bring to the aid of the squatter class the whole
of the popular sympathy of the country.

In 1844, Sir George Gipps, the then Governor of New
South Wales, either with the object of replenishing an empty
Treasury, as is alleged by Dr. Lang, or with the view of giving
he squatter a permanent holding in the land, such as might
operate as an inducement to him to ' settle ' instead of merely
to ' encamp,' and so that at the same time the monopolisation
of the surface of the country by licensees might be prevented,
issued a set of regulations under which it became obligatory
on the squatters to purchase a small portion of their runs
every eight years, at a minimum price of 1*l*. per acre. Also
they were required to take out, not *one* 10*l*. licence to cover
their occupancy of tracts of land, however large, but a separate
10*l*. licence for each area occupied by them which possessed an
estimated capacity for carrying 4,000 sheep. The sting of
these regulations consisted, not in the extra *amount* imposed
by them on the pastoral interest, but in the fact that they were
framed and gazetted without concert, consultation, or even
prior intimation to the Legislature.

The colonists had for long been loud in their claims to administer their own land and the revenues derived from it.
They were daily becoming more self-assertive in their demand
to be permitted to regulate their own affairs in every respect,
and therefore regarded with extreme jealousy any action on
the part of the Government which savoured in the slightest
degree of prerogative. Under the circumstances, it may

readily be believed that these regulations were excellently calculated to provoke in them deep and righteous indignation. However desirable the measures resolved upon might be in themselves was a matter of small importance. Their significance from a political point of view, as imposing taxes upon the people without even the pretence of the consent of their representatives in the Council having been asked or obtained, was alone to be considered. The colonists had been insulted by the contemptuous treatment accorded to their representatives, as well as unfairly treated by unconstitutional action. There was felt to be imminent danger lest the precedent supplied by the Executive of imposing taxation without the concurrence of the Legislative Council—to whom the initiative of recommending taxation belonged—might be extended to every interest in the colony whenever a deficiency of funds had to be made up to the Treasury, and that concurrently with this liability there was no real check upon the extravagance of the home Government.

The squatter cause was at once converted into the cause of the people. The after-action of the Legislative Council in refusing to reinstate the Act for the assessment of live stock, and in expressing their determination not to tax their fellow-colonists ' in a department in which the Executive took upon itself to increase their taxation at its pleasure,' was received with popular acclamation, and the apprehension of further arbitrary proceedings similar to the regulations banded together all classes of the community in common hostility to their arch-enemies the Imperial Government and the imperial representative.

' But,' says Westgarth, ' the circumstance that was eventually attended with most important effects was the formation of " The Pastoral Association." The original object of this body was to place the squatting interest upon a more secure and satisfactory footing. The pecuniary amount involved in the change effected by the Executive was regarded as quite unimportant in the contest. Prosperity dawned apace upon the squatters. They would admit that the rate was not unreasonable, although, perhaps, imposed prematurely; but they protested against the principle by which an irresponsible authority of its own accord, without any notice, without any guaranteed principle of action, could thus impose changes upon a great colonial interest involving an important body of the public. The object therefore was twofold—first, to obtain a guarantee against such arbitrary changes in future, and secondly, to secure the occupants of the pastoral lands against the uncertain and unconstitutional influence of the Commissioners of Crown Lands, who had already been enacting some vexatious and fantastic proceedings among their numerous tenantry. . . . But the views of the squatters enlarged with the prosperity of their cause. By the original understanding, they held their lands until these territories were otherwise required in the progress of the colony, making of them in the meantime what advantage they could, and being subject to no charge save the trifling one for licence and assessment. To render these holdings more satisfactory they had asked for protection against the arbitrary power of the Crown and its agents the Commissioners. They now resolved the still superior position of holding the lands, not only against Commissioners and fellow-squatters, but against the colonial public. When it was resolved to agitate the question before Parliament and the home Government, the squatters had already determined to make a stand for definitive and exclusive leases of the waste lands. The proposal of a term of fourteen years, although at first a subject of some sceptical merriment, became at length a familiar theme ; and as they arrayed the forces they could bring to bear upon the home Government in the battle, hope gradually dawned upon the horizon, and eventually became reality and victory.'[1]

The home Government had through its representative thus put the entire colony in antagonism to itself. It had by its arbitrary mode of acting identified the squatters' cause with that of the community. By so doing it had stimulated pretentious claims, at first deemed worthy of uncriticising derision, and now it was to pose as the ready tool of a class whom, by injudicious treatment, it had stirred up to vigorous

[1] Westgarth's *Victoria, late Australia Felix*, pp. 103, 104.

action for the purpose of procuring for itself alone, to the in-expressible injury of the community, a set of privileges as un-just to the colony as unexpected by the squatters themselves.

Taking advantage of the political support which the peculiar complexion assumed by the land question had for the time assured to them, the squatters pressed their claims upon the home Government with renewed insistance, and, largely by dint of private backstairs influence, they procured for them-selves in 1846 an Act of the Imperial Parliament, followed up in the succeeding year by the famous Orders in Council, by which an amount of injury was inflicted upon the colonial population, especially in Victoria (then known as Port Phillip) which no excuse can palliate or lapse of time thoroughly obviate. The chief features of the Orders in Council of 1847 founded upon the imperial Act were, first, the division of all the Crown lands into three classes—namely, the settled, inter-mediate, and unsettled districts.

The settled lands comprehended that small part of the colony already divided into nineteen counties, and all lands within certain distances of chief towns and other valuable parts of the country. In Victoria, for example, a circuit of twenty-five miles round Melbourne, of fifteen miles round Geelong, and of ten miles round Portland, was to be considered as being within the settled district, as were also lands within three miles inland from the sea-coast. The intermediate dis-tricts comprised the other counties then established or to be established prior to December 31, 1848. The unsettled districts embraced the remainder of the territory.

Secondly, leases to the squatters. The local Government was empowered to expose the runs situated within the settled districts to auction for a lease for each year. The occupants of the intermediate lands were to have eight years' leases, sub-ject to sixty days' notice at yearly intervals, regarding such parts as were required for sale, and those who had runs in the unsettled districts were to be entitled to fourteen years' leases, with a right, if the lands were still unsold, to a second term of fourteen years.

No one in the colony objected to the squatters having

leases made out to them for definite terms of moderate length. It was clearly enough perceived of what vast importance the pastoral interest was to the development of the colony; and it was recognised as being for the welfare of the community that, especially in remote regions, the squatters should have a fair measure of encouragement given them to improve their runs to the best of their capacity; but it was firmly held by the people as an axiomatic principle that the leases should confer nothing beyond *the mere right to graze*. In the popular view the occupant under lease was not to be invested with rights of an exclusive nature over the timber or stone quarries of his run; nor was he to be empowered to prevent the public from searching for minerals thereon, or to impound at will such cattle of neighbouring cultivators as might stray into his domain. The right to use the grass for a certain fixed period was the only right that the people were willing to give, or that the squatter, who had paid highly for his live stock but nothing for his land, could in reason expect. His property was in his sheep and cattle. With them he had been accustomed to wander on from one grazing ground to another until he found unoccupied pasture to suit him, when he built him a homestead and settled down, but all merely as a *stock*, not a *land* proprietor. 'Let him keep his stock,' said the popular voice, 'as a property which belongs to him on every principle of right and justice. Let him even have a recognised exclusive right to depasture his flocks and herds for definite periods of time over such lands as may be necessary for the most profitable production of wool and tallow. Let him keep what he has got by purchase; let a right be conferred upon him to feed his flocks over particular areas in return for the benefits derived by the community at large from the successful results of his occupation.' Thus far the people were in favour of leases, but no further. They wished to encourage the squatters in the successful prosecution of the business of grazing, but they were resolved not to give more than was necessary for the purposes of that business. The grass and water *were* necessary; the soil, the timber, and the impounding rights of the landlord *were not*; for, as the entire population of New South Wales was in 1847 less than 190,000, while that of Victoria was scarcely over 42,000, there was no possible risk of trespassing being carried on on a scale sufficient to impair the grazing capacity of any run, and therefore there was no reason why the squatter should have protecting powers given to him. Moreover, the vast majority of the respective populations of the two divisions resided in Sydney or Melbourne, so there was not the slightest reason to apprehend that any injury would be done to the squatters' business by encroachments on the boundaries of their runs for many years to come. If these were the popular views, what were those of the squatters? Strange to say, they were precisely the same! As will be seen, the injurious effects of the Orders in Council were far more felt in Victoria than in New South Wales, and yet the Victorian squatters had had no hand in the agitation and misrepresentation which procured the Orders. At the very outside they wished for mere grazing leases in lieu of the old licences, and the Orders in Council were for them an unasked-for boon.

But had it been merely a question between leasing a grazing right and leasing the land itself, it is possible enough that the people might have consented to the latter mode if that had stood alone, in the hope that the acquisition of self-government, that seemed now a near prospect, would enable them to correct any injurious results. But the leases were, in the Orders, only the foundation for the regulation that both in the intermediate and in the unsettled districts the lessees might, at any time during the currency of their leases, exercise a *pre-emptive right* over any portion of their runs at 1*l.* per acre. This pre-emptive right was the keystone of the system promulgated in the Orders. A few hundred men were to be permitted to monopolise three-fourths of the whole available territory of New South Wales and Victoria at 1*l.* per acre, while in the settled portion, where the pre-emptive right was not exercisable, the price of land, under the influence of the competition forced on purchasers by the narrowness of the limits open to free bidding, would average many-fold the price of twenty shillings per acre.

It may be as well now to consider the whole question in its most typical form as affecting Victoria rather than the older colony. ' In New South Wales the interspersed areas of unalienated land were either too sterile or too remote to be the subject of much contention, and the vast extent of lands beyond the boundaries might be generally described to the same effect.' In Victoria, on the other hand, the country in nearly every direction was beautiful, fertile, and available for man ; and the land sales had been only commenced, the quantity previously sold being a very inconsiderable fraction of the territory.

According to the latest computation, the area of Victoria is 87,884 square miles, or 56,245,760 acres, and is therefore slightly less than that of Great Britain. Of this extent the land contained in the settled district covered an area of rather more than 2,000,000 acres, and the intermediate and un-settled districts therefore extended over 56,000,000 acres, only a part of which was occupied when the Orders were issued, but the whole of which was then made subject to the opera-tion of pre-emptive rights. Within the comparatively small limits of the settled districts were centred nearly the whole population of the colony, grouped together, principally, in the large towns of Melbourne, Geelong, and Portland. For reasons of convenience, the land returns made to the Victorian Legislature of the lands sold up to July 1851 may be used to illustrate the principal points in the situation. By that re-turn it appeared that of holders of 25,000 acres and upwards there were :—

				£		Acres
339	squatters, who paying an-nually in the aggregate			3,470	held for this sum	4,599,304
256	do.	do.		3,420	do.	12,443,121
54	do.	do.		990	do.	7,751,707
11	do.	do.		320	do.	4,670,108
Totals 660	do.	do.		£8,200	do.	29,464,240

Besides these there were seven persons who refused to return the quantities of land they held. This shows an enormous disproportion between the lands occupied by the squatters,[1]

[1] The total amount of stock returned as depastured over this immense

which were locked up from the people by pre-emptive rights, and the small area over which the members of a rapidly-growing population could only acquire land by raising prices by free bidding against each other. Over the whole of these twenty-nine millions and a half of acres—more than a moiety of the lands of the colony—these 660 occupiers were given pre-emptive rights, and not only that, but any man could, under the Orders, take up the unoccupied remainder of the unsettled districts, and the simple fact of his doing so and paying a small licence fee would entitle him to the right to purchase the land at 1*l*. per acre. True, it was provided that a valuation should be made of the land over which the pre-emptive right was exercisable, but good entertainment and a certain fellow-feeling between the squatter and the Valuing Commissioner, as well as a little judicious hoodwinking, could easily be brought to bear to secure a valuation which might be low or high according as the squatter's pleasure was to buy himself or to prevent others from buying.

It cannot be denied that the Orders were in great part due to the extreme ignorance of local conditions that distinguished the framers of them. Misrepresentation on the part of the agents of the Pastoral Association at home had led the imperial authorities to believe that beyond the settled districts the lands of the colony were utterly worthless. Thus Port Phillip was classed with the barren parts of New South Wales, and the fertile lands of the former were made subject to rules framed primarily to suit the waste territory of the latter. Driblets of limited extent were here and there reserved in the intermediate districts in the supposed interests of the agricultural population, and nothing could be more suggestive of the culpable recklessness of the authors of the Orders than the way in which these reservations were determined. Let Dr. Lang give us an example :—

territory, exceptionally rich as a large portion of it was in nutritious grasses, and not affected by lengthened droughts, was not more than 5,550,000. In Hayter's *Victorian Year Book* the total quantity for 1852 is put down at 7,000,000, but I prefer taking the returns of the day, whether accurate or not, as more thoroughly exemplifying the position which the land conflict assumed in the minds of men at the time.

From Sydney to the Tropic of Capricorn— that is, for ten degrees of latitude, or nearly 700 miles along the sea coast—there are not fewer than twelve rivers, all available to a certain extent for steam navigation, on one of which, the Richmond river, in latitude 28½° south, and on its principal tributaries, there are not fewer than 300 miles of navigable water. Now, I suggested that a clause should be inserted into the Orders in Council, exempting all lands within four miles of navigable water from the operation of the Squatting Act. A measure of that kind would have encouraged and promoted the settlement of an agricultural community in the very locality in which the land, while unavailable for squatting purposes, is usually best adapted for cultivation, and in which the facilities for steam navigation render the settlement of such a population highly desirable.

But the Emigration and Land Commissioners, refining upon my ideas, as they thought, but in entire ignorance of the subject, made it an Order in Council that two miles on either side of the Richmond river down to its mouth should be reserved from the operation of the Squatting Act for the settlement of an agricultural population. Had my suggestion been simply embodied as it stood in the Orders in Council, numerous families of cedar-cutters then on the river, who were left unfortunately to a life of vagabondism, dissipation, and ruin, would have purchased small farms by its navigable waters, transferring the country into a perfect garden and themselves into an orderly and virtuous population. But the Richmond river, running parallel to the coast line, for twenty miles from its mouth is still within five miles of the sea, and the whole of the intervening land on either side of it is a dismal swamp affording no means of sustenance either for man or beast.[1]

According to their own computation, the squatters paid in the aggregate for their enormous holdings the amount of 30,000*l*. annually, partly in payment for licences, and partly in payment of an assessment of one halfpenny per sheep. No other payments were made by them to the colony for the privilege of depasturing, and everything, over and above the cost of carriage and superintendence, that their flocks could produce went into their pockets as clear profit. As the price of wool then averaged from 3s. to 4s. 6d. per pound, while each sheep might be expected to give two or three pounds of wool, to say nothing of the proceeds of sales of young stock, which even in these expensive days of wire-fencing and land-taxing usually cover the entire yearly expenses of a station, and not to mention the gain from boiling down into tallow, the profit must, to say the least, have constituted a handsome return for an average annual payment of 1*l. per thousand acres.*

In comparison with the thousandth part of a pound paid yearly per acre, the purchase price imposed as a condition of the pre-emptive right may seem high, and, so far as regarded great part of New South Wales, and every here and there small tracts in Victoria, it was undoubtedly so high as to be prohibitive to any purchaser. But the major portion of Victoria was considered to be worth far more than 1*l.* per acre to any man who had the means to stock or cultivate it. Up to July 1851 the average price realised for lands sold in the colony by public auction had been over 3*l.* per acre ; and taking private sales together with the others, the average had been 2*l.* per acre. Of course the high price of town and suburban lots in and about the principal towns had helped to raise the average, but against this must be set the fact that large quantities of land had been sold in blocks of 5,000 to 20,000 acres at upset price in the days when the upset price was 5*s.* and afterwards 12*s.* per acre, and at the time when the population was a mere fraction of what it was in 1851. Further, in the intermediate and unsettled districts were many localities where land forming part of squatters' runs was, by reason of its proximity to a township or market centre, in eager demand at prices varying from 5*l.* or 8*l.* to 100*l.* per acre. Although, therefore, a squatter holding several thousand acres might, through want of capital, be unable to purchase his holding outright, his lease and pre-emptive right together might be the means of keeping land locked up for which many bidders would be anxious to compete. The squatter, too, could almost certainly procure an advance on his ' clip ' to the full value of it from bankers and agents, and could purchase portions of his run in chessboard pattern, enclosing the water frontages so as to render the remaining portions of it worthless to a purchaser. He had another advantage given him which was quite as operative as the actual payment of money to keep his run in his own hands. If he improved his run a purchaser would have to compensate him for improvements by paying an increased price. So by digging a few water-holes, forming a rough road at small expense, or by fencing in part of his outlying boundaries, he could get his whole run valued at a price far above the capacity of any but the wealthiest capitalists. Or, again, he might purchase at the Government price a few acres in an exceptionally advantageous position, and so force an unwilling purchaser, to whom the land was a necessity, to buy those acres at an enormous advance. 'This,' said Mr. John Bingley in a letter of complaint to Earl Grey, ' is no hypothetical case, but one which to a certain extent has been already realised. A squatter in the neighbourhood of Colac had, as he himself reports, acquired by his privilege of pre-emption a section of land adjoining that township, and commanding all its supply of water, at the Government minimum price, while the next adjoining section, being divided into small portions, was sold at prices varying from 5l. to 20l. per acre a few days previous to his purchase, and within a week after he authorised an agent to offer it at 5l. per acre to persons who had attempted in vain to purchase it direct from the Crown at a regular land sale. These facts, incredible as they appear, I am prepared to prove on the spot by the oath of the gentleman whose application to purchase was refused and to whom the land has since been offered by the purchaser at 5l. per acre.' Mr. Bingley's illustration went to the very root of the general popular complaint, and typified a condition of things which was not only usual but which was the necessary consequence of the perfunctory drawing-up of the Orders in Council. Why this should have been so is capable of easy demonstration.

The Orders were published in New South Wales in October 1847, and regulations were made under them directing claims for leases by existing occupiers to be handed in within six months from that date. By an oversight, however, which would have been extraordinary had not the fault been that of a Government department at home which knew nothing about the Colonies, and was absolutely careless as to what complications might arise from ill-considered legislation, *no provision whatever had been made for establishing proper boundaries between the several districts, and no survey had ever been made of the limits of the several runs.* In the sparsely-peopled, uncleared, and largely unexplored territories over which rights of lease and pre-emption were given to a handful of men, no survey had been made, and approximate areas or supposititious boundaries could not be made the basis of descriptions of particular runs even to the satisfaction of the squatters themselves. The whole of an immense area might have but a small water frontage, and no squatter would tamely submit to a mode of description which might include within his neighbour's run the cherished portion of water frontage which he considered essential to the success of his own grazing business. By the end of 1849, more than a year and a quarter after the local publication of the Orders, the classification of the settled, intermediate, and unsettled districts had been determined ; but the far larger matter of the limits of runs was still left undecided.

The applications for leases having been sent in and gazetted, a local Act[1] was passed in New South Wales under which Commissioners were appointed to examine into the boundary claims. About one-seventh of the total number of applications were disputed by the lodging of caveats against them, and the Commissioners had every prospect of plenty of work. Surveys were now to be made at a cost pre-ordained by the Governor of 2*l.* per linear mile, a rate which was so ridiculously excessive that six months later—after full time for a consideration that might have been accorded beforehand —it was reduced to ten shillings a linear mile, a rate as far below as the existing one was above existing requirements. This low rate was of itself sufficient to ensure indefinite pro- traction of the surveying operations, and, independently of that, it was soon found that no practicable extension of the survey staff could effect the object without interminable delay. Shortly afterwards, it being evident that a considerable time

---

[1] Disputed Boundaries Act, June 1848.

must elapse before leases could issue, even under the most favourable circumstances, the Governor issued a notice sanctioning the purchase under pre-emptive right of certain portions of runs, beyond the ' settled ' districts, for which proper applications for leases had been sent in.

In the meantime two additional Orders in Council[1] had been issued authorising the squatters to transfer their leases under certain conditions, and extending the privilege of limited pre-emption to occupants of Crown lands beyond the settled districts for other than pastoral purposes, as well as to certain squatters whose runs had been unexpectedly included by the Orders within the settled districts, and also authorising the issue of annual leases to occupants of Crown lands for other than pastoral purposes throughout the colony. The regulations ultimately issued in Victoria, after separation, to carry out this Order, bore date December 9, 1851.

The nature of the main hindrances which were necessarily opposed to the prompt issue of leases may now be briefly stated in Lieutenant-Governor La Trobe's own words :—[2]

The nature of the legal instrument contemplated, and of the conditions under which it was to be held, demanded, in the words of a Government notice on this subject, ' that the boundaries should be sufficiently defined to satisfy the rule of the law which holds any grant or conveyance from the Crown to be absolutely null and void if the property to be conveyed be not described with certainty and correctness.' Of the 826 claims first enrolled up to June 30, 1848, it is not probable that one-eighth part assigned boundaries of this character. The great majority were neither accompanied by a clear definition of boundary or area ; and even where attempts were made to give the former there was every probability that one line or other might be disputed. Many were of the vaguest description. When the circumstances under which the country was so recently taken up are considered, this can scarcely be matter of surprise.

Moreover, before any detailed surveys of runs preparatory to the issue of leases could be undertaken, it was necessary, not only that the general features of the province, which included many rugged and

<hr>

[1] July 18, 1849; published in the colony in April 1850. Second notice, June 19, 1850; published in the colony in February 1851.

[2] Despatch of September 3, 1852.

mountainous tracts, should be correctly laid down, but that the proposed reserves to be exempted from lease should be clearly defined. Every practicable extension of the Survey Department made to this end could only secure a certain progress. The latter duty involved a far closer knowledge of the details of the country than could be possibly obtained without much time and labour.

The disputed Boundary Act of June 1848, and the trouble and expense which it entailed upon both the Government and individuals, was not productive of the advantages which might have been anticipated. In fact, as far as Port Phillip was concerned, the time had hardly arrived when it could have been made generally effective. It is true, as I have before stated, a certain number of caveats were entered, examinations made, and decisions given. But a great number of these were felt, both by the Commissioners and the parties concerned, to be inconclusive and unsatisfactory, from the fact that no actual survey of boundaries or of lines in dispute had been made, or could be achieved under the circumstances. Further, it was generally conceded that a very large number of questionable boundaries were never brought forward for supposed adjustment, in many cases because one or other of the parties really interested would not take the trouble to come forward, and in others because until actual survey of what was really claimed on either hand the existence of any cause for dispute might remain unsuspected. There are large tracts of country in the province without any marked physical features whatever sufficient to form or clearly indicate boundaries of runs, not only on the plains but in the ranges; and where this is the case nothing but actual survey will obviate discrepancies and overlappings and render the limits of runs undoubted.

To make matters worse, and to throw yet greater doubt upon the effect of the measure, and the decisions arrived at by the Caveat Commissioners on examination of disputes, as far as might be, purely upon their merits and bearings upon the Government regulations and prescriptions, divers of these decisions were reversed by actions at law.

Thus it happened that the Home Government, by their Orders of 1847, had given away territories which the terms of their own notice [1] had precluded them from dealing with either by way of lease or grant. They were pledged to issue leases to the squatters, and yet they could not carry their pledge into execution until vast regions, of the physical features of which they were for the most part totally ignorant,

[1] January 1, 1850.

had been accurately surveyed by a very limited surveying staff. Without the very slightest knowledge of the capacity or resources of the country, without having made the smallest effort to ascertain either the one or the other, with not the most remote conception of the topography of the land beyond the outskirts of Sydney and Melbourne, the Home Government had promised the whole of it to a few hundred men, and ignorantly regardless of what might be its value in the immediate future, they had placed upon it a fixed, unalterable price. Even the mode of sale urgently pressed upon the colonial authorities by successive Secretaries of State as essential to colonial prosperity—that by public auction—had been made to give way to the system of sale most condemned by them—that by private valuation between the Crown and the vendee. And all this merely to gratify the wildest dreams, as they themselves regarded them, of a small clique, whose hope in asking much had been to obtain a little, and who were now to be rewarded with a more than ample recognition of their demands—a recognition which was certain to place them in bitter antagonism to the vast majority of the population, and to provoke a spirit of uncompromising hostility to the Home Government itself. And for whom was this monstrous injustice perpetrated? 'For a few men,' said John Pascoe Fawkner, 'who have not done any one act for this colony or for this people to entitle them to such undue advantages as they claim—namely, to hold possession of nearly 60,000,000 acres of land, a great part of which is rich agricultural land, for which to the extent of from 3l. to 4l. per acre would have been given at public auction, had not the squatter interfered and prevented the sale after the lands were advertised, and people collected at the auction-room from fifty miles distant prepared to buy these lands.'

'The squatter,' he adds, 'has not done any act to entitle him to hold his eight or nine hundredth part of near 60,000,000 acres for his proportionate share of 14,000l. a year'—the extreme total amount paid for licences, on the

---

[1] Letter to the Governor in 1852.

squatters' own showing—'and it is a well-known fact that the land cultivated by the squatters is worth far more than this sum yearly, 5s. per acre being the lowest sum annually paid in the interior for poor land to graze stock upon—that is to say, wherever the lands *are* sold.

'The squatter has not made any roads, nor paid for making any; the squatter has not paid any money to import emigrants from Great Britain or Ireland, but he has done so to import pagans and savages from China, from India, and from the South Sea Islands.[1]

'The present squatters, with very few exceptions, did not explore the country, did not venture their lives amongst the simple aborigines; and the early squatters who did assist to found this country and open up this colony received no reward or encouragement save a yearly licence to graze their flocks and herds; and the men in truth and sober fact who have ousted the earlier settlers have been rewarded with what should have fallen to the real squatter settlers who explored the country.'

Principally owing to the initiative of Mr. Robert Lowe,[2] a measure was passed disenabling the Governor from issuing leases until the boundaries had been properly determined in accordance with the notice of January 1850. A few days subsequent to the promulgation of the famous Orders in Council, but before the six months within which applications for leases were to be sent in, proclamation had been made of the sale by public auction of certain lots of land in the county of Grant. These lands had been surveyed, and marked out for general sale when occasion offered, five or six years previously. Under the regulations then existing it had been competent to the Government at any time to bring them into the market, although until they were sold they were left in the occupation and covered by the annual depasturing licence of the licensees; and this was their position at the time when

[1] The importation of yellow-skinned and dark-skinned labour does not appear to me at all reprehensible. However, it was odious to Mr. Fawkner, whose letter is expressive of the popular feeling of that day. [Author.]
[2] Now Lord Sherbrooke.

they were, at the request of private individuals, applied for to be sold. These lands, as it happened, turned out to be in the intermediate district, and therefore the licensees applied to have them withdrawn from sale on the ground that they were entitled to a lease of them. The opinion of the law officers of the colony was in favour of the sale being held, but the colonial Government, aware of the home bias in favour of the squatters, decided to avoid the chance of possible censure by withdrawing the lands from auction. No doubt it was questionable in the extreme whether, under the Orders in Council, the land could legally be sold, but a strong local Government, if its own sympathies had been with the popular cause, would never have consented to a withdrawal fraught with consequences certain to be fatal to the immediate prospects of the settlement of the colony. For the withdrawal was a precedent which, if acted upon in other cases, would have the inevitable effect of locking up from sale all the lands in the intermediate districts for which leases might be claimed. Several other cases, precisely similar to this first one, afterwards occurred. In all of them it was contended by the advocates of popular rights that until the leases had been actually issued outside purchasers were entitled to bid for lands in the intermediate district, while it was maintained on the other side that the conditional promise of a lease was equivalent to its actual issue.

That the promise was in no case unconditional can hardly admit of a doubt, for the Governor could, under his powers, exercise some discretion as to the persons to whom he should grant leases, and he had an unfettered authority as to the duration of the lease within the maximum limits specified in the Orders. If, then, under any conceivable circumstances, the Governor had a discretionary power of withholding a lease, no man could assert a right to one until the discretion had been determined in his favour; and until the Governor had irrevocably fixed the duration of a lease, no man could say, as matter of law, that he was in the virtual position of a lessee for a definite term, and that at the particular moment at which a sale took place he was possessed of rights paramount to those of the vendor—the Government—so as to oblige the latter to withdraw the land from sale. Moreover, the opinion of the Attorney-General of Victoria [1] was that it did not admit of question that the Governor might make sale of these lands if they were required ' for facilitating the settlement of the colony.' On the first point the law officers subsequently gave another opinion contradictory of their previous one, now stating that ' we are of opinion that until a lease of the land has been granted and has either expired by lapse of time, or been determined by notice as provided in the Orders, no portion of it could be legally put up for sale.'

Action was immediately taken in accordance with this opinion, and, says Mr. La Trobe,[2]

The consequence has been unfavourable to the interests of the public.

The Government has considered itself disabled from effecting sales in every instance where the individual, whose temporary interest might be supposed affected, thought proper to exercise the right thus conceded him of keeping land out of the market for what might be an indefinite period.

Not only has individual enterprise received a check, but the gradual development of the resources of the country, in one quarter or other, has been seriously retarded, the public interests and requirements being temporarily set aside and made subservient to what must, in truth, be considered the private interests of individuals.

This state of things has been productive of considerable dissatisfaction, and I think that the concession now made in favour of the squatter, enabling him to exercise a right which he could, in strict law, only expect to exercise after the issue of his lease, at the same time that the public remains strictly shut out from the exercise of the privilege of purchase of land in the 'intermediate' district, which would be secured to it by the provision of the Orders in Council after that lease were issued, may form a very just subject of complaint. . . .

There are localities marked as reserves, portions of which are urgently required for the public use, were it only for the establishment of inns and other facilities to the settlement of the country districts, which the gradual growth of the province requires, but which, under the circumstances stated, cannot be made available for sale for

---

[1] Mr. W. G. Plunket's opinion in 1848.
[2] Despatch of July 22, 1850.

an indefinite period, at the same time that the obstacles which stand in the way of the issue of occupation licences disables the Government from attending to the public wants by that temporary expedient.

This was the expression of the opinion of a Governor by no means celebrated for his popular sympathies, and who by his position was bound to criticise existing regulations with mildness rather than with acerbity.

The people were prevented from getting at the land outside the settled district except by purchasing at an enormous advance on 1*l.* per acre the land, or the rights to it, secured to the squatters at that price. But how fared it with the squatters? The situation was productive of the greatest dissatisfaction even to the members of that specially favoured class.

Let us take their own view of the position in which the Orders had placed them. They divide the effects following from the delay in the issue of leases under two heads, diametrically differing from each other in kind, as follows :—

1. By reference to Lord Grey's despatch dated November 29, 1846, it will be seen that the special object contemplated by the new Orders in Council was to present inducements to the settler to make permanent improvements on his run, so as to accommodate a larger amount of stock; but it is notorious that few persons have engaged in such enterprises, from the uncertainty of their position, and the doubts which they have justly entertained as to the issue of leases, and consequently they cannot be said to have enjoyed all the privileges intended to have been conferred upon them ; neither have they been able to dispose of their stock and stations to the same advantage in the public market of the colony as they would have done had the faith of the Government been fulfilled.

2. On the other hand, there are persons who have placed a more unlimited faith in the pledges of the Government, and have made improvements on their runs, or purchased new runs, on the expectation of a definite and guaranteed enjoyment for a number of years. Such cases present examples of vested interests created on the faith of the Crown, and ought not to be disturbed on any consideration of mere expediency, without an equivalent compensation.[1]

Such, then, was the result so far of the unjustifiable and

---

[1] Minute of arguments addressed to the Lieutenant-Governor at an audience afforded by a number of squatters on August 3, 1852.

ill-conceived measures of the home Government for depriving the then and the future population, in perpetuity, of the lands of the colony. Never was there a more solid proof of the folly of attempting to direct the affairs of the colony from a department of State many thousands of miles distant. The representations of a small knot of New South Wales squatters who knew little or nothing of the circumstances of the neighbouring colony were held, at the Colonial Office, to be all that was requisite to justify the adoption of the same measures for both colonies.

It was barely a decade since Batman and Fawkner had inaugurated the settlement of Victoria. We know now how little was known of the interior of the country within the first ten or twelve years, for although individuals had penetrated to remote parts of it, scarcely one of them was capable of scientifically investigating the future possibilities of the soil or of devoting himself to the most elementary form of surveying, and but few of them troubled themselves to record their experiences for the benefit of the general public. So far as official knowledge was concerned, any systematic classification of the broad general features of the colonies was entirely supposititious. Distances and heights were approximate only. Rivers were mapped out where their courses were surmised to be ; and it was a moot point whether the greater part of the land far inland was covered with dense scrub, whether it was a collection of barren stony ridges, or abounding in rich agricultural and pastoral soils. Of the geological character of the interior nobody did or could know anything. Whether the colony rejoiced in golden treasures and in other minerals were matters as to which no one could do more than hazard a conjecture. This dearth of knowledge might well have rendered the official mind fearful of legislating for the colony, until at least *some* information was procurable to allow of the formation of opinions as to what the country was really like and what might be expected from it. Instead of this, the home Government rushed into legislation to be applied to Port Phillip, not legislation of a tentative order, but of a kind which was to regulate at once, decisively and unalterably, the

whole future of the colony, and such as, if they had possessed
a small share of local knowledge, the law-makers would themselves have condemned as the extreme of lunacy.

The Orders in Council satisfied nobody. They had raised
up hopes on the one hand which could not be satisfied, and
had, on the other hand, excited sullen discontent capable of
ripening into a more active form by taking from the people
that which they regarded as their own property. 'The
further acquisition of land through great part of the colony
was thenceforth to assume the aspect of an incessant battle
with parties in actual possession, who either set their disturbers
at defiance by pre-emptive ingenuities, or challenged them to
prove an adequate public necessity for the interference with
their rights in the ungracious task of destroying a vocation
that had been the mainspring of the colony.' [1]

How vast were the evil consequences which might be produced by the carrying out of the Orders in their integrity was
not fully perceived until the discovery of gold brought a sudden and vast rush of population. The gold-fields were almost
uniformly in those intermediate and unsettled districts where
the public had been forbidden to trespass. Now was confusion
worse confounded. The surveying staff went off to the diggings
like all the rest of the world, so no surveying could be done,
and the prospect of the issue of leases became more remote
every day. But the tension of the situation became greater,
for although many diggers were successful, a great many were
remarkably unfortunate, and these last felt keenly how greatly
the locking up of the lands contributed to the cost of living
on the gold-fields. A tent full of stores was second in value
only to a tent full of the gold itself. Flour, which could be
purchased in Melbourne at 20*l.* a ton, was sold in Bendigo at
the rate of 200*l.* a ton. These high prices were largely instrumental in causing, even whilst the yield of gold remained un-
diminished, a substantial subtraction from average gains; and
they were to a large extent due to the chaotic state to which
the Orders in Council had reduced the country during the past
four years, so that no proper roads had within that period

[1] Westgarth's *Victoria, late Australia Felix*, p. 120.

been constructed even in the settled districts. In June 1852 the rates of carriage rose to 120l. per ton, and contracts were said to have been freely made at 150l. per ton. The squatters afterwards took to themselves great credit for having supplied an abundance of beef and mutton to the crowds of gold-diggers, but it was a virtue that brought large profits in the way of enhanced prices of meat, and it opened the eyes of the diggers to the vast capabilities of profit rendered possible to those who had the exclusive possession of the land, inspiring them with a wish to possess themselves of a portion of it, while it also forcibly impressed them with the fact that pastoral settlement had prevented agricultural settlement, and that consequently agricultural produce was only obtainable at vast expense. How important it was that agricultural produce should be supplied from the neighbourhood of the growing towns rapidly arising in the mining districts will at once appear from the consideration that during six months of 1852 no less than three-quarters of a million sterling were paid for the *mere carriage* of the necessaries of life to the gold-fields—exclusive of beef and mutton, which were supplied, so to speak, on the premises.

Besides this, the miners found themselves obliged to pay 30s. a month each for a piece of ground measuring sixty-four square feet, in the midst of land for which the squatters were paying less than a farthing per acre, with the right of buying the fee simple of the whole, enhanced as it might be in value by contiguity to the mining township, at the ridiculously low price of 1l. per acre.

It has been seen how under two additional Orders in Council[1] the squatters had been empowered to transfer their leases, or rather their rights to leases, under certain conditions, and also to exercise their pre-emptive rights over a portion of their runs independently of the after issue of leases. It was therefore open to them to deal with their lands pretty much as if they had been made over to them. For they might either sell a portion or the whole of their rights to lease, or

[1] Published locally on April 26, 1850, and February 1851, respectively.

they might, where not entitled to do so, lock their lands up
from purchase; or, again, they might buy up a part of their
runs at 1*l.* an acre, and sell it again to a competing crowd
who could not get a large supply put up to public auction, in
small driblets at a great profit. These pre-emptive rights had
been exercised to a considerable extent over the more fertile
lands in the neighbourhood of the gold-fields, and miners or
farmers wishing to acquire land in these districts could only
do so by buying it direct at fancy prices from the squatters
who had just got it at the minimum price. Every one at the
gold-fields—that is, nine-tenths at least of the whole population—was interested in getting cheap tillage and an immediate
supply of produce in the vicinity. The money derived from
the sale of lands prior to the Orders of 1847 had been expended
in great measure in introducing labour for the squatters, and
very little of it had been devoted to purposes of road-making
or other internal improvements; hence the extravagant rates
of 80*l.*, 100*l.*, and even 150*l.* per ton, charged to the miners
for the carriage of agricultural produce and other requisites
of existence; and, as one way of reducing the cost of mining
so as to make it a profitable occupation, it was absolutely
necessary to inaugurate extensive farming around the gold-
fields themselves. So men were found willing to pay the
high prices for agricultural lands about Bendigo, Mount
Alexander, and Ballarat demanded by the squatters. But
when they had got the land they found that farming was by no
means such a profitable speculation as they had anticipated.
For every farmer had to possess a certain stock of horses,
cattle, sheep, and pigs, requiring pasturage over a considerable
acreage. The commonage reserves for this purpose were
absurdly inadequate, and the stock had to be fed on the produce, which otherwise would have been eagerly bought in the
market. Around the dearly-purchased farm lay rich pasture
land on which, as yet, no sheep had ever fed—for, as has been
observed, the flocks and herds in the possession of the squatters
were totally insufficient to cover the worst grazing land in
Victoria, while the rich grasses of the western district in
which lay the principal gold-fields, could have supplied food

for many times the number of head depastured on them. But the Orders in Council were strict and precise in preventing the buyers of land and their tenants from grazing on any un-bought lands. The farmer, therefore, when he put his work-ing team, for example, out to graze, had either to undergo the expense and labour of fencing his boundaries around, and of superintending their proper repair, or he had to run the risk of his team straying on to the adjoining ' waste lands ' so called. The squatter, on his part, was prompt to pounce on these four-footed trespassers and to charge fourpence damage, and frequently from one shilling to ten shillings per head for driving the plough-horses and oxen to the pound, even where it was less than a mile distant. These proceedings being profitable to the squatter, but ruinous to the farmer, engen-dered constant disputes ; and as the magistrates before whom they were determined were themselves of the squatter class, and animated by feelings of uncompromising hostility to farmers and miners, the decisions in these cases tended still further to aggravate the bad blood between the different sets of colonists.

The settled districts contained, by computation, rather over 2,000,000 acres, and it was contended by the monopolists that the land situate within them were those that should be sold, if required ' for facilitating the settlement of the colony,' before the lands in the intermediate and unsettled districts could be touched. But a great part of the settled district was sterile and utterly unfitted for agriculture. Besides, it was far from the region where the conflux of miners had formed the chief centres of demand. It would indeed be a novel rule of political economy that should lay down the advisability of production being conducted at the most remote distances from the pur-chasing market, if baldly stated ; but it was attempted to apply it in all its literalness to the colony of Victoria. The consequences were such as might without difficulty have been foreseen. In one part of the country, where the customary barrenness had given place to an area of rich well-watered soil, crops were rotting on the ground, partly because of the immense cost of procuring labour from the distant gold-fields

to harvest them, partly because there was no market immediately adjacent to which the farm produce could be taken
without the risk of spoiling in the transit. In another part
were closely-packed masses of men craving for agricultural
food, and who, unable to procure it cheap and fresh from the
fertile waste around, had to pay enormous prices for it when,
stale and unnutritious, it finally arrived at the gold-fields after
a lengthy toilsome transit. So the districts which did not
want farmers were full of them, and in those where farmers
were urgently wanted farms could not be got except by
private contract involving so large an expenditure and such
harassing restrictions that would-be purchasers were frightened
off, and it resulted that the supply of farm produce from the
neighbourhood could rarely suffice for the local demand.
Many hundreds, perhaps thousands, of people—shepherds,
miners, and persons of all sorts—had frugally saved their
earnings in the hope of buying land on which they could set
up as farmers, and in the reaction of their disappointment at
finding that they could not acquire land in the only parts of
the colony where farming could pay, they recklessly set to work
to 'knock down their cheques,' as the expression was, in one
long bout of drink. These proceedings on their part were
welcomed and encouraged by the squatters, who saw that by
this improvidence men of small means were again obliged to
earn a livelihood as labourers, and they congratulated themselves on the circumstance as ensuring to them an unfailing
supply of labour, while at the same time giving them increased
facilities for extending their own monopoly. Thus the limitation of the purchasable area of land contributed to the formation of habits of vice which it was directly to the supposed
interest of the squatter to stimulate by insisting still further
on his privileges.

'Extend the settled districts,' clamoured the people, ' to
parts more settled than the settled districts themselves.' But
this extension would have endangered the application of the
economical rule—of discouraging production except at the
greatest possible distances from markets—to which the home
and local Governments had given their adhesion ; so the plan

went no further than discussion and adverse vote in the squatter-driven Legislative Council of the day. Besides, to extend the settled districts would have been to encroach on the principle sanctioned by the Orders in Council, and such a thing was not to be contemplated with equanimity.

The necessity for such extension was becoming more apparent every day. The demand for land in the interior was rising with the advent of each fresh emigrant shipload, and while a larger number of people than ever were on the gold-fields, a larger proportion of the whole were beginning to find gold-mining an unprofitable pursuit, and were looking eagerly around for the opportunity of acquiring small blocks of land on easy terms in the unsettled districts. The squatters' terms rose responsive to the demand. They could now lease un-stocked areas, for rentals varying from 100*l.* to 500*l.* a year, to other persons desirous of taking to the grazing business, and could sell or let small lots for agriculture at proportionately high rates. Also, by reason of the enormous quantities of land that had been thrown open to them for purchase at the minimum price of 1*l.* per acre, without competition, the value of lands of a similar kind which had been purchased at public auction at a much higher rate had been sensibly depreciated, to the great injury of the proprietors. And this because, on the thing of most fluctuating value in the colony, the land, the Government had put a value fixed as between itself and a few individuals, while those few in turn might retail it as what it was—*the one thing* in the colony that was most susceptible to extreme variation in value.

In an old settled country there might be comparatively little difficulty in estimating the value of land over a short term of years; but even there any attempt to settle beforehand the price that land might be worth a quarter of a century on, could never be more than conjectural. Within the last twenty or thirty years the variations and the ultimate rise in land values in many of the most thickly-populated districts of England have been such as no prophet could have ventured to predict at the beginning of the period, and it would be equally impossible to forecast any future value with confidence. But in a new country situated as Victoria was, undergoing changes of unexampled rapidity and subjected to the influence of an extraordinary course of events, nothing could be more un-certain than the value of land property.

'It is impossible,' says Mr. La Trobe, 'to value that the value of which has never been tested, and for the estimate of which no certain and fixed data of any description exist. The land which to-day is valued and fixed at 1*l.* is seen before a month's end to be estimated at 50*l.*' Yet it was this virgin territory, teeming with wealth of all kinds, of which the value could by no possibility be conjectured even for the moment, and which a slight preliminary examination might have ascer-tained as excellently fitted for the future home of thousands upon thousands of English men and women, that, without a moment's hesitation on the part of a home Government which delighted to pose ' as trustee for the inhabitants of the empire [1] of the vast colonial possessions, et cetera,' was made over to a handful of squatters, in defiance of the rights of future generations as well as of those of the then scanty population. Not that plenty of warning was withheld from the Govern-ment as to the gross impolicy and injustice of the application of the Orders to Victoria, not only by the oldest settler then living in that colony, John Pascoe Fawkner, but by their own representative Governor—to say nothing of numerously-signed petitions forcibly presenting the true situation and foreshadow-ing the more immediate inevitable consequences.

A few extracts from the correspondence in the Blue-Books will best exemplify the nature of the warnings conveyed, the relative positions of the squatters and the people, and also afford cogent illustrations of some of the salient points at issue. Nor will the language be found intemperate or the pro-positions on the popular side at all illiberal :—

Only fancy [writes Mr. Fawkner [2]] the fee simple of this fine pro-vince vested in one thousand persons- -a country capable of supporting in peace, plenty, and contentment many millions of the human family.

My advice is, and it is the counsel of an old colonist, one of the

---

[1] Despatch from Earl Grey in 1851.
[2] Letter to Earl Grey, written at commencement of 1851.

year 1803, that in no instance shall a lease be given to any man for more than fifty thousand acres, and that no man shall hold more than one lease.

Facts are good weapons I trust, and these are facts, my Lord.

In 1835, a poor but industrious man came over to Port Phillip to settle, shortly after I had founded Melbourne; that is, he brought with him fifty-three sheep, as he himself then told me, of his own, and a flock of some hundreds of which he was only overseer. Shortly after his arrival, say in 1836, another stockholder landed with four hundred sheep. The man with the four hundred sheep was shut in and kept closed until he had only about seven thousand to eight thousand acres of land on which to run his flocks and herd; but the man of fifty-three sheep, as I find by the returns published in 1848, claimed in the unsettled districts no less than four runs, each of fifty thousand acres, and another run in the settled districts of say twenty to twenty-five thousand acres.

Thus you see the wisdom of the officers holding power here, and the grasping spirit of the monopolist.

I have no hesitation in saying that one of those runs of fifty thousand acres was quite competent to the agistment of all the sheep this man then had, and that the other four runs authorised by the local Government to this forestaller were not occupied by sufficient stock to consume the grass; consequently a serious loss was inflicted on the colony, for many persons were prevented from becoming stockholders, and from benefiting themselves, as well as providing for and inducing their friends to emigrate.

If these people get their leases of these vast quantities of land they will stock them very leisurely, or else they will partly ruin the new-comer by selling or letting him parts of these runs at very high, nay at enormous, rates as compared with the sums they pay to the Crown. This is daily taking place; the squatters when they sell their right of grazing, a ten pound a year licence, frequently charge from one to five hundred pounds for their right. What right? how acquired? Let them show, I say—a right only got by favouritism upon monopoly.

Then, if leases are granted, great care must be taken that the right of the leaseholder only extends to the use of the land for the sole purpose of grazing.

Already, my Lord, it is whispered amongst the class squatter, that they will not allow people to cut timber on the lands they thus claim to hold; and now it is a fact that may perhaps astonish you, but the local Government let a piece of land known as the Stringy Bark Ranges to a squatter for ten pounds a year.

These ranges are covered with timber fit for house and ship building, and each pair of industrious sawyers and woodcutters have to pay the sum of fifteen pounds a year for the privilege of cutting any of the timber.

I lately presented a petition to the local authorities here, handed to me for that purpose by a committee of the body of sawyers and woodcutters, in which they assert, and I believe it to be true, that these industrious men pay about one thousand a year for only a part of the same land for which the squatter pays simply ten pounds a year. And the squatter and the local Government forbid these working-men to feed the cattle that draw their timber to town on the wild grass of these land—a monstrous injustice.

This, my Lord, is a great fact, and plainly points out to you the vast good you have done by holding the authority over these lands in your own hands.

But look at this question. The woods and mines and minerals, and all other rights over these lands, must be withheld from the squatter; all, all except the right of grazing his stock, and residing thereon; or how are we, who bought our lands and paid from one to four, five, aye, to sixty pounds an acre—how are we to obtain timber, &c. for our various wants? Why, solely by buying of the squatter, who pays less than one halfpenny an acre of yearly rent; whereas we landholders have paid from twenty shillings up to above sixty pounds (in villages) per acre to the Crown.

Mr. Fawkner goes on to show that the total amount of the squatter's licence and assessment fees is not equal in the year to the interest on the amount actually paid for their small holdings by the ordinary agricultural settlers, and he asks :—

Who has the most right to privileges and immunities? The man who, for every square mile of land he holds, pays from six hundred and forty pounds and upwards, or the man who only pays ten pounds a year for the use of twelve thousand eight hundred acres, upon which he exercises all the rights of ownership?

Now listen to Mr. La Trobe : [1]—

The propriety of granting a lease to the occupant of the waste lands of the Crown for pastoral purposes within the 'unsettled districts' for the long term of fourteen years need not in itself be subject to question, provided due care were taken that such continued licensed

---

[1] Despatch of September 3, 1852.

occupation carried with it no other advantage, which might prove, sooner or later, inimical to the general interests. But Section six orders that during the lease the land shall be saleable only to the occupant ; and this brings me to the question of pre-emptive right. With a certain class of colonists the concession of such pre-emptive right of purchase, under any circumstances, is held to have been uncalled for, and opposed to the general interest ; yet I have never been led to question the propriety of such concession to the stockholder, to the extent of the purchase of one or two sections containing homesteads or *bonâ fide* improvements ; and for the purpose of raising what is required to supply the wants of the station, even though it might to a defined and limited extent involve a departure from the general system of open sale by auction.

But beyond this I am not disposed to go, and I think the arguments that may be adduced, under a full acquaintance with the local circumstances of the colony, against any such wide extension of the ' pre-emptive right ' as that contemplated by the Orders in Council, whether in the ' intermediate ' or ' unsettled districts,' are not to be lightly disposed of. I think I shall be borne out in asserting that beyond a firm assurance that he would not be disturbed in his occupation of the waste land of the colony for pastoral purposes so long as the land comprised in his run was not really required for sale or other appropriation in due regard to general interests, and further, the acquisition, without the necessity of open competition, of the land containing homesteads and improvements, the settlers of this province, as a body, had formed neither wish nor expectation. In fact, that the extension of the ' pre-emptive right ' over the whole of the land covered by their lease, whether in the ' intermediate ' or the ' unsettled districts,' with the exception of such portion as the Crown may be considered legally empowered to reserve from, or withdraw from, occupation, under the 9th section, &c., was neither asked for nor dreamed of in this colony, either by the settler or by the Executive Government. I speak for myself. At this very hour, I believe that if the truth were told the acquisition and maintenance of such a privilege, unless claimed now as a matter of conceded right which may seem to be attacked, would be a matter of indifference to the great majority of the class in question, and that, if even left undisturbed, the cases in which the privilege would be exercised to any extent would be very few in number ;—always taking it for granted that maintenance and better carrying out of *purely pastoral pursuits,* which I assume was originally intended to form the primary, if not the sole, object of its exercise, were the *bonâ fide* end which the purchaser might have in view.   As matters stand, however, no provision has been made to secure that this shall be the case.

I think I shall be borne out in asserting, that beyond such homesteads, sections, &c., land purely and solely fitted for pastoral purposes, wherever situated, would not be in one instance in a hundred purchased by the lessee, and in the instance where it might be purchased it would be with other views than the mere advantages which its acquisition might lend to pastoral pursuits, and because the extraordinary or ordinary march of events gave that land a present or prospective value which would render its acquisition desirable.   The question arises then, if such be the case, why should the lessee of the Crown have the advantage of that purchase under a pre-emptive right?   I cannot, for my part, assign a satisfactory answer.

'I am constrained,' he adds, 'to look upon the whole question as one of a very serious character, and to conclude that the revision of the Orders in Council of March 1847, as far as it may legally be practicable, is most undoubtedly called for.'

And how were these representations received at home ? To Mr. Fawkner came a contemptuous reply from Earl Grey, while the views of the Lieutenant-Governor were not allowed to influence the latest official decision—which was, to make the commencement of the term of each lease run from the future date of its actual issue, instead of from the date of the promulgation of the Orders.   The request of the squatters, made in the latter part of 1852, for the extension of the date of commencing the lease, was, in the state of the colony at the time, about as impudent a proposition as could have been put forward.   The squatters could hardly have dared to hope that it would be granted, and yet granted it was in the terms of the petition, while all representations in the popular interest were completely ignored.

The leases were not, in fact, actually issued ; but a legacy of claims to leases, which met with bitter opposition and with a counteracting wave of sweeping anti-squatter legislation that has often threatened to run to a height of unreasonableness in some measure approaching to that of the Orders in Council themselves, was handed down to the first representative Victorian Assemblies.   The Orders to a large extent failed of their immediate object, as measures of glaring injustice must inevitably do in a community vigorous enough to claim the right of self-government at a very early period of its career, but they thoroughly succeeded in turning the inhabitants of the young colony into two hostile bodies, and in importing periodical convulsions into the whole political, social, and commercial life of the colony. Instead of all the colonists working together for a common object, the one class has uniformly sought to defeat or delay the constructive and reforming policy of the other. This last has in its turn persistently endeavoured to ride with roughshod violence over the privileges and prejudices of the party still in possession of the lands of the colony. The assertion of the rights of the people, which under the natural circumstances of forward progress would have been an irresistible, gradual, and peaceful process, has been made to assume the aspect of unfair encroachment upon established concessions. As the pressure of population upon obtainable space has increased, so the dividing line between the landed proprietors and the bulk of the people has become more strongly accentuated ; and the growing numbers of each succeeding generation can but furnish a fairer reason and a fresh excuse for the modification of the land system in a popular direction. The evils of the monopolisation of land in a comparatively few hands become daily more apparent, as population grows apace and gives greater preponderance to the power of the growing masses, with whom increasing rent, decreasing wages, and an envious regard of the luxurious position occupied by a small caste of landowners, operate as inducements to endeavour to secure for themselves the possession of the soil which almost hourly confers great and apparently never-ending advantages. The bitterness of the strife is yet to come. A country fitted by nature for the support of millions has as yet acquired but a small modicum of population in proportion to its undoubted capacity. The boundaries within which industrious cultivators of small capital can settle themselves at trifling preliminary cost are speedily becoming insufficient for existing demands. A vigorous population is for the time being almost stationary in numbers as compared with the rapid rate of increase in adjoining colonies, where large quantities of available land are obtainable on easy terms. Rents are rising, while wages and the purchasing powers of wages are diminishing as the inevitable result of a monopoly of landholding in a few hands, such as must woefully cramp the energy which would gladly devote itself to the development of the vast resources of the country. To New South Wales, to South Australia, to Queensland, go emigrants in plenty—all in the well-grounded confidence that the reward of their labour will be for them the acquisition of a remunerative block; but to Victoria they go not but in scanty shiploads, and the emigration from that colony more than balances the immigration to it. And why but because, in Victoria alone of all the colonies of the Australasian group, none but capitalists can hope to purchase a share in the soil!

Victoria is still prosperous, but relatively to the other colonies less prosperous than she was. It is no longer to her that her neighbours must concede the right of virtual headship, at one time acquired for her by the energy of a population not circumscribed or hedged in by artificial bounds. That it is in her power to regain her position of supremacy there need be no doubt; but it can only be by recourse to more efficient methods of legislation with regard to the masters of the land than have been resorted to so far. So far, the many-acred landowner still bears with ever-increasing weight on the broad backs of the Victorian people, and every effort to dispossess him of his monopoly has reacted injuriously on his necessitous assailants. May the experience of the past give better direction to the endeavours of the future, so that by temperate measures of orderly pressure on the one hand, of timely concession on the other, the evils of the struggle which violent proceedings may engender may be happily averted!

It may at some time be my task to trace in extenso the long-continued struggle between the landowners and the people of Victoria that has strewn the path of legislation with obstacles ever since the boon of self-government was accorded to the infant colony, and which for many a year to come may invest with virulent animosity the political struggles of the more matured State. In the foregoing pages I have but briefly sketched the cause and growth of a land system fraught with disastrous results to a people unjustly deprived of a fair heritage.

Fortunate it was for the maintenance of the imperial tie that within a very short time after the real pressure of the Orders in Council had come to be realised, the charge of regulating their own land policy was handed over to the colonists themselves. Popular indignation now found a safety vent in constitutional agitation, and the Orders were deprived of their grosser features in relation to the future working of the land system. Had the Orders been maintained in their integrity by the distant imperial authority, the waning loyalty of the injured colony would have set itself in firm opposition to the power of the Crown, and had the execution of the principle of the Orders been then persisted in, violent disruption from England would have taken the place of the peaceable connexion which now subsists. And who can say that the other Australasian colonies would not have followed the vigorous lead?

The Imperial Government in Australia had begun by propagating crime and infamy throughout its dependency; it had ended by perpetrating one of the most glaring acts of injustice to which the annals of England give recital. Beginning with a strenuous attempt to fashion Australia into an Elysium of vice for hardened criminals, the supreme effort of Government to close the chapter of imperial rule over the older colonies, by establishing the curse of a landowning monopoly, was in consistent keeping with the accustomed tenor of its way. From first to last no system could have been better devised to ensure the forcible disseverance of the relations between ourselves and the lands beneath the Southern Cross.

The work of emigration is one that calls for the constant exercise of careful supervision, watchful forethought, and ready attention. The task of effecting the settlement of a country is infinitely more difficult of satisfactory accomplishment than is the business of transporting emigrants to distant colonies. So difficult is it, in fact, that the qualifications necessary, even to initiate settlement, cannot by any possibility be possessed

by any far distant body of State officials. Intimate acquaintance with local, geological, geographical, and topographical features; extensive knowledge of the probable resources of the
new country, and of the readiest means for developing them;
knowledge of climate and of climatic influence upon the manners
and customs of the colonial population; of difficulties to be en-
countered; of individual and general requirements; above all,
an absorbing interest in, and complete identification with, the
progress of the youthful community—these are amongst the
qualifications which legislators bent upon framing a scheme of
settlement for a country ought to possess, and such as a remote
Government department cannot possess. Nor can even the
local Government, however zealous in the cause of colonial
prosperity, be fitted to plan out any but a temporary arrangement to suit the necessities of the hour, and that, too, one
liable to be varied from day to day.

In a new country, individuals certainly ought to be allowed
to be the best judges of their own requirements, and it can
only be by giving the freest play to the expression of the
largest number of individual wishes that the preliminary
knowledge for even the most temporary scheme of settlement
can be acquired. Wakefield tells us that what a colony
principally stands in need of at the outset of its career is
'plenty of good government.' Granted—if good, but government can never be more than comparatively good; that is, in
its best form it cannot pretend to perfection, but only to a
greater degree of efficiency than in its worst form. It seems,
on the contrary, to be greatly to the advantage of the young
colony to have as little Government direction as possible, and
that that Government should rest on the widest and most
popular basis. It is only a Government of this popular description that can pretend to prescribe for the wants of the
colonists, and that can be prevented from mapping out audacious plans to control the arrangements of future generations.
So soon as a Government does this last, it becomes dangerous;
for in inventing legislation for the future it takes as its guide
merely the experiences and facts of the day, and the plans
formed by it for the settlement of a sparsely-peopled territory

are in the highest degree unlikely to be accepted when elbow-room becomes scarcer. The temptation to colonise on a plan must present powerful attractions to those to whose keeping is confided a wholesale supply of colonies. To form one plan for the whole, and to follow it without reference to the distinguishing features of each; or to make the plan adopted for each colony, if discrimination is so far exercised, an invariable one, is a far simpler and less laborious mode of transacting the official business of the Colonial Office than it is to lend attention to varying special circumstances calling for separate treatment on new lines. The less that is known of the Colonies, the bolder is the plan and the greater the local obstacles to its practical working.

In young colonies the land is everything; and to settle what is to be done with the land is to attempt to arrange beforehand the future tendency of legislation. Let it be conceded that rules should be made as occasion requires, to regulate to a limited and necessary extent the rights of individual landlords and the legal relations between them and the landless majority. But this gradual method of tentative legislation is nothing else than the gradual codification of requirements and inter-relations resolving themselves by degrees into the system best adapted for the country and the people. It is the assimilating of an evolutionary process, which as it grows contains within itself all the elements of stability derivable from a foundation of custom and habit; and as its rise is slow and noiseless, so its continuance will be long-lived and popular. The fear, indeed, is lest the system thus evolved should become too strong; lest it should so ingrain itself into the prejudices of a part of the people and so weld itself into the institutions of the country that the claims of those interested in the maintenance of the land system should become, in time, demands for the extension of peculiar privileges against an increasing outcry for popular and sweeping modifications of the land laws. This is a danger inherent in the constitution of imperfect human nature—that rights based on custom should insensibly lead to the assertion of exclusive rights. As population crowds closer against the boundaries of the acred magnate, so will his lot appear more enviable to the thickening mass ; so will the value of his possessorship become more actual and more visible to himself, and so will he claim for himself a closer-bound network of legal protection. No forms and no amount of legislation can prevent this tendency, and its development must be awaited with patient apprehension. But in the ordinary course of events, in a popularly-governed country, the evil will not be an all-absorbing one until a matured and prosperous commonalty has advanced far on the stage of progress, and has arrived at a height of political intelligence, based on the lessons of experience, which may enable it skilfully to unloose, instead of violently to dissever, the environing cords of an oppressive land system.

To fetter the rising life of a people with a pre-arranged land system is but to stimulate from the outset the worst passions of the people ; to goad the community into unfitness for thoughtful, organised political action ; to raise up opposing classes throughout the country, and to pre-ordain bitter, intemperate conflicts between them.

Let it be remembered that there is not in Australia a supreme despotic authority against whom all sorts and conditions of men must be banded together in common cause. In England, noble and vassal were united in joint antagonism to overweening kingly power. This is not the case in Australia. There, no universal cause of freedom induces sympathetic forbearance between the large landowner and the working-man. There, each has to oppose the other, and each strives to do his best for himself and his worst for his opponent. Each day lends increasing bitterness to the conflict between them. The flame may lull for awhile, but it may one day burst forth into fiercer volume, which in its spread may involve the universe in vast disturbance.

CHAPTER VIII.

WAKEFIELDISM—'THE WAKEFIELD GAMBLE.'

APOLOGY is unnecessary for putting before the reader a Memorandum drawn up by Governor Sir George Gipps as an introduction to the comparatively few remarks I would make on the subject that his observations almost exhaust. The Memorandum is strong evidence of the penetrating, caustic intelligence of a Governor who ruled the then united colonies of New South Wales and Port Phillip at a very critical period of their history, and who, had he been able to bring his force of will under subjection to his reasoning powers, must infallibly have elicited the admiration of his contemporaries as a wise and fearless administrator.

But the chief value of the document consists in its exhaustive treatment of questions which will probably ever be subjects of unsatisfied discussion, and which at the time were hotly contested between those who advocated or opposed the doctrines of Gibbon Wakefield.

It is rarely given to any one man to identify his name with the successful promotion of more than one great principle. Wakefield's ' System of Colonisation ' endeavoured to do a vast number of things which never can be done *on system*, and he elaborated every detail with so great a regard to its ready-made perfection as to almost ensure the complete failure of the whole whenever and wherever it might be put into practice. He wished to make of colonisation an exact science, in which human beings might be treated as numerals with defined and invariable values from the moment of their being ranged on colonial soil, instead of regarding it as a haphazard process, even under the most careful superintending rules, and as one which could best acquire vitality by being left as much as possible to itself.

But all these fanciful speculations may be left out of sight in view of the great and useful principles underlying the whole. These were, that the land in new colonies should not, as previously, be recklessly granted away, but that every acre of it should be sold, and that the funds so derived should be appropriated to the purpose of introducing emigrants. The colony would thus be made self-supporting, and emigration itself would receive a certain degree of systematisation, regulated in accordance with local interest by being placed under the charge of the colonists themselves. These principles were undoubtedly of great value, but it unfortunately happened that their importance was almost obscured by the prominence given to other principles, not only of no value at all, but, in the case of some, of positively injurious tendency. The establishment of definite ratios between land and labour in a country where there was neither the one nor the other, and the discovery of the best means of restraining a vigorous young nationality from overstepping a narrow boundary which did not exist, were put in the foreground as the chief ends to be attained in the formation of a colony—and with singularly disastrous results.

One of the main contentions of Wakefield was that land should not be sold by public action, but at a fixed uniform price per acre. The question has been vigorously threshed out by many a colonial Legislature, where it has been in turn the theme of the orator, the stalking-horse of the demagogue, the text of political factions, and the study of publicists. But it has never been more lucidly or vigorously criticised than in those sentences of the master of epigrammatic despatch-writing whose Memorandum may now be allowed to speak for itself on this and on other subjects connected with the history of land tenure in Australia.

The disposal of lands in the Australian colonies has become a
matter of such importance, not only to the colonies themselves, but to
the people of the United Kingdom, that any information on the subject derived from authentic sources must, it is presumed, be an object
of interest to Her Majesty's Government.

The question of the way in which the lands should be disposed of,
or rather of the best method of disposing of them, is very distinct
from that of the way in which the money derived from the sale of
them shall be spent. On this latter question there is little, if any,
difference of opinion. All parties are agreed that the largest possible
portion of the proceeds ought to be spent in the importation of
labourers from the United Kingdom to the colonies. The desire that
it should be so spent is certainly not less intense in New South Wales
than in South Australia; whilst, on the other hand, the pretension of
being able to apply the gross proceeds of the land sales to the purposes
of immigration, without even deducting the expense of the survey and
sale of the lands, has been given up by the persons with whom it
originated. It might perhaps very fairly be even further argued, that
whilst the money derived from the sale of agricultural or pastoral
lands should be applied to the importation of labour, the proceeds
derived from the sale of lands in towns should be applied to public
purposes in the towns themselves; and that even in the country some
portion of the proceeds should be applied to the making of roads or
the erection of places of worship; but this is a question on the discussion of which it is not proposed at present to enter. The different
methods in which lands may be disposed of may now be considered as
reduced to two—one is that of sale by auction, the other that of disposing of them at a fixed price.

The sale of land by auction was introduced into New South Wales
in 1831, the minimum price at which any could be sold being fixed at
5s. per acre.

This minimum price was decidedly too low; but still, little if any
evil would have resulted from it if the distinction between the minimum price and the upset price had been sufficiently preserved.

In practice, however, the minimum price was made almost univer-

---

[1] Sir George Gipps to Lord John Russell, December 19, 1840.

sally the upset price ; and such large quantities of land were brought
into the market at that upset price, that there was a complete glut of
it. This glut was considerably increased, if not entirely occasioned,
by the practice of allowing land to be brought to sale on the demand
of any one who chose to apply for it, without even the precaution of
forcing such person to buy it at the upset price, if no one offered
more.

Under such circumstances the land seldom produced at auction
more than 5s. per acre, and the impression became general in the
colony that the Government did not desire to get more for it.

At a trial in the Supreme Court in 1836, it was even deposed that
the Government officer under whose direction the sales were conducted
had declared that the Government did not wish to get for it a higher
price than 5s. per acre.

In 1839 the minimum price was raised to 12s., and the practice
introduced of varying the upset price according to the presumed value
of the land, making it, as a general rule, from 10 to 20 per cent. less
than the last selling price of land of the same quality and in the same
locality ; and in the Port Phillip district, land was only brought to
sale at the discretion of Government, applications from individuals not
being received or attended to.

Under this improved system, the rise in the price of land was very
rapid, and the productiveness of the land sales proportionally increased.

The average price of all land sold in the old parts of the colony
was, in 1838, 5s. 7½d. ; in 1840, 1l. 0s. 6¼d. In the Port Phillip
district, the average of all lands was—

	£	s.	d.
In 1838		17	9½
In 1840	2	12	10

The total amount of land sold was, in the old parts of the colony—

In the year 1838 . . .	278,508 acres.
And in 1840	94,568 ,,

and in the Port Phillip district—

1838	38,694 acres.
1840	82,898 ,,

The general results are shown in the following Return :—

	Years	Country Lands			Town Allotments			Country Lands and Town Allotments		
		Acres	Price per acre	Sum	Acres	Price per acre	Sum	Acres	Price per acre	Sum
			£ s. d.	£ s. d.	A. R. P.	£ s. d.	£ s. d.		£ s. d.	£ s. d.
Old parts of the colony	1838	278,323	5 4¾	75,159 5 11	185 3 26	1 7 4	3,228 13 5	278,509	0 5 7½	78,387 19 4
	1839	198,198	8 1¾	80,836 7 5	231 0 22	29 0 11½	6,714 2 3	198,429	0 8 9¾	87,550 9 8
	1840	94,878	13 1¾	62,360 5 10	513 1 25	69 3 7¾	35,518 13 9	95,391	1 0 6¼	97,878 19 7
Port Phillip	1837	—	—	—	87 3 20	81 5 8¼	7,142 18 0	88	81 5 8	7,142 18 0
	1838	38,653	13 3	25,587 17 9	41 1 12	213 11 7½	8,826 5 4	38,694	0 17 9½	34,414 3 1
	1839	38,283	1 11 11	61,102 14 6	65 1 8	137 19 0	9,008 2 8	38,348	1 16 6¾	70,110 17 2
	1840	82,729	1 12 11	136,367 15 8	169 2 16	487 16 2	82,732 10 0	82,899	2 12 10	210,100 5 8

In explanation of this return, it is, perhaps, proper to observe that the rise in the minimum price of country land from 5s. to 12s. produced for a time an indisposition on the part of the public to purchase such land, and that a great deal of money which might otherwise have been laid out in the purchase of ordinary land came to be invested in town allotments; in fact, a sort of rage for speculation in town allotments ensued, the consequence of which was the great increase in the price of them that is shown in the return.

The practice of selling land at a fixed price was introduced in South Australia in 1836 or 1837, and the system was based upon a theory of which the leading points appear to be—

1. That there is some assignable ratio between land and labour, and that therefore the price of land should be regulated by the cost of conveying labourers to the country where the land is situated.

2. That the occupation of land should be made difficult, instead of easy, in order to ensure the combination of labour, and to prevent the dispersion of the settlers; also to prevent persons from becoming proprietors or cultivators on their own account who properly belong to the class of labourers.

3. That in order to secure the early cultivation of good land, or, in other words, to secure the cultivation of lands in the order of their natural advantages, all land should be disposed of at the same price.

The South Australian plan of disposing of lands was moreover marked with two peculiar features, which contributed greatly to make it acceptable to persons intending to emigrate from the United Kingdom; one was the system of special surveys, the other the disposal of building allotments in new towns by means of a lottery or raffle, the tickets of which lottery were given gratuitously, or next to gratuitously, to the purchasers of a certain number of country acres.

The first of these inventions secured very great advantages to early settlers. The second added to the attractions of the scheme some of that excitement which is produced in the human mind by gambling.

That both acted powerfully in the first settlement of South Australia cannot be doubted; but as it is not proposed to introduce either of them at Port Phillip, it may be, perhaps, concluded that they are no longer to form a part of what is called the South Australian system.

Nevertheless, in the settlement which has recently been formed on the South Australian principle at Port Nicholson, the same plan has been pursued: to each purchaser of 100 acres of land a lottery ticket was given, by which he had a good chance of obtaining a prize of a thousand pounds; indeed, it is asserted on good authority that many of the prizes in this lottery have already sold for sums varying from 100*l.* to 1,000*l.*

The invention of special surveys was certainly well calculated to advance one of the main objects of the system, that of causing the lands to be occupied in the order of their natural advantages, for under it any person might demand to have a survey made of 15,000 acres in the best locality he could select, on binding himself to take no more than 4,000; which 4,000 he might select as he chose, provided only that he took them in portions of not less than 80 acres each. With such a privilege, a purchaser of course selected all the good land, and left the bad.

The system of special surveys, as at first introduced into South Australia, was not even guarded by the precaution of preventing a purchaser from selecting a narrow strip of land along the bank of a river, and thus possessing himself of a vast extent of what is called ' water frontage' at a price infinitely below its value.

It is well known in New South Wales that whoever has the water frontage on any river has the command of all the land in the rear of it, often for many miles, or of the lands which are familiarly called ' the back run.'

Even in the early days of the colony, when grants of land were made with the greatest profusion, so well was the value of water frontage understood, that the extent of any grant of land along the bank of a river was never allowed to be more than one-fourth of the breadth of it, measured at right angles to the course of the river.

Thus, though the Governor for the time being had the power of granting four square miles, under certain conditions and qualifications, these four square miles (or 2,560 acres) could never carry with them more than one mile of water frontage.

When land was no longer given away, but sold, this regulation of the Government was considerably relaxed; but even at present in New South Wales no person can, in pastoral districts (and the whole country, with very few exceptions, is pastoral), obtain a mile of water frontage unless he buy all the land to the rear to the extent at least of a mile.

For such a square mile, or section, as it is called, even if he get it at auction at the present minimum price of 12*s.* per acre, he must pay 384*l.*; but for good land of this sort he would, in all probability, have to pay at auction at least 500*l.*

In South Australia, where land is divided into sections of 80 acres each, he might get the same extent of water frontage for 100*l.*, or he might have to pay for it 320*l.*, according as his special survey had been measured for him by a friendly or unfriendly surveyor.

In New South Wales he would have to buy the whole square mile (A); in South Australia he would have to buy either the two sections abutting on the river, as shown in (B), or the four, as shown in (C),

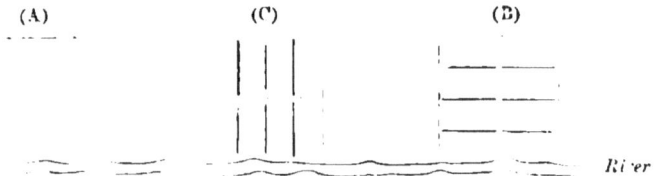

(A)   (C)   (B)

River

according as the surveyor had divided the land.   In either case he will get it cheaper than he could in New South Wales; it would therefore be a fallacy to say that land is dearer in South Australia than in New South Wales, even if other documents did not exist to prove that during the year 1840, at least, the price obtained for land in New South Wales has considerably exceeded what it is sold for in South Australia.

Having got possession of the water frontage, the purchaser may be perfectly sure of remaining in undisturbed possession of his back run for many years, and his danger of being molested will be reduced in proportion as the price, whether minimum or fixed, of land is increased.   Few persons in New South Wales will give 20*s.* an acre for grazing land, devoid of water frontage; and it may be doubted whether many will be found to do it (except in the neighbourhood of towns) either in South Australia or Port Phillip.

Old settlers in New South Wales, indeed, who were often forced to purchase their back run, to prevent its falling into the hands of strangers, when the minimum price of land was 5*s.*, feel secured in their possession of it for years without purchase, now that the minimum price is raised to 12*s.* per acre.

The theory of forcing persons to cultivate, or even to occupy, lands in the order of their natural advantages, seems altogether to fail in Australia, where not the hundredth part of the land sold by the Government is purchased with any intention of cultivating it, and where scarcely one acre in a thousand is cultivated of the land that is occupied without being purchased.

The Australian wool-grower or grazier cultivates very little, and desires to cultivate no more than is necessary to feed his herdsmen or shepherds; his great aim is to secure water, the scarcity of water being, as is well known, the great characteristic of the country.

T

In a colony like Demerara, where land is used for scarcely any purpose but cultivation, and cultivation too of the most expensive sort, the theory might perhaps be practically applied ; but to a pastoral country like Australia, it is evidently altogether inapplicable.

It may be essential, however, here to observe, that wherever land is of a quality or in a locality which renders it fit for cultivation, as in districts of superior fertility, or in the neighbourhood of towns, it is usually divided into much smaller lots than sections of square miles. Such smaller divisions are called ' cultivation allotments ' (the word section being made use of only for grazing land), and they are made to vary from 20 to 320 acres. When in the neighbourhood of large towns, such as Melbourne, they are called suburban allotments.

But if the theory by which it is sought to make persons cultivate lands in Australia in the natural order of their advantages be altogether incapable of good, that which would seek to prevent the dispersion of the people is only incapable of mischief because it is utterly impossible to reduce it to practice. As well might it be attempted to confine the Arabs of the Desert within a circle traced upon their sands, as to confine the graziers or wool-growers of New South Wales within any bounds that can possibly be assigned to them ; and as certainly as the Arabs would be starved, so also would the flocks and herds of New South Wales if they were so confined, and the prosperity of the country be at an end.

The time will come, if the colony continue to prosper, when it may be more advisable (that is to say, more profitable) for a proprietor to improve the land he holds, so as to make its produce suffice for his increasing flocks, than to seek (as is the present practice) for new lands in distant regions ; but it may, perhaps, be wiser to let this time arrive naturally, as it will, than to attempt to accelerate it by any contrivances.

The largest landholders of New South Wales have not land enough of their own for their flocks ; there is scarcely a man of any property who has not a cattle run, or a sheep station, beyond the boundaries— that is to say, upon the unalienated lands of the Crown.

The evils, therefore, that have resulted in New South Wales from the lavish grants of land which were made in former years are evils only as they affect the revenue ; could all these grants be resumed, the Government would have them now to sell, but no further advantage would be derived from the resumption of them. Moreover, under the present system of selling land by auction, at an upset price, not fixed, but made to vary so as generally to bear a proportion to the prices already realised, it is scarcely to be feared that persons will purchase any undue quantity of land, or more than it is salutary for them to hold.

The last advantage sought to be derived from a uniform price of land is that persons on arriving in the colony may at once acquire the land they want, without being exposed to delay or to competition at auction.

More may be advanced in favour of the system on this ground than on any other, for whilst on the other points it can be proved almost to demonstration that the system of selling by auction is the best, it may be admitted that the supposed certainty of being able to settle at once on their own land on arriving in the colony has had some considerable effect in inducing people to emigrate from England.

The supposed advantage when strictly examined will, however, prove to be altogether delusive. So long as the delusion lasts, it doubtless produces its effect; but such is the case also with other delusions.

It is in reality an attempt to put, by artificial means, a newly-arrived emigrant on a par with the settler who has gained experience in the colony; and it may safely be asserted that this is what no measures, however artificially devised, can accomplish.

Let us suppose a person to have paid in England 100l. or 1,000l., and to arrive in New South Wales with an order to take immediate possession of his land, how is he to proceed? He may be put into possession of such land as the Government may choose to give him: or he may with others draw lots, or throw dice, for a number of portions to be distributed amongst a given number of them; or, lastly, he may be left to make his own selection.

The first mode will assuredly not give him satisfaction; the second, it is hoped for the sake of public morality, will never be adopted; and, consequently, the third is the only one that remains to be seriously examined.

He arrives a stranger in a strange country, and he has to choose his 100 acres out of any land that may be open to his selection. If only small districts, or a small number of districts, be open to him, he will infallibly find that all the good land has been previously taken, and occupied by those who, residing on the spot and having far better means of information of the comparative value of land than he can pretend to have, had an exceedingly great advantage over him; if, on the contrary, a vast extent of land be opened to him, he will be so puzzled how to choose, and so much afraid of choosing wrong, that he will in all probability waste his time, as well as his resources, before he makes up his mind to choose at all. Land indeed he will be able to get, but unless he be perfectly indifferent to the quality of his land, his difficulty in determining where to settle himself will be still almost as great as ever. This has been completely exemplified in New South Wales. A person arriving in New South Wales with an order for land from the Commissioners in England will be in precisely the same condition that a person formerly was who (during the time of gratuitous grants) arrived with an order for land from the Secretary of State; also in the same situation that military and naval settlers were in up to the end of the year 1833, permission having been granted them to select land at 5s. an acre, precisely on the same grounds that it is now proposed to give it to emigrants generally at 20s. per acre—namely, that they might avoid the delay and inconvenience of waiting for an auction. So great, however, in either case was the delay which usually occurred in their making their choice, that it was found necessary to prescribe a limit within which they were required to choose: and, though the period of four months was fixed as the limit, applications for an extension of the time were very frequent, and generally complied with; whilst amongst military or naval settlers the practice of late became almost universal of selling their right of selection to persons who had more experience than themselves. As it was with one class of men so will it be with the other; it is in the nature of things that it should be so, for the selection of a spot on which to fix for life is a matter of too great importance to be done in a hurry.

From one or other of those difficulties it seems impossible to escape; if small districts only of the colony be opened successively to purchasers at the fixed price of 1l. per acre, all the good land will be bought up by speculators on the spot; if extensive districts be opened, a new-comer must be so perplexed in making his selection that he will lose as much time or more than he would do if he had to buy at auction, where, though he might be opposed, he would not be so likely to be misled. If it be sought to meet this difficulty by reserving entire districts or parishes for settlers from the United Kingdom, and by not allowing persons on the spot to select out of such parishes or districts, the regulation would be very easily evaded by the employment of agents in England; and it may probably be pretty safely assumed that, however prudent, politic, wise, or ingenious may be the regulations laid down by the Commissioners in England, the speculators or land sharks in New South Wales will be ingenious enough to defeat them.

It may further here be remarked that it is by no means desirable for persons on their first arrival in Australia to become purchasers of land. The settler who has only a few hundreds of pounds at command will, in general, find on his arrival that he was wrong in thinking to invest any portion of his capital in land, and his first endeavour will probably be to disembarrass himself of his land order by selling it for what it will fetch. So long as land is rising in the market he will be able to sell it at a premium, and if land orders are to take precedence according to their date, the buying of them will become a source of very profitable speculation. The newly-arrived emigrant may not be able to wait for his land, but the speculator, or land shark, can wait, and of course he will wait until land that he likes be opened : if, on the contrary, the priority in choice be not in any way dependent on the priority of date, then a real scramble will ensue, in which it is also only reasonable to suppose that the experienced land shark will have an advantage over the inexperienced and newly-arrived emigrant; in fact, the whole scheme seems, as it was before said, to be conceived in the delusion that it is possible by any artificial means, such as regulations of Government, to put the one upon a par with the other.

It has hitherto been assumed, that the lands open to selection at a uniform price are to be limited to such quantities as may from time to time be proclaimed by the Government; also that no land is to be opened that is not surveyed.

If this be the case, a fresh source of pressure from without will be opened to the Government. Persons will not be content to buy refuse lands, as they will be called, after the best lots of any district have been culled out ; but the opening of new lands will be constantly demanded, and the authority of the Secretary of State will be adduced to prove that it is the intention of Her Majesty's Government that nobody is to buy inferior land.

It may be reasonable to ask, will the local Government be strong or steady enough to resist such demands, and if not, will any surveying staff that can be sent out from England be strong enough to supply the demand ? If, on the contrary, unsurveyed lands are to be open to selection, the chaotic confusion into which the colony will be thrown is beyond conception.

A very large proportion of the land which is to form the new district of Port Phillip is already in the licensed occupation of the squatters of New South Wales, a class of persons whom it would be wrong to confound with those who bear the same name in America, and who are generally persons of mean repute and of small means, who have taken unauthorised possession of patches of land. Amongst the squatters of New South Wales are the wealthiest of the land occupying, with the permission of Government, thousands and tens of thousands of acres. Young men of good family and connexions in England, officers of the army and navy, graduates of Oxford and Cambridge, are also in no small number amongst them.

At the end of 1839, the cattle depastured beyond the boundaries was returned as follows, though probably the real quantity was much greater:—

Sheep	1,334,593
Horned cattle . . .	371,699
Horses	7,088

The number of acres in cultivation was also returned as 7,287.

If unsurveyed lands are to be open to selection, or if the South Australian system of special surveys is to be introduced, all the lands of which our squatters are in the licensed occupation, the houses, or huts, folds, and stock-yards which they have built, the provision-fields which they have cultivated, the streams or pools at which they water their cattle, may henceforth be wrested from them by any one who can run faster than they to the Land Office, and there deposit a few pounds.

It is true that the occupiers or squatters themselves will have an equal chance with the rest : but they will have only an equal chance, and therefore it is that there must be a scramble. It is true also, that the squatters have at present no secured possession of their lands, nor even any right of pre-emption over them. They are well aware that they have not, and they know that such lands will eventually be taken from them, or that they will have to purchase them at an advanced price. But they have always reckoned on having some time to prepare themselves for such an event; they have considered that the Government would continue to act upon the same system which has been so long in use, and that the country would be opened successively to location, one district after another; that even when the evil day came they would have a fair chance with others at a fair auction; and that no person could at any rate get possession of their lands, with the improvements they had made on them, without paying to the Government the value of them. But under the new system (if it be to extend to unsurveyed as well as to surveyed lands) the unhappy squatter may see his lands and his improvements wrested from him by his nearest neighbour or by his bitterest enemy, and himself reduced to ruin, unless he can in his turn beggar somebody else ; and he will not even have the poor consolation of knowing that the public revenue is a gainer by his loss. The lands for which he would (if allowed time to do so) willingly give 20*l.* per acre, will be sold for twenty shillings before he can look around him.

The matter is of too great importance to be hastily dismissed; therefore, even at the risk of some repetition, the principles on which the new system is founded must be again examined.

First. There is, it is said, some definable ratio between land and labour, and therefore the price of land should be regulated by the price at which labour can be supplied, in such quantity, that the profits derived from land and labour may be at a maximum. The proposition, as applied to Australia, may be enounced somewhat in the following terms. In order to obtain a maximum quantity of produce from a given quantity of labour, that labour must be employed in the ratio or proportion of three men to 100 acres. But these men must have (or ought at least to have) each a wife; consequently, to cultivate 100 acres of land in the most advantageous manner six persons must be sent from the United Kingdom to Australia.

But the passage of these people will cost 100*l.*, therefore the 100 acres ought to be sold for 100*l.*; and the value of land is consequently at once authoritatively fixed at 1*l.* per acre. This is henceforth to be the sufficient price: anything more is too much, anything less is too little.

If the assumed facts be true, the conclusion that no land should be sold for the purpose of cultivation at a less price than 1*l.* per acre may seem to follow, but why none should be sold for more, if more can be obtained for it, does not seem quite so satisfactorily proved.

It might be convenient to the three labourers and their wives to have a blacksmith, or a carpenter, or a tailor in their neighbourhood : and any extra price obtained for the land might be employed in supplying one. But 1*l.* per acre is said to be the sufficient price, and therefore they must get tailors or blacksmiths as they can.

Without at all questioning the accuracy of the ratio of labour to land, which requires three men to 100 acres when that land is to be cultivated, it is quite sufficient to repeat that scarcely one-hundredth part of the land sold by the Government in Australia is ever purchased for the purpose of being cultivated.

Australia is essentially a pastoral country, and must remain such for ages.

Allowing, therefore, the above ratio to hold good in respect to land purchased for the purposes of cultivation, it remains to be inquired what the sufficient price of pastoral land would be upon the same principle.

A shepherd in New South Wales commonly takes care of from

700 to 1,000 sheep; but as 600 are considered the proper number for a flock, no more than 600 shall be assumed as under his charge.

To obtain a maximum return of wool and mutton from the flock, it is necessary that an extent of four acres for each sheep, or 2,400 acres for each flock, should be allowed.

The shepherd must have (or ought at least to have) a wife; consequently it will be necessary to provide for the passage of two persons from Europe, instead of one. Their passage will cost 40l., which consequently ought to be the price of the 2,400 acres of land; therefore the sufficient price of land is 4d. per acre: anything more than 4d. is too much; anything less than 4d. is too little.

By introducing different elements into the calculation, such as the probability of either the agriculturists or shepherds having children as well as wives, and by affording in a greater or less degree the assistance of carpenters, blacksmiths, &c., any sum whatsoever might just as well be called the sufficient price as either 4d. or 20s.

The only sufficient price of any commodity formerly used to be considered that which it would sell for when judiciously brought to market; and any attempt to control by laws or regulations the value of things in the market was out lately considered contrary to the clearest principles of political economy.

The lands at Port Phillip are now bought eagerly at prices varying from 12s. to 500l.; and surely it may be asked why, when persons are found to buy them at such prices, they should all be sold indiscriminately at 20s.

Had Port Phillip been opened on the South Australian system, a loss would already have been sustained of 179,000l. out of 331,000l. which has been realised. If the recent Order had been put in force without waiting for further instructions from the Secretary of State, a further loss of 800,000l. and upwards would, according to the estimate formed by the chief officers of the Government of New South Wales, have been incurred in less probably than three weeks from the promulgation of the Order.

Amongst the numerous articles of which a new settler stands in need, there are perhaps very few which it would not be more for his advantage to have at a fixed price than land; it is rarely advantageous in any part of Australia for a newly-arrived emigrant to become a proprietor of land, unless his capital be considerable.

It would be far more advantageous to him to be supplied with sheep or oxen at a fixed price, or, on his first arrival in Sydney, that the price of his lodgings should be so regulated.

The second great object of the South Australian system is to ensure the cultivation of the lands in the order of their natural advantages; and this is supposed to be secured by means of the uniform price.

That the uniform price secures the appropriation of the best land first is pretty evident; that it secures even the occupation of them is doubtful; that it secures the cultivation of them is very much more than doubtful. If there be any great advantage in selling all the good land first, then the system of special surveys ought not to be abandoned. It is true that the system requires the survey of 15,000 acres in order to secure the sale of 4,000; that it increases the dispersion of the agriculturists, and therefore renders combination or co-operation amongst them difficult; that it lays each small settler under the necessity of making a road for himself; but still it seems to secure the object of selling the best land first, and therefore it should, according to the new theory, be good.

The third great principle of the South Australian system is that of checking the dispersion of the settlers (and therefore at variance with special surveys, the tendency of which is to create dispersion), so as to enable them to combine their efforts; and this is acknowledged as far as agricultural purposes are concerned to be most desirable; but Australia, it must be once more observed, is not an agricultural but a pastoral country, and dispersion is essential to its prosperity. Whatever the inconveniences (and without doubt they are many) which dispersion brings with it, the country must be content to bear with.

In order to prevent dispersion the South Australian system proposes to put a high price upon land when it is sold, and either to prevent the occupation of unsold land (squatting) or to render such occupation difficult.

That land should be sold at a high price, or at a much higher price than it formerly was, is equally the argument herein maintained as it is the argument of the South Australians. In fact, the main object of this paper is to ensure a higher price than can be obtained in South Australia by getting rid of the South Australian maximum, a fixed price being evidently a maximum, as well as a minimum.

That the occupation of the unsettled lands of the colony should be rendered difficult instead of easy is a very different proposition, and as it is directly opposed to the squatting system of New South Wales, some further explanation of this latter system may be necessary.

The occupation of the unsold lands of the Crown was, probably, in the first instance made easy because the Government in the early days of the colony scarcely thought it worth while to prevent it. Under the easy permissive occupancy thus introduced, however, the flocks and herds of New South Wales now stray over an extent of country 900 miles long by 400 broad; and it may safely be said that all the power of the Government would not suffice to bring them back within the narrower limits.[1] One great advantage (possibly an unforeseen one) which has grown out of this system is that persons make money beyond the boundaries, with which they afterwards purchase land within them. The desire to be possessed of a portion of the solid globe is strong in all men; and the additional importance which is given to a man in New South Wales, as elsewhere, by being ranked as a landed proprietor is found quite sufficient to ensure the sale of land faster than in all probability it could be sold if the price to be paid for it were not produced on the land itself. Another great advantage of this extensive system of authorised squatting is, that the flocks and the herds of New South Wales have increased under it to a degree that is almost unprecedented. The older settlements have, under it, become the hive from which swarms of sheep and cattle have been driven, to give a value to the lands of Port Phillip and South Australia which, without them, would to this day have been an unprofitable wilderness.

It is this system which has in reality enabled South Australia to avoid the fate of Swan River, for if South Australia has prospered more than Swan River, it is principally, if not solely, because it is nearer to New South Wales. The enterprising colonists who first drove sheep and cattle from New South Wales to South Australia rescued that colony from ruin.

It is under this system, moreover, that New South Wales, after having, without the expense of one shilling to the mother-country, and without the aid of borrowed money, silently founded a settlement of unexampled prosperity at Port Phillip, is now rendering similar services to Great Britain in securing to her the islands of New Zealand.

Before this paper is brought to a conclusion, it will be necessary to say a few words on the subject of town allotments.

The original plan in South Australia was, as has been observed, to play at dice for them. This has been given up: and in order to get rid of the embarrassment which the disposal of them in any other way (except the prohibited one of auction) would occasion, they are

---

[1] Mr. E. G. Wakefield, when examined before a Committee of the House of Commons in 1836, said, in answer to Question No. 634, ' That he considered it not more difficult to prevent squatting in the Colonies than it is to prevent it in the Principality of (Old) Wales.'

to be got rid of altogether; in other words, the formation of all minor towns is to be left to private enterprise. As this is a return to the natural order of things, and to the way in which most towns in the Old World have been formed, the proposal is objectionable only in as far as it tends to reduce the average price of lands, and consequently to lessen the revenue derived from the sale of land in the colony. It has already been shown, that in the old parts of New South Wales, though the average price of country land was only, for the year 1840, 13s. 1¾d. per acre, the general average of all land was, by means of town allotments, brought up to 20s. 6¼d.

In the new districts of New South Wales, it is not intended entirely to do away with Government towns, though very few are to be founded, and such only as are likely to become the seats of district administrations.

In these towns land is to be sold at 100l. per acre, whilst beyond the town the uniform price is to be 1l. per acre.

Whatever limits, therefore, may be assigned to the town, there must be a boundary within which all land is to be sold at 100l. per acre, and beyond it at 1l. per acre. A state of things will therefore be produced somewhat of the same nature as would arise in London, if a regulation could by possibility be enforced that all land beyond Hyde Park Corner should be sold for the one-hundredth part of the price of land in Piccadilly, and that all the land east of Hyde Park Corner, from Piccadilly to St. Giles's, should be sold at the same price.

I have, &c.

Sydney: Dec. 19, 1840.　　　　　　(Signed)　　　G. GIPPS.

To attempt to concentrate the population of a new colony within narrow artificial limits is to endeavour to inflict the most serious injury upon the young community. Every deduction from the liberty of man as a free agent is, in an economical sense, a diminution of his power; and to restrain the natural enterprise of colonists by confining their action within limited bounds is to minimise working power by preventing energy from having the free scope which, in the ordinary course of events, would develop it to the highest extent. The mere effort at concentration is well calculated to repress the natural inclination to wander far afield in the hope of bettering one's condition—an inclination which if unrestrained will in all certainty be productive of the best results. Forced concentration obliges the more enterprising portion of the settlers to relinquish the advantage of appropriating the most fertile land within their reach, in order to secure the real or supposed benefits of congregation. It forbids the pioneer to war with the wilderness around, and to keep ever enlarging the area of settlement, until population has crept close to its restricted boundary, and is beginning, in the proximity of a vast uninhabited territory, to undergo the bitter experience of an old and over-peopled State. The labourer is reduced to be the slave of a certain set of regulations devised with a view to curb his enterprise and activity and to destroy his sense of self-reliance by the exercise of his capabilities being made dependent upon Government direction ; and thus State vacillation, incompetency, and hesitancy are substituted for individual energy founded upon the wholesome instincts of self-interest.

Fertile soil is the machine with which the settler works, and to make him put up with a less fertile instead of a more fertile machine is to diminish his productive power. The concentration theory, where put into practice, could not fail to limit the settler's choice of land, and therefore to circumscribe his productive powers.

It is strange indeed that so vigorous and acute a thinker as Gibbon Wakefield should have advanced so palpably erroneous a theory as that artificial concentration of colonists could be productive of other than most disadvantageous consequences. It is still harder to conceive how, with his varied colonial experience and great critical ability, he could ever have reasoned himself into the belief that forced concentration would be possible, as a system, in a State composed of free people.

A certain amount of herding round a common centre there will always be amongst every people and in every locality under the sun, so soon as mankind has advanced a step beyond the pastoral stage, and has begun to recognise the advantages derivable from combination and division of labour ; and day by day the gregarious tendency more prominently asserts itself. But, together with this natural process of concentration, an overflow of population is surely dispersing itself further and further from the common centre; for natural concentration is in itself the promoter of dispersal. Dispersal is a consequence, and if checked, the concentration becomes forced and unhealthy. It was to prevent this natural overflow that Wakefield directed his efforts.

It need never be feared that any considerable number of persons in a new colony will acquire the habit of wandering far, or at all, beyond the bounds of location, so as to place themselves out of the reach of markets. Some men there are, of the celebrated Daniel Boone type, who, for reasons of their own, endeavour to interpose a wide intervening margin between themselves and civilisation, but neither do they count for anything in the economical life of a nation, nor are they amenable to laws intended to regulate the more settled society. It was not, in truth, against the wanderings of men such as these that Wakefield directed his 'concentration' policy, but his was a subtler, if an equally visionary, aim. He had seen capital lying idle and valueless for want of labour to give it vitality, and he hastily jumped to the conclusion that labour should be bound down as a servile handmaid to capital. In his view, if labour were confined within a definite area, capital would be attracted to it, and so the greatest development would be afforded to local resources. He thought that the convenience of capitalists ought alone to be consulted, and that labour was to be regarded as the mechanical tool of capital. In accordance with his theory he devised a fantastic set of rules providing for the introduction into his ideal colony of capital and labour in certain whimsical quantities, pre-arranged as 'due proportions.' To ensure the 'due proportion,' it was necessary to have a 'sufficient price' for land—a price just enough to prevent the labourer from leaving his employer in order to settle on a block of his own, and just enough to allow of the sum paid for any block being exactly equivalent to the cost of importing the right amount of labour to work the purchased land in the most efficient manner. He attempted, in short, to organise that of which no organised plan is possible outside the limits of a State bound over at once to s' ivery and despotism ; where prices, wages, and the whole social existence of a community may be predetermined by the undisputed fiat of a meddlesome absolute ruler.

The truth is that this careful elaboration of ideas was due to an extraordinary confusion of thought which, in Wakefield's case, must have proceeded rather from persistent attachment to a cherished prejudice than to his perception of a balance of reason in its favour. If, he thought, capital was being wasted for want of labour, it must follow that labour was suffering from absence of capital. There was a reciprocal action between the two, a co-relation, which rendered the operations of the one profitless without the aid of the other. Therefore, he argued, that as capital might employ many labourers, while impecunious labourers could not employ the capital which they had not got, capital was necessarily the more valuable member of the co-partnership, and that consequently its possessors ought to be put into the position of being able to use it to the best advantage for themselves. The theory when worked out came to this—that a new colony ought from its earliest foundation to be handed over to the fostering care of speculative capitalists.

To enter into the questions so vehemently disputed between rival schools of economists as to the relations between capital and labour, or to argue for or against the strongly-held but as strongly-reprobated creed that wages are invariably advanced out of capital, is foreign to my immediate purpose. Without trending on that debatable ground, it may be observed that in a virgin territory the chief, at first the only, means of producing wealth is by physical toil. Hardy labourers, inspired by the stimulus to exertion arising from the conviction that they are working for their own individual benefit, are the colonists who, in the first stages of settlement, are best fitted for making the most of the material resources of the colony. Gradual development, gradual settlement, form the elements of the society into which capital naturally flows to give direction and cohesiveness to the efforts of the labourer. Capital then sets itself to attract labour as the only means of acquiring for itself a value ; and so in the

earlier stages of the formation of a society we find the
capitalist seeking for labour rather than labour seeking for
capital. The first developing power is labour ; and therefore
to commence the process of settlement by placing it in forced
subordination to capital is to discourage the immigration of
labourers, and at the same time to place labour in a position
in which it can afford no aid to capital except as a fettered.
and consequently a more or less unwilling, inefficient
agent. On the other hand, to encourage the expenditure of
capital on a virgin soil before the work of the labourer has
laid the foundation of future prosperity is merely to court the
operations of ' land sharks,' who make no effort to cultivate or
improve the land, but who use their capital for purely speculative purposes. The more encouragement there is given to
the latter course—and it is the only course *certain* to result
from the plan of giving over a new colony to capitalists—the
more speedy and overwhelming will be the ruin of *bonâ fide*
settlers.

Let us summarise the leading propositions advanced by
Wakefield on these points. First we are told ' that the prosperity of new colonies depends mainly upon the abundance of
available labour at the command of capitalists in proportion
to the extent of territory offered ; ' or, to adopt Merivale's
rendering of the proposition, ' that it is desirable to provide
colonists requiring land with a greater supply of labourers to
work on their own account than their capital would naturally
attract.'

I have tried to show, in the foregoing pages, that the prosperity of new colonies is dependent upon exactly opposite
considerations ; and if Merivale's translation is the true
rendering. it is hardly necessary to say more than that
capitalists could never be provided with an amount of labour
beyond the attracting power of their capital, unless the labour
was *forced* and the country reduced to a state of slavery—
contingencies which Wakefield certainly did not contemplate
as desirable.[1]

---

[1] Of course Wakefield never really meant to initiate slavery as the
principal feature of his model colony ; but it is not easy to see how a

The second proposition is ' that this abundance of labour is to be secured by introducing labourers from the mother-country and other well-peopled regions, and by taking care to keep them in the condition of labourers living by wages for some considerable time.'

Taking the two propositions together, we find that an equilibrium is to be established between the quantity of land purchased, the amount of capital seeking employment, and the supply of labour to carry out the work to be done by the capital. If labour would not be employed, then it must be forced into employment, and yet the labourer was to be a free agent. The single proposition thus formed seems as intricate, as difficult of correct statement, and as impossible of being practically applied, as could well be desired. It is a problem for which there is no apparent solution but rejection, for each step in its examination is beset with increasing difficulty.

If human beings were mere implements of trade to be stored up ready for future use against the call of the all-powerful capitalist, and to be put aside as inanimate tools when the work expected from them had been accomplished : or, to put it in another way, if a number of human beings, incapable of acting or thinking for themselves, were to be forced to emigrate and to give their services to any capitalist who might come forward, the possibility might be imagined of establishing the equilibrium between land, labour, and capital so devoutly wished for by Wakefield, till, at any rate, the advent of new comers without capital, but gifted with intelligence, endowed at the same time with freedom of action, and allowed unrestrained power of access to fertile and easily available lands. The equilibrium would *then* be immediately disarranged, and beneficially so for the colony ; for can any one doubt that the labour of these free immigrants would, in a brief space of time, yield far more valuable results than would accrue from the previous combination of capital and forced labour ?

ready-made labour force for capitalists can be formed and maintained in a new country, without a degree of compulsion which, for the time it exists, is nothing if it is not slavery.

If, then, immigrants are to be introduced just in proportion to the wants of capitalists, it follows that no immigrants should be allowed to come in, in excess of the proportionate number, for fear of disarranging the equilibrium. That is, the supposed wants of capitalists and not the real requirements of the colony are alone to be provided for.

Again, as the labourers obtained and planted on the land, in pursuance of the system, were not to be prevented from land prospecting after a certain time, there was every chance of capitalists losing the services of their labourers *after* that time. The funds for the introduction of labourers, so far as any one man's land was concerned, have been exhausted in bringing on his land the labouring immigrants first placed on it, and who have now, we will suppose, left him. If he could not afford to get more labour himself out of his private resources, he would probably find himself with an estate which, in view of the contingency of his labourers leaving him at the end of the ' certain time,' he had worked to its utmost producing power, and which consequently now required more labour than ever if it was to afford him a living at all. The chances of his being able to get labour out of his private resources were at least doubtful, for the ' certain time ' allowed—two or three years—was probably not more than enough to give him a partial return of his expended capital, even under the most exhausting mode of cultivating the soil. It is likely enough that he would, instead, claim a fresh supply of labourers as an obligation due to him from the State, and that a number of men combining to make such a claim would procure its concession—at the expense of the community. Thus the system of ' State aid,' or ' protection ' to the landowning capitalist, would be further extended.

The other alternative before him was to buy fresh land further afield and to leave his first purchase neglected behind him. This, if ' protection ' was withheld from him, would be the alternative nearly every fresh settler would be forced to choose unless his land had been so remarkably prolific of produce, and his produce so capable of being exchanged under altogether exceptionally favourable circumstances, during the

U

' certain time ' as to have left him a large surplus of available funds wherewith to procure fresh labourers to replace those who had deserted him. Again, another alternative was that he should submit to be taxed for the purpose of importing fresh labour; but the experience of the history of new colonies only slightly peopled does not favour the supposition that direct taxation would be endured. The position, then, of the vast majority of landowners would be this—they would not be able to import fresh labour from their private savings ; the natural increase of population in the colony during the ' certain time ' would be totally insufficient to supply the gaps in labour occasioned on the whole aggregate of properties ; and their owners could not afford, or would refuse, to be taxed directly to the full extent that would be required if a fresh supply of labour was to be imported. So they would have to disperse to fresh fields, repeating a similar process so long as they had endurance enough to put up with the system. Thus dispersal would be forced on instead of concentration.

There are, of course, other means of procuring a fresh labour supply, of which the most obvious one is by raising a State loan for the purpose, and this method will be treated of later on.

Even in the oldest and most settled countries, an equilibrium between land, capital, and labour, such as Wakefield and Colonel Torrens based their principles upon, is a term without a meaning. For such an equilibrium to be possible, land, capital, and labour must bear a certain fixed and constant ratio to each other, so that any one of them can always be expressed in terms of each of the others ; but that is a condition which never has existed, nor ever can exist, so long as fresh labour, increased efficiency of labour, or an extension of the field of employment, daily produce fresh wealth capable of employment as capital.

Wealth is the product of the development by labour of the resources of the land. The more unfettered is the action of labour, the greater is the production of wealth. The less free scope there is for labour, the smaller will be the amount of wealth produced. Capital is that portion of wealth which furnishes the power of combining the operations of labour, or else of specialising and subdividing labour into particular channels, and so of procuring a larger remuneration for itself from the increased efficiency it gives to labour. The relation between the two, then, and between land which has not, as yet, become the subject of rent, is that of parallel and allied forces to a large extent mutually interdependent; but it is not represented by the balance between opposing forces necessary to constitute an equilibrium.

Be the technical argument worth what it may, there are other and more serious objections to be advanced against the plan of the compulsory subordination of the labourer to the capitalist.

The plan amounts to a proposal to 'protect' capital at the expense of labour; that is, to increase the profits of the capitalist by preventing labour from applying itself to develop local resources under the far-seeing stimulus of individual self-interest. The effect of such a restriction, if it were capable of being enforced in a new colony, would be to retard the prosperity of the young society, by preventing the natural production of infinite wealth, in order to localise a labour supply for the capitals from time to time introduced into the colony for purposes of speculation. But labour would not be *attracted* to a country where it was forcibly localised, because both freedom of action and the hope of acquiring a block of land—the two chief incentives to the emigration of labourers worth their salt—would be, to say the least, considerably interfered with; and also because of the distrust that would be felt by the would-be emigrant labourer in the future of a colony whose first legislation was in favour of 'protection' to the capitalist. Ergo, the plan which would ensure a constant supply of labour to the capitalist would necessitate the country, where such a state of things was contemplated, being rendered unpopular with the best individuals of the working class, and would require a staff of forced labourers—convicts, for example—to be recruited in order to satisfy the requirements of capitalists. So we come back again into the vicious circle of slavery in some form or other if a country is to start its business with an established ready-made equilibrium between land, capital, and labour.

In the longest-settled countries it is quite impossible to strike *even a proportion* between capital and labour definitely. The ratio between the two is always a varying one, and this no one could see more clearly than did Wakefield himself when he prominently put forward the proposition that the rate of wages is regulated rather by the extension or contraction of the field of employment than by any imaginary or actual proportion between capital and labour. He rejected the idea of a *proportion*, but he schooled himself into belief in an equilibrium, although equilibrium must of necessity be dependent on adjustment of proportion.

In plain reason, then, the only possible conclusion seems to be that an ' equilibrium ' between capital and labour is a term without a meaning, and that the ' most convenient proportions ' between the two are those which actual requirements call forth. To endeavour to establish a proportion, an equilibrium, or what you will, by previous regulation, is to demolish the whole basis of natural formation on which either of them, if possible of being found, *could alone* rest. I would conclude this portion of the discussion by remarking that if it is impossible to establish, by previous arrangement, an ' equilibrium ' between capital and labour, it is equally impossible to pre-arrange one between land, capital, and labour ; because, for the purpose of the equation, land has an equal value for both.

Unless, then, forced labour is resorted to, the supply of labourers in a new country where capital is ' protected ' is likely to prove insufficient and inefficient. Under these circumstances, the introduction of masses of capital is certain to be attended with the very consequences that Wakefield most wished to avoid. For the capitalist, unable to find labour when he bought land, would do so merely as a speculator in its prospective value. He would buy the best lands in contiguity to the centre of settlement, and he would endeavour to keep it out of the market until his resale would give him a large profit. In the meanwhile he would keep his land as 'waste,' uncultivated, unimproved, and without any means of communication across it. The longer he so kept it, or the greater the numbers of capitalist purchasers who kept their lands in this state, the further would it be necessary for the *bonâ fide* settler to go in order to find a block for himself. Settlers of limited means, but who, as is the invariable rule with new colonists, have resolved upon acquiring land immediately on arrival—not for speculative purposes, but for purposes of cultivation and residence—these men, the very life-blood of the young settlement, must, if they would really wish to settle down and develop the riches of the soil, go far away from the common centre; and thus again dispersal would be promoted instead of concentration.

But this would be a forced, not a natural dispersal, and it would be effected in the most expensive way for the colony, by leaving interposed an uncleared, unroaded area between the dispersed cultivators and their market.

Dispersal, as has been said, will never proceed on any considerable scale beyond the range of markets; so it would result that when the best land outside the uncultivated area possessed by speculators had been taken up, the value of the area between outside cultivation and the centre of settlement would be greatly increased by the demand of would-be fresh cultivators, unless new markets had grown up inland—an unlikely occurrence. The speculators would then be able to sell their land at enormous profit, and that, to the injury of the new purchaser, whose pecuniary means for cultivation would be diminished by just the extra price paid for his land. This profit would go into the speculators' pocket, and would not, therefore, be available to the State for the purpose of procuring fresh immigrants. The introduction of capital on a favoured basis, without provision made for a staff of forced labourers, would then have resulted in forced dispersal, in great gain to the land shark, and in incalculable economical loss to the community.

It is possible enough that Wakefield foresaw these consequences, and that it was with a view to avoid them that he endeavoured to provide labour on a quasi-compulsory footing. But he did *not see* that compulsion would be ineffectual in a new country unless supported by a complete system of slavery; and as he did not contemplate or provide for *that*, every detail of his plan broke down utterly and hopelessly— except the sound principle of selling, instead of giving away, the land.

The reign of the capitalist was to be secured by a 'sufficient price' being put upon land. The sufficient price was to be one that would answer two conditions. First, it was to prevent the premature purchase of land by individuals of the labouring class; second, it was to be a price that would enable the purchaser of land to command the necessary quantity of labour.

In old countries, the purchase price which land bears is regulated by the capitalised amount of its rental value over a short period of time. The yearly rent derivable from the land is a thing that it is comparatively easy to estimate from time to time. But, at best, the value so taken is but an arbitrary one, and does not hold good for periods of any considerable length. Even in the oldest and most settled countries rent varies from day to day, according to improvements in existing modes of production, according to the development of some new centre of industry, to discoveries of mineral wealth, to increased facilities for exchange, and to numberless other causes. Whatever basis of valuation may be taken is therefore, even there, evidently a very shifting one.

But the value of wild land in a new colony is, properly speaking, nothing. The purchaser only hopes that by the application of labour and capital it may be rendered otherwise. To endeavour to make its price suffice for the two objects in view must, then, be either to ignore its value altogether by placing on it a price fixed without reference to the supposed value of the land, or to fix an arbitrary value for the land for all time, without having any guide to indicate what its *present* value may be. The only rough test that could be given—

namely, the average price bid for land over a period of time—
was forbidden by the system, so it is necessary to suppose that
the price fixed referred merely to the attainment of the objects
described, and not at all to the value of the land.

This was actually the case. Proceeding on the assumption that a certain number of labourers were required for a
certain number of acres, Wakefield fixed his sufficient price by
taking as a basis the quantity of labour presumed to be necessary to produce the best working results.

Now nothing is more certain than that Nature permits of
no such ascertained proportion of labourers to acres. To discover such a proportion, even approximately, it would be
requisite to gauge accurately qualities of soils, as well as the
capabilities of every individual labourer, climatic influences
and variations, and every circumstance that might in any way
affect, not only land cultivation, but general industrial operations ; to do, in short, what no one in his senses would attempt
to do.

Further argument against so impossible a systematisation
is perhaps not called for. The weakness of the theory is
apparent enough from the mere statement of it. It is as
follows :—' The quantity of labour necessary for an acre of
land must determine what is the sufficient price for that acre ;
that, and no other price, is to be given for it, and the quantity
of labour by which the price is determined must be imported
to cultivate that acre.' The labourers are to be forced, or
induced, to stay on that particular acre, and, as nothing is said
as to the rate of wages to be paid in such a case, it may be
presumed that Wakefield did not think the question of wages
worth consideration. It might well be, however, that the
landowner called upon to receive a number of labourers proportioned to his acreage would regard wage-paying in a
serious light ; for his 1*l*. per acre—supposing that to be the
sufficient price—would involve not only the acquisition of so
much land, but also the obligation of feeding, housing, and
waging the ' proportionate ' amount of human flesh and blood
imported for him.

The only reasonable view to take of what ought to be a

' sufficient ' price seems to be that the price which a purchaser is willing to give for the land is the true ' sufficient ' price. This could only be ascertained by sale at public auction ; and with all the evils attaching to that system, it appears to be, on the whole, the fairest, where security is taken that the land bought shall be substantially improved or cultivated by the purchaser. But if sale by public auction is deemed undesirable, and if the ' sufficient ' price theory is still insisted on, the price fixed should be based on the advisability of extending settlement as fast and as far as the natural conditions of the country will allow of with *bonâ fide* settlers ; as, also, with the view of collecting a revenue, from sales of land, large enough to cover the general expenses of government and of opening up the country.

This was the view afterwards taken by the more popular section of colonial legislators, who in advocating a fixed uniform price system were desirous of seeing it in operation, because they believed that it would induce labouring men to become purchasers of land, and would at the same time discourage the land speculations of capitalists. To them, the capitalist, Wakefield's delight, was an object of aversion. I do not maintain that the colonists, if they had adopted the proposed system, would have succeeded in discouraging land-jobbing [1] and encouraging settlement, but it is a curiously instructive commentary upon Wakefield's line of reasoning that, although the system was, in fact, Wakefield's own, the reasons put forward for its adoption, first by him and afterwards by the colonists, were diametrically opposed to each other. Wakefield wished for it in order to encourage land speculation as the greatest blessing ; the colonists wanted it because they believed it would be the readiest means of putting an end to land speculation, which they looked upon as the greatest curse of the colony.

[1] Unfortunately, no enactment has ever yet been framed which has had more than a temporary effect in doing so. Land, the thing of most increasing value, is ever the most attractive bait for the speculator, and by one means or another he has always succeeded in evading the most stringent laws devised to check him.

The Wakefield colonisers were in too great a hurry. They wanted to establish in new colonies an exact reproduction of the economical condition of old countries. In the Old World, capital was a more gainful possession than in the New, because it could always command an unfailing supply of cheap labour ; therefore it was supposed that capital could be made vastly more profitable in the Colonies if labour could there be secured to it. Undoubtedly so ; but the 'if' was a fatal bar to the theory.

The relations between capital and labour, at home, were the results of gradual growth over a period coeval with that of the life of the nation itself ; and to import those relations, in the shape of regulations, was to attempt to supersede the process of natural development by clapping the oldest head on to the youngest shoulders, in the hope of its fitting there. Naturally it did nothing of the sort.

A country must go through many initial stages of adversity before it can attain to the height of prosperity fondly imagined by Wakefield as its necessary starting-point. Any efforts to anticipate the evolutionary process by previous regulation of the grandmotherly despotic type must ultimately delay the attainment of prosperity just in proportion as it forces it on for a time. Supposing labour had been compulsorily concentrated within defined limits in servitude to capital in Melbourne, or even on the squatters' runs (if capitalists had been allowed to squat anywhere—a license in opposition to the strict theory, but permitted as a supplement), when would the gold discoveries have taken place ? and for how long would the rush of population consequent on these discoveries have been delayed ? Nay, would not the rapid development of Melbourne itself have been sensibly retarded, the settled districts themselves prevented from progressing, and cultivation limited to a very small area ?

The example of South Australia has shown the danger of accumulating immigrants on a newly-occupied spot to find employment, instead of encouraging them freely to disperse until an effective demand for labour stimulates a certain degree of concentration.

'It was from the conviction of the difficulty of preventing labourers from disseminating themselves over the country as landowners that the suggestion was pressed on the Colonial Society, in 1830, of fixing a comparatively high price on Government land, in order at once to furnish a fund that might be exclusively appropriated to immigration purposes, and to prevent the poorer immigrants from acquiring a dominion over the soil on too easy terms, and from becoming occupants in lieu of labourers. The first-fruit of the project was the foundation of South Australia.'[1]

The principles of the system on which it was founded were, to use Merivale's summary—

1. That the prosperity of the Colonies mainly depends upon the abundance of available labour at the command of capitalists, in proportion to the extent of territory occupied.

2. That this abundance is to be secured by introducing labourers from outside, and taking care to keep them in the condition of labourers living by wages, for some considerable time — at least two or three years, according to Colonel Torrens.

3. That the revenue derived from the sale of new land is the fund out of which the cost of introducing them is best defrayed.

4. That the most convenient way of preventing them from rising too rapidly from the condition of labourers into that of independent landowners is, to sell the land at a sufficiently high price.

5. That the *entire* proceeds of the land sales ought to be devoted to the purpose of obtaining immigrants, and that only by devoting the whole, and not any portion, will the exact equilibrium between land, labour, and capital be secured.

6. That the sale of land should be at a fixed uniform price per acre for all qualities and all situations, and not by auction.

7. (Which is not necessarily connected with the others, and is rather a deduction than a principle.) That this system

[1] Merivale on Colonisation, Lecture XIX.

will tend to concentrate the population and to check that inconvenient dispersion which is apt to take place in new colonies.

The projectors put these principles forward as a connected system, of which no link could be injured without rendering the chain valueless.

This bundle of red-tape was energetically wound round the virgin territory of South Australia. By an Act of the Imperial Parliament, a Governor and Council were appointed for the colony. Also a Board of Commissioners was constituted to regulate the disposal of land and to arrange the management of emigration. The *whole* of the land fund was to be applied to emigration.

No specific provision was made for preparatory works, but 50,000*l*. was to be levied on land, on the security of the land fund, for defraying the necessary 'costs, charges, and expenses of founding the colony.' The Commissioners were also empowered to raise 200,000*l*. on the security of the '*future colonial revenue*,' while the future land fund was to serve as a collateral security.

The settlement was to be self-supporting, and the self-supporting principle was to be initiated by the borrowing of money in anticipation of future revenues. In practice, however, the notion of raising 200,000*l*. on the future revenue from an unbroken soil, even at 10 per cent., was found impossible. Only 39,000*l*. had been borrowed under the power up to 1838, when a new Act was passed giving increased borrowing facilities.[1] By it, all the funds of the colony were to be made security for loans ; nevertheless, so that the total debt due from the general fund to the land fund should never, at the end of any one year, exceed one-third of the whole amount of the land fund for that year.

The general revenue was almost certain not to be sufficient to meet even local requirements for years to come, so the whole system rested on the veriest speculation. Nothing was real but the land fund, and that was appropriated. Therefore

[1] 1 & 2 Victoria, c. 60.

the general revenue must be forced into existence by making the land fund larger. To effect this every means of speculation was resorted to. ' The original price of town lands in Adelaide was 12s. per acre ; only three days before the completion of the plan of the town 560 sections were sold at an average of 6l. 3s. per acre ; and in 1839, it was thought that those in the best situations were worth 1,000l. to 2,000l. per acre.' [1]

By the end of 1838 the colony numbered, as its population, some 6,000 persons. The price of land had been raised from 12s. to 1l. Nearly 50,000l. had been raised by the sale of land and applied to the introduction of immigrants, but almost the whole of the sales up to that period had been effected in England and were purely speculative.

In 1839, the colony was apparently in the full swing of prosperity. Over 5,000 immigrants arrived from the United Kingdom in that year, while 50,000 acres of the land of the colony were sold in England, and some 100,000 in the colony itself, at 1l. per acre. Up to the end of 1839, 125,000l. had been borrowed on the credit of future revenues out of the 200,000l. authorised to be raised under the Act.[2] The average interest on the amount borrowed was 10 per cent., while the revenue was inadequate to meet even the local expenses, or the charges for the civil list and the police department.

Now follows an extraordinary chapter of financial extravagance. ' The one thing needful,' said the Commissioners, ' is to give high bounties on the introduction of capital ; ' Adelaide must at all costs be made a good port, land must be surveyed and sold as fast as it could be got rid off. With the enormous cost of labour the expense of surveying rose to 10s. per acre. Thousands of emigrants arrived, and entailed a heavy burden on the Government before they could find employment. Whether from ostentation or necessity, the disbursements for the police department were twice as high in this colony without convicts as in New South Wales.

[1] Fourth Report of the Commissioners.
[2] 4 & 5 Wm. IV. c. 95.

Everything was done on a similar scale of reckless extravagance. A Government House was erected at a cost of 25,000*l.* Within four years from the foundation of the colony, the expenditure was at the rate of 140,000*l.* per annum,[1] on an actual revenue of 20,000*l.* In 1840 the Governor drew bills on the Commissioners for 123,000*l.* The original Commissioners for South Australia had been lately superseded by a general Board of Land and Emigration Commissioners, who refused to accept the bills. Then came the crash ; the colony became bankrupt, and emigration and land sales ceased in August 1840.

Parliament interfered, and empowered the home Government to advance a very considerable sum on security of the colonial revenue. So ended the ' self-supporting ' part of the scheme.

Merivale accounts for the collapse—firstly, because South Australia was not a country calculated by nature to ·become suddenly rich ; secondly, because no ' preparation ' (roading, bridging, &c.) had been made ; thirdly (and this cause was the most injurious of all), because of the unnatural encouragement given to speculation, and to its inseparable companion—extravagance. Further, he says :—' Time was wasted and the interest of capital sacrificed in land-jobbing operations which might have been profitably employed in sheep-farming and agriculture.'

' A community urged on by the spirit of speculation, which they (the Commissioners) sought in every way to encourage, cannot be morally or socially healthy. The one thing needful, thought they, is to encourage the rapid influx of capital, by high bounties, . . . and they never thought of the tide of evils which flow in along with a rapid influx of capital, when that capital is not gradually attracted by the opening field of employment, but comes in hopes of finding or creating such a field. The wealthier immigrants, finding no useful occupation for their means, took to land-jobbing, *i.e.* gambling, while waiting for it. The poorer immigrants, attracted by the hope

---

[1] In the last quarter of 1840, the Government expenditure was at the rate of 240,000*l.* per annum.

of large wages, were disappointed by the high prices, and found even the high sums which they actually realised insufficient to satisfy their anticipations.'

In 1840, 8,000 people, nearly half the population of the colony, were congregated at Adelaide. ' At the end of 1842, one-third of the houses in Adelaide were deserted ; their tenants, the surplus population created by the land-jobbers, had turned to the cultivation of the soil. Now, instead of paying 270,000*l.* in one year (1839) for the necessaries of life, the only want of the colonists was a market. Wheat was at 2*s.* 6*d.* a bushel ; sheep were fattened with it. Communication with the other Australian colonies soon rectified this.' [1]

The land sales fell from 170,000 acres in 1839 to about 600 in 1843. The new Governor, Captain Grey, reduced the expenditure in a single year from 90,000*l.* to 30,000*l.,* and nearly 2,000 persons were thrown on the Governor's hands as absolute paupers at the end of the first year of his administration.

' In a year or two more the colonists were poor indeed ; but they were out of debt, and working their way to prosperity ; for the Governor by his sturdiness and far-sighted economy had redeemed their financial position—though not until the self-supporting system appears to have cost the mother-country about 200,000*l.*' [2]

Never was there a system more fraught with all the elements necessary to failure ; the whole of it was a reckless gamble. From its very foundation the whole colony was put in pawn, and its first struggles were efforts to free itself from pre-contracted debts. To do this it had, by previous arrangement, to plunge headlong into the wildest speculation, and financial ruin was achieved before the infant settlement had got a fair start. At the same time the policy of the system was towards concentration to such an extent that individual prospecting, the great agent for the development of the country, was completely paralysed. Thus the only possible means of

[1] Report of the Land and Emigration Board for 1840.
[2] Merivale on Colonisation, Lecture XIX.

making the country quickly rich, and so of paying off debt, was prevented from operating in that direction.

The colony was, as has been said, to be self-supporting; and the best way of achieving that end was thought to be—to get money *anyhow*. In pursuance of this view, every effort was made to encourage the purchase of the lands of the colony by people at home, and agencies were established in England where maps of South Australia—plans of an unknown and unsurveyed territory—were displayed, in order to attract, not emigrants, but speculators. These last came forward in shoals, and brought up the vacant spaces on the maps with fervid zeal. Nothing was further from their intention than to go out themselves to the colony, and their sole hope was to resell the pieces of paper they had marked out for themselves, at an advance, as soon as possible. 'Large profits and quick returns;' such was the principle on which the landowning rights in South Australian soil were jobbed about, and for a while a roaring trade was driven merrily along.

The collapse that speedily took place was probably owing at least as much to this plan of selling land to speculators outside the colony as to any other cause; for, apart from the evil consequences of the speculation itself, the system was framed to encourage speculation to the utmost possible extent. Thus, sale by public auction was not to be permitted because purchasers at home could not be present at auction sales. Instead thereof, the land was to be sold at a fixed uniform price of 1*l*. per acre. Other reasons, doubtless, were present to the minds of the promoters in advocating the fixed uniform price regulation, but they are dealt with in Sir George Gipps's Memorandum in a way that absolves me from the necessity of further treating of them. The price fixed was, of course, the 'sufficient price,' and under that name, its evils, when directed to procure the dominion of the capitalist, have been already adverted to at considerable length. For and against the uniform fixed price theory when standing by itself, without reference to Wakefield's views in regard to the results to be derived from it, there is enough to be said to require lengthy and separate treatment, but the discussion would be foreign to the purpose of this work. It is enough to venture the observation- that sale by public auction, where the purchaser is put under conditions, and where the laws are rigidly enforced against illegal combinations to raise or lower prices, is a mode of disposing of land far preferable to that of sale at a fixed uniform price. Also, that the latter system, as applied, with the definite object prescribed, to South Australia, was productive of grievous misfortune to that colony.

Nothing could be more objectionable than the proposition to devote the entire proceeds of the land fund to the introduction of emigrants. If the land fund should be devoted in its entirety to that one purpose in any colony, the question arises, out of what fund preliminary surveying, roading, and other public works are to be carried on. Taxation on imports or exports must be resorted to for providing the means ; or else the colony must raise a foreign public loan. The advocates of the 'equilibrium' theory could not propose the former expedient, because they did not approve of indirect taxation ; and the carrying out of their theory forbade the imposition of direct taxation. Direct taxation would, in effect, have been an addition put on to the price the purchaser had paid for his land. The price, then, would have been *more* than sufficient to establish the 'equilibrium,' and as the 'equilibrium' was very delicately balanced, the slightest addition to the price of land would have upset it altogether, beyond the reconstructing powers of the most ingenious designers. So the Wakefieldians were driven to raise a public loan by way of initiating the colony into the practice of ' self-support.'

Injury upon injury. The failure of the loan policy in South Australia was undoubtedly assisted by the general framework of the system on which it was founded, more than by any extraneous cause ; but even though, under more favourable circumstances, it might not have been so signally unsuccessful, there can be little doubt that the mere fact of a colony starting on its career pledged to a loaning principle furnished an unfavourable augury for its future prosperity.

To a young country, strong in its confidence in its own

resources, and believing itself the possessor of inexhaustible wealth, but wanting an immediate supply of ready-money to enable it to open shop, to borrow money abroad seems the most economical way of getting it. The interest may be high—or low, what matters it? If low, it is a proof of the general outside belief in the credit of the colony, and a sign that lenders will not readily recall their principals. If high— well then; both principal and interest will soon be paid off, and there will be an end of the business.

The reasoning is hopeful, and creditable to local patriotism; but how stands the case really?

The interest on the loan may be less than the rate current in the colony itself, and the actual charge on that account may be insignificant. So much the worse, for the less the burden is felt, the greater is the danger of encouragement to fresh loan transactions, which the colony will not be willing to pay off at maturity except by the time-honoured, injurious expedient of raising new loans to pay off old debts.

Further, the knowledge that money can be borrowed is tolerably certain to generate spendthrift habits in young communities, already disposed to extravagance by the consciousness of the ease and certainty with which the virgin soil can be made to yield a fortune. A great many of the early settlers, too, are totally regardless of the future of the colony, and regard purely their own welfare, whether in opposition to that of the community or not. All causes combine to promote careless expenditure, and soon the colonists proceed to the erection of public works on a scale altogether unnecessary—but which in time becomes almost necessary—in order that the large numbers of labourers engaged on the works may be kept provided with the Government employment and Government pay that they have now come to consider as their due. The picture may be indefinitely extended and filled in with an extraordinary train of indirect consequences.

A Government will think twice before committing itself to expenditure, however likely to prove reproductive in the future, if it has only to rely, for the purpose, upon funds raised in the colony itself; but it will scarcely hesitate if any temporary extravagance can be made good by a loan, which can in all probability be raised at far below the average rate of interest prevailing in the colony. On the contrary, the éclat consequent on successfully floating such a loan on better terms than their predecessors has the effect of inducing competition in loan-mongering amongst responsible ministers. On the mass of the people, too, the effect is demoralising. Estimates are not criticised by them with any great severity, except for party purposes, when it is known that money can always be borrowed abroad to set everything right; and the country in its ignorance points with pride to its high credit abroad, and to the stability of its position as evidenced by the high rate of indebtedness per head. The new loans are looked upon as certain panaceas for distress, and as certain guarantees of prosperity. People laugh at the burden of four to five per cent., when for their own personal borrowings they pay interest at the rate of eight or ten per cent. Extravagance and waste become the inevitable rule in the department of public works, and decay and corruption become inseparable from the conduct of the public service. A steady opposition to direct taxation is gradually set on foot, and strengthened with each fresh proof of improved facility of loaning power. Local bodies, in turn, begin to borrow from the central Government, and the evils of the system are disseminated through the length and breadth of the community; while last but not least, is the imminent risk of the colony resorting to heavy indirect taxation and protective duties, in order to attempt the clearance of the growing burden of the yearly interest on its loans.

Even the application of a *fixed portion* of the land fund to emigration purposes is objectionable. The sum so applied may amount, in bad times, to far more than sufficient for its purpose, and yet, unless conscientiously administered, it may, in great part, find a mysterious path into the capacious pockets of shipowners or agents. This risk must always be run, but it may be to a certain extent minimised, if the fund allotted to emigration purposes is one based on actual emigra-

tion statistics, or on the view of the local demand for emigrants taken by the majority of members of the colonial
legislature in discussion on the estimates. If actual statistics
of past emigration be looked at in considering the amount
that ought actually to be expended on emigration, the sum
necessary will be found, since 1852, to bear a very small proportion to the average annual revenues from land sales in
each and all of the older colonies. Moreover, since that date,
State-assisted emigration has only accounted for a fraction of
the total number of emigrants. Also it is a matter of no-
toriety that a great part of the fund devoted to State-assisted
emigration was lavished in a variety of ways in 'pickings and
stealings,' and much of the remainder was expended in re-
lieving the mother-country of paupers, criminals, and infirm
people.

No system, however ingeniously devised by the colonists
themselves, deeply interested as they were in procuring full
value for immigration funds sent home, ever yet sufficed to
prevent fraud, and misappropriation of the money, from being
largely carried on, and we may find that in Victoria, at a time
when she possessed a population barely as large as that of a
fair sized provincial town at home, one of the earliest expressions of the popular will was directed to the material curtailment of the scale of State-aided emigration. Even under the
limited scale under which that colony consented to continue
the system, it was thought expedient to exact from the emigration agent sent to England the enormous security of
10,000l., as a guarantee for his proper administration of the
funds entrusted to him. And yet this was an agent selected
by the colony for his presumed integrity and fitness for the
post. It almost seems then, on the whole, that the smaller
the proportion of the land fund allotted to immigration, the
better for the colony; because the expenditure of small sums
is capable of being more rigidly checked, while giving less
opening to peculation, than would be the case with a larger
amount. Whether this be so or not, however, it is clear that
the amount should always be carefully scrutinised, and that to
sanction a vote for a larger amount than may be called for by

ascertained requirements may prove a serious blunder. That Wakefield's views in appropriating to immigration the whole of the indefinite revenue derivable from land was an erroneous one, has been conclusively demonstrated in the histories of the Australian colonies.

It only remains now to briefly refer once again to Wakefield's desire to prevent the labourer from rising too rapidly to a superior position. He was to be prevented from rising by a network of State-framed discouragement being imposed upon him. That is to say, he was to accept State superintendence or dictation as the rule for his direction in his private aims. The labourer who had traversed half the globe to seek for freedom, was, on arriving at his destination, to renounce even the degree of freedom that he had experienced at home. Surely not a 'consummation devoutly to be wished,' and least of all desirable in a new country, where vigorous independence on the part of the working-man is the most important factor in its political and economical progress.

How are widely disseminated centres of local and municipal government to grow up, if the labouring and artisan classes— those most actively interested in decentralised self-government —are confined within narrow limits and subjected to Government dictation in the conduct of their private affairs? The spirit of independence dies out under the withering blight, and with it decays, not only the hopeful vigour of the energetic worker, but also the healthy interest which he would, if left to himself, throw into the consideration of all questions connected with the government of the colony.

Is it unreasonable to hazard the suggestion that it was in the hope of such a result that the home Government consented to allow of the application of Wakefield's theories to South Australia? It is certain that for some time the Imperial Governors would not consent to their being put into practice, not because they deemed the economical regulations impracticable, but because the whole system seemed to aim at effecting too great a transfer of power to the colonial population. When at length they conceded to Wakefield an opportunity of trying his system in a modified form, they had previously satisfied themselves that the principles on which it was based were in no degree calculated to stimulate political activity in the minds of the colonists. Their supposition as to this was correct in one way, but at the same time, it is likely enough that had any new attempts been made from home to revive the system in its original form, after it had collapsed under its own cumbrous weight, a very active degree of hostility would have been excited against it in the colony; and the unexpected result of the forced separation of South Australia from England—if the settlement had not been entirely abandoned—might have formed the fitting termination to the history of the ' Great Wakefield Gamble.'

CHAPTER IX.

SYSTEMATIC FLEECING.—' HIGH PRICE' IN VICTORIA, LATE
PORT PHILLIP.

WE are assured by Merivale that the good fortune of Port
Phillip was owing mainly to the high price of its land. He
says :—' The increasing capital of Van Diemen's Land, unable
to find sufficient profit in that island, where so much had been
appropriated, found a new field in this adjacent region. Its
land has sold at the great average price of thirty shillings per
acre. If land had been given away at low prices, capitalists
would not have got the land at all : it would have been appropriated for the most part by numerous settlers, if they had
had equal chances of obtaining it with the rich, and in the
next place the few capitalists who might have settled there
could not by their united efforts have procured labour half so
cheaply or effectually as the Government has been able to do
it for them, besides the other advantages which the territory
has derived from the application of its land fund to other
branches of necessary expenditure.' [1]

Merivale believed that the future prosperity of colonies
was best secured by the monopolisation of the public lands in
the hands of capitalists, and like most devotees to a theory, he
doubted not that whatever height of prosperity the colony might
rise to, would be due entirely to the operation of ' high price '
in procuring that monopolisation. It is fortunately not a
matter of difficulty to show that while monopoly was the effect
of which ' high price ' was the cause, yet both together tended
in no small degree to retard the progress of Port Phillip or
Victoria in onward prosperity.

[1] Merivale on Colonisation, Lecture XIX.

Victoria speedily became prosperous, and its lands sold from the first at high prices. Therefore, according to Merivale, prosperity was the consequence of high price. A very slight examination of the early land history of Australia will probably suffice for the complete restatement of the proposition. It will then be seen that Port Phillip owed most or all of its early success to the fact that it was started into being by unsystematised private enterprise, instead of on a fanciful systematic basis, and that its progress might have been far greater and more stable had it not been for 'the high average price to which the lands were raised by means which may fairly be written down as artificial.

It was in Governor Bourke's reign in 1831, that the system of selling instead of granting land in New South Wales was first initiated. Former Governors had been in the habit of giving away land as they pleased, and charges of impartiality and injustice in the distribution were freely indulged in by disappointed applicants, and in many cases with good reason. The right of giving away land involving, as it did, an onerous responsibility, was a weighty charge to be given up to the keeping of Governors completely irresponsible to the colony, and it furnished them with an overwhelming power of patronage which, if they had not to some extent made it available for the furtherance of their own private whims or predilections, would have argued in them integrity almost more than human. By orders from home, Bourke was deprived of the power of granting land in any quantity or to any person whatever, except to a specified extent for schools, churches, glebes, or other public purposes. Crown lands were now to be sold by public auction, and none were to be sold at all unless applied for by an intending purchaser. A minimum upset price of five shillings per acre was fixed for country lands.

In 1839 the upset price was raised to twelve shillings, and again in 1843 to twenty shillings per acre. ' At the time when the change was first made, from grant to sale, a pledge had been virtually given to the colonists that the revenue from the sale of land should be appropriated mainly towards the encouragement and promotion of the emigration of virtuous and industrious families, and individuals from Great Britain and Ireland; and considering the original character of the colony as a general receptacle for the accumulated criminality of the empire, no appropriation of that revenue could possibly have been more judicious on the one hand, or more important in the eye of enlightened philanthropy, on the other. For there was thus provided the means of infusing, to almost any conceivable extent, the salutary ingredient of a virtuous and industrious population into the mass of a convict colony, and of thereby elevating that colony, in a period of time comparatively short, to the rank of an intelligent, respectable, and religious community.' [1]

This promise was, however, not fulfilled, for up to the end of Sir Richard Bourke's governorship, out of a total revenue from land during the six years of 439,625*l*., only about one-fifth or 91,167*l*. was found to have been expended on immigration during that period.

Sir George Gipps entered on his administration in 1838, and during his reign the free (that is, not convict or freed) immigrants and the native-born population together outnumbered the other classes, and all the more prominent traces of the convict origin of the colony disappeared. Now was the time to affiliate the free immigrant, in especial, to the soil, by giving him the opportunity of settling on the land, and now was just the time chosen by the Imperial Governor for interposing difficulties in the way of his acquiring land. The price was fixed at a minimum of 1*l*. per acre, in itself a price by no means prohibitive. The object of the Governor seems to have been to fill the Treasury, and to impress the value of his stewardship upon the home authorities, by showing the largest possible revenue from the smallest possible area. He played the part of the ' land-shark ' to perfection, and as long as he could show an overflowing balance-sheet, his proceedings met with the applause of his titular superior. The expedient adopted was to throw a very limited quantity of land into the market at one time, and competition amongst a lot of eager buyers soon ran prices up to heights more satisfactory to the

[1] Lang's *New South Wales*, vol. i. p. 262.

governing powers than to the purchaser. Port Phillip was, at that time, a part of New South Wales, and the rush of population thither indicated to Sir George Gipps the most desirable spot in all Australia for fleecing the early settlers by means of high land prices.

The immediate consequence of limiting the quantity of land in the market to a very small amount was to compel the unfortunate immigrants, who were almost *obliged* to obtain land or building allotments, to bid against each other till the price of land rose to fancy height. They were thus ' crippled in their means, involved in debt, and in many instances hopelessly ruined, while millions of acres of the richest land around them were lying utterly waste. Mr. Richard Howitt, who went out amongst the first emigrants to Port Phillip, but who left the country in disgust after a few years' trial, on finding that he had been all but ruined in the very midst of all the elements of prosperity and plenty, through the absurd policy of the local Government in regard to the disposal of the waste lands, published a work [1] in which he details his own bitter experiences on the subject, and in which the reader will find that these statements have been by no means exaggerated.' [2]

Another favourite device of Sir George Gipps was to place a high upset price upon all town allotments. The evils of this were heavily enough felt in the towns already formed, but they pressed more grievously upon the would-be inhabitants of those inland towns which as yet only existed on the map. There labour and necessaries were far dearer than in the established chief towns on the coast, and in addition to the tax thus entailed upon the slender resources of the local settler, he had to pay high rents to recoup their outlay to the speculative purchasers of lots in the unformed town.

Says Dr. Lang : [3] ' The evil consequences of this injudicious policy, in addition to the serious evil of crippling the immigrants by depriving them of their available means, were two-fold. First, the allotments actually purchased in the towns

---

[1] *First Impressions of Australia Felix*, by R. Howitt.
[2] Lang's *New South Wales*, vol. i. p. 287.   [3] *Ibid.* p. 287-8.

were in numerous cases cut up by the calculating speculator who purchased them into insignificant fragments, to be resold to a humbler class of purchasers at an exorbitant profit ; and numerous narrow lanes and *culs-de-sac* were thus formed, in which the labouring population, by whom the buildings erected on these fragmentary allotments were chiefly inhabited, were very soon almost as densely crowded together as in some of the largest capital cities or manufacturing towns of Europe—an arrangement which in a comparatively warm climate like that of New South Wales constitutes a perfect nursery of fever and other forms of contagious or epidemical disease. Second, knowing people bought large suburban allotments, which they obtained at comparatively low prices— at 2l. or 5l. an acre—beyond the limits of Sir George Gipps' towns, and cutting them up into half-acre or quarter-acre allotments, immediately advertised other towns, as rivals to the Governor's, in their immediate neighbourhood. Hence it is that all the principal towns of the era of the Government of Sir George Gipps, from Geelong and Portland, in latitude 38° south, to Brisbane and Ipswich in the Moreton Bay country, in latitude 27° south, resemble respectively so many hens and chickens, each consisting of a larger town in the centre with a number of smaller ones all around it. In this way the peculiar advantages of towns—the concentration of the population within a reasonable space, and the consequent ability of the inhabitants to provide for themselves all the requisite public improvements at a comparatively trifling cost—were lost on the one hand, while all the disadvantages of the country—distance and discomfort—were entailed upon the community on the other.'

The money thus extracted from the pockets of the settlers was employed in bringing out fresh batches of immigrants who, as they were landed, formed an additional formidable body of competing land buyers, who, by force of necessity, had no alternative but that of trying to get blocks of land at high prices. For this purpose they could get money freely advanced by the numerous banks then recently established, and so the immigrants were afforded every facility for plunging headlong into debt, and bought not only land that they *did* want, but land that they did not require except for purposes of mere speculation.

The good fortune of the colony was, to all appearance, great about the year 1839; but the structure of prosperity was but a house of cards ready to topple over at a touch. Fortunate it was in effect, though disastrous at the moment, that just about this time Sir George Gipps exerted a pressure upon the local banks, which brought down with a run the artificial edifice built up of high prices and wholesale credit, for every day that it remained erect the mischief was spreading itself over a wider area.

The manner of the collapse is briefly told by Lang :—

The local Government [he tells us] were at this period in the habit of depositing the large amounts that accrued from the different land sales in the different banks of the colony, and charging interest on these deposits at the rate of four per cent.; but Sir George Gipps, speculating doubtless on the soundness and permanency of the wonderful prosperity which the colony was exhibiting under the extraordinary influx of capital, and desiring to secure the largest share of that prosperity for the State, insisted upon having either seven or seven and a half per cent. in future as the interest on the Government balances in the banks; and as these establishments were now working against each other, his imperious mandate had to be obeyed, under the penalty of a withdrawal of the Government funds from the refractory establishment.

To enable them to pay this high interest and to make a large profit besides, the banks had to enlarge their discounts, and to take security for their advances in the descending scale of *best, better, and good*, till they crossed the line of safety and included a great many which had not even the positive degree of this commercial quality to recommend them, but which were notoriously *bad, worse, and worst*.

With these extraordinary facilities for all sorts of money operations, the rage for speculation, not only in land and town allotments, but in sheep, cattle, and horses, reached a much greater height than it had ever done, even during the sheep and cattle mania of the era of Sir Ralph Darling; and the most unbounded extravagance of living was in many instances the natural accompaniment of so unnatural a state of things. Everybody bought land and town allotments, or sheep, cattle, and horses at enormous prices; adopting at the same time a scale of domestic expenditure proportioned to the profits they expected to realise, and giving their promissory notes for due payment to the banks, or mortgaging their lands and houses to one or other of the loan and trust companies for sums not unfrequently far below their real value. One mercantile house in Sydney, which of course fell when the storm came, and great was the fall of it, had purchased land on speculation at Port Phillip to the extent of upwards of 100,000*l.* ; and a property which was mortgaged to one of the companies for 10,000*l.*, and which afterwards fell into the hands of the company, realised to its proprietors not more than 100*l.* a year.[1]

The upshot of all this might have been foreseen, and was experienced at length in full force. The purchase of Government lands and town allotments declined apace, and then ceased entirely. The obligations to the banks and other lending companies, as well as to private individuals, fell due ; and land and stock and other property of all kinds were forced upon a falling market to meet them. These articles of property consequently declined rapidly in value, falling as far below the average of former years as they had been unmaturally raised above it ; and all but universal bankruptcy ensued. A flock of sheep was actually sold by the sheriff at this period, in satisfaction of a comparatively small debt, at sixpence per head ; while another flock, the property of one of the oldest merchants in the colony, was purchased at so low a price (one shilling and sixpence per head) that within two months after the sale, which took place in September, just before shearing time, the fortunate purchaser realised upwards of 250*l.* more than the whole amount of his purchase money from the wool alone. In another similar case, cattle which had been bought at six guineas a piece were sold at seven shillings and sixpence each ; and horses, that cost sixty guineas, brought only sixteen or seventeen shillings, while a house in Sydney, for which 5,000*l.* had been offered and refused very shortly before, was sold for 1,200*l.*[2]

The local writers of that day could furnish an infinite number of such examples, if examples were needed, to prove that everything and everybody was insolvent. The prosperity raised on a system of artificial high price had been but a bubble, to which the slightest prick was fatal.

It was calculated that the losses immediately consequent on the collapse were equivalent to ten pounds per head of the colonial population. So universal was the ruin that bank-

[1] Lang's *New South Wales*, vol. i. pp. 291-3.
[2] *Ibid.* p. 293.

ruptcy ceased to be considered a disgrace, because it was no longer a distinction.

Strange as it may seem, the real prosperity of the colony had been materially advancing during this period of inflation. The seasons had been unusually good, the flocks and herds of the colony had been multiplying with rapidity, and during the whole time the necessaries of life were abundant and cheap. At this period, too, pastoral pursuits had acquired an extra value by reason of the discovery of the boiling-down process for extracting tallow from the carcasses of dead stock.

This last was unsystematised, unforced, natural prosperity, and it formed the basis on which the industrial future of the colony was gradually to erect itself.

It has been seen how injurious to the colony were the effects of high speculative prices, how general was the speculation in the settled districts, and how vast the ruin its collapse produced. Are we to believe Dr. Lang and evidence like to his, given by contemporary chroniclers of the period, or are we to accept Merivale's assertion that the progress of colonisation in Australia ' was almost entirely free (thanks to the rigid provision of its institution) from those evils which have so extensively arisen from the engrossing of land by speculators in free grant or low price colonies ? '

That free grant is an erroneous and highly-dangerous system may be readily admitted, but that high price, as tried in Victoria, contributed to the prosperity of that colony, is a statement directly contradicted by the most glaring and indisputable facts.

Again, Merivale observes : ' The success of high price in Australia was owing to the small cost of clearing, and to the facility the even surface of the land gave for roads, or rather for dispensing with roads, in the first stages of settlement. The easy acquisition of pastoral lands, and the rapidity with which wealth had been created by sheep-farming, has furnished a continual stimulus to agriculture and a constant field for the employment of surplus labour. The mere purchase-money of the land has formed consequently a very considerable part of the purchaser's expenditure. He can afford to pay to the

land fund what the Canadian farmer had to devote to clearing. . . . . He consequently reaps the full benefit of his expenditure by the importation of immigrants.'

Merivale is here treating of a period anterior to the time
when the squatters acquired pre-emptive rights over their runs.
Hardly a single acre had, up to then, been bought by the
pastoral interest; therefore, it is not easy to see how ' high
price' could have contributed to the success of the interest
which was then the backbone of the colony. The number of
labourers required to do the work of a sheep or cattle station
is extraordinarily small in comparison to acreage, and a very
small portion of the land fund would have sufficed to bring
out all the labour demanded by the squatters. Squatting, or
rather its favoured conditions and profitable results, had undoubtedly the effect of attracting many men of superior position to the colony, but it certainly did little or nothing
towards bringing labouring emigrants there or towards giving
them employment on their arrival.

Had Merivale known the actual circumstances of the
colony, he could never have advanced so untenable an argument as that high price assisted pastoral pursuits, and that
pastoral pursuits ' furnished a stimulus to agriculture.' This
last it did not do, for even before the date of the Orders in
Council—when, as has been seen, the position of the squatters
was made the means of directly discouraging agricultural pursuits—the squatting stations were always possessed of their
own cultivation paddocks, on which they grew produce for
their own consumption, and therefore even then they gave no
direct assistance or stimulus to the farming interest.

The assertion made by Merivale is really a roundabout
attempt to prove that whatever degree of prosperity farming
had attained to, was mainly ascribable to the operation of
' high price.' The benefit of high price to the farmer was
supposed to be that it enabled enough labouring emigrants to
be imported to give him a constant certain supply of labour,
while at the same time it prevented the labourer from rushing
to acquire a block of land immediately on landing in the
colony.

Now, in so far as high prices given for farming land— by which I mean the artificially enhanced prices which Merivale eulogises—were concerned, their first effect was to reduce the quantity of land which the farmer might have got under a system which would have induced cheaper prices, and also to reduce the private capital which he might otherwise have made available for improvements. He was, therefore, driven to borrow money at high rates, as a preliminary to the successful prosecution of his business. He was thus greatly handicapped at starting, and it is exceedingly doubtful whether he was benefited at all by the use made of the purchase-money to import labouring emigrants. It may safely be asserted that he would have got his labour cheaper than he actually did—even had the land revenue for emigration purposes been far smaller than it was during the high price period—if the smaller revenue had been raised in a natural, non-speculative manner.

As evidence in support of this last assertion, it may be as well to glance at some of the ascertained consequences of artificial 'high price' in Port Phillip.

The highest average prices and the greatest amount of land revenues were together derived from the purchase of town and suburban lots for building purposes. The immigrants, as they landed, were eagerly competed for by the buyers of these lots, with the result that the labouring immigrants, who would under ordinary circumstances at once have gone up country, were turned into bricklayers, plasterers, &c., at enormously high wages, and were consequently very well satisfied to remain in Melbourne. The farmers, heavily fleeced by the high prices they had paid for their land and by the heavy weight of advances under which they lay, could not afford to offer wages equal to those given by the builders, and could at the best only employ one labourer instead of two.

The builders, in order to recoup themselves for their large expenditure—for which they too were, as a rule, under heavy advances—had to charge exorbitant rents. The traders in the principal towns found their high rents a serious tax upon their profits, and were therefore under the necessity of selling their goods at high prices, at a time when, the community generally being out of pocket—a necessary consequence of the speculative craze—every one was more anxious to sell something of his own than to buy what some one else had to sell him. The farmers under these circumstances were either obliged to resort to the roughest and most unproductive methods of agriculture, or they had to procure agricultural implements, at great cost, from a remote seaport town. Thus they too had to pay in enhanced prices for the difficulties in which Melbourne and Geelong had been placed by the system which gave a speculative value to town lots ; and thus an artificially stimulated speculation, engendered by the high prices produced by the system of limiting the quantity of land open for sale below the popular demand, acted adversely alike on those interests furthest away in point of distance from the chief centre of speculation, and on those nearest to them.

Plenty of immigrants were brought into the country by means of the land fund, but as they remained in the seaport towns, the farmer got but small return for his purchase money in the shape of the immigrant labour he was supposed to have paid for when he bought his land. His ' high price ' therefore did not benefit him just in the very particular in which Merivale assures us that he derived most advantage from it.

If a considerable portion of the land revenue had been appropriated to road-making—an amount proportioned to the high prices paid for farms in the most naturally favoured of the agricultural districts—a boon would have been conferred on the farmers which would have largely compensated them for their extravagant outlay in purchase. But the policy of the Government was to make use of the funds to bring in fresh supplies of immigrants to swell the lists of competitors for lands. So the farmer had to have extra teams of oxen and horses to do the work of the heavy transport of his produce to the nearest large markets, instead of employing a smaller stud to do the work of easy transport over good roads. All this increased cost constituted a heavy deduction from the profit on his produce and left him a miserably small margin wherewith to carry on the struggle for existence.

To the economist the following tables will be full of interest, as showing at a glance the effect produced upon the cost of transport by improved means of communication. It shows how preferable the lot of the agriculturists might have been compared to what it actually was, during a period when communications were hardly opened at all between Melbourne and the farming districts not more than a hundred miles distant. The comparison in the tables is between railway and road prices. To estimate the true position of the Port Phillip farmer in and about 1840–2 it must be borne in mind that then there were few or no roads, so that the length and difficulties of transport were far greater than in 1857; and so also was the risk of loss or damage of the produce carried.

TABLE SHOWING THE COMPARATIVE EFFECTS ON PRICES OF PRODUCE, IN 1857, BY TRANSPORT OVER ROADS AS CONTRASTED WITH TRANSPORT OVER RAILWAYS.

Table I., showing effect on prices of produce by transport over Roads.

	Flour per ton			Wheat per bushel		Potatoes per ton			Tallow per ton			Hay per ton		
	£	s.	d.	s.	d.	£	s.	d.	£	s.	d.	£	s.	d.
Price at market . . .	22	0	0	8	0	6	10	0	40	0	0	8	0	0
Value, 20 miles from market	19	6	8	6	$6\frac{6}{7}$	3	16	8	37	6	8	5	6	8
,, 40 ,, ,,	16	13	4	5	$1\frac{5}{7}$	1	3	4	34	13	4	2	13	4
,, 60 ,, ,,	14	0	0	3	$8\frac{4}{7}$	not given			32	0	0	not given		
,, 80 ,, ,,	11	6	8	2	$3\frac{3}{7}$	,,			29	6	8	,,		
,, 100 ,, ,,	8	13	4	0	$9\frac{2}{7}$	,,			26	13	4	,,		

Table II., showing effect on prices of produce by transport by Rail.

	Flour per ton			Wheat per bushel		Potatoes per ton			Tallow per ton			Hay per ton		
	£	s.	d.	s.	d.	£	s.	d.	£	s.	d.	£	s.	d.
Price at market . . .	22	0	0	8	0	6	10	0	40	0	0	8	0	0
Value, 20 miles from market	21	13	4	7	$9\frac{6}{7}$	6	3	4	39	13	4	7	13	0
,, 40 ,, ,,	21	6	8	7	$7\frac{5}{7}$	5	16	8	39	6	8	7	6	8
,, 60 ,, ,,	21	0	0	7	$5\frac{4}{7}$	5	10	0	39	0	0	7	0	0
,, 80 ,, ,,	20	13	4	7	$3\frac{3}{7}$	5	3	4	38	16	4	6	13	4
,, 100 ,, ,,	20	16	8	7	$1\frac{2}{7}$	4	16	8	38	6	8	6	6	8
,, 120 ,, ,,	20	0	0	6	$11\frac{1}{7}$	4	10	0	38	0	0	6	0	0
,, 140 ,, ,,	19	13	4	6	$9\frac{1}{14}$	4	3	4	37	13	4	5	13	4

The tables [1] furnish an excellent illustration of the immense benefit derivable by settlers in a young colony from the material quickening and cheapening of existing modes of transport, and point with equal force to the immense disadvantage under which the country labours when supplied with inferior means of communication. We find, from the first table, that in the case of some articles, the necessity of having to transport them in drays over roads, for even the short distance of from twenty to twenty-five miles, was enough to bring down their value to one-half of the ' price at market,' and if we may draw an inference from the omissions in the table it would appear that at a greater distance than forty miles the expense and delay of sending potatoes and hay to market was sufficient to prevent the attempt being made at all—by road, On the other hand, it is evident from Table II. that better modes of transport were instrumental in stirring up the energies of farmers at remote distances from Melbourne, to raise and to send thither produce which otherwise would have been either not raised at all, or else left to rot on the ground for want of a market to which they could be conveyed with profit. It is obvious from the tables that the best means of encouraging agricultural pursuits would have been by making good roads, and had a considerable portion of the large revenue derived from the sale of land been applied to the purpose of making good roads at a time when there were none, or of improving bad ones later on, the high price of land might have really benefited the colony. As it was, the land revenue being devoted to no other purpose than the introduction of immigrants, the new arrivals found no resource open to them —after their first rush to the diggings—in the remote rural districts : for the want of roads prevented the possibility of their working there profitably as farmers, and they had therefore to return to Melbourne, to swell the multitude struggling for room in the already unnaturally distended metropolis.

The ' high price ' system as practised in Port Phillip was a

[1] The tables are included in a return made to the Victorian Parliament in 1857-8.

but too successful effort to fill the Treasury, in order to import additional crowds to replenish it more vigorously at greater expense to themselves. Those venerated appearances of prosperity, plenty of money and plenty of people, were to furnish the world with proofs of the thoughtful wisdom of the colonial Governor, and everything was to be strained to subserve this end. No matter that the money was extracted from people who beggared themselves in paying it, and that the fresh immigrants were fleeced, as soon as landed, by the grasping policy of the Government land shark. Plenty of money in the Treasury, plenty of people in the colony : that was the text of the perpetual self-laudation of the Imperial representative, and which procured for him the esteem of an enraptured Colonial Office—until the crash came, and with it an empty Treasury, a bankrupt colony, and a sharp contraction of prices to nothing at all. In the history of the mad speculation, the reckless extravagance, the impeded industry and the total collapse of Port Phillip, read the necessary sequel of ' high price ' and the bitter converse of Merivale's mistaken eulogy.

CHAPTER X.

PART I.—THE DUAL HOUSE SYSTEM IN AUSTRALIA.
PART II.—PAYMENT OF MEMBERS AND COLONIAL
CORRUPTION.

PART I.

IN a foregoing chapter,[1] reference has been made to the unsatisfactory results to which the establishment of the Dual House system in the Australian colonies, under their paper constitutions, has given rise. It may be worth while here to allude to the system at slightly further length, mainly with a view to indicate the obstacles which interfere with its smooth working in the colonies, and which give colour to the local objections to the system.

In England, the House of Lords is representative of a long-established and influential caste which, while the cause of the people against the encroachments of monarchy was its own, did yeoman service for the national liberties. The right of peers to an important share in the legislation of the country was therefore recognised as being the natural outcome of efforts made by them to curtail the powers of despotic authority, and there was thus some reason for the existence of the House of Lords *ab initio*, although there may be none for its continuance on an hereditary basis. But in Australia there was absolutely no reason, beyond English precedent, for he establishment of Upper Houses. There was not, in the Australian colonies originally, any recognised separate class demanding for itself special legislative rights or even desiring burden itself with the cares of legislation. Unfortunately the effect of setting up Upper Houses there has been to foster amongst wealthy and influential colonists the belief that they

[1] Chapter V., *ante*,

occupy a peculiarly lofty position as of right, and that it is necessary to conduct themselves as if there is no identification possible between their own prosperity and that of the general body of the people. In other words, the institution of an Upper House, in the one case, was due to the pre-existence of a class whose members occupied the position of popular leaders ; in the other, there were no similar circumstances to justify the erection of Upper Houses, but the consequence of their establishment has been to procure the rise and growth of a class straining after an exceptional and privileged position for itself.

It may be well that colonial self-government should have begun on the Dual House system, for the difficulty of working it on that footing has been exposed from the outset ; and being a part of a ready-made paper constitution, it will be far easier to remedy or modify it than if it had been gradually evolved by the necessities of the nation. That the system has acted injuriously for the immediate interests of the colonists, seems evident enough. Life in Australia, and notably in Victoria, is now divested of much of its former ease for the working class. By slow but certain degrees, the struggle for existence is beginning there to assume acuter phases. Men and women work harder than they used to do and for smaller returns. For the working man, any one of the Australian colonies is still a paradise, but a paradise where exhausting toil and thought for the morrow are gradually trending upon the normal conditions of 'a fair day's work for a fair day's wage.' And why ? Let anyone who cares to supply a ready answer peruse the parliamentary records of Victoria, the colony which has been foremost in political activity. There he will read a tale of Reform Bills rejected, of Land Bills thrown out, of Education Bills mangled, of bitter class hatreds engendered, of long-continued commercial depression produced and maintained, of universal discontent and trouble, caused mainly by the anti-popular action of the Legislative Council—the House of Lords of Victoria. Consistently and constantly that Council has striven to limit the rights and to depress the condition of the people, by favouring the opposing claims of a small class, until it has at length succeeded in establishing an almost stationary condition of industrial existence as the normal characteristic of the colony, in place of the rapid forward development, which ' Protectionism ' by itself could not have wholly checked.

' Such seems to be the disposition of man, that whatever makes a distinction produces rivalry,' and the tendency of Upper Houses to embrace the unpopular cause is undoubtedly strengthened by placing them in juxtaposition with Lower Houses representative of the people. A distinction is made between the functions of the two bodies, and rivalry—the rivalry of enmity—follows as of course.

So long as the Dual House system, on its present basis, remains unaltered in Victoria, an unsettled, restless condition and consequent industrial depression will be stimulated by the purely selfish action of one of the two Houses, and we may fairly conclude from past evidence, as well as from the nature of the case, that the House whose selfishness will be the most powerful to retard the progress of the colony, will be the one that sets itself in opposition to measures designed for the extension of the privileges of the people. At the same time, the Lower House—the Assembly —has been and probably will continue to be impelled, by the merest spirit of opposition to the Council and all its works, to make its legislative proposals extravagant and unreasonable, rather than moderate and therefore acceptable. For this the Dual House system is responsible, and from its existence is derived the tendency of Victorians to make of the course of legislation a mere struggle for mastery between the two Houses, and to appeal, on disputed questions, rather to the passions than to the good sense of the community. With regard to this, take, for instance, the question of Free Trade *versus* Protection. The Legislative Council in Victoria has usually advocated Free Trade principles, while the Lower House has given its adhesion to Protectionist measures. In the Free Trade endeavours of the Council we have, it may be observed, a notable exception to the general anti-popular

tenour of its legislation ; still the fact need not be credited to
the beneficent intentions or to the greater wisdom of the
Council. On the contrary, the difference between the two
Houses on this particular point is little more than evidence of
the unworkability of the Dual House system. For it is probably
the bitter antagonism between the two Houses that produces
so essential a difference of view ; and with regard to many
other important questions, divergencies of opinion between
Council and Assembly are to be largely accounted for by the
prevalence of this feeling of mutual hostility. But assuming
it to be otherwise ; supposing the Free Trade-ism of the Council
to be due to a pure and intelligent desire to forward the prosperity of the colony, the fact, if fact it be, may place the
Council in a more favourable light, but it does not advance the
argument in favour of the Dual House system any further.
For the hoisting of the Free Trade banner by the Council does
little beyond exciting the Assembly to an extravagant extreme
of Protectionism ; and Protectionist policy, being associated in
the minds of the people with the maintenance of the power of
the Assembly as long as the Council is anti-Protectionist, is
pursued by them with an insistance fervent enough to override
the adverse vote of their natural enemy, the Council. So with
land legislation ; each House strains every nerve to gain the
mastery over the other, only in a more marked degree. In
this case the breach is wider, because each side is firmly convinced of the justice of its own cause ; but, in either case, the
proposals for legislation and the opposition to them at length
come to assume an extreme form, and the colony is divided
into two hostile camps, one for the Council policy, right or
wrong, the other for the Assembly policy, wrong or right.

There are one or two considerations which affect the working of the Dual House system in Australia which it is necessary
to bear in mind, as constituting an all important difference
between the system as practised there, and as established in
England. Let me begin my allusion to them by asking what
would be said in England if it were seriously proposed to
accord to peers the right to vote for members of the House of
Commons ? Surely the majority of the nation would scout the

proposition as intolerable, so long as the peers had a House of
their own. Yet in England the admission of the right of peers
to vote for members of Parliament would, in all probability, have
little or no direct effect on the composition of the Lower House,
because the number of peers is too limited to permit of their
exercising any numerical influence over parliamentary elections.
But in the Colonies, the electors who have the exclusive right to
vote for members of the Council have also the right to vote for
members of the Assembly. Besides, *there* the number of electors
for the Council forms a large proportion of the total electorate :
so, as they can duplicate their votes by voting for Assembly as
well as for Council members, it is evident that they may acquire
a preponderating share of power by exercising a great direct
influence over the election of the Assembly, in addition to
choosing members for that house which is supposed to be
peculiarly representative of their own views. By the operation of this system of voting, the Council is furnished with a
certain number of supporters in the Assembly, and its position
for insisting on its own course is strengthened, a result all
sufficient to excite the dislike of those electors who possess only
the right of voting for Assembly members, to a dual system
which appears to them to trick them out of the logical consequence of their natural numerical preponderance.

There is yet another consideration worthy of mention. In
the Australian colonies, members of the Legislative Councils
are not, as in England, men of a class long recognised as
being, in point of social standing, far above the commonalty.
There is none of that instinctive reverence for a member of
Council that the average Englishman feels for a peer. The
lowliest in the land does not feel himself separated from the
most highly placed by an impassable social gulf, as he does in
England, and the member of Council is not regarded with any
peculiar respect, either by reason of his membership or of his
position in society. Where such comparatively small differences
of level are found, the community is naturally unwilling to
surrender exceptional advantages to any portion of its citizens,
and is inclined to watch jealously the proceedings of those to
whom special privileges have been given.

On the other hand, the privileged class casts an equally suspicious eye upon the community, and is quick to stigmatise each assertion of popular claims as an unwarrantable interference with its own rights. Hence, the extreme bitterness of the contests between the two Houses in colonies where political activity is great, and where the magnitude of the cause at issue comprises directly and palpably the dearest interests of the entire population.

It is far from my intention to enter into a discussion of the benefits or evils that might be expected from a system of government by one House. All schemes for government on a popular basis are little more than so many make-shift compromises, and are therefore necessarily highly imperfect and open to criticism. That any scheme should work fairly well is all that can be expected. The opinion that a one House system in the Colonies would fulfil that condition may be an erroneous one; but there can be little room for doubt that the dual system, as it prevails to-day in the Colonies, must be greatly modified if it is to continue to exist at all, or to produce results satisfactory to the mass of the colonists. It is in Victoria that its unworkability has, so far, been most keenly felt. It needs only a greater pressure of population on space, in the other Australian colonies, to stimulate political activity in them to a high degree, and to bring home to each of them the consequent necessity for radically altering the Dual House arrangements in their existing constitutions.

Rule by two Houses is too often a convenient synonym for the worst form of rule by one alone—the one that thwarts the popular will. It was so wholly in England not so very long ago; it is still so to a very pronounced extent on all questions which do not command a very large share of public interest, and on which the Lords believe they may safely differ from the House of Commons. On all Irish matters, for instance, until the interest of the public is fairly aroused, the sole legislative body is the House of Lords—the uncompromising opponent of the progress and prosperity of Ireland. As with England, so with the Colonies. The Council in any colony—

the House of the few—can at all times cripple the legislative functions of the House of the many, and if this difficulty is to be successfully met, the interminable power of the Upper House to defeat or mangle Bills sent up from the Lower House, must be strictly bounded by some reasonable limit. If it be thought wise to retain the principle of the Dual House system, provision must be made that the will of a proportionate majority of the people's representatives shall become the law of the land without further reference to a hostile Council ; or that a twice or thrice passed measure, which has been rejected by the Council as often as passed by the Assembly, need not be again submitted to the criticism of the obstructive House.

In all probability, future modifications will proceed upon the lines indicated, but it is in the highest degree improbable that they will be effected except at the cost of much political and social disturbance, and of many a legislative dead-lock.

PART II.

PAYMENT OF MEMBERS AND COLONIAL CORRUPTION.

So much misconception prevails amongst Englishmen as to the effect produced by payment of members of colonial Legislatures, in stimulating the growth of corrupt practices in all departments of colonial politics, that an examination of the subject which may tend to place in a clearer light the reason of the practice, and the absence of any necessary connection between it and political corruption, may be fitly enough introduced into a work that deals, to some extent, with various incidents attaching to colonial self-government. At any rate, the interest taken by many politicians and writers in the subject is unquestionably great, and that alone may serve as a sufficient excuse for dealing with it here.

Englishmen are never tired of prating of the corruption that distinguishes the working of self-government in the

Australian colonies. It is certain that it is present there, for all governments must pass through certain stages of the corruption malady before the process of fermentation has been perfected and the mass works itself clear. But colonial corruption is integrity of the brightest and most conspicuous type, when brought into comparison with that which distinguished parliamentary government in England up to some fifty years back. At that date, too, political and parliamentary proceedings were model expositions of immaculate purity, when compared with the jobberies actively assisted by the advisers of His Gracious Majesty King George III. of ever blessed memory, and influentially supported by the royal countenance. If we wish to find more recent examples of gross corruption, let us turn not to colonial or American history for those of greatest magnitude, but to the recorded proceedings of European States administered by individual wills. Let us instance the late French Empire, the past and present Russian despotisms, the rule of a Spanish Queen, of petty Italian despots, of a Turkish Sultan ; let us place them side by side with colonial illustrations, or even let us cull incidents at random from the last general election in our own purified and reformed country, if we would see that by comparison with them colonial and American corruption furnishes a lofty standard of morality, to which less popularly-governed countries have as yet failed to attain. Of courtesy, the courtesy that obscures the plain meaning of ordinary language, the veneer that conceals the hidden thought and gives colour to a false sentiment, there is in European States enough and to spare, and in the Australasian colonies a very meagre supply. But these æsthetic refinements are scarcely proof of excellence in political arrangements, or even of the absence of corruption. They are rather indicative of the absorption of power by a leisure class, versed exclusively in the amenities of discourse, than significant of the healthy participation of the lower orders in the government of the country, through the medium of popular, energetic, and earnest representatives.

It was during the period when parliamentary eloquence in

England was most plentifully besprinkled with classical tropes and similes, when polish of language and style were the convenient substitutes for profundity of thought or depth of sympathy with popular needs, that corruption and jobbery ran their greatest riot. Language, not legislation, assertion of privilege, not performance of a delegated duty, were the chief requisites for parliamentary success; and corruption in all things, not correction of abuses, was the invariable object to which the struggles of everyday political life were directed. How could it be otherwise when all power and all influence were monopolised by a small but rapacious clique?

The more limited the basis of representation, the less limited is the monarchy of a ruling class composed of men of wealth and leisure, whose guiding principle is the preservation of their own narrow monopoly of the right to misrule. The more pronounced their general tone of courtesy, the less likely is it that they concern themselves with discussing questions of popular reform; for as soon as they do this, violent language is sure to take the place of studied courtliness of expression.

The revenue, the multitudinous sinecure posts of emolument, the seats in Parliament, were conveniently apportioned between the members of one small ruling class; and debate was rather confined to general declamation, or to contests of invective between rival leaders on points of personal interest, than used as an instrument for ventilating and asserting urgent popular demands. There was none of the 'sæva indignatio' which is the invariable accompaniment of conflict between distinct classes at opposite ends of the social scale. The voice of the people was unheard in the House of Commons, and there was nothing to interfere with the general tone of suavity and harmony of the assembly. Courtesy was, however, an incident of the situation rather than a merit. For no sooner had the wants of the lower orders found forcible expression, than the polished classical orators were found capable of descending to a depth of abusive and incendiary language with which colonial debaters would with difficulty vie, and such as would not be tolerated in any colonial legislative House.

The truth is, that general suavity of bearing or polish of language, when characteristic of a popular legislative assembly, are indications of a spirit of contentment with existing conditions, and of a general desire to do as little as possible towards reforming them. What business has to be transacted is done mechanically, perfunctorily, and badly, according to recognised forms. Such a body can never be representative of the people at large, for if it were so, it would be overwhelmed with business, and that of a type that, where there is an aristocratic opposition, is eminently productive of envy, hatred, malice, and all uncharitableness. A courteous legislative assembly, therefore, must be one which is not under popular control. It is, therefore, practically unchecked in its power of disposing of public offices, or of appropriating the public money according to its own sense of the fitness of things. Who can doubt that power so unlimited and centralised would be utilised by the possessors of it entirely or chiefly for their own benefit? that the habit of doing so would, in time, acquire the strength of an organised system, to be branded by an unappreciative posterity with the name of—Corruption?

'In a democratic country,' says an Australian writer, 'corruption exists only as a parasite or adventitious disease, caused by a number of dishonest men trying to live by politics in any possible way. In England, it existed as a system established for the purpose of poisoning the springs of government, and diverting them from their several channels solely for the benefit of a ruling caste, who saw power slipping from their hands, and were ready to resort to the most degrading means to retain it.' The reasoning seems to be, that the prominent cause of corruption is Australia is attributable to the fact that politicians *there* make a trade of their calling. But one may perhaps be permitted to doubt, while agreeing generally with these conclusions, whether the cause assigned as peculiarly productive of corruption in Australia is not equally the cause of it everywhere where it exists.

During the period of English history just glanced at, what were politics but a trade—and that too the *sole* trade of a class? Bargain and sale of office, of places of trust, of

parliamentary boroughs, of church dignities, of all appointments great or small, whether in the Army, or Navy, the Law,
the Church, or the Civil Service, and nothing but bargain and
sale, go far to establish politics on general trade principles.
The wholesale dealers were the Lord Chancellors and heads
of departments; the retail dealers were the boroughmongers,
members of Parliament, minor officials, and a host of subordinate agents. A roaring trade was politics, but its palmy
days are over, and the self-seeking colonial politician of to-day
can but hope to do a little underhand risky dabbling in the
local trade of politics, in feeble imitation of the open, remunerative, and extensive dealings of Englishmen more
fortunate in their time and opportunity.

Between the trading politician and the professional politician there is this world-wide difference, that the one lives by
politics, the other *for* them. As a plunderer on an extensive
scale, the first is out of date nowadays, and the last is by
no means necessarily immoral in his aims, but may, and in
the colonies generally does, become a valuable custodian of
the charge imposed upon him by his constituency. Professional politicians are frequent enough there, and it is the
fashion both to cry down the pretensions of such to dis-
interestedness or capacity, and to attribute their choice of a
calling to the payments they derive, in most of the colonies,
as members of one or both of the legislative Houses. Undoubtedly many of them would not seek for membership if
they were not remunerated for their services; but it is contrary
to the fact that the majority of them are worthless, or disposed
to be public wreckers. If a certain number of reckless, self-
seeking men are attracted to politics in the colonies to gratify
ambition on trade principles, it is because of the large amount
of patronage unfortunately thrown into the hands of political
men—a consideration quite outside the inducement offered by
the small salaries paid to members of the legislative bodies.

It we set to work to reason ourselves into the belief that
legislation, the most important because the most comprehensive in its scope, and the most wide-reaching in its effects,
of all businesses, is to be carried on at the expense of con-

centration of energy and specialisation of function, if, in brief, we arrive at the conviction that it is better to have two Houses to do legislative business badly than to have one to do it comparatively well, we shall have little or no difficulty in adding, as an additional article to our creed, that the less individual members care and know about the matters they are chosen to transact, the more wisely and effectively will legislation be conducted. But if imagination fails to grasp the line of reasoning by which the major premiss is supported, it is difficult to follow out the conclusion, except on the general supposition that everything that is right in private life is wrong in public life. That that is a principle consecrated by use may be unhesitatingly admitted; but that it is a sound one may be stoutly denied.

In legislation, as in ordinary affairs, it is desirable that the men chosen for the purpose of moulding the national laws should find their chief interest in politics as a business, rather than as a recreation. The more they know about the business delegated to their charge, and the more they are inclined to stick to it, as one calling for unremitting attention and thought, the better for the country at large. But how are such men to be procured in sufficiently large numbers to constitute the sense of any legislative body, unless inducements to competition for membership are held out to make political life attractive as a profession? Look at the personnel of our own House of Commons. If the recurrence of the same names in the lists of members year after year, election after election, does not mean that a majority of the House of Commons consists of professional politicians, what does it mean? It means unfortunately just the opposite, if work is to be taken as the test of the applicability of the term, for it is certain that very few of these members can pretend that they come up to Westminster to practice politics. They come, not to a workroom, but to a playground, where there are few workers and plenty of playfellows. They are professional politicians of a sort, the worst sort; for they neither know nor care anything about the duties of their profession. More corresponding to the model professional politician are the men who live but for politics, and who, by strict attention to business, attain by degrees to the highest offices of the State. But how infinitesimally meagre a minority of their fellow members do these professors represent. The rest were better out of the House, to make room for others anxious for and interested in the national business. So long, however, as the House of Commons is the leisure-lounge of the rich, so long will every means be adopted by the drones to prevent any considerable number of poorer but more earnest politicians from supplanting them.

'An unpaid legislature,' says John Stuart Mill, 'and an unpaid magistracy, are institutions essentially aristocratic—contrivances for keeping legislation and judicature exclusively in the hands of those who can afford to serve without pay. . . . Of the able men the country produces, nine-tenths at least are of the class who cannot serve without pay. . . . In political as in all other monopolies, if you would stimulate exertion you must throw open all monopolies.' The cry against professional politicians is a cry against entrusting the national business to those most interested in carrying it on in the best possible way, in order to keep it as an exclusive possession for those interested in doing it in the most careless, that is, in the worst possible way. To offer an inducement to capable and earnest men to become legislators is the readiest means for breaking down the monopoly of uncaring, whip-driven, rich legislators. And why not offer it? 'Because,' say the monopolists, 'the form of inducement suggested—a money payment—can procure none but corrupt legislators.' Let us be reasonable. The proceedings of a paid member will be watchfully scanned by his constituents. Is corruption the necessary or probable course of tactics to which poor men responsible—probably more so than if unpaid—to a keen-eyed constituency, will resort? Is it not certain that bribery, corruption, and treating are the weapons on which our wealthy legislators can rely in the last resort if so disposed? and is it not equally certain that without those means of nursing and fostering venal boroughs, corruption, in the style we are accustomed to in England, would be impossible?

Let it not be supposed that bribery represents merely the

power of wealth to secure the return of a member. By just so much as it secures the return of one does it prevent the return of another. When, therefore, wealthy legislators unite their efforts to keep less wealthy politicians out in the cold, by refusing to sanction the payment of their services, what is this but bringing the power of wealth to bear in the most extended form of bribery, aimed too at the suppression of popular rights ? The present system affords a fine field for the exercise of every variety of corruptive influence, but to say that 'payment of members' would probably eventuate in corruption is to rashly foreshadow an agreement between what Paley would call 'opposite improbabilities.' The hard facts are against such a supposition ; deductive reasoning is opposed to it ; there is no connection between one and the other, so it may safely enough be dismissed from consideration.

If it be wrong to pay those who make the laws, why should it be right to pay those who carry them into execution ? Why should the money-prize attached to Ministerial offices be so great as to constitute a potent attraction, even to men of considerable wealth, to make politics their sole profession, if the objection to payment of private members is that it would induce them to turn their attention to nothing but politics ? The principle of payment to the Executive is exactly the same as that which regulates the payment of a bank clerk—that is, to secure the services of the best men available and to make it their interest to attend faithfully and assiduously to their duties. Is not the carrying out of laws dependent on their being framed efficiently to secure their end? If so, then why should it be necessary to stimulate the due execution and not the right framing of a law ? 'All very well,' it will be said, 'but high Ministerial officers receive, not payment for their services, but salaries to enable them to support high social positions.' Is it really true that Lord Chancellors, Prime Ministers, and others are heavily subsidised in order to give a round of balls and garden parties ? If so, then Lord Chancellors and Ministers should be qualified for their posts by their capacities for social dissipa-

Z

tion, and youth and volatility should confer the right to administer the high departments of State.

We know that this part of the Constitutional theory has not yet sunk to so low a level. We know that high official position requires a high expenditure to support its manifold duties, but these duties are *official*, not social, and are paid for as being all in the day's work. High official salaries are paid partly for the maintenance of Ministerial salons on-a respectable footing, as an official, not a social necessity : and these salaries carry with them the obligation of advancing the national business. The drawing-room work is but a part of the office work, and is paid for as such. Leave hair-splitting as to terms on one side and it is evident that the salary, remuneration, payment, or what you will, is given to secure efficient service—not only to secure it, but to attract it, for the latter is implied in the former—to attract men, that is, to politics as a profession by the offer of a large money payment. It may be said that these payments *do* have the effect of stimulating the best efforts of individual members, or that at any rate they are devised so as to operate in that direction. If that is the case, it must be admitted that the Constitutional theory is not averse to the payment of members, but that its intention is to induce every member to devote himself exclusively to politics ; in other words, to become a professional politician – that the existing system, in effect, contemplates general professionalism in politics as an object to be attained. We know that members of the House of Commons used to be paid in order to secure their attendance, and as Constitutional theories seem never to wear out through decrepitude, it may reasonably be presumed that what was once desirable in the view of the Constitution is so still, only with the difference that Ministerial salaries are now substituted as inducements to political work instead of individual payments being made with that object. Would that the result accorded with the expectation, but it is clear that only a very few men, of exceptional talent and industry, can hope to arrive at the highest dignities of the State, and that the official payments are no premium on the exercise of the talents and industry of the nineteen members out of every twenty who cherish membership as a privilege instead of regarding it as a duty, however much they may stimulate intrigues among the would-be official individual 'outs' to grasp at the sweets of Office. The working of the system proclaims, in effect, that a very limited number of men are to be encouraged to become professional politicians for the sake of place and office, while very large numbers of men are to be discouraged from taking any interest in current questions by the inducements to become professional *working* politicians being withdrawn from them. This last effect is produced by the exclusion from membership of all who are not wealthy enough to legislate without being paid for it, quite as much as by the fact that the prizes are hopelessly beyond the reach of the vast majority of actual members.

In a youthful and widespread community the necessity for paying the members of the local Parliament is most easily apparent. Inferior means of locomotion and communication prevent the candidature of men pursuing busy avocations requiring constant personal supervision and residing at remote distances from the place of assembly. The representation is therefore chiefly confined to men living within the city which is the seat of government. It was found that in Victoria, in 1858, out of a total number of sixty members of Assembly no fewer than forty-five were residents in Melbourne. In all the Australian colonies, as well as at the Cape or in Canada, the great majority of members of the respective Assemblies were resident in the several capitals and knew little or nothing of the country beyond the urban limits. To secure adequate representation for the country district, it was absolutely necessary to compensate country members for having to employ paid superintendence for their private concerns; otherwise the entire conduct of affairs would have continued to be monopolised by a knot of metropolitan lawyers.

But is not the reason for the advocacy of payment of members in England the same as it was in the Colonies? Is it not the cost of representation in our own country that prevents representation from being representative? Distances may be short and easily traversible in quick-running trains, but still the fact that most men cannot delegate their private duties to others, in order to enter on political life without incurring heavy additional expense, reduces the question to one of cost just as is the case in new colonies.

Supposing a wealthy class, enjoying plenty of leisure, to be established in the youthful colony ; supposing railway and other modes of communication to be brought to a high point of perfection, then it may be said that the original reason for payment of members of the Colonial Legislature falls to the ground. By no means is this so. Let the rich men become legislators if they can, but let poorer men have inducements to strive for the honour and burden if they will. If it was politic to pay members once, it is right to pay them still, for the principle—the extension of representation over the widest possible area to all sorts and conditions of men, so as to get the benefit of the most diversified intelligence—holds good equally now as then.

A paid member must, it is said, be a delegate. If by this is meant a delegate with a *general* mandate, why not ? Is it disgraceful to redeem pledges given on the hustings, or to conform to the wishes of a constituency with which one can conscientiously sympathise, preferably to becoming the tool of a party leader ? Those who declaim against the evils of delegation seem to think that it is better for a man to be the delegate of his own political chief rather than of the con-stituency to which he stands pledged. The mind obedient to the crack of the party whip is all honour and purity according to them ; while he who, in accordance with his convictions and promises, keeps faith with the majority who elected him to serve a purpose is the personification of dis-honest sycophancy. He may wreck his own hopes of personal advancement by so doing ; and yet we are told that the mem-ber who regards the interests of his constituents as of prior importance to his own is necessarily devoid of the first princi-ples of honour.

It is usually assumed—why it is impossible to say—that delegates who would endeavour to give effect to the instructions of their constituents must necessarily surrender their right of private judgment. Even if so—and the supposition is by no means an admission—how would delegates compare in point of morality with the present unpaid members of the House of Commons? Do these last never surrender their private judgment, nay, even their firmest convictions, according to the exigencies of party tactics? Is it not constantly and notoriously the case that party, not principles, moves, not measures, convenience, not conviction, regulate the political lives of our blameless senators? Pledges may be broken by them, principles trampled on by them, to suit the whims of an intriguing party leader, and yet 'are they all, all honourable men.' 'Let the system of representation be what it may,' says John Stuart Mill, 'it will be converted into one of mere delegation if the electors so choose. As long as they are free not to vote, and free to vote as they like, they cannot be prevented from making their vote dependent on any condition they think fit to annex to it.' In effect members of Parliament will become delegates if it suits the convenience of the nation that they should be such, whether they receive payment or not.

But is it certain that paid members would of necessity become delegates either in a general or particular sense? The probabilities are not all in favour of such a result. Ministers in receipt of payment are not delegates, however nearly a Premier, who has to submit the outlines of every proposition for the approval of the country, may resemble one by virtue of his position. Why then should private members become delegates as a consequence of being paid? Whether they would so become or not would depend upon the fund out of which they were paid. If out of the imperial revenue, they would probably be much on the same footing with their constituents as they are at present; if out of local funds, it is more likely that they would become delegates, but only in a general sense. At any rate, a member so paid would be more of a delegate than he is at present, for he would certainly feel himself under a greater sense of responsibility to his constituency ; while the latter, in turn, would be more jealous of the proceedings of its salaried representative, and would be able to secure from him better service. Payment out of local funds would probably in time take the form of payment by results—a principle which it might be as well to establish in politics as in other things as being far and away the most equitable, unless we are to reject the belief that constituencies are as a rule the best judges of their own concerns and of the services rendered to them by their representatives.

To speculate thus is to wander off into a future which may be far distant. In those countries, whether European, American, or colonial, where members of the legislative bodies receive payment for their services, no representative has as yet become the delegate in all things of his constituency. The inconvenience of such a system, even with much shortened Parliamentary terms, would be too great to allow of the practical application of such a method of representation. The members of the States-General of the Dutch United Provinces were delegates of the most particular type; but in our own times such an arrangement as referring back to constituents for instructions on every point of principle that might arise would be out of the question. Locomotion and means of communication may be quicker than they were, but they have not been quickened so much in proportion as has the political intelligence and activity of modern nations. A general mandate renewable periodically may be possible and even desirable, but a particular mandate for every detail of legislation would be found unworkable in practice as involving constant inconvenience and political ferment on the one hand, constant risk and expense on the other.

A Parliament, the members of which are paid, need not by any means be a perfect assemblage, but it will in all probability contain a far greater percentage of men of serious purpose than are to be found in an unpaid legislative chamber. It might possibly consist of men to whom the annual payment would be a matter of small consideration; but even in that case it would throw open the entrance to political life to a keener competition than can be expected in England at present. The mere dread of being supplanted by a large number of possible rivals would stimulate the energies and the liberal instincts of members, however wealthy. The system, too, would tend to prevent the re-election of men who had shown themselves incapable of work or unwilling to undertake it, of those who obstructed legislation for obstruction's sake, or who turned the political debating-ground into an arena for the continual exhibition of private animosity.

Payment of members is not an ideally perfect system. Nothing is in political arrangements. The most that can be expected of the best is that it will not work as badly as the worst. But this system of paying members is not so bad as the one prevailing in England to-day. It has, on the whole, worked well in the countries in which it is in use, and that is high praise considering the adverse conditions interfering with its fair working. In the Australian colonies in especial, excessive centralisation in the hands of Government of business undertakings usually conducted in other countries by private enterprise has introduced an element of corruption into political dealings which is usually placed to the account of 'payment of members' by people too careless to analyse cause and effect. In the United States the system is held answerable for evils entirely unconnected with it as a consequence, but which permeate through the political and social life of the people. The immense area of patronage thrown open to every member of the Legislature, as the result of the periodical redistribution of every official appointment, down to that of the pettiest post-office clerk in the most remote corner of the Union, furnishes an incentive to men to become political jobbers, incentives such as the small salaries of members of the Legislature could never furnish.

It is unfortunate that a vicious principle can never be associated with another, however harmless in itself, without impairing the benefits that might have flowed from the unhampered operation of the latter. Good and bad are confounded together in sweeping condemnation by indiscriminating mankind, ever ready to accept what they are willing to believe. In Australia, and also in the United States, 'payment of members' and 'manhood suffrage,' the two bugbears of wise and wealthy men of leisure, are written down by them as the authors of all the evils attendant on the otherwise excellent working of thoroughly democratic forms of government, because it suits their inclinations that there the fault should be placed. The allegation is a false one. It may be unhesitatingly asserted that no one who has attentively and impartially seen for himself the actual political conditions of those countries can fail to be satisfied that the two alleged causes of evil are, by themselves, at once beneficial and necessary to their prosperity.

There is nothing so calculated to infuse activity of political interest throughout a community as the throwing open of the possibility of entrance to the Legislature to worth unaccompanied by wealth, to all men of ability, however devoid of grace of manner and polish of diction. It is one of the most satisfactory features of a liberal system of self-government in the Colonies that it has introduced to public life a number of men who, at home, would probably never have had an opportunity of an audience outside the limited circle of their immediate acquaintances. That these men have done excellent, useful work ; that they have taken the initiative in all the great reforming acts which mark the difference between Home and colonial legislation, is conclusively shown by the local Hansards and the local division-lists. It is because men of a class which is part and parcel of the working mass of the people make up a large proportion of the members of the colonial Assemblies that legislation in the various parts of Australia has always been, by comparison with our own, drastic, popular, and to the point. All the power implied in working-men membership of ascertaining the requirements of the multitude, and applying to them effectual remedies, is notably absent from the English Legislature, and prolonged outside agitation has consequently to be resorted to if urgent reforms are to be pressed through Parliament. There, they have to make their way against opposing class prejudices of members who, though convinced of the necessity of popular measures, are unwilling to concede their expediency, or who, however earnest in support, must lack the knowledge which practical experience of working class life can alone give. However well informed, these last are never more than an insignificant minority which may give shape, but cannot impart life, to the measures it advocates. So, popular legislation is rendered slow, partial, and shifty ; ambiguous, too, in meaning and construction, instead of being terse, clear, and easily workable.

Colonial statutes cannot claim an absolute degree of efficiency or thoroughness, but the materials for improving them are always to hand, and it takes but little time in the Colonies for a badly-framed measure to be superseded by a better. The men whose chief interest is in forward progress are present in force in the Legislative Assemblies, and are ready and eager to push on reforms to completion. Not to finality—for such a state is neither to be expected or desired. but so as to comprehend the popular wants of the day. This is the stamp of member of which every legislative body terming itself representative stands in the greatest need ; because the aim of legislation should be to give as fair play to the legitimate aspirations of the lower orders as to those of the upper classes. Many will differ *in toto* from this view. ‘Let laws be made,’ they will tell us, ‘for the behoof of the propertied classes, as those who have the greatest stake in the country, and let the law-makers be of the “great stake” class, men who have everything to lose and nothing to gain.’ They assert, in effect, that the wealthy interests of the kingdom are those which are most in need of privilege-conferring legislation. Is it in any sense true that those who have nothing to gain are as interested in good legislation as those who have all to gain ? Which of any two men has the greatest stake at issue, depending upon the course that Government may take ; the man who need anticipate no more than decreased luxury, even from the worst of measures, or he to whom bad government brings scanty food and low wages ?—the man of leisure, indifferent to the wish to better his condition, or the humble toiler, feverishly anxious to avail himself of every slice of legislation that may by possibility afford him a fresh avenue for subsistence ? The answer is too plain for argument. The man who has the greatest stake in the establishment of the best or worst form of government is undoubtedly he who has all to gain, and whose nothing to lose is all his livelihood. Listen to Jeremy Bentham :—' Property, it is continually said, is the only bond of pledge and attachment to the country. Not it, indeed. Want of property is a much stronger one. He who has property can change the shape of it and carry it with him to another country whenever he pleases. He who has no property can do no such thing. In the eyes of those who live by the labour of others, the existence of those by whose labour they live is indeed of no value ; not so in the eyes of the labourers themselves. Life is not worth more to yawners than to labourers, and their own country is the only country in which they can so much as hope to live. Among a hundred of them are no ten exceptions to this, you will find.'

Which is the class whose well-being is most beneficial to the State ? The class of those who by their work increase the national wealth and prosperity, or of those who add nothing to either ? Should Parliaments legislate for the benefit of bread-wasters or of bread-winners—if legislation *must* be preferential ? of idle consumers or of thrifty producers ? of men who have the means of procuring every luxury, or of those who must struggle and toil to avoid starvation ? of the men who enjoy fortunes, or of those who are adding to the resources of the nation by striving for a competence ?

Heaven forbid that there should be exclusive legislation for one set of men more than for another—the country has had centuries of it—but if it must incline to one side or the other, let it lean in favour of those who are most willing but least able to help themselves, rather than towards those who have no wants that they cannot easily supply for themselves. Let the working-man have his full share of representation. If that cannot be hoped for while membership of the Legislature is tabooed to all save the representatives of the rich, who need no preponderance of representation, let means be taken to give the working-man a working majority of his own kidney. If it cannot be done so long as members are not paid, by all means let them be paid. It has been done in the greatest of all free countries, in the most progressive of all communities, in the United States and in Australia. Those portions of the globe derive their unexampled prosperity from the reign of the working-man, rendered possible by the system of payment of members.

The privileges of the wealthy stand on the most secure footing where the working-man is king, for the kingship is representative of those whose interest is the universal interest. There, the demands of the rich for exclusive social and political supremacy may be scouted as fanciful, their would-be social distinctions may be ignored as presumptuous; but where the paid member, the poor man's representative, holds undisputed sway, legitimate rights are best preserved and equitable claims of property chiefly respected.[1]

[1] The above (Part II.) appeared as an article in the *Westminster Review* for July 1883.

CHAPTER XI.

PERHAPS some future historian will be tempted to enter into colonial history more thoroughly than I have done, with a view to demonstrate how each one of the colonies could furnish its all-compelling ' Bonds of Disunion ' in the incidents of its direct subordination to or legislative connection with England. For my part, I have confined myself to treating of those only of our colonies which appear to me most typical for the purposes of this book, and which present a comparison ready to hand between their condition to-day under self-government, and but a few years ago under the direct rule of the imperial power. On the subject of the administration of our Crown colonies I have said nothing, for, however injurious to them may be the application of the principle of government from a distant centre, the considerations relating to them must materially differ from those which are suggested by the experiences and circumstances of free colonial communities, composed of populations of British race.

I have alluded in the introductory chapter to the question of Imperial Federation, and have in doing so claimed for this work that it would show in unmistakable fashion that the tendency of centralised imperial rule over the principal British colonies was to create feelings of distrust between the mother-country and her dependencies that would, if the imperial system had been persisted in, have led to acts of positive hostility on either side such as might in all likelihood have resulted in the disruption of the Empire. I have there also given my reasons for supposing that no Federal Council, however carefully limited its functions might be to matters of imperial concern, could fail to intermeddle with the internal concerns of the Colonies. Also I have, I trust, established a fair ground for supposing that if such a Council were to be attempted to be formed, it is doubtful in the extreme whether the Colonies would be willing to concede a preponderating share of authority in it to England; that it would be still more doubtful whether in course of time England would not find herself under the necessity of taking only a subordinate part in its deliberations; and that if England's claim to the foremost position should be rejected the entire federation scheme would fall to the ground.

If centralisation of colonial rule in London has been tried in times past and found miserably wanting in all the requisites of good government, is it likely that even in a modified form it would give happier results in the future? That is the question to which I would now supply an answer by dealing further with the suggestions of the advocates of federation; for federation, if accomplished on the lines laid down, can mean nothing short of centralisation of colonial rule in the hands of the federal leader.

It may be as well to deal briefly with plans having for their immediate object the representation of the Colonies in the House of Commons, for no serious-minded person can suppose that either England or the Colonies would consent to their being put into practice. The vote of a ' corner ' composed of colonial representatives might sound the death-knell of the most popular Ministry and the most urgently-needed measures of the day, and the bare possibility of such a contingency is sufficient of itself to condemn the proposed arrangement. If the experiment were ever to be tried, the colonial members might possibly be found useful for party purposes; but as in order to be really representative the number of colonial members must periodically increase in proportion to the expanding populations of the Colonies, it might result that alien representatives despatched from the Antipodes, from Canada, and from the Cape, would in time become the arbiters of English political measures and the controllers of English Legislatures.

The probability, however, is that the claim of the colonial members to a voice in general legislation would speedily be voted intolerable, and that their right of interference would soon be limited to criticisms on colonial measures—criticisms to which the House of Commons would be disposed to pay only a scant and ignorant attention that would bring prominently before colonial populations the contempt accorded to the treatment of their affairs at home. The Colonies are daily becoming proportionately more imperious than England herself, and can any one in his senses suppose that they would yield to English members of Parliament the power of regulating any matters relating to the Colonies while the right of making their votes felt in English politics was denied to colonial representatives? Those who think so mistake indeed the dispositions of free colonists.

But one word more from another point of view. Nothing can more conclusively show the incapacity of the English Legislature for dealing with any but purely English business than does London legislation for Ireland. Irish members have but to be sincere in the expression of beliefs founded on acquaintance with the real condition of Ireland to have every abusive epithet at the command of an unsympathetic English press indignantly showered upon them. They have only to be impassioned in defence of the local liberties of their country to be treated with contumely and the accusation of the foulest motives. They have but to insist on procuring indispensable, drastic measures of reform in order to be denied access to the House of Commons; and when the Irish party has been thus temporarily gagged, measures of unreasoning coercion, such as under no circumstances would be allowed to be applied to England, are presented to Ireland as the expression of the sense of the United Parliament of Great Britain and Ireland. Even when, in submission to absolute necessity, the House of Commons finds itself forced to concede to Ireland the very reforms for insisting on which the more zealous of the Irish members have suffered contemptuous expulsion and arbitrary imprisonment, it can balance the pain of the concession by the comforting assurance that the House of Lords may be safely relied upon to cut to shreds whatever beneficial features any portion of Irish legislation may contain. What does this show but that the narrow barrier of St. George's Channel is wide enough to prevent Irish matters from being either intelligently or considerately treated in England? also that England is quite unfitted to legislate for any but its own requirements. Then how would it be with Colonies separated from England by the half-distance of the globe? Long intervals of distance cannot fail to promote a complete paralysis of interest between countries remote from one another, and ignorance coming to the aid of lack of interest would speedily ensure a type of legislation as unpalatable to the colony whose representatives would be in a minority in the British Parliament as English Irish legislation is to the Irish. The stronger the colonial opposition the harsher and more accentuated would grow the hostility between the home and the colonial members, and the more embittered the conflict between the home and the colonial press, until the worst features of Irish mismanagement would be attempted to be reproduced in our dealings with the Colonies—a mode of treatment that the latter would certainly not tolerate.

The plan breaks down hopelessly under examination, and it is rejected even by so ardent an imperialist as Earl Grey.[1] That nobleman gives as his main reason for its rejection, that the colonial members when on the Opposition side of the House would be debarred from free communication with the advisers of the Crown—a technical point of its kind, but powerful enough of itself to be a fatal bar. He might have added, had he been disposed to deal more broadly with the question, that it would be open to colonial members on the Government benches to attain to the highest offices of the State, and that it might happen that those members might at some time form the majority of an English Ministry. In such a case the interest and the business of the colonial

[1] See Earl Grey's article in the *Nineteenth Century* for June 1879.

members elevated to office would be no longer with the Colonies, but would be mainly confined to English legislation— a condition of things that would be considered unbearable by both England and the Colonies. Either, then, colonial members must be introduced into the home Parliament on an exclusive basis, or they must be left out altogether. The former plan would be productive of conditions intolerable to the Colonies, and the adoption of the latter would ultimately become necessary—only it might under certain circumstances present the appearance of a forcible expulsion of colonial members.

Let it be here again repeated that the attention of legislators ought to be devoted, primarily, and as exclusively as possible, to the concerns of their own country. Government is at best but an inefficient machine, and its inefficiency is to be measured by its opportunities for legislation. The smaller the area which any governing body has to administer, the smaller is the chance of misgovernment and error. On the other hand, the greater the multiplicity of interest for which a governing body is to be provided, the more probable it is that government will be a series of unsatisfactory mistakes. It must surely be admitted that even popular Governments of the best description can but furnish as their record of legislation a series of hand-to-mouth compromises—compromises based on views of temporary expediency; that to make of Acts of Parliament fairly effective machines for any immediate purpose in view must require the concentrated intelligence, attention, and concurrence of the vast majority of a nation for long antecedent periods ; and that fresh circumstances are perpetually arising in the nation's life which demand for their consideration indefatigable toil, the minutest examination, and the most thoughtful application of principles old or new. Admit this, and the conclusion is unavoidable that a country which would govern itself decently well cannot afford to devote its attention to its Imperial rather than to its own local concerns.

Not so, however, thinks Earl Grey. In his opinion the Imperial interest is first and foremost. He would therefore employ the valuable time of the advisers of the Crown in interfering with the commercial regulations of the Colonies in order to assimilate English and colonial customs tariffs on a Free Trade basis. According to him, the protectionist tariffs of most-of our colonies are antagonistic to the interests of England as well as destructive of their own. Of this there can be no reasonable doubt; but it is impossible to believe with Earl Grey that either remonstrance or dictatorial legislation from a Council at home, or from the Crown itself, will for a moment tend to bring the colonists to wiser views. On the contrary, any proceedings on England's part directed to that end will only stimulate colonial protectionists to greater excesses. Nationalities rarely or never arrive at sound economical principles for their own government until internal pressure—the growing contrast between progress and poverty —demands Free Trade as the only remedy for a distressed condition. In England Free Trade was scouted as an absurdity until it was seen to be the natural, the sole efficacious antidote for the people's emptiness of stomach. Sheer starvation it was that brought conviction of the folly of Protection, and sheer necessity alone will bring conviction to protectionist colonies. So long as the masses of the colonial populations are well-to-do, so long will we find that English exhortations to Free Trade will be regarded by them as impertinent interferences with their rights of internal legislation, and the hand that would administer the healing medicine will be repulsed with a vigour proportioned to the strength of the intention to force a remedy upon them. No amount of imperial legislation or advice could make the Colonies Free Traders, but it might and very probably would lead them into the adoption of an aggravated system of Protection specially directed against ourselves.

Again, Earl Grey would cement the political tie between England and her Colonies by forming a Council of colonial agents at home with power to advise the Crown on matters of imperial concern. But let us ask his lordship how he proposes to work out his project. Is the Crown to act on the advice of the colonial agents in Council or not? If the former, then the imperial politics of any one colony must either be regulated by the vote of a majority of the members of the Council—however unpalatable the decision arrived at may be to the colony affected, and however little to its taste the composition of the majority may be—or else the Crown will be enabled to exercise its own discretion and so to arrogate to itself the right to direct colonial policy. There can be no doubt whatever that no one of our colonies would consent to place any part of its external policy under the charge of a Colonial Council formed as suggested, nor would the Colonies for a moment permit the Crown to regulate for them matters of which they would be apt to consider themselves the most competent judges.

The imperial policy of a realm is but a conventional term for the general tenour of the aggregate of the local policies of different parts of the whole empire, and to effect an alteration in imperial policy is therefore equivalent to effecting a modification in the local policy of each colony to the extent required for the new departure. For instance, in this very matter of commercial policy to which Earl Grey specially invites attention, it must be evident that a system of Free Trade throughout the empire could not be erected without radically altering the fiscal arrangements of nearly every one of our colonies. Or take the question of a mutual association for offensive and defensive purposes. As the essence of the proposition relating to that is, that every part of the empire should furnish its proportionate quota to the expenses of the imperial armament, it follows that a portion of each colonial revenue must yearly be voted for the purpose, and that can only be done by local taxation direct or indirect in each colony; in other words, local colonial legislation must always be the groundwork of imperial policy, and to impose the latter upon the Colonies would be equivalent to demanding from them adaptations of their local principles of legislation to imperial requirements.

But suppose, as is only too probable, that any one of the colonies distinctly refuses to acquiesce in the measures advised by the Council or sanctioned by the Crown, does Earl

Grey imagine that the rest of the Confederation is to set to work to coerce the recalcitrant member into submission ? We are wiser than we were in the days when Earl Grey himself ineffectually attempted to make the Colonies the catspaw of Downing Street ; and it cannot seriously be supposed that coercion in any form or shape would ever be resorted to. If coercion were to be attempted, the unwieldy confederation must infallibly fall to pieces. The Australian colonies, some years ago, were frank enough to inform us that they would no longer consent to have their hands tied by clauses in their Constitution Acts binding them down to a specified course with regard to differential duties between colony and colony. We pocketed the affront and let them do as they pleased, and so we would have to do again under similar circumstances. Whatever course might approve it-self to the Crown or to a majority of the Council would, then, be merely the declaration of an abstract principle incapable of being enforced except at the risk of the certain disintegra-tion of the empire ; and being, in fact, unaccompanied by a compelling sanction, would be as valueless as the resolutions of a village debating club. Worse than that, the assertion of a policy which could not be imposed on any dissenting member of the Confederation would certainly bring the decrees of the central consultative body, as we may call it, into well-merited contempt, to the loss of the dignity and real power of the imperial Government which endorsed those decrees as the embodiment of its own imperial policy.

Federation and centralisation are convertible terms. To federate the empire for particular purposes would be to rule its constituent members from London for *all* purposes ; for, as has been shown, imperial and local politics are the reciprocals of each other, and interference with the one is intermeddling with the other. The colonists themselves are quick enough to perceive that this is so, and this is promi-nently the conviction in the Australian colonies, no one of which has yet been able to agree upon a plan of inter-colonial federation with any other colony in its own group because of the impossibility of separating local from inter-colonial

A A 2

interests. If two adjacent colonies, between whose laws, usages, occupations, and institutions there is a very general similarity, and in both of which there is a strong belief in the advantages derivable from federation between them, cannot find a *via media* for a loose federal union, is it reasonable to suppose that far-distant colonies—between whom and the mother-country there is no apparent community of interest; whose laws differ widely even in principle from the laws of England; whose inhabitants are rapidly diverging even in physical type from the type of the parent stem, and whose satisfaction with their present systems of government is intensified by contrast between their present circumstances under self-rule and their past unprosperity when subordinated to the domination of Downing Street—would ever of their own consent commit themselves to any scheme of federal union with England which might subject them once again to be made the sport of the whims of English officials—or of future Earl Greys ?

Some colonists there undoubtedly are who would willingly consent to any plan which might perchance bring them into closer contact with the English official world. And what manner of men are these ? Land-monopolising colonists who would crown the edifice of their wealth with those titular distinctions which sycophantic loyalty conjoined with large possessions may expect to claim from appreciative British Ministers, and who see their opportunity in drawing closer the connecting link with England ; greedy politicians hankering after marks of imperial favour which may enable them to display the appearance of a respectability which their own characters cannot supply ; and the generality of men composing the small castes who in each colony set themselves in bitter opposition to the aspirations of colonial populations. These are men the excess of whose vaunted loyalty to English institutions is a proof of their disloyalty to the laws of the community in which they live, as well as evidence of their ignorance of the realities of English life, and these are the men who alone among colonists give assent and feeble vigour to impossible schemes for imperial federation.

Highly-coloured pictures of the power and magnificence of the federated empire are always pleasing to the drawer, and long may they remain so. But it is impossible to regard them except as allegorical sketches where playful fancy revels in extravagance of conception. If such an empire could not co-here for a day, it is needless to examine the effect its existence might produce on the universe subordinated to its federated might. But suppose for the moment that federation for purposes of imperial offence and defence has become a possibility. Then it behoves us to consider the result. For argument's sake let us assume several premisses standing greatly in need of proof. Assume, for instance, that at first the contributions of the Colonies to the imperial armament fund are contentedly paid ; that no colony cements the alliance by reserving to itself the right to grumble over the payment of its quota ; that each of the colonies is willing at the commencement to submit to the dictation of the mother-country as to the objects to be attained at any time by the federal forces ; and that the separate contributions may be yearly raised without interference with the principle of local self-government in any of the colonies. The schemes most plausibly advanced for the purpose of federal armament are two in number. In one it is suggested that England should furnish the men, ships, and *matériel* of war, and that the Colonies should supply the funds for the purely colonial portion of the military and naval expenditure. In the other it is insisted that each colony should form its own army and navy, and should allow of the employment of both by England for imperial purposes.

It is evident that under either plan the mother-country would be rendered vulnerable in her remotest and weakest colonies—at just the very points in her armour, in fact, which she can least easily defend. It must also be evident that in order to make the empire invulnerable at any point, the armaments to be kept on foot must be of enormous proportions and must be maintained at enormous expense.

The military danger would be great, the military preparations would at length become intolerable, and would be first felt to be so by the colonies militarily most secure. The colony which by reason of its superior population or resources had contributed the largest amount to the federal armament fund, or which, under the alternative plan, had provided the largest local armament for itself, and could fairly claim to be the strongest of the colonies, would, in all probability, be the first to complain of any addition to its burdens for the purpose of defending a weak and poor dependency which could ill afford either men or money. Does it not follow as of course that the imperial armament must be curtailed in its dimensions, and so the defensive power of the empire must be weakened? or else, that the objecting colony will promptly release itself from the federal tie? What other consequence could result? And yet, the curtailment of armaments would mean the submission of the leader of the federation to the dictation of one of its parts, and would imply an amenability to dictation from every other of its parts such as would introduce endless confusion into the whole principle of imperial leadership; while the withdrawal of the objecting colony from the federation would mean the addition of our strongest colony to the list of our possible enemies, and would demand more extensive armament than ever to meet the increased danger. The strength of a chain is that of its weakest link; the circumstances that led to the first withdrawal would by repetition speedily force on other defections, and thus the necessity of strengthening the weakest suburb of the empire would wreck the scheme *in toto.*

A country that believes itself to be in little danger of invasion by any outside Power will be apt to think itself entitled to proportion its armaments to its own apprehension of risk, and although it has been assumed, for argument's sake, that the Colonies might consent to arm themselves or to pay for armaments on a scale deemed fitting by imperial authorities, it would be contrary to all probability to suppose that they would for any length of time continue to provide men or money on a scale which would appear to them unnecessarily high. In the end the federal armament scheme would come to this, that each colony would arm itself for its own and not for imperial requirements.

But notwithstanding what has just been said, let us once more make an extreme assumption. Suppose the federal armament to be maintained for awhile on the most bloated scale. It is difficult indeed to see how the strength of the empire could fail to deteriorate under the weight. The men and money given up to the military exigencies of the empire would, in all the Colonies, constitute an important subtraction from their productive powers. The direct economical loss thus perpetually being incurred would perhaps do more to weaken the Colonies than vast armaments would do to strengthen them. But beyond and besides the direct economical loss there would be a still more serious disadvantage consequent on the maintenance of federal forces for imperial purposes, and this I would here advert to.

If a colony is justified in believing that it can always rely upon imperial aid to extricate it from a difficult position, it is tolerably certain that it will neither show any very serious disposition to avoid unnecessary risks, nor hesitate to call upon the imperial forces to extricate it from the danger it has courted, preferably to stirring a finger in its own defence. How often have our African colonies, relying confidently on our assistance, rushed headlong into quarrels which, if they had had to provide their own means of defence, they would have avoided or peacefully settled? How often has the certainty of speedy military aid from England impelled them to some fresh advance into a hostile country, or incited them to some reckless outrage against a friendly neighbour? How far, in consequence, have the frontiers of those colonies been advanced beyond the ability of the colonists themselves to maintain or defend them?

On the one hand, the self-dependent proclivities of the colonists have been repressed by their belief in the certainty of imperial backing, and they will never be developed while England is ready at hand to help them. On the other hand their greed for more territory than they can pretend to guard has been aggravated by the frequent opportunities afforded them by British military assistance of gratifying their grasping propensities. They have been taught by the unwise fostering of England to advance, not peacefully and therefore substantially, not by pressing forward their boundaries foot by foot in the manner of the irresistible advance of the American settlers from the Atlantic to the Pacific, but by the uncertain and unstable process of military conquest. Yet withal, can the British African colonists pretend to a tithe of the ability of the unassisted Dutch Boers for military purposes? They cannot, because they have never been brought up in the sturdy training-school of self-help. Can they pretend to a record of successful progress to compare with that of the early North-American colonies over a corresponding period of settlement, beset though the latter were with perilous obstacles to advancement? Again they cannot, and for no other reason than that the African colonists have never been called upon to fight their own battles as the Americans were. The imperial assistance so freely supplied to South Africa has had nothing but injurious results. It has left behind it a crop of quarrels ripe for the harvesting, an unnatural extension of territory beyond the unaided power of the colonists to defend—an extension to straggling boundaries begirt with tribes whom our military policy has rendered warlike and hostile ; and last, but not least, it has been effectual in retarding the growth of a spirit of self-reliance amongst the colonists themselves.

How was it with New Zealand? So long as the assistance of the imperial forces was accorded to it, the colony made comparatively slight forward progress ; so soon as the New Zealand colonists were thrown on their own resources and left to fight their own battles, self-reliance based on the necessity of existence effected the victory which the British soldiery could not achieve. When the regiments were withdrawn and the colonists had to make the best of the situation for themselves, the efforts of the Maoris were speedily quelled by volunteers, not more valorous than the soldiery, but far more interested in a satisfactory solution of the native difficulty ; and from thenceforth commenced an unchecked era of extraordinary prosperity. New Zealand and South Africa, in their recent history, have impressed upon us maxims which may be of great value in our future dealings with the Colonies, and they are these :—Leave a nationality, however young and immature, to fight its own battles, and it will satisfactorily work out its own destinies. Give it the unnatural stimulus of a belief in the military aid of an imperial Power, and though its frontier may be unnaturally distended so as to give it an appearance of prosperous advance, the foundation of its prosperity will be for the time a treacherous shifting quicksand, momentarily threatening to engulf the superincumbent structure.

What has imperial military assistance done for the Colonies, wherever applied, whether in Africa, New Zealand, or Canada ? Has it not prevented the early development of the industrial might which alone can irresistibly war with the wilderness and with the savage ? The progress of New Zealand since the entire withdrawal of the imperial forces has been out of all proportion to its advance under their protection, while Canada has exhibited a healthy vigour since the curtailment of the imperial military force maintained within its borders, such as it never gave evidence of when England was ever ready to rush into a quarrel on behalf of some fancied colonial necessity ; and the Cape Colonists will show a similar spirit when they are compelled to rely upon their own resources, but not till then.

Consider, again, the periodic disturbance each fresh military expedition inflicts upon the peaceful march of ordinary trade in the Colonies ; look at the inducements thus given to thrifty colonists to become unscrupulous contractors for the supply of stores and means of transport to the expeditionary force, and at the tendency thus imparted to the colonial mind to regard wars as blessings productive of great and easily-earned pecuniary profit. Hence, the colonists come to welcome war as an excellent commercial speculation in which their risks are small, their personal responsibility nothing, and their gains enormous. Into what pernicious courses this feeling, if widely spread, may lead a young community, it is needless to inquire. Suffice it to say that it does not seem as if South Africa, for example, can ever be peaceful so long as its colonists get handsomely paid for creating disturbances which they are not themselves called upon to terminate.

Even if the colony had to pay the bill, there must still be always a number of influential people interested in promoting war when they are certain that a sufficient military force will be furnished by the imperial Power to make the war successful, and therefore popular; and it seems altogether impossible to escape from the conclusion that federation for purposes of imperial armament would involve a constant supply of small local wars as long as any part of the federation could furnish a surplus of troops to be sent to the assistance of any bellicose member. But, more important by far, it would mean the temporary utter extinction of those principles of self-reliance and self-help without which no nationality can become great and prosperous, and the indefinite weakening of colonial strength and resources by the periodic paralysis inflicted at intervals on regular, industrial, and commercial occupations.

We are sometimes assured that federation of the empire for commercial purposes would induce an immense increase in the trade of the empire—because 'trade follows the flag.' How? when? and why? let me ask. Is it erroneous to suppose that trade seeks the most profitable and surest market— the market where exchanges are effected on the best and safest terms, whatever the flag that floats over it? If English ships are the chief carriers of goods, is it not because private English shipowners supply the greatest facilities for the carriage of cargoes? *Private English shipowners,* I repeat; for it is since British shipping has been emancipated from the weight of regulations, which kept the shipping interest as a kind of a State industry in close dependence on the State and made the national flag a symbol of State direction of English commerce, that the commencement of the development of our present great carrying trade fairly dates. The emphasis is important as showing that our carrying trade is not the consequence of hoisting the British flag on our ships, but that it is due to causes not necessarily connected with the cover of any particular flag—namely, to the activity and enterprise of individuals associated together. But suppose the contention I uphold to be untenable, what.

let me ask again, is the conclusion to be deduced from the fact that not only our Colonies but *all* nations employ our ships as carriers in preference to their own? Obviously it must be that 'trade does *not* follow the flag' in the carrying trade any more than for the purpose of finding a market.

The flag of Free Trade—the common property of all nations if they so will—is the flag that commerce most eagerly follows. Were the United States, with their vast resources of exchangeable wealth ready to hand, to unfurl the Free Trade banner side by side with the Stars and Stripes, then commerce from all parts of the most closely confederated of empires would rush to the States in perhaps larger volume than it now does even to England's open markets.

Finally, we are told that the stream of emigration would follow the flag of the Confederation. The assertion is a bold one, because in contrariety to the lessons which he who runs may read in the records of emigration past and present. Over the period of forty years from 1840 to 1880, it was ascertained that considerably more than two-thirds of the emigrants from the United Kingdom went direct to the United States, besides large numbers who made their way thither by Canadian routes. They went to the States because they saw, or thought they saw, readier prospects of bettering themselves there than anywhere else—and *that* must be the main reason which will always determine the set of the tide of emigration in any given direction. The matter is almost too plain for argument.

From a very early date in English emigration history the primary desire of emigrants was to escape from the immediate influence of the national flag; and whether that be now their main object in leaving their native land or not, it is certain that the majority of them do not emigrate with the view of *following* the British flag. Let those who think that it would be otherwise were the empire federated, and as a consequence of federation—those on whom lies the *onus probandi*—advance, if they can, a single reasonable ground for a supposition opposed to the suggestions of all previous experience.

Let us by all means endeavour to promote good-will and harmony between England and her Colonies, nor let us patiently labour out schemes which may force the disruption of the powerful ties of mutual interest and affection now firmly linking together the remotest portions of the empire. Let us be warned by the evil results of centralised colonial government in the past to avoid the merest semblance of the re-introduction of the principle of centralised rule in the future. Only by leaving the free Colonies alone to work out their own destinies can we expect to retain them in permanent union with ourselves. But if, instead of playing the passive part which experience and reason would alike suggest, England should attempt to interfere where she has neither the right nor the power to intermeddle, to command where she has no claim to obedience, and neither the means nor the ability to put her decrees into execution—to attempt, in short, ' to bring the Colonies into firmer dependence '—she will infallibly find each fresh endeavour powerful as an incentive to permanent disunion between herself and her loyal and friendly self-governing Colonies.

LONDON : PRINTED BY
SPOTTISWOODE AND CO., NEW-STREET SQUARE
AND PARLIAMENT STREET

APRIL 1883.

GENERAL LISTS OF NEW WORKS

PUBLISHED BY

MESSRS. LONGMANS, GREEN & CO.

PATERNOSTER ROW, LONDON.

—◦◦;⚬;◦◦—

HISTORY, POLITICS, HISTORICAL MEMOIRS, &c.

Arnold's Lectures on Modern History. 8vo. 7s. 6d.
Bagehot's Literary Studies, edited by Hutton. 2 vols, 8vo. 28s.
Beaconsfield's (Lord) Speeches, by Kebbel. 2 vols. 8vo. 32s.
Bingham's Marriages of the Bonapartes. 2 vols. crown 8vo. 21s.
Bramston & Leroy's Historic Winchester. Crown 8vo. 6s.
Buckle's History of Civilisation. 3 vols. crown 8vo. 24s.
Chesney's Waterloo Lectures. 8vo. 10s. 6d.
Doyle's English in America. 8vo. 18s.
Dun's American Food and Farming. Crown 8vo. 10s. 6d.
Epochs of Ancient History :—
>   Beesly's Gracchi, Marius, and Sulla. 2s. 6d.
>   Capes's Age of the Antonines, 2s. 6d.
>   — Early Roman Empire. 2s. 6d.
>   Cox's Athenian Empire, 2s. 6d.
>   — Greeks and Persians, 2s. 6d.
>   Curteis's Rise of the Macedonian Empire, 2s. 6d.
>   Ihne's Rome to its Capture by the Gauls, 2s. 6d.
>   Merivale's Roman Triumvirates. 2s. 6d.
>   Sankey's Spartan and Theban Supremacies, 2s. 6d.
>   Smith's Rome and Carthage, the Punic Wars, 2s. 6d.
Epochs of English History, complete in One Volume. Fcp. 8vo. 5s.
>   Browning's Modern England, 1820–1875, 9d.
>   Creighton's Shilling History of England (Introductory Volume).
>   Fcp. 8vo. 1s.
>   Creighton's (Mrs.) England a Continental Power, 1066–1216, 9d.
>   Creighton's (Rev. M.) Tudors and the Reformation, 1485–1603, 9d.
>   Gardiner's (Mrs.) Struggle against Absolute Monarchy, 1603–
>   1688, 9d.
>   Rowley's Rise of the People, 1215–1485, 9d.
>   Rowley's Settlement of the Constitution, 1689–1784, 9d.
>   Tancock's England during the American & European Wars,
>   1765–1820, 9d.
>   York-Powell's Early England to the Conquest, 1s.
Epochs of Modern History :—
>   Church's Beginning of the Middle Ages, 2s. 6d.
>   Cox's Crusades, 2s. 6d.
>   Creighton's Age of Elizabeth, 2s. 6d.

London, LONGMANS & CO.

Epochs of Modern History—*continued*.
    Gairdner's Houses of Lancaster and York, 2*s.* 6*d.*
    Gardiner's Puritan Revolution, 2*s.* 6*d.*
    — Thirty Years' War, 2*s.* 6*d.*
    — (Mrs.) French Revolution, 1789-1795, 2*s.* 6*d.*
    Hale's Fall of the Stuarts, 2*s.* 6*d.*
    Johnson's Normans in Europe, 2*s.* 6*d.*
    Longman's Frederick the Great and the Seven Years' War, 2*s.* 6*d.*
    Ludlow's War of American Independence, 2*s.* 6*d.*
    M'Carthy's Epoch of Reform, 1830-1850, 2*s.* 6*d.*
    Morris's Age of Queen Anne, 2*s.* 6*d.*
    Seebohm's Protestant Revolution, 2*s.* 6*d.*
    Stubbs's Early Plantagenets, 2*s.* 6*d.*
    Warburton's Edward III., 2*s.* 6*d.*

Froude's English in Ireland in the 18th Century. 3 vols. crown 8vo. 18*s.*
    — History of England. Popular Edition. 12 vols. crown 8vo. 3*s.* 6*d.* each.
    — Julius Cæsar, a Sketch. 8vo. 16*s.*
Gardiner's England under Buckingham and Charles I., 1624-1628. 2 vols. 8vo. 24*s.*
    — Personal Government of Charles I., 1628-1637. 2 vols. 8vo. 24*s.*
    — Outline of English History, B.C. 55-A.D. 1880. Fcp. 8vo. 2*s.* 6*d.*
Greville's Journal of the Reigns of George IV. & William IV. ˙3 vols. 8vo. 36*s.*
Ihne's History of Rome. 5 vols. 8vo. £3. 17*s.*
Lecky's History of England. Vols. I. & II. 1700-1760. 8vo. 36*s.* Vols. III. & IV. 1760-1780. 8vo. 36*s.*
    — History of European Morals. 2 vols. crown 8vo. 16*s.*
    — — — Rationalism in Europe. 2 vols. crown 8vo. 16*s.*
Lowes's History of Philosophy. 2 vols. 8vo. 32*s.*
Longman's Lectures on the History of England. 8vo. 15*s.*
    — Life and Times of Edward III. 2 vols. 8vo. 28*s.*
Macaulay's Complete Works. Library Edition. 8 vols. 8vo. £5. 5*s.*   Cabinet Edition. 16 vols. crown 8vo. £4. 16*s.*
    — History of England :—
    Student's Edition. 2 vols. cr. 8vo. 12*s.* | Cabinet Edition. 8 vols. post 8vo. 48*s.*
    People's Edition. 4 vols. cr. 8vo. 16*s.* | Library Edition. 5 vols. 8vo. £4.
Macaulay's Critical and Historical Essays. Cheap Edition. Crown 8vo 2*s.* 6*d.*
    Student's Edition. 1 vol. cr. 8vo. 6*s.* | Cabinet Edition. 4 vols. post 8vo. 24*s.*
    People's Edition. 2 vols. cr. 8vo. 8*s.* | Library Edition. 3 vols. 8vo. 36*s.*
May's Constitutional History of England, 1760-1870. 3 vols. crown 8vo. 18*s.*
    — Democracy in Europe. 2 vols. 8vo. 32*s.*
Merivale's Fall of the Roman Republic. 12mo. 7*s.* 6*d.*
    — General History of Rome, B.C. 753-A.D. 476. Crown 8vo. 7*s.* 6d.
    — History of the Romans under the Empire. 8 vols. post 8vo. 48*s.*
Orsi's Recollections of the last Half-Century. Crown 8vo. 7*s.* 6*d.*
Rawlinson's Ancient Egypt. 2 vols. 8vo. 63*s.*
    — Seventh Great Oriental Monarchy—The Sassanians. 8vo. 28*s.*
Seebohm's Oxford Reformers—Colet, Erasmus, & More. 8vo. 14*s.*
Short's History of the Church of England. Crown 8vo. 7*s.* 6*d.*
Smith's Carthage and the Carthaginians. Crown 8vo. 10*s.* 6*d.*
Taylor's Manual of the History of India. Crown 8vo. 7*s.* 6*d.*
Trevelyan's Early History of Charles James Fox. Crown 8vo. 6*s.*
Walpole's History of England, 1815-1841. 3 vols. 8vo. £2. 14*s.*

London, LONGMANS & CO.

BIOGRAPHICAL WORKS.

Bagehot's Biographical Studies. 1 vol. 8vo. 12s.

Bain's Biography of James Mill. Crown 8vo. Portrait, 5s.
— Criticism and Recollections of J. S. Mill. Crown 8vo. 2s. 6d.

Burke's Vicissitudes of Families. 2 vols. crown 8vo. 21s.

Carlyle's Reminiscences, edited by J. A. Froude. 2 vols. crown 8vo. 18s.
— (Mrs.) Letters and Memorials. 3 vols. 8vo. 36s.

Cates's Dictionary of General Biography. Medium 8vo. 28s.

Froude's Thomas Carlyle, 1795-1835. 2 vols. 8vo. with Portraits and Plates, 32s.

Gleig's Life of the Duke of Wellington. Crown 8vo. 6s.

Halliwell-Phillipps's Outlines of Shakespeare's Life. 8vo. 7s. 6d.

Jerrold's Life of Napoleon the Third. 4 vols. 8vo. £3. 18s.

Lecky's Leaders of Public Opinion in Ireland. Crown 8vo. 7s. 6d.

Life (The) and Letters of Lord Macaulay. By his Nephew, G. Otto Trevelyan, M.P. Popular Edition, 1 vol. crown 8vo. 6s. Cabinet Edition, 2 vols. post 8vo. 12s. Library Edition, 2 vols. 8vo. 36s.

Marshman's Memoirs of Havelock. Crown 8vo. 3s. 6d.

Memoir of Augustus De Morgan, By his Wife. 8vo. 14s.

Mendelssohn's Letters. Translated by Lady Wallace. 2 vols. cr. 3vo. 5s. each.

Mill's (John Stuart) Autobiography. 8vo. 7s. 6d.

Mozley's Reminiscences of Oriel College. 2 vols. crown 8vo. 18s.

Newman's Apologia pro Vitâ Suâ. Crown 8vo. 6s.

Overton's Life &c. of William Law. 8vo. 15s.

Skobeleff & the Slavonic Cause. By O. K. 8vo. Portrait, 14s.

Southey's Correspondence with Caroline Bowles. 8vo. 14s.

Spedding's Letters and Life of Francis Bacon. 7 vols. 8vo. £4. 4s.

Stephen's Essays in Ecclesiastical Biography. Crown 8vo. 7s. 6d.

MENTAL AND POLITICAL PHILOSOPHY.

Amos's View of the Science of Jurisprudence. 8vo. 18s.
— Fifty Years of the English Constitution, 1830-1880. Crown 8vo. 10s. 6d.
— Primer of the English Constitution. Crown 8vo. 6s.

Bacon's Essays, with Annotations by Whately. 8vo. 10s. 6d.
— Promus, edited by Mrs. H. Pott. 8vo. 16s.
— Works, edited by Spedding. 7 vols. 8vo. 73s. 6d.

Bagehot's Economic Studies, edited by Hutton. 8vo. 10s. 6d.

Bain's Logic, Deductive and Inductive. Crown 8vo. 10s. 6d.
    PART I. Deduction, 4s. | PART II. Induction, 6s. 6d.

Bolland & Lang's Aristotle's Politics. Crown 8vo. 7s. 6d.

Grant's Ethics of Aristotle ; Greek Text, English Notes. 2 vols. 8vo. 32s.

Hodgson's Philosophy of Reflection. 2 vols. 8vo. 21s.

Kalisch's Path and Goal. 8vo. 12s. 6d.

Leslie's Essays in Political and Moral Philosophy. 8vo. 10s. 6d.

Lewis on Authority in Matters of Opinion. 8vo. 14s.

Macaulay's Speeches corrected by Himself. Crown 8vo. 3s. 6d.

Macleod's Economical Philosophy. Vol. I. 8vo. 15s. Vol. II. Part I. 12s.

Mill on Representative Government. Crown 8vo. 2s.
— on Liberty. Crown 8vo. 1s. 4d.

London, LONGMANS & CO.

Mill's Analysis of the Phenomena of the Human Mind. 2 vols. 8vo. 28s.
- Dissertations and Discussions. 4 vols. 8vo. 46s. 6d.
- Essays on Unsettled Questions of Political Economy. 8vo. 6s. 6d.
- Examination of Hamilton's Philosophy. 8vo. 16s.
- Logic, Ratiocinative and Inductive. 2 vols. 8vo. 25s.
- Principles of Political Economy. 2 vols. 8vo. 30s. 1 vol. crown 8vo. 5s.
- Subjection of Women. Crown 8vo. 6s.
- Utilitarianism. 8vo. 5s.

Müller's (Max) Chips from a German Workshop. 4 vols. 8vo. 36s.
- — Selected Essays on Language, Mythology, and Religion. 2 vols. crown 8vo. 16s.

Sandars's Institutes of Justinian, with English Notes. 8vo. 18s.

Seth & Haldane's Philosophical Essays. 8vo. 9s.

Swinburne's Picture Logic. Post 8vo. 5s.

Thomson's Outline of Necessary Laws of Thought. Crown 8vo. 6s.

Tocqueville's Democracy in America, translated by Reeve. 2 vols. crown 8vo. 16s.

Twiss's Law of Nations in Time of War. Second Edition, 8vo. 21s.

Whately's Elements of Logic. 8vo. 10s. 6d. Crown 8vo. 4s. 6d.
- — Rhetoric. 8vo. 10s. 6d. Crown 8vo. 4s. 6d.
- English Synonymes. Fcp. 8vo. 3s.

Williams's Nicomachean Ethics of Aristotle translated. Crown 8vo. 7s. 6d.

Zeller's Socrates and the Socratic Schools. Crown 8vo. 10s. 6d.
- Stoics, Epicureans, and Sceptics. Crown 8vo. 15s.
- Plato and the Older Academy. Crown 8vo. 18s.
- Pre-Socratic Schools. 2 vols. crown 8vo. 30s.

MISCELLANEOUS AND CRITICAL WORKS.

Arnold's (Dr. Thomas) Miscellaneous Works. 8vo. 7s. 6d.
- (T.) Manual of English Literature. Crown 8vo. 7s. 6d.
- English Poetry and Prose. Crown 8vo. 6s.

Bain's Emotions and the Will. 8vo. 15s.
- Mental and Moral Science. Crown 8vo. 10s. 6d.
- Senses and the Intellect. 8vo. 15s.

Beaconsfield (Lord), The Wit and Wisdom of. Crown 8vo. 6s.

Becker's *Charicles* and *Gallus*, by Metcalfe. Post 8vo. 7s. 6d. each.

Blackley's German and English Dictionary. Post 8vo. 7s. 6d.

Contanseau's Practical French & English Dictionary. Post 8vo. 7s. 6d.
- Pocket French and English Dictionary. Square 18mo. 3s. 6d.

Farrar's Language and Languages. Crown 8vo. 6s.

Froude's Short Studies on Great Subjects. 3 vols. crown 8vo. 18s.
- — — Fourth Series. 8vo. 12s.

Hobart's Medical Language of St. Luke. 8vo. 16s.

Hume's Essays, edited by Green & Grose. 2 vols. 8vo. 28s.
- Treatise on Human Nature, edited by Green & Grose. 2 vols. 8vo. 28s.

Latham's Handbook of the English Language. Crown 8vo. 6s.

Liddell & Scott's Greek-English Lexicon. 4to. 36s.
- Abridged Greek-English Lexicon. Square 12mo. 7s. 6d.

Longman's Pocket German and English Dictionary. 18mo. 5s.

Macaulay's Miscellaneous Writings. 2 vols. 8vo. 21s. 1 vol. crown 8vo. 4s. 6d.
- Miscellaneous Writings and Speeches. Crown 8vo. 6s.
- Miscellaneous Writings, Speeches, Lays of Ancient Rome, &c. Cabinet Edition. 4 vols. crown 8vo. 24s.

London, LONGMANS & CO.

Mahaffy's Classical Greek Literature. Crown 8vo. Vol. I. the Poets, 7s. 6d. Vol. II. the Prose Writers, 7s. 6d.
Millard's Grammar of Elocution. Fcp. 8vo. 3s. 6d.
Milner's Country Pleasures. Crown 8vo. 6s.
Müller's (Max) Lectures on the Science of Language. 2 vols. crown 8vo. 16s.
— — Lectures on India. 8vo. 12s. 6d.
Owen's Evenings with the Skeptics. 2 vols. 8vo. 32s.
Rich's Dictionary of Roman and Greek Antiquities. Crown 8vo. 7s. 6d.
Rogers's Eclipse of Faith. Fcp. 8vo. 5s.
— Defence of the Eclipse of Faith Fcp. 8vo. 3s. 6d.
Roget's Thesaurus of English Words and Phrases. Crown 8vo. 10s. 6d.
Selections from the Writings of Lord Macaulay. Crown 8vo. 6s.
Simcox's Latin Literature. 2 vols. 8vo. 32s.
White & Riddle's Large Latin-English Dictionary. 4to. 21s.
White's Concise Latin-English Dictionary. Royal 8vo. 12s.
— Junior Student's Lat.-Eng. and Eng.-Lat. Dictionary. Square 12mo. 12s.
Separately { The English-Latin Dictionary, 5s. 6d. The Latin-English Dictionary, 7s. 6d.
Wilson's Studies of Modern Mind &c. 8vo. 12s.
Wit and Wisdom of the Rev. Sydney Smith. Crown 8vo. 3s. 6d.
Witt's Myths of Hellas, translated by F. M. Younghusband. Crown 8vo.
Yonge's English-Greek Lexicon. Square 12mo. 8s. 6d. 4to. 21s.
The Essays and Contributions of A. K. H. B. Crown 8vo.
Autumn Holidays of a Country Parson. 3s. 6d.
Changed Aspects of Unchanged Truths. 3s. 6d.
Common-place Philosopher in Town and Country. 3s. 6d.
Counsel and Comfort spoken from a City Pulpit. 3s. 6d.
Critical Essays of a Country Parson. 3s. 6d.
Graver Thoughts of a Country Parson. Three Series, 3s. 6d. each.
Landscapes, Churches, and Moralities. 3s. 6d.
Leisure Hours in Town. 3s. 6d. Lessons of Middle Age. 3s. 6d.
Our Little Life. Essays Consolatory and Domestic. 3s. 6d.
Present-day Thoughts. 3s. 6d.
Recreations of a Country Parson. Three Series, 3s. 6d. each.
Seaside Musings on Sundays and Week-Days. 3s. 6d.
Sunday Afternoons in the Parish Church of a University City. 3s. 6d.

ASTRONOMY, METEOROLOGY, GEOGRAPHY, &c.

Freeman's Historical Geography of Europe. 2 vols. 8vo. 31s. 6d.
Herschel's Outlines of Astronomy. Square crown 8vo. 12s.
Keith Johnston's Dictionary of Geography, or General Gazetteer. 8vo. 42s.
Nelson's Work on the Moon. Medium 8vo. 31s. 6d.
Proctor's Essays on Astronomy. 8vo. 12s. Proctor's Moon. Crown 8vo. 10s. 6d.
— Larger Star Atlas. Folio. 15s. or Maps only, 12s. 6d.
— New Star Atlas. Crown 8vo. 5s. Orbs Around Us. Crown 8vo. 7s. 6d.
— Other Worlds than Ours. Crown 8vo. 10s. 6d.
— Sun. Crown 8vo. 14s. Universe of Stars. 8vo. 10s. 6d.
— Transits of Venus, 8vo. 8s. 6d. Studies of Venus-Transits, 8vo. 5s.
Smith's Air and Rain. 8vo. 24s.
The Public Schools Atlas of Ancient Geography. Imperial 8vo. 7s. 6d.
The Public Schools Atlas of Modern Geography. Imperial 8vo. 5s.
Webb's Celestial Objects for Common Telescopes. Crown 8vo. 9s.

London, LONGMANS & CO.

6 General Lists of New Works.

NATURAL HISTORY & POPULAR SCIENCE.

Arnott's Elements of Physics or Natural Philosophy. Crown 8vo. 12s. 6d.
Brande's Dictionary of Science, Literature, and Art. 3 vols. medium 8vo. 63s.
Decaisne and Le Maout's General System of Botany. Imperial 8vo. 31s. 6d
Dixon's Rural Bird Life. Crown 8vo. Illustrations, 5s.
Edmonds's Elementary Botany. Fcp. 8vo. 2s.
Evans's Bronze Implements of Great Britain. 8vo. 25s.
Ganot's Elementary Treatise on Physics, by Atkinson. Large crown 8vo. 15s
— Natural Philosophy, by Atkinson. Crown 8vo. 7s. 6d.
Goodeve's Elements of Mechanism. Crown 8vo. 6s.
Grove's Correlation of Physical Forces. 8vo. 15s.
Hartwig's Aerial World. 8vo. 10s. 6d. Polar World. 8vo. 10s 6d.
— Sea and its Living Wonders. 8vo. 10s. 6d.
— Subterranean World. 8vo. 10s. 6d. Tropical World. 8vo. 10s. 6d
Haughton's Six Lectures on Physical Geography. 8vo. 15s.
Heer's Primæval World of Switzerland. 2 vols. 8vo. 12s.
Helmholtz's Lectures on Scientific Subjects. 2 vols. cr. 8vo. 7s. 6d. each.
Hullah's Lectures on the History of Modern Music. 8vo. 8s. 6d.
— Transition Period of Musical History. 8vo. 10s. 6d.
Keller's Lake Dwellings of Switzerland. by Lee. 2 vols. royal 8vo. 42s.
Lloyd's Treatise on Magnetism. 8vo. 10s. 6d.
— — on the Wave-Theory of Light. 8vo. 10s. 6d.
Loudon's Encyclopædia of Plants. 8vo. 42s.
Lubbock on the Origin of Civilisation & Primitive Condition of Man. 8vo. 18s.
Macalister's Zoology and Morphology of Vertebrate Animals. 8vo. 10s. 6d.
Nicols' Puzzle of Life. Crown 8vo. 3s. 6d.
Owen's Comparative Anatomy and Physiology of the Vertebrate Animals. 3 vols. 8vo. 73s. 6d.
— Experimental Physiology. Crown 8vo. 5s.
Proctor's Light Science for Leisure Hours. 3 Series, crown 8vo. 7s. 6d. each.
Rivers's Orchard House. Sixteenth Edition. Crown 8vo. 5s.
— Rose Amateur's Guide. Fcp. 8vo. 4s. 6d.
Stanley's Familiar History of British Birds. Crown 8vo. 6s.
Text-Books of Science, Mechanical and Physical.
  Abney's Photography, 3s. 6d.
  Anderson's (Sir John) Strength of Materials, 3s. 6d.
  Armstrong's Organic Chemistry, 3s. 6d.
  Ball's Astronomy, 6s.
  Barry's Railway Appliances, 3s. 6d.
  Bauerman's Systematic Mineralogy, 6s.
  Bloxam & Huntington's Metals, 5s.
  Glazebrook's Physical Optics, 6s.
  Gore's Electro-Metallurgy, 6s.
  Griffin's Algebra and Trigonometry, 3s. 6d.
  Jenkin's Electricity and Magnetism, 3s. 6d.
  Maxwell's Theory of Heat, 3s. 6d.
  Merrifield's Technical Arithmetic and Mensuration, 3s. 6d.
  Miller's Inorganic Chemistry, 3s. 6d.
  Preece & Sivewright's Telegraphy, 3s. 6d.
  Rutley's Study of Rocks, 4s. 6d.
  Shelley's Workshop Appliances, 3s. 6d.

London, LONGMANS & CO.

Text-Books of Science, Mechanical and Physical—*continued*.

Thomé's Structural and Physiological Botany, 6*s*.
Thorpe's Quantitative Chemical Analysis, 4*s*. 6*d*.
Thorpe & Muir's Qualitative Analysis, 3*s*. 6*d*.
Tilden's Chemical Philosophy, 3*s*. 6*d*.
Unwin's Machine Design, 6*s*.
Watson's Plane and Solid Geometry, 3*s*. 6*d*.
Tyndall's Floating Matter of the Air. Crown 8vo. 7*s*. 6*d*.
— Fragments of Science. 2 vols. post 8vo. 16*s*.
— Heat a Mode of Motion. Crown 8vo. 12*s*.
— Notes on Electrical Phenomena. Crown 8vo. 1*s*. sewed, 1*s*. 6*d*. cloth.
— Notes of Lectures on Light. Crown 8vo. 1*s*. sewed, 1*s*. 6*d*. cloth.
— Lectures on Light delivered in America. Crown 8vo. 7*s*. 6*d*.
— Lessons in Electricity. Crown 8vo. 2*s*. 6*d*.
— Sound, New Edition, including Recent Researches. Crown 8vo.
Von Cotta on Rocks, by Lawrence. Post 8vo. 14*s*.
Wood's Bible Animals. With 112 Vignettes. 8vo. 14*s*.
— Common British Insects. Crown 8vo. 3*s*. 6*d*.
— Homes Without Hands. 8vo. 14*s*. Insects Abroad. 8vo. 14*s*.
— Insects at Home. With 700 Illustrations. 8vo. 14*s*.
— Out of Doors. Crown 8vo. 5*s*.
— Strange Dwellings. Crown 8vo. 5*s*. Sunbeam Edition, 4to. 6*d*.

CHEMISTRY & PHYSIOLOGY.

Buckton's Health in the House, Lectures on Elementary Physiology. Cr. 8vo. 2*s*
Jago's Inorganic Chemistry, Theoretical and Practical. Fcp. 8vo. 2*s*.
Miller's Elements of Chemistry, Theoretical and Practical. 3 vols. 8vo. Part I.
Chemical Physics, 16*s*. Part II. Inorganic Chemistry, 24*s*. Part III. Organic
Chemistry, price 31*s*. 6*d*.
Reynolds's Experimental Chemistry. Fcp. 8vo. Part I. 1*s*. 6*d*. Part II. 2*s*. 6*d*.
Thudichum's Annals of Chemical Medicine. Vols. I. & II. 8vo. 14*s*. each.
Tilden's Practical Chemistry. Fcp. 8vo. 1*s*. 6*d*.
Watts's Dictionary of Chemistry. 9 vols. medium 8vo. £15. 2*s*. 6*d*.

THE FINE ARTS & ILLUSTRATED EDITIONS.

Dresser's Arts and Art Industries of Japan. Square crown 8vo. 31*s*. 6*d*.
Eastlake's Notes on the Brera Gallery, Milan. Crown 8vo. 5*s*.
— Notes on the Louvre Gallery, Paris. Crown 8vo. 7*s*. 6*d*.
Hulme's Art-Instruction in England. Fcp. 8vo. 3*s*. 6*d*.
Jameson's Sacred and Legendary Art. 6 vols. square crown 8vo.
Legends of the Madonna. 1 vol. 21*s*.
— — — Monastic Orders. 1 vol. 21*s*.
— — — Saints and Martyrs. 2 vols. 31*s*. 6*d*.
— — — Saviour. Completed by Lady Eastlake. 2 vols. 42*s*.
Longman's Three Cathedrals Dedicated to St. Paul. Square crown 8vo. 21*s*.
Macaulay's Lays of Ancient Rome, illustrated by Scharf. Fcp. 4to. 21*s*.
— — — illustrated by Weguelin. Crown 8vo. 6*s*.
Macfarren's Lectures on Harmony. 8vo. 12*s*.
Moore's Irish Melodies. With 161 Plates by D. Maclise, R.A. Super-royal 8vo. 21*s*.
— Lalla Rookh, illustrated by Tenniel. Square crown 8vo. 10*s*. 6*d*.
New Testament (The) illustrated with Woodcuts. New Edition, in course of
publication in 18 Monthly Parts, 1*s*. each. Quarto.
Perry on Greek and Roman Sculpture. With 280 Illustrations engraved on
Wood. Square crown 8vo. 31*s*. 6*d*.

London, LONGMANS & CO.

THE USEFUL ARTS, MANUFACTURES, &c.

Barry & Bramwell's Railways and Locomotives. 8vo. 21s.
Bourne's Catechism of the Steam Engine. Fcp. 8vo. 6s.
— Examples of Steam, Air, and Gas Engines. 4to. 70s.
— Handbook of the Steam Engine. Fcp. 8vo. 9s.
— Recent Improvements in the Steam Engine. Fcp. 8vo. 6s.
— Treatise on the Steam Engine. 4to. 42s.
Brassey's British Navy, in 5 vols. 8vo. with many Illustrations. VOL. I. Ship-building for the Purposes of War, 10s. 6d. VOLS. II. & III. 3s. 6d. each.
Cresy's Encyclopædia of Civil Engineering. 8vo. 25s.
Culley's Handbook of Practical Telegraphy. 8vo. 16s.
Eastlake's Household Taste in Furniture, &c. Square crown 8vo. 14s.
Fairbairn's Useful Information for Engineers. 3 vols. crown 8vo. 31s. 6d.
— Mills and Millwork. 1 vol. 8vo. 25s.
Gwilt's Encyclopædia of Architecture. 8vo. 52s. 6d.
Kerl's Metallurgy, adapted by Crookes and Röhrig. 3 vols. 8vo. £4. 19s.
London's Encyclopædia of Agriculture. 8vo. 21s.
— — — Gardening. 8vo. 21s.
Mitchell's Manual of Practical Assaying. 8vo. 31s. 6d.
Northcott's Lathes and Turning. 8vo. 18s.
Payen's Industrial Chemistry Edited by B. H. Paul, Ph.D. 8vo. 42s.
Piesse's Art of Perfumery. Fourth Edition. Square crown 8vo. 21s.
Sennett's Treatise on the Marine Steam Engine. 8vo. 21s.
Stoney's Theory of Strains in Girders. Royal 8vo. 36s.
Ure's Dictionary of Arts, Manufactures, & Mines. 4 vols. medium 8vo. £7. 7s.
Ville on Artificial Manures. By Crookes. 8vo. 21s.

RELIGIOUS & MORAL WORKS.

Abbey & Overton's English Church in the Eighteenth Century. 2 vols. 8vo. 36s.
Arnold's (Rev. Dr. Thomas) Sermons. 6 vols. crown 8vo. 5s. each.
Bishop Jeremy Taylor's Entire Works. With Life by Bishop Heber. Edited by the Rev. C. P. Eden. 10 vols. 8vo. £5. 5s.
Boultbee's Commentary on the 39 Articles. Crown 8vo. 6s.
— History of the Church of England, Pre-Reformation Period. 8vo. 15s.
Bray's Elements of Morality. Fcp. 8vo. 2s. 6d.
Browne's (Bishop) Exposition of the 39 Articles. 8vo. 16s.
Calvert's Wife's Manual. Crown 8vo. 6s.
Christ our Ideal. 8vo. 8s. 6d.
Colenso's Lectures on the Pentateuch and the Moabite Stone. 8vo. 12s.
Colenso on the Pentateuch and Book of Joshua. Crown 8vo. 6s.
Conder's Handbook of the Bible. Post 8vo. 7s. 6d.
Conybeare & Howson's Life and Letters of St. Paul :—
    Library Edition, with all the Original Illustrations, Maps, Landscapes on Steel, Woodcuts, &c. 2 vols. 4to. 42s.
    Intermediate Edition, with a Selection of Maps, Plates, and Woodcuts. 2 vols. square crown 8vo. 21s.
    Student's Edition, revised and condensed, with 46 Illustrations and Maps. 1 vol. crown 8vo. 7s. 6d.
Creighton's History of the Papacy during the Reformation. 2 vols. 8vo. 32s.
Davidson's Introduction to the Study of the New Testament. 2 vols. 8vo. 30s.

London, LONGMANS & CO.

Ellicott's (Bishop) Commentary on St. Paul's Epistles. 8vo. Galatians, 8*s.* 6*d.*
Ephesians, 8*s.* 6*d.* Pastoral Epistles, 10*s.* 6*d.* Philippians, Colossians and
Philemon, 10*s.* 6*d.* Thessalonians, 7*s.* 6*d.*
Ellicott's Lectures on the Life of our Lord. 8vo. 12*s.*
Ewald's Christ and His Time, translated by J. F. Smith. 8vo. 16*s.*
— History of Israel, translated by Carpenter. 5 vols. 8vo. 63*s.*
— Antiquities of Israel, translated by Solly. 8vo. 12*s.* 6*d.*
Gospel (The) for the Nineteenth Century. 4th Edition. 8vo. 10*s.* 6*d.*
Hopkins's Christ the Consoler. Fcp. 8vo. 2*s.* 6*d.*
Jukes's New Man and the Eternal Life. Crown 8vo. 6*s.*
— Second Death and the Restitution of all Things. Crown 8vo. 3*s.* 6*d.*
— Types of Genesis. Crown 8vo. 7*s.* 6*d.*
Kalisch's Bible Studies. PART I. the Prophecies of Balaam. 8vo. 10*s.* 6*d.*
— — — PART II. the Book of Jonah. 8vo. 10*s.* 6*d.*
— Historical and Critical Commentary on the Old Testament; with a
New Translation. Vol. I. *Genesis*, 8vo. 18*s.* or adapted for the General
Reader, 12*s.* Vol. II. *Exodus*, 15*s.* or adapted for the General Reader, 12*s.*
Vol. III. *Leviticus*, Part I. 15*s.* or adapted for the General Reader, 8*s.*
Vol. IV. *Leviticus*, Part II. 15*s.* or adapted for the General Reader, 8*s.*
Keary's Outlines of Primitive Belief. 8vo. 18*s.*
Lyra Germanica : Hymns translated by Miss Winkworth. Fcp. 8vo. 5*s.*
Manning's Temporal Mission of the Holy Ghost. Crown 8vo. 8*s.* 6*d.*
Martineau's Endeavours after the Christian Life. Crown 8vo. 7*s.* 6*d.*
— Hymns of Praise and Prayer. Crown 8vo. 4*s.* 6*d.* 32mo. 1*s.* 6*d.*
— Sermons, Hours of Thought on Sacred Things. 2 vols. 7*s.* 6*d.* each.
Mill's Three Essays on Religion. 8vo. 10*s.* 6*d.*
Monsell's Spiritual Songs for Sundays and Holidays. Fcp. 8vo. 5*s.* 18mo. 2*s.*
Müller's (Max) Origin & Growth of Religion. Crown 8vo. 7*s.* 6*d.*
— Science of Religion. Crown 8vo. 7*s.* 6*d.*
Newman's Apologia pro Vitâ Suâ. Crown 8vo. 6*s.*
Passing Thoughts on Religion. By Miss Sewell. Fcp. 8vo. 3*s.* 6*d.*
Sewell's (Miss) Preparation for the Holy Communion. 32mo. 3*s.*
— — Private Devotions for Young Persons. 18mo. 2*s.*
Seymour's Hebrew Psalter. Crown 8vo. 7*s.* 6*d.*
Smith's Voyage and Shipwreck of St. Paul. Crown 8vo. 7*s.* 6*d.*
Supernatural Religion. Complete Edition. 3 vols. 8vo. 36*s.*
Thoughts for the Age. By Miss Sewell. Fcp. 8vo. 3*s.* 6*d.*
Whately's Lessons on the Christian Evidences. 18mo. 6*d.*
White's Four Gospels in Greek, with Greek-English Lexicon. 32mo. 5*s.*

TRAVELS, VOYAGES, &c.

Baker's Rifle and Hound in Ceylon. Crown 8vo. 7*s.* 6*d.*
— Eight Years in Ceylon. Crown 8vo. 7*s.* 6*d.*
Ball's Alpine Guide. 3 vols. post 8vo. with Maps and Illustrations :—I. Western
Alps, 6*s.* 6*d.* II. Central Alps, 7*s.* 6*d.* III. Eastern Alps, 10*s.* 6*d.*
Ball on Alpine Travelling, and on the Geology of the Alps, 1*s.*
Brassey's Sunshine and Storm in the East. Crown 8vo. 7*s.* 6*d.*
— Voyage in the Yacht 'Sunbeam.' Crown 8vo. 7*s.* 6*d.* School Edition,
fcp. 8vo. 2*s.* Popular Edition, 4to. 6*d.*

London, LONGMANS & CO.

Freeman's Impressions of the United States of America. Crown 8vo. 6s.
Hassall's San Remo and the Western Riviera. Crown 8vo. 10s. 6d.
Macnamara's Medical Geography of India. 8vo. 21s.
Miller's Wintering in the Riviera. Post 8vo. Illustrations, 7s. 6d.
The Alpine Club Map of Switzerland. In Four Sheets. 42s.
Three in Norway. By Two of Them. Crown 8vo. Illustrations, 6s.
Weld's Sacred Palmlands. Crown 8vo. 10s. 6d.

WORKS OF FICTION.

Arden, a Novel. By A. Mary F. Robinson. 2 vols. crown 8vo. 12s.
Hester, a Novel. By Mrs. Hope. 2 vols. crown 8vo. 12s.
In the Olden Time. By the Author of ' Mademoiselle Mori.' 2 vols. crown 8vo. 12s.
Messer Agnolo's Household. By Leader Scott. Crown 8vo. 6s.
Cabinet Edition of Novels and Tales by the Earl of Beaconsfield, K.G. 11 vols.
    crown 8vo. price 6s. each.
Cabinet Edition of Stories and Tales by Miss Sewell. Crown 8vo. cloth extra,
    gilt edges, price 3s. 6d. each :—

Amy Herbert. Cleve Hall.	A Glimpse of the World.
The Earl's Daughter.	Katharine Ashton.
Experience of Life.	Laneton Parsonage.
Gertrude. Ivors.	Margaret Percival. Ursula.

Novels and Tales by the Earl of Beaconsfield, K.G. Hughenden Edition, with 2
    Portraits on Steel and 11 Vignettes on Wood. 11 vols. crown 8vo. £2. 2s.

Lothair. Coningsby.	Contarini Fleming.
Sybil. Tancred.	Alroy, Ixion, &c.
Venetia. Henrietta Temple.	The Young Duke, &c.
Vivian Grey. Endymion.	

The Modern Novelist's Library. Each Work in crown 8vo. A Single Volume,
    complete in itself, price 2s. boards, or 2s. 6d. cloth :—

By the Earl of Beaconsfield, K.G.	Kate Coventry.
Lothair. Coningsby.	The Gladiators.
Sybil. Tancred.	Good for Nothing.
Venetia. Henrietta Temple.	Holmby House.
Contarini Fleming.	The Interpreter.
Alroy, Ixion, &c.	The Queen's Maries.
The Young Duke, &c.	
Vivian Grey. Endymion.	By Various Writers.
By Anthony Trollope.	The Atelier du Lys.
Barchester Towers.	Atherstone Priory.
The Warden.	The Burgomaster's Family.
	Elsa and her Vulture.
By Major Whyte-Melville.	Mademoiselle Mori.
Digby Grand.	The Six Sisters of the Valleys.
General Bounce.	Unawares.

Novels and Tales of the Earl of Beaconsfield, K.G. Modern Novelist's Library
    Edition, complete in 11 vols. crown 8vo. price £1. 13s. cloth extra.
Oliphant's (Mrs.) In Trust. Crown 8vo. 6s.
Whispers from Fairy Land. By Lord Brabourne. With 9 Illustrations. Crown
    8vo. 3s. 6d.
Higgledy-Piggledy. By Lord Brabourne. With 9 Illustrations. Crown 8vo. 3s. 6d.

POETRY & THE DRAMA.

Bailey's Festus, a Poem. Crown 8vo. 12s. 6d.
Bowdler's Family Shakspeare. Medium 8vo. 14s. 6 vols. fcp. 8vo. 21s.
Cayley's Iliad of Homer, Homometrically translated. 8vo. 12s. 6d.

London, LONGMANS & CO.

Conington's Æneid of Virgil, translated into English Verse. Crown 8vo. 9s.
—   Prose Translation of Virgil's Poems. Crown 8vo. 9s.
Goethe's Faust, translated by Birds. Large crown 8vo. 12s. 6d.
—   — translated by Webb. 8vo. 12s. 6d.
—   — edited by Selss. Crown 8vo. 5s.
Ingelow's Poems. New Edition. 2 vols. fcp. 8vo. 12s.
Macaulay's Lays of Ancient Rome, with Ivry and the Armada. 16mo. 3s. 6d.
The same, Cheap Edition, fcp. 8vo. 1s. sewed, 1s. 6d. cloth, 2s. 6d. cloth extra.
Moore's Poetical Works, 1 vol. ruby type. Post 8vo. 6s.
Southey's Poetical Works. Medium 8vo. 14s.

RURAL SPORTS, HORSE & CATTLE MANAGEMENT, &c.

Dead Shot (The), by Marksman. Crown 8vo. 10s. 6d.
Fitzwygram's Horses and Stables. 8vo. 10s. 6d.
Francis's Treatise on Fishing in all its Branches. Post 8vo. 15s.
Horses and Roads. By Free-Lance. Crown 8vo. 6s.
Howitt's Visits to Remarkable Places. Crown 8vo. 7s. 6d.
Miles's Horse's Foot, and How to Keep it Sound. Imperial 8vo. 12s. 6d.
—   Plain Treatise on Horse-Shoeing. Post 8vo. 2s. 6d.
—   Stables and Stable-Fittings. Imperial 8vo. 15s.
—   Remarks on Horses' Teeth. Post 8vo. 1s. 6d.
Milner's Country Pleasures. Crown 8vo. 6s.
Nevile's Horses and Riding. Crown 8vo. 6s.
Ronalds's Fly-Fisher's Entomology. 8vo. 14s.
Steel's Diseases of the Ox, being a Manual of Bovine Pathology. 8vo. 15s.
Stonehenge's Dog in Health and Disease. Square crown 8vo. 7s. 6d.
—   Greyhound. Square crown 8vo. 15s.
Wilcocks's Sea-Fisherman. Post 8vo. 12s. 6d.
Youatt's Work on the Dog. 8vo. 6s.
—   — — — Horse. 8vo. 7s. 6d.

WORKS OF UTILITY & GENERAL INFORMATION.

Acton's Modern Cookery for Private Families. Fcp. 8vo. 4s. 6d.
Black's Practical Treatise on Brewing. 8vo. 10s. 6d.
Buckton's Food and Home Cookery. Crown 8vo. 2s. 6d.
Bull on the Maternal Management of Children. Fcp. 8vo. 1s. 6d.
Bull's Hints to Mothers on the Management of their Health during the Period of Pregnancy and in the Lying-in Room. Fcp. 8vo. 1s. 6d.
Campbell-Walker's Correct Card, or How to Play at Whist. Fcp. 8vo. 3s. 6d.
Johnson's (W. & J. H.) Patentee's Manual. Fourth Edition. 8vo. 10s. 6d.
Johnston's Land Law Ireland Act. Crown 8vo. 1s.
Longman's Chess Openings. Fcp. 8vo. 2s. 6d.
Macleod's Economics for Beginners. Small crown 8vo. 2s. 6d.
—   Elements of Banking. Fourth Edition. Crown 8vo. 5s.
—   Elements of Economics. 2 vols. small crown 8vo. VOL. I. 7s. 6d.
—   Theory and Practice of Banking. 2 vols. 8vo. 26s.

London, LONGMANS & CO.

M'Culloch's Dictionary of Commerce and Commercial Navigation. 8vo. 63s.
Maunder's Biographical Treasury. Fcp. 8vo. 6s.
  —   Historical Treasury. Fcp. 8vo. 6s.
  —   Scientific and Literary Treasury. Fcp. 8vo. 6s.
  —   Treasury of Bible Knowledge, edited by Ayre. Fcp. 8vo. 6s.
  —   Treasury of Botany, edited by Lindley & Moore. Two Parts, 12s.
  —   Treasury of Geography. Fcp. 8vo. 6s.
  —   Treasury of Knowledge and Library of Reference. Fcp. 8vo. 6s.
  —   Treasury of Natural History. Fcp. 8vo. 6s.
Pewtner's Comprehensive Specifier ; Building-Artificers' Work. Crown 8vo. 6s.
Pole's Theory of the Modern Scientific Game of Whist. Fcp. 8vo. 2s. 6d.
Quain's Dictionary of Medicine. Medium 8vo. 31s. 6d.
Reeve's Cookery and Housekeeping. Crown 8vo. 7s. 6d.
Scott's Farm Valuer. Crown 8vo. 5s.
  —   Rents and Purchases. Crown 8vo. 6s.
Smith's Handbook for Midwives. Crown 8vo. 5s.
The Cabinet Lawyer, a Popular Digest of the Laws of England. Fcp. 8vo. 9s.
Ville on Artificial Manures, by Crookes. 8vo. 21s.
Willich's Popular Tables, by Marriott. Crown 8vo. 10s.
Wilson on Banking Reform. 8vo. 7s. 6d.

MUSICAL WORKS BY JOHN HULLAH, LL.D.

Hullah's Method of Teaching Singing. Crown 8vo. 2s. 6d.
Exercises and Figures in the same. Crown 8vo. 1s. sewed, or 1s. 2d. limp cloth ;
    or 2 Parts, 6d. each sewed, or 8d. each limp cloth.
Large Sheets, containing the ' Exercises and Figures in Hullah's Method,' in
    Two Parcels of Eight, price 6s. each.
Chromatic Scale, with the Inflected Syllables, on Large Sheet. 1s. 6d.
Card of Chromatic Scale. 1d.
Grammar of Musical Harmony. Royal 8vo. price 3s. sewed and 4s. 6d. cloth ; or
    in 2 Parts, each 1s. 6d.
Exercises to Grammar of Musical Harmony. 1s.
Grammar of Counterpoint. Part I. super-royal 8vo. 2s. 6d.
Wilhem's Manual of Singing. Parts I. & II. 2s. 6d. or together, 5s.
Exercises and Figures contained in Parts I. and II. of Wilhem's Manual. Books
    I. & II. each 8d.
Large Sheets, Nos. 1 to 8, containing the Figures in Part I. of Wilhem's Manual,
    in a Parcel, 8s.
Large Sheets, Nos. 9 to 40, containing the Exercises in Part I. of Wilhem's
    Manual, in Four Parcels of Eight Nos. each, per Parcel, 6s.
Large Sheets, Nos. 41 to 52, containing the Figures in Part II. in a Parcel, 9s.
Hymns for the Young, set to Music. Royal 8vo. 8d. sewed, or 1s. 6d. cloth.
Infant School Songs. 6d.
Notation, the Musical Alphabet. Crown 8vo. 6d.
Old English Songs for Schools, Harmonised. 6d.
Rudiments of Musical Grammar. Royal 8vo. 3s.
School Songs for 2 and 3 Voices. 2 Books, 8vo. each 6d.
A Short Treatise on the Stave. 2s.
Lectures on the History of Modern Music. 8vo. 9s. 6d.
Lectures on the Transition Period of Musical History. 8vo. 10s. 6d.

London, LONGMANS & CO.

Spottiswoode & Co. Printers, New-street Square, London.

www.ingramcontent.com/pod-product-compliance
Lightning Source LLC
Chambersburg PA
CBHW030905270326
41929CB00008B/578